汽车技术英语全图解

吴拓 编

化学工业出版社
·北京·

内容简介

本书通过"文字说明+实物图示"的形式,中英对照、直观形象地讲解了汽车技术相关知识。全书共分两大部分9个单元。第Ⅰ部分汽车结构,涉及汽车整体构造、汽车发动机、汽车底盘和汽车电气设备;第Ⅱ部分汽车维修与保养,涉及汽车保养概述、发动机的维修、底盘的维修、汽车电气的维修和汽车美容。本书体现了现代汽车工业的新概念、新特点、新技术及新发展,双色印刷,重点突出,能帮助相关技术人员较为系统地学习汽车专业英语知识。

本书既可供汽车行业的技术人员和维修、销售人员学习参考,也可作为高等院校汽车专业的专业英语教材。

图书在版编目(CIP)数据

汽车技术英语全图解/吴拓编 . —北京:化学工业出版社,2021.4
ISBN 978-7-122-38466-9

Ⅰ. ①汽… Ⅱ. ①吴… Ⅲ. ①汽车工程-英语 Ⅳ. ①U46

中国版本图书馆 CIP 数据核字(2021)第 018977 号

责任编辑:贾　娜　毛振威　　　　　　　　　　　装帧设计:王晓宇
责任校对:边　涛

出版发行:化学工业出版社(北京市东城区青年湖南街 13 号　邮政编码 100011)
印　　刷:三河市航远印刷有限公司
装　　订:三河市宇新装订厂
787mm×1092mm　1/16　印张 13$\frac{3}{4}$　字数 339 千字　2021 年 7 月北京第 1 版第 1 次印刷

购书咨询:010-64518888　　　　　　　售后服务:010-64518899
网　　址:http://www.cip.com.cn
凡购买本书,如有缺损质量问题,本社销售中心负责调换。

定　　价:69.80 元　　　　　　　　　　　　　　　　　　　版权所有　违者必究

前言

近年来，随着我国国民经济的快速发展，人民生活水平日益提高，生活质量不断改善，我国人民对汽车的需求越来越旺盛。世界各国的汽车公司竞相来我国开展销售和联合制造业务。我国自己的汽车制造业也方兴未艾，正在走向世界。虽然我国仍不是汽车工业强国，但汽车核心技术的研发、国际市场的拓展已成燎原之势。我国已成为世界上最大的汽车市场和汽车生产国之一。

众所周知，不仅进口和出口汽车的使用说明书、维修手册、仪表板显示等都用英文表达或标注，而且各大汽车公司向汽车维修站提供的技术指导也都是用英文发布的。因此，为了与国际接轨，汽车行业需要更多既懂汽车专业知识，又有一定英语基础的人才。为了帮助汽车行业的技术人员和高等院校汽车专业的学生学习汽车技术英语，提高专业英语阅读和翻译能力，快速准确地维修进口汽车和开展汽车国际贸易业务，特编写本书。

全书共分两大部分9个单元。第Ⅰ部分汽车结构，涉及汽车整体构造、汽车发动机、汽车底盘和汽车电气设备；第Ⅱ部分汽车维修与保养，涉及汽车保养概述、发动机的维修、底盘的维修、汽车电气的维修和汽车美容。附录还列举了常用汽车专业术语和常用汽车英语缩略语。本书既充分体现了汽车知识的完整性、系统性，也体现了现代汽车工业的新概念、新特点、新技术及其新发展。本书有如下特点：

1. 主旨明确，知识全面。鉴于汽车技术英语的词义和语法比较简单，如今读者的英语水平完全够用，本书主要是通过中英文对照和图解的方式，帮助读者扩充汽车技术英语词汇量。内容涵盖汽车构造、汽车维修与汽车美容等各个方面，能帮助相关技术人员较为全面、系统地学习汽车技术英语知识，熟练掌握2000个左右汽车技术专业英语词汇，以便阅读和翻译英文的汽车操作说明书和有关技术手册。

2. 图文并茂，版式新颖。所有内容都有文字说明和实物图示，中英对照，直观形象，通俗易懂；专业词汇的词义在课文一侧对应位置列出，方便即时学习；阅读材料中的重要词汇与表达加有译注，便于通读和理解。

3. 内容精炼，简约实用。笔者编写本书时尤其注重实用性，课文和阅读材料尽量选用专业词汇较多、关系密切的内容。

4. 双色版面，美观清晰。本书采用双色印刷，汽车技术英语词汇、其他重要词汇与短语等均用红色字体显示，突出重点。

5. 既适于自学，又适应教学。本书既适于汽车行业的工程技术人员和维修、销售人员自学汽车技术英语，也适合高等院校汽车专业的学生学习汽车专业英语。

由于编者水平所限，书中疏漏在所难免，恳请读者多提宝贵意见！

编　者

CONTENTS 目录

Part Ⅰ Structure of Automobile 汽车结构 /001

Unit 1 Whole Structure of Automobile 汽车整体构造 002

Unit 2 Automobile Engine 汽车发动机 006

Section 2.1 Engine Structure, Operating Principle and Classification
发动机的结构、工作原理及分类 ……………………………… 006

Section 2.2 The Power Mechanism of the Engine 发动机的动力机构 ……… 012

Section 2.3 Engine Fuel System 发动机燃油系统 ……………………………… 016

Section 2.4 Engine Ignition System 发动机点火系统 ………………………… 020

Section 2.5 Engine Starting System 发动机起动系统 ………………………… 027

Section 2.6 Engine Cooling and Lubricating Systems 发动机冷却与润滑系统 … 036

Section 2.7 Engine Valve Train 发动机配气机构 ……………………………… 043

Unit 3 Automotive Chassis 汽车底盘 049

Section 3.1 Power Train System 传动系统 ……………………………………… 050

Section 3.2 Vehicle Clutch 汽车离合器 ………………………………………… 057

Section 3.3 Automobile Running Gear 行驶系统 ……………………………… 062

Section 3.4 Differential 差速器 …………………………………………………… 068

Section 3.5 Automobile Steering System 转向系统 …………………………… 070

Section 3.6 Four-wheel Steering 四轮转向 ……………………………………… 077

Section 3.7 Braking System 制动系统 …………………………………………… 081

Unit 4 Auto Electrical Equipment 汽车电气设备 089

    Section 4.1 Auto Electric Appliance 汽车电气 ……………………………… 089

    Section 4.2 Vehicle Air Conditioning 汽车空调 ………………………………… 103

    Section 4.3 Safeguard System 安全保护系统 …………………………………… 105

Part Ⅱ Automobile Service and Maintenance /111
汽车维修与保养

Unit 5 Summarize of Auto Maintenance 汽车保养概述 112

    Section 5.1 Factors Influencing the Stability and Control of Vehicle

               影响车辆稳定性和操作性的因素 ……………………………… 112

    Section 5.2 Maintenance Technique of Car Exterior 汽车外表保养技巧 ………… 116

    Section 5.3 Paint Your Car at Home 自己漆车 ……………………………………… 120

    Section 5.4 Auto Repair Equipment 汽车维修装备 ………………………………… 122

Unit 6 Engine Maintenance 发动机的维修 129

    Section 6.1 Fuel-system Service and Maintenance 燃油系统的维修与保养 …… 129

    Section 6.2 Cooling-system and Lubricating-system Service and Maintenance

               冷却系统与润滑系统的维修与保养 …………………………… 132

    Section 6.3 Ignition-system and Starting-system Service and Maintenance

               点火系统和起动系统的维修与保养 …………………………… 136

Unit 7 Chassis Maintenance 底盘的维修 141

    Section 7.1 Clutch System and Transmission Troubleshooting

               离合器与变速箱的检修 ………………………………………… 141

Section 7.2　Steering System Service　转向系统的维修 …………………… 146

Section 7.3　Brake System Service　制动系统的维修 …………………… 151

Unit 8　Vehicle Electric Maintenance　汽车电气的维修　　154

Section 8.1　Vehicle Information Displaying System Service

　　　　　　汽车信息显示系统的检修 ………………………………… 154

Section 8.2　Lighting System Service　照明系统的维修 …………………… 159

Section 8.3　Air Conditioning System Detection and Service

　　　　　　空调系统的检测与维修 …………………………………… 163

Unit 9　Car Beauty　汽车美容　　170

Section 9.1　Clean Car Interior　内饰美容 ………………………………… 170

Section 9.2　Car Body Care　车身美容 …………………………………… 172

Section 9.3　Car's Accessorizing　汽车装饰 ……………………………… 175

Appendix　附录　　181

Appendix Ⅰ　Common Terminology on Automobile　常用汽车专业术语 ……… 181

Appendix Ⅱ　Common English-Chinese Abbreviations on Automobile

　　　　　　　常用汽车英语缩略语 …………………………………… 194

References　参考文献　　212

Part I
Structure of Automobile
汽车结构

Unit 1

Whole Structure of Automobile

汽车整体构造

The perspective view of car is shown in Fig. 1-1.

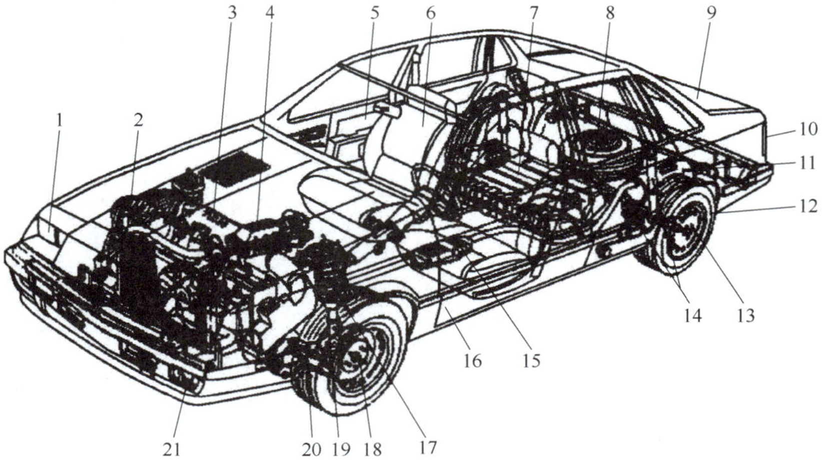

Fig. 1-1 Perspective view of car 汽车透视图
1—Head lamp 前照灯；2—Radiator 散热器；3—Engine 发动机；4—Air cleaner 空气滤清器；5—Door 车门；6—Seat 座椅；7—Fuel tank 燃油箱；8—Spare tire 备胎；9—Body 车身；10—Tail light 尾灯；11—Muffler 消声器；12—Tire 轮胎；13—Wheel cover 车轮装饰罩；14—Rear suspension 后悬架；15—Catalytic converter 三元催化转化器；16—Front sill panel 前门槛板；17—Front suspension 前悬架；18—Front wheel hub 前轮毂；19—Front brake 前制动器；20—Control arm 控制臂；21—Turn signal lamp 转向信号灯

chassis：底盘
electrical system：电气系统
fuel：燃料
lubricating：润滑
cooling：冷却
ignition：点火
starting：起动
internal combustion engine：内燃发动机
cylinder：气缸
convert：转化
expanding force：膨胀力
explosion：爆炸
rotary force：旋转力
propel：驱使

As everyone knows, the automobile generally is composed of four sections such as engine, chassis, body and electrical system（as is shown in Fig. 1-2）.

The engine is the source of power that makes the wheels go around and the car move. It includes the fuel, lubricating, cooling, ignition and starting systems. Generally, an automobile is operated by internal combustion engine. The internal combustion engine burns fuel within the cylinders and converts the expanding force of the combustion or "explosion" into rotary force used to propel the vehicle.

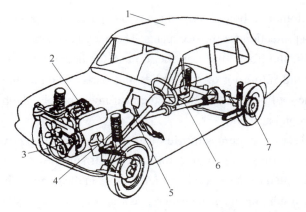

Fig. 1-2 Layout of a modern automobile 现代汽车示意图
1—Body 车身；2—Engine 发动机；3—Electrical equipment 电气装置；4—Suspension 悬架；
5—Steering 转向总成；6—Transmission 变速器；7—Brake 刹车

The chassis is a framework used to assemble auto components on it. The chassis itself is divided into four systems like transmission system, suspension system, steering system and brake system.

The transmission system applies to the components needed to transfer the drive from the engine to the road wheels. The main components are clutch, gearbox, drive shaft, final drive and differential. The primary purpose of the suspension system is to increase strength and durability of components and to meet customers' requirements for riding comfort and driving safety. In automobile suspension, the major component is springs. The springs used on today's vehicles are engineered in a wide variety of types, sizes, rates and capacities. Spring types include leaf springs, coil springs and torsion bars prings. Springs are paired off on vehicles in various combinations and are attached to vehicle by different mounting techniques. The function of the steering system is to provide the driver with a mean for controlling the direction of the vehicle as it moves. The steering system consists of steering wheel, steering shaft, worm, gear sector, pitman arm, drag link, steering knuckle arm, king pin, steering arms, tie rod, front axle and steering knuckle. They enable the car to change the direction by means of turning and moving forth and back. The automobile brake system is a friction device to change power into heat. When the brakes are applied, they convert the power of momentum of the moving vehicle（kinetic energy) into heat by means of friction, thus retarding the motion of the vehicle. Structurally, an automotive brake system contains these major parts like brake drum, brake shoe, brake lining, etc. Functionally, an automotive brake system can be divided into wheel brake mechanism and parking brake mechanism.

framework：框架
transmission system：传动系
suspension system：悬挂系
steering system：转向系
brake system：制动系
clutch：离合器
gearbox：变速箱
drive shaft：驱动轴
final drive：主减速器
differential：差速器
leaf spring：钢板弹簧
coil spring：螺旋弹簧
torsion bar spring：扭杆弹簧
steering wheel：方向盘
steering shaft：转向轴
worm：蜗杆
gear sector：扇形齿轮
pitman arm：转向摇臂
drag link：拉杆
steering knuckle arm：转向节臂
king pin：转向销
steering arm：转向臂
tie rod：横拉杆
front axle：前桥
steering knuckle：转向节
retard：减速
brake drum：制动鼓
brake shoe：闸瓦
brake lining：刹车蹄片
parking brake mechanism：停车制动机构

hood：引擎盖
fender：挡泥板
roof panel：
（车）顶板
instrument panel：
仪表盘
bumper：保险杠
luggage compartment：
行李厢
ignite：点火
air-fuel mixture：空气燃料混合气
horn：喇叭

The automobile body serves the obvious purpose of providing shelter, comfort and protection for the occupants. The body is generally classified into four sections: the front, the rear, the top and the underbody. These sections can further fall into a lot of assemblies and parts, such as the hood, the fenders, the roof panels, the door, the instrument panel, the bumpers and the luggage compartment.

The electric system supplies lighting and driving power for the automobile. It cranks the engine for starting. It supplies the high-voltage surges that ignite the compressed air-fuel mixture in the combustion chambers. The electric system includes the battery, generator, starting system, ignition system, lighting system, horn system, radio and other devices.

In summary, the automobile description above seems to conclude that though automobiles are quite different in design, but they are basically similar in structure.

Reference Version 参考译文

如图 1-1 所示为汽车透视图。

众所周知，汽车一般由发动机、底盘、车身及电气系统四部分组成（如图 1-2 所示）。

发动机是使车轮转动，从而驱动汽车行驶的动力来源，它包括燃料系统、润滑系统、冷却系统、点火系统和起动系统。汽车一般采用内燃发动机。内燃发动机在气缸里燃烧燃料，将内燃所产生的膨胀力转变成旋转力用以推动车辆前进。

底盘是一个用以总装汽车部件的框架。底盘本身可以分成四个系统，即传动系统、悬挂系统、转向系统和制动系统。

传动系统运用所需部件将发动机产生的动力传递到车轮。它的主要部件有离合器、变速器、传动轴、后桥和差速器。悬挂系统的主要目的是提高零部件的强度和寿命，并满足用户对车辆乘坐舒适性和驾驶安全性的需求。汽车悬挂系统上的主要部件是弹簧。目前车辆上使用的弹簧被设计制造成许多不同的型号、大小、标准及负载。弹簧类型包括钢板弹簧、螺旋弹簧和扭杆弹簧。弹簧以各种组合形式在车辆上配套使用，并用不同的装配技术将弹簧装在车辆上。转向系统的用途是在驾驶员的操纵下控制汽车行驶的方向。转向系统包括转向盘、转向轴、蜗杆、扇形齿轮、转向摇臂、直拉杆、转向节臂、主销、转向臂、转向横拉杆、前轴和转向节。这些零部件前后移动或转动，就可使汽车改变运动方向。汽车制动系统是一种将动能转变为热能的摩擦装置。当使用制动器时，制动器通过摩擦将行驶车辆的动能转变成热能，从而使车辆运动停止。从结构上来讲，汽车制动系统含有制动鼓、制动蹄片、制动器摩擦衬片等几个主要部件。从功能上讲，汽车制动系统可分为行车制动机构和驻车制动机构。

车身的基本功能就是向乘员提供保护，使其乘坐舒适并保证安全。车身一般分为四个部分：车前部、车后部、车顶部和车下部。这些部分可以进一步细分为许多的部件，如发动机盖板、挡泥板、车身顶板、车门、仪表板、汽车保险杠和行李厢。

电气系统向汽车提供照明与驱动电力。它能起动发动机，提供高压电脉冲点燃燃烧室中空气和燃油的高压混合气等。电气系统包括电池、发电机、起动系统、点火系统、照明系统、喇叭、收音机以及其他装置。

综上所述，尽管汽车的设计变化很大，然而汽车的构造基本上是一样的。

Unit 2

Automobile Engine
汽车发动机

Section 2.1

Engine Structure, Operating Principle and Classification
发动机的结构、工作原理及分类

kernel component:
核心部件
overhead camshaft:
顶置凸轮轴

(1) Engine structure

The engine, so to speak, is kernel component of automobile. It consists of fuel system, starting system, lubrication system, cooling system, valve train, etc. Fig. 2-1 shows a V-6 engine with dual overhead camshafts.

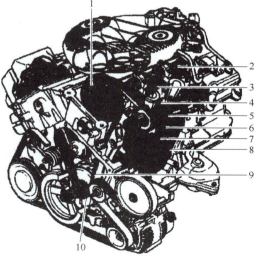

Fig. 2-1　V-6 engine with dual overhead camshafts 带双顶置凸轮轴的 V-6 发动机
1—Camshaft sprocket 凸轮轴链轮；2—Camshaft 凸轮轴；3—Valve spring 气门弹簧；
4—Intake valve 进气门；5—Exhaust valve 排气门；6—Piston 活塞；7—Connecting rod 连杆；
8—Crankshaft 曲轴；9—Timing chain 正时链；10—Crankshaft sprocket 曲轴链轮

Components and parts composed engine is shown in Fig. 2-2.

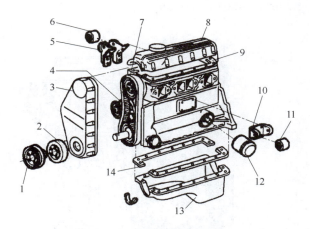

Fig. 2-2 Engine components 发动机的零部件

1—Crankshaft pulley 曲轴带盘；2—Vibration damper 减振器；3—Timing belt cover 正时带罩；
4—Tensioning pulley 张紧轮；5—Rear engine mount 发动机后悬置座；
6—Rear engine mount insulator 发动机后悬置隔振套；7—Timing belt 正时带；
8—Valve cover 气门室盖；9—Valve cover gasket 气门室盖衬垫；
10—Front engine mount 发动机前悬置座；11—Front engine mount insulator 发动机前悬置隔振套；
12—Oil filter 机油滤清器；13—Oil pan 油底壳；14—Oil pan gasket 油底壳密封垫

(2) Engine operating principle

The majority of engines in motor vehicles today use internal combustion engines. It comes into being huge power after mixture and burning of gasoline and air. Air enters the engine through the air cleaner and proceeds to the throttle plate. You control the amount of air that passes through the throttle plate and into the engine with the gas pedal. It is then distributed through a series of passages called the intake manifold, to each cylinder. At some point after the air cleaner, fuel is added to the air-stream by either a fuel injection system. The blended fuel (gas-oil ratio: 14.7∶1) triggers explosion by spark plug ignition in air cylinder, and makes piston move so that do work.

Fig. 2-3 shows a inline four-cylinders gasoline engine.

The internal combustion engine is the one most commonly used in the automotive field. The internal combustion engine, as its name indicates, bums fuel within the cylinders and converts the expanding force of the combustion into rotary force used to propel the vehicle. The actions taking place in the engine cylinder can be classified into four stages, or strokes. "Stroke" refers to piston movement: a stroke occurs when the piston moves from one limiting position to the other. The upper limit of piston movement is called TDC (top dead center). The lower limit of piston movement is called BDC (bottom dead center). A stroke is piston movement from TDC to BDC

air cleaner: 空气滤清器
throttle plate: 节气门
gas pedal: 油门踏板
intake manifold: 进气歧管
air-stream: 气流
fuel injection system: 燃料喷射系统
gas-oil ratio: 气油比
spark plug: 火花塞
do work: 做功

top dead center: 上止点
bottom dead center: 下止点

or from BDC to TDC. In other words, the piston completes a stroke each time it changes its direction of motion.

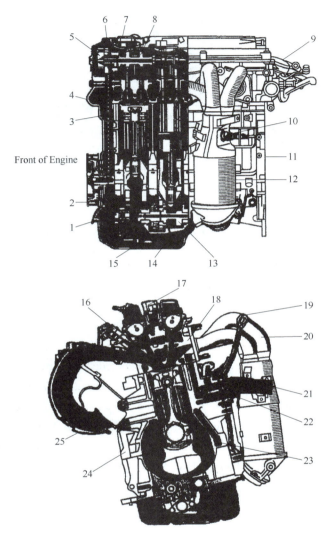

Fig. 2-3　Inline four-cylinders gasoline engine 直列四缸汽油发动机
1—Oil pump 机油泵；2—Camshaft timing sprocket 凸轮轴正时链轮；3—Timing chain 正时链；
4—Timing chain cover 正时链罩；5—VVT controller 可变配气正时调节器；
6—Cylinder head cover 气门室罩；7—Oil filler cap 加机油口盖；8—Camshaf 凸轮轴；
9—Throttle body 节气门体；10—O_2 S=Oxygen sensor 氧传感器；11—Rear of engine 发动机后面；
12—Catalytic converter 三元催化转化器；13—Balance shaft 平衡轴；14—Oil pan 油底壳；
15—Oil strainer 机油集滤器；16—Injector 喷油器；17—Ignition coil with igniter 带点火器的点火线圈；18—Cylinder head 气缸盖；19—Oil dipstick 机油尺；20—Exhaust manifold 排气歧管；
21—Outlet spout 出水管；22—Thermostat 节温器；23—Jacket 水套；
24—Cylinder block 气缸体；25—Intake manifold 进气歧管

Where the entire cycle of events in the cylinder requires four strokes（or two crankshaft revolutions）, the engine is called a four-stroke-cycle engine.

The four-stroke-cycle engine is also called the Otto cycle engine, in honor of the German engineer, Dr. Nikolaus Otto, who first applied the principle in 1876. The four piston strokes are intake, compression, power and exhaust, as is shown in Fig. 2-4.

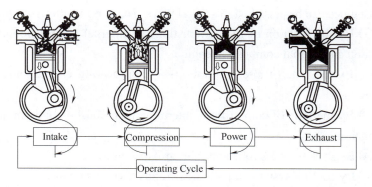

Fig. 2-4　The operation of a four-stroke cycle engine　四冲程发动机的工作过程

　　Intake stroke. On the intake stroke, the intake valve has opened, the piston is moving downward, and a mixture of air and vaporized gasoline is delivered to the cylinder by the fuel system and carburetor is entering the cylinder through the valve port.

　　Compression stroke. After the piston reaches BDC, or the lower limit of its travel, it begins to move upward. As this happens, the intake valve closes. The exhaust valve is also closed, so that the cylinder is sealed. As the piston moves upward, the air-fuel mixture is compressed. By the time the piston reaches TDC, the mixture has been compressed to as little as one-tenth of its original volume, or even less. When the air-fuel mixture is compressed, not only does the pressure in the cylinder to up, but the temperature of the mixture also increases.

　　Power stroke. As the piston reaches TDC on the compression stroke, an electric spark is produced at the spark plug. The ignition system delivers a high-voltage surge of electricity to the spark plug to produce the spark. The spark ignites the air fuel mixture. It now begins to burn very rapidly, and the cylinder pressure increases to as much as 3~5MPa or even more. This terrific push against the piston forces it downward, and a power impulse is transmitted through the connecting rod to the crankpin on the crankshaft. The crankshaft is rotated as the piston is pushed down by the pressure above it.

　　Exhaust stroke. As the piston reaches BDC again, the exhaust valve opens. Now, as the piston moves up on the exhaust stroke, it forces the burned gases out of the cylinder through the exhaust-valve port. Then, when the piston reaches TDC, the exhaust valve closes and the intake valve opens.

four-stroke-cycle：四冲程循环

intake stroke：进气冲程
vaporized：汽化的
carburetor：汽化器；化油器
valve port：气门口
compression stroke：压缩冲程

power stroke：做功冲程；动力冲程
ignition system：点火系统
high-voltage surge：高压脉冲
connecting rod：连杆

exhaust stroke：排气冲程
exhaust-valve：排气门

Now, a fresh charge of air-fuel mixture will be drawn in to the cylinder as the piston moves down again toward BDC. This four-stroke cycle of piston within the cylinder is repeated time and again to put the vehicle forward.

(3) Engine classification

Engines can be classified in several ways. The classifications are follow:

① By the location of tile combustion: an internal combustion engine (ICE) and an external combustion engine.

② By the type of internal motion: a reciprocating engine and rotary engine.

③ By the type of combustion: intermittent combustion and continuous combustion.

④ By stroke: two-stroke and four-stroke engines.

⑤ By cooling system: liquid-cooled and air-cooled engines.

⑥ By fuel systems: gasoline and diesel engines.

⑦ By ignition systems: spark-ignition and compression-ignition engines.

In addition, the cylinder and camshaft of automobile engines is also designed diversified arrangement.

① Cylinder arrangement. Depending upon the vehicle either an in-line, V or opposed cylinder arrangement can be used. The engines usually have 4, 6, 8, or 12 cylinders.

② Camshaft arrangement. Many engines have the camshaft located within the block. Nearly all automobiles now use engines that have an overhead camshaft. Dual camshaft (two camshaft) engine is designed so that one operates the intake valves, while the second operates the exhaust valves.

---

reciprocating: 活塞式

liquid-cooled: 液冷的
air-cooled: 风冷的

diversified arrangement: 多样化的排列
in-line: 直列；直排

camshaft: 凸轮轴

overhead camshaft: 顶置凸轮轴

Reference Version　参考译文

(1) 发动机的结构

发动机，可以说是汽车的核心部件。它由燃料供给系统、起动系统、润滑系统、冷却系统、配气机构等组成。图 2-1 所示为一台带双顶置凸轮轴的 V-6 发动机。

组成发动机的零部件如图 2-2 所示。

(2) 发动机的工作原理

现代汽车大多使用内燃发动机，它是通过汽油和空气的混合、燃烧后产生出巨大的动力。空气通过空气滤清器进入发动机，并进入节气门。通过油门踏板，你能控制经过节气门进入发动机的空气量。空气通过进气歧管进入各个气缸。在空气滤清器后的某处，燃油通过燃料喷射系统加入到气流中。混合燃料（气油比 14.7:1）在气缸中由火花塞点火引发爆炸，推动活塞运动做功。

图 2-3 所示为一直列四缸汽车发动机。

在汽车领域里，内燃机是用得最为普遍的一种。顾名思义，内燃机是在气缸里燃烧燃料，将内燃的膨胀力转变成推动汽车前进的旋转力。发动机气缸内的工作过程可以分为四个行程或冲程。冲程指活塞的运动，即活塞从某一限定位置到另一限定位置的运动。活塞运动的上限称为 TDC（上止点），下限称为 BDC（下止点）。一个冲程就是活塞从上止点到下止点，或从下止点到上止点的运动。换句话说，活塞每完成一个行程，就要改变一次其运动的方向。

发动机气缸中的全部工作过程分为四个冲程的（即曲轴旋转两周），叫做四冲程循环发动机。为纪念德国工程师尼科拉斯·奥托博士于 1876 年首次运用四冲程循环原理，四冲程循环发动机也叫奥托循环发动机。发动机的四个活塞冲程是进气、压缩、做功和排气，如图 2-4 所示。

进气冲程：在进气冲程中，进气门打开，活塞向下移动，由燃料系统和化油器提供的适当浓度可燃混合气通过进气门进入气缸。

压缩冲程：在活塞到达下止点或活塞下限时，活塞开始向上运动。同时，进气门关闭，排气门也关闭，所以这时的气缸是封闭的。当活塞向上运动时(这时是由转动的曲轴和连杆推动活塞)，可燃混合气被压缩。当活塞到达上止点时，可燃混合气被压缩到只有原体积的十分之一，甚至更少。当油气混合燃料被压缩时，不仅气缸里的压力上升，可燃混合气的温度也随之增加了。

做功冲程：活塞到达压缩行程的上止点时，火花塞产生电火花。电火花是由点火系统向火花塞提供高压电脉冲而产生的。电火花点燃可燃混合气。可燃混合气开始发生剧烈燃烧，气缸内压力达到 3～5MPa，甚至更高。作用于活塞上强大的推动力推动活塞向下运动，并将这一推力通过连杆传到曲轴上的连杆辅颈上。因此，当活塞受压向下运动时，推动曲轴转动。

排气冲程：活塞再一次到达下止点时，排气门打开。同时，活塞向上移动，将废气经排气门排出气缸。随后，活塞达到上止点，排气门关闭，进气门打开。

当活塞又一次向下移动到达下止点时，新鲜可燃混合气被吸入气缸。气缸活塞的四个冲程就这样不断重复，便可推动着汽车前进。

（3）发动机的分类

发动机可以按不同的方式进行分类，其分类方式如下。
① 根据燃烧发生的位置可分为内燃机和外燃机。
② 按照内部运动的不同可分为往复活塞式发动机和旋转式发动机。
③ 按燃烧的类型可分为间歇燃烧和连续燃烧。
④ 按冲程数可分为两冲程发动机和四冲程发动机。
⑤ 按冷却方式不同可分为液冷发动机和风冷发动机。
⑥ 按燃料不同可分为汽油机和柴油机。
⑦ 按点火方式不同可分为点燃式发动机和压燃式发动机。

此外，汽车发动机的气缸和凸轮轴还被设计成多种排列形式。

① 气缸的排列形式。气缸可以采用直列、V 形，或者对置式布置。发动机通常有 4 缸、6 缸、8 缸或 12 缸。

② 凸轮轴的排列形式。发动机的凸轮轴大多位于气缸体内部。几乎所有的汽车都采用顶置凸轮式发动机。双凸轮轴设计的发动机中，一根凸轮轴控制进气门，另一根控制排气门。

Section 2.2
The Power Mechanism of the Engine 发动机的动力机构

power mechanism：动力机构
connecting rod assembly：曲轴连杆总成
cylinder block：气缸体
flywheel：飞轮
crankcase：曲轴箱
cast alloy iron：铸造合金
wear characteristic：磨损特性
rigid：刚度
withstand：经受起
potential energy：势能
kinetic energy：动能
piston head：活塞顶部
piston ring：活塞环
piston land：活塞环槽脊
piston skirt：活塞裙部
piston pin hole：活塞销孔
crown：顶冠
turbulence：涡流；湍流
narrow groove：窄槽
top ring：顶环
heat dam：绝热槽
compression ring：压缩环；气环
oil-control ring：油环
cylinder wall：缸壁
oil drainage：泄油

In a reciprocating engine，the power mechanism is called the crankshaft and connecting rod assembly. In this assembly，all of the major units such as the engine crankcase and cylinder block，the piston and connecting rod，the crankshaft and flywheel work together to convert thermal energy into mechanical energy used to drive the vehicle.

The engine crankcase and block are usually cast into one piece and therefore can be seemed as the largest and most intricate piece of metal in automobile. They are usually made of high-grade cast alloy iron to improve wear characteristics of the cylinder. This major unit must be strong and rigid enough to withstand any bending or distortion.

The piston converts the potential energy of the fuel into the kinetic energy that turns the crankshaft. The piston is a cylindrical shaped hollow part that moves up and down inside the engines cylinder. The piston is composed of piston head，piston rings，piston lands，piston skirt and piston pin hole（see Fig. 2-5）. The piston head or "crown" is the top surface against which the explosive force is exerted. It may be flat，concave，and convex or any one of a great variety of shapes to promote turbulence or help control combustion. In some application，a narrow groove is cut into the piston above the top ring to serve as a "heat dam" to reduce the amount of heat reaching the top ring. The piston rings carried in the ring groove are of two basic types：compression ring and oil-control ring. The upper ring or rings are to prevent compression leakage；the lower ring or rings control the amount of oil being deposited on the cylinder wall. The lower groove or grooves often have holes or slots in the bottom of the grooves to permits oil drainage from behind the rings. The piston lands are parts of piston between the ring grooves. The lands provide a seating surface for the sides of piston rings.

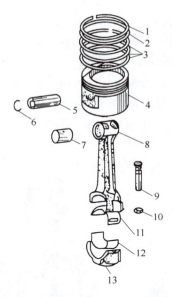

Fig. 2-5　Piston and connecting-rod 活塞和连杆
1，2—Compression ring 压缩环；3—Oil ring 油环；4—Piston 活塞；5—Piston pin 活塞销；
6—Piston-pin ring 活塞销环；7—Connecting rod bushing 连杆衬套；8—Connecting rod 连杆；
9—Connecting rod bolt 连杆螺栓；10—Connecting rod nut 连杆螺母；11，12—Crank bearing
half shell 曲柄轴承哈夫瓦；13—Connecting rod cap 连杆大头盖

  The main section of a piston is known as the skirts. It forms a bearing area in contact with the cylinder wall. The piston pin hole in the piston also serves as a bearing for the piston pin, which is used to connect the connecting rod. In addition, because pistons operate under exceedingly difficult mechanical and thermal conditions, piston must be strong enough to stand the force of the expansion, yet light enough to avoid excessive inertia forces when their direction of travel is reversed twice each revolution. Piston must be able to withstand the heat from the burning air-fuel mixture, plus the heat generated by friction.

  The connecting rod is attached to the crankshaft at one end and to the piston at the other end. In operation, the connecting rod is subjected to both gas pressure and inertia loads, and therefore, it must be adequately strong and rigid and light in weight as well. So they are generally fabricated from high quality steel. The connecting rod is in form of a bar with ring shaped heads at its end. They are composed of connecting rod small end, connecting rod shank, connecting rod big end, connecting rod cap, and connecting rod bearing half shells. To avoid misplacing the rod caps during assembly, the connecting rods and their mating caps are marked on one side with serial numbers, starting with the first rod from the radiator, to identify their location in the engine.

in contact with：与……有关联

expansion：膨胀
inertia：惯性

attached to：附属于

inertia load：惯性负载
fabricate：制造
high quality steel：优质钢

serial number：序列号
radiator：水箱

identify：识别

serve to：起……作用
handle：控制
entire power output：全功率输出
wear：磨损
bending：弯曲
tensional strain：张力应变
wear-resistant：耐磨性
high-strong iron：高强度铁
main bearing journal：曲轴主轴颈
rod journal：连杆轴颈
crank arm bearing：曲臂轴承
counter-balanced weight：平衡配重

The crankshaft serves to change the reciprocating motion of the piston into rotary motion and handles the entire power output. The periodic gas and inertia forces taken by the crankshaft may cause it to suffer wear and bending and tensional strains. The crankshaft therefore must be adequately strong and wear-resistant. So the crankshaft is either forged from a high quality steel or cast in a high-strong iron. The crankshaft shown is actually made up of various parts such as main bearing journal, rod journal, crank arm bearing, counter-balanced weight and flywheel end (see Fig. 2-6).

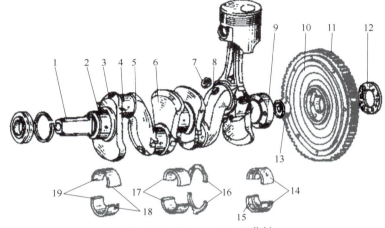

Fig. 2-6　The crankshaft 曲轴

1—Crankshaft front end 曲轴前端；2—Front main journal 前主轴颈；3—Oil passage hole 油道孔；4—Crank pin 曲柄销；5—Crank web 曲柄臂；6—Counter weight 平衡锤；7—Oil passage plug 油道塞；8—Oil passage 油道；9—Crankshaft collar 曲轴颈圈；10—Flywheel 飞轮；11—Flywheel gear ring 飞轮齿圈；12—Flywheel lock plate 飞轮锁片；13—Clutch shaft bearing 离合器轴轴承；14—Rear main bearing half shell 后主轴承哈夫瓦；15—Oil groove 油槽；16—Crankshaft thrust 曲轴塞；17—Central main bearing half shell 中心主轴承哈夫瓦；18—Bearing half shell 轴承哈夫瓦；19—Front main bearing half shell 前主轴承哈夫瓦

The flywheel is a relatively heavy metal wheel，which is firmly attached to the crankshaft. Its function is to help the engine to run smoothly by absorbing some of the energy during the power stroke and releasing it during the other strokes.

indentation：压痕
bell housing：飞轮壳；钟形罩

In the front face of the flywheel，there is a shallow indentation used to determine the position of the piston in the first cylinder. When this indentation is aligned with a special hole provided in the bell housing, the piston is at top dead center (TDC) or indicates the start of fuel injection into the first cylinder. The flywheels of some engines also carry marks indicating the serial numbers of the cylinders where the compression occurs. The flywheel marks and indentation are used for setting the valve and ignition systems relative to prescribed positions of the crankshaft.

In conclusion, the connecting rod and crankshaft mechanism of the engine is composed of various units, and each of these units has its own functions in producing power for vehicles.

Reference Version 参考译文

在活塞式发动机中，动力机构称为曲柄连杆总成。在装配时，全部主单元，诸如发动机曲轴箱和气缸体，活塞和连杆，曲轴和飞轮，协调一致进行转换，将热能转换成机械能，用以驱动车辆。

发动机曲轴箱通常铸成一体，因此看起来就像汽车的一个最大、最复杂的金属件。它们用优质的铸造合金制造，以增强气缸的耐磨性。这个主要组件具有足以经受任何弯曲和变形的强度和刚度。

活塞将燃料的势能转换为曲轴转动的动能。活塞是一个圆柱形的在发动机气缸内上下运动的异形中空零件。活塞由活塞顶部、活塞环、活塞环槽脊、活塞裙部、活塞销孔组成（参见图 2-5）。活塞头或顶冠是抵御爆炸力的顶面，它可以是平面、凹面、凸面或者其他产生涡流或者帮助控制燃烧的各种形状。在某些应用中，顶环切有一条窄槽作为绝热槽以减少热量传到顶环。活塞环的环槽有两种基本类型：气环和油环。上环阻止压缩气体泄漏，下环控制气缸壁上的油量。下环槽脊常允许在槽底部从后面环渗入的泄油。活塞环槽脊是两个环槽之间的活塞部分，是为活塞环提供支撑的基础表面。

活塞的主干称之为裙部，它形成一个与活塞缸壁相关联的面积。活塞的活塞销孔同样也为连接连杆的活塞销轴承发挥作用。此外，因为活塞在非常艰难的机械和热力条件下运作，必须具有足以经受膨胀力的强度，以及具有足够小的与其行进方向相反的极度惯性力。活塞必须能够经受得起来自空气燃料混合气的热量，加上摩擦产生的热量。

连杆的一端连着曲轴，另一端连着活塞。在运行时，连杆承受着气体压力和惯性负载，因此它必须有足够的强度和刚度，而且重量轻才好，所以通常它们由优质钢制造。连杆的端部都整饬成环状头形。它们由连杆小端、连杆柄、连杆大端、连杆盖、连杆轴承哈夫瓦组成。为了避免连杆盖装错位置，特地在连杆与它们相配合的盖的一侧打上序列号记号。首先从水箱开始，再连接到发动机的识别位置。

曲轴起着将活塞的往复运动变成旋转运动并使之全功率输出的作用。周期性的气压和惯性力迫使曲轴遭受磨损、弯曲和张力应变，因而曲轴必须保持足够的强度和耐磨性，所以曲轴用优质钢锻造或者用高强度铁镶铸而成。事实上，曲轴由各种零件，诸如曲轴主轴颈、连杆轴颈、曲臂轴承、平衡配重以及飞轮等组成（见图 2-6）。

飞轮是个比较重的金属轮，牢固地附着在曲轴上。它的功能是帮助发动机平衡地运行，将一个动力冲程吸收的一些能量在另一个冲程时释放它。

在飞轮正面有用来确定活塞在第一个气缸位置的压痕，当压痕对准飞轮壳上的特殊小孔时，活塞就位于上死点，或者表明燃油喷射到了第一个气缸。有的发动机飞轮还带有表示重现压缩的气缸序列号。飞轮的记号和压痕用来设置气门和点火系统的位置，相当于指定曲轴的位置。

总之，发动机的连杆和曲轴机构由各种部件组成，每个部件在为发动机提供动力的过程中都有各自的功能。

Section 2.3
Engine Fuel System
发动机燃油系统

critical：决定性的

The fuel system is critical to operation of engine. The fuel system has the job of supplying a combustible mixture of air and fuel to the engine. All automobile have some forms of fuel supply system. There are three functions of the fuel system in an automobile. First of all，it must be able to store fuel. Second，it must be able to move the fuel from the fuel tank to the engine. Third，it must mix the fuel with the air in such a way as to be used by the engine. Moreover，the system must perform these functions regardless of the outside temperature，altitude，and speed of the vehicle. The typical fuel system consists of the fuel tank，fuel pump，fuel filter，carburetor and fuel lines. All automobile have some forms of fuel delivery system，as is shown in Fig. 2-7.

fuel tank：燃料箱
regardless of：不管
altitude：海拔高度
fuel filter：燃油过滤器
carburetor：化油器；汽化器

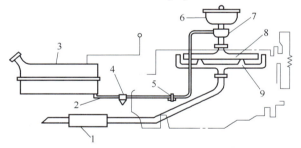

Fig. 2-7　Fuel delivery system 燃油供给系统
1—Muffler 消音器；2—Fuel line 燃油管道；3—Fuel tank 燃油箱；4—Fuel filter 燃油滤清器；
5—Fuel pump 燃油泵；6—Air filter 空气滤清器；7—Carburetor 汽化器；
8—Intake manifold 进气歧管；9—Exhaust manifold 排气歧管

injection system：注射系统
fuel delivery system：供油系统
vacuum：真空
air-fuel ratio：空气燃料比
float system：浮子系统
choke system：节流系统
acceleration system：加速系统
idle system：怠速系统

We will discuss the three basic types of automotive fuel systems：carburetor，gasoline injection system and diesel injection system.

The components of carburetor fuel system are the fuel tank，the fuel pump，the fuel delivery system and the carburetor. The carburetor uses engine vacuum to draw fuel into the engine. All carburetors have six functioning systems that will precisely match the air-fuel ratio requirements on any given engine condition. They are the float system，the main system，the choke system，the power system，the acceleration system and the idle system.

The primary difference between the gasoline injection system and the carburetor system is that fuel is measured into the intake manifold by using how much fuel injectors. Modern gasoline injection systems use a computer and sensors to determine the amount of fuel required for different engine conditions. Computer and sensors read the throttle valve position, the temperature of air entering the engine, the engine coolant temperature, the condensation of oxygen inside the exhaust pipe and other important conditions (see Fig. 2-8). Fig. 2-9 shows a common rail injection diesel.

primary difference：第一差别；主要区别
intake manifold：进气歧管
throttle valve：节流阀；节气门
engine coolant temperature：发动机冷却液温度
condensation：凝结
exhaust pipe：排气管

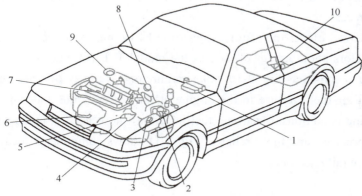

Fig. 2-8　Fuel injection system 燃油喷射系统
1—ECU 电子控制模块；2—Air flow meter 空气流量计；3—EFI main relay 电子控制燃油喷射主继电器；4—Water temperature sensor 水温传感器；5—Cold start injector time switch 冷起动喷射定时开关；6—Oxygen sensor 氧传感器；7—Injector 喷油嘴；8—Ignition coil 点火线圈；9—Throttle position sensor 节气门位置传感器；10—Fuel pump 燃油泵

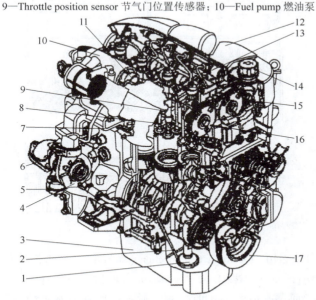

Fig. 2-9　Common rail injection diesel 共轨喷射柴油机
1—Oil strainer 机油集滤器；2—Oil dipstick 机油尺；3—Oil pan 油底壳；4—Turbocharger 涡轮增压器；5—Waste gate 废气旁通阀；6—To exhaust manifold 到排气歧管；7—Intake manifold 进气歧管；8—Valve 气门；9—Injector 喷油器；10—Cylinder head cover 缸盖罩；11—Camshaft 凸轮轴；12—Trim cover 装饰罩；13—Common rail 共轨；14—Oil filler cap 加机油口盖；15—Timing chain 正时链；16—Timing sprocket 正时链轮；17—Crankshaft pulley 曲轴带轮

filter：过滤器
feed pump：进料泵
governor：调速器
timer：计时器
nozzle：喷嘴
firing order：点火顺序
in-line type：直列式
distributor type：分电盘；分配器
out of date：过时的；废弃的

In the diesel fuel system, the feed pump draws the fuel from the fuel tank. It pushes fuel through the fuel filter into the injection pump. The injection pump assembly consists of the feed pump, governor, timer and injection pump. When the injection pump establishes high pressure, it sends fuel to the injectors (nozzles) according to the firing order. At the same time, the injectors inject fuel into the cylinders. There are two types of injection pumps: the in-line type and the distributor type in modern cars.

Now, electronic fuel injection (EFI) has made conventional carburetors about as out of date as the model T. Electronic fuel injection system is shown as Fig. 2-10, like carburetor, is a way of delivering the correct air-fuel mixture to the engine at the correct time under different operating conditions. Electronic fuel injection, however, is much simple, more precise, and more reliable. Fig. 2-11 shows components location of common rail injection system.

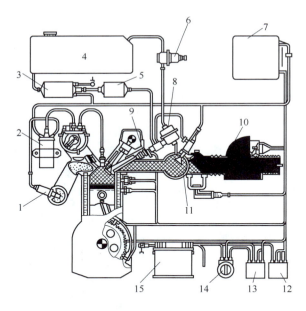

Fig. 2-10　Electronic fuel injection system 电控燃料喷射系统
1—Oxygen sensor 氧传感器；2—Ignition coil 点火线圈；3—Fuel pump 燃油泵；
4—Fuel tank 燃油箱；5—Fuel filter 燃油滤清器；6—Pulsation damper 脉动缓冲器；
7—ECU 电子控制模块；8—Pressure regulator 压力调节器；9—Fuel injector 燃油喷射器；
10—Air flow meter 空气流量计；11—Cold start injector 冷起动喷射器；
12—Pump relay 泵继电器；13—Main relay 主继电器；
14—Ignition switch 点火开关；15—Battery 电池

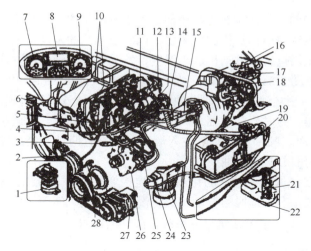

Fig. 2-11 Components location of common rail injection system
共轨喷射系统零部件位置

1—EGR modulator check valve 废气再循环调制器单向阀；2—Electromagnetical fan 电磁风扇；3—Coolant temperature sensor 冷却液温度传感器；4—Glow plug 预热塞；5—Electronic injector 电子喷油器；6—Camshaft position sensor 凸轮轴位置传感器；7—Speedmeter and odometer 车速里程表；8—Display 显示器；9—Engine tachometer 发动机转速表；10—Camshaft sprocket 凸轮轴链轮；11—Common rail 共轨；12—Rail pressure sensor 轨压传感器；13—Intake air pressure and temperature sensor 进气压力与温度传感器；14—Throttle assembly 节气门总成；15—Low pressure fuel pipe 低压油管；16—Brake pedal position sensor 制动踏板位置传感器；17—Clutch pedal position sensor 离合器踏板位置传感器；18—Accelerator pedal position sensor 加速踏板位置传感器；19—Battery 蓄电池；20—ECC（electronic controlled centre）电控中心；21—Fuel gauge sender 燃油表传感器；22—Fuel tank 燃油箱；23—Fuel filter 燃油滤清器；24—Common fitting 共用接头；25—Fuel pressure regulator 燃油压力调节器；26—High pressure pump 高压泵；27—A/C compressor 空调压缩机；28—Engine speed sensor 发动机转速传感器

Reference Version 参考译文

　　燃油系统对发动机的运行是至关重要的。燃料供给系统的作用是为发动机提供被称为可燃混合气的汽油与空气混合物。所有的汽车都有燃料供给系统。它有三种功能：首先，它必须能够储存燃料；第二，它必须能够将燃料从油箱传送到发动机；第三，它必须将空气和燃油混合以供发动机使用。此外，燃料供给系统必须在车辆处于不同环境温度、海拔和速度的条件下完成上述工作。典型的燃料供给系统由油箱、燃油泵、汽油滤清器、化油器和油管组成，如图 2-7 所示。

　　下面我们将讨论三种基本类型的汽车燃油系统：化油器、汽油喷射系统和柴油喷射系统。

　　化油器式燃油系统的部件包括油箱、燃油泵、燃油传输系统和化油器。化油器在发动机真空状态下将燃料吸入发动机。所有的化油器都有六个工作系统，它们可以根据任何给定的发动机工况精确匹配空燃比。六个工作系统分别是浮子系统、主供油系统、节流系统、动力系统、加速系统和怠速系统。

汽油喷射系统和化油器系统的主要区别在于，燃油进入进气歧管的测量是采用几个燃料喷射器进行的。现代汽油喷射系统使用计算机和传感器，以确定不同的发动机工况所需的燃油量。计算机和传感器读取节气门位置、发动机进气温度、发动机冷却液温度、排气管中氧的浓度以及其他重要的指标，见图2-8。图2-9所示为一共轨喷射柴油机。

在柴油机燃油系统中，输油泵从油箱中吸取燃油，然后通过燃油滤清器再送入喷油泵。喷油泵总成包括输油泵、调速器、定时器和喷油泵。当喷油泵建立了高压，它就按工作顺序将燃油送至喷油器（喷嘴）。同时，喷油器往气缸注入燃油。通常有两种类型的喷油泵：柱塞式喷油泵和在新型汽车中使用的分配式喷油泵。

现在，电控燃料喷射系统已经取代了传统的化油器。电控燃料喷射系统如图2-10所示，它和化油器一样，都是在不同的工况下适时给发动机提供燃油混合气。然而，电控燃料喷射系统更简单、精确、可靠。图2-11表示了共轨喷射系统零部件的位置。

Section 2.4
Engine Ignition System
发动机点火系统

high tension voltage：
高电压
timely：适时地

(1) Engine ignition system

Engine ignition system is an important constituent part of engine, its function is to transform the voltage from the battery to high tension voltage, and timely introduce the electricity into the engine cylinder in accordance with the work order of the engine cylinder to ignite the air-fuel mixture by spark, so that the engine can be started normally, as is shown in Fig 2-12.

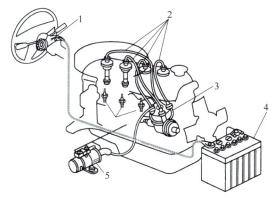

Fig. 2-12　Ignition system 点火系统
1—Ignition switch 点火开关；2—High-tension cords 高压线圈；
3—Distributor 分电器；4—Battery 蓄电池；5—Ignition coil 点火线圈

primary：初级的
secondary：次级的
ignition switch：
点火开关
ballast resistor：附加电阻
ignition coil：点火线圈

The two main sections of the ignition system are the primary and secondary circuits (see Fig. 2-13). The primary circuit includes the battery, the ignition switch, the ballast resistor, the ignition coil (primary coil winding) and the distributor points. The secondary circuit is the high voltage section. It includes the ignition coil (secondary coil winding) and the high tension wire, the distributor rotor and the spark plug.

distributor point: 分电盘触点
distributor rotor: 分电器转子
spark plug: 火花塞

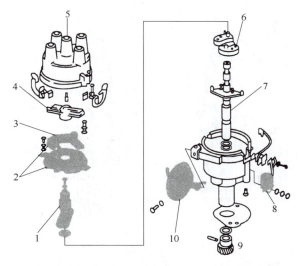

Fig. 2-13　Primary and secondary circuits 主、次电路
1—Distributor cam 分电器凸轮；2—Breaker points 继电器触点；3—Breaker arm 继电器臂；
4—Distributor rotor 转子；5—Distributor cap 分电器盖；6—Weights 配重；
7—Distributor shaft 分电器轴；8—Condenser 电容器；9—Driving gear 驱动齿轮；
10—Vacuum advancer 真空提前机构

There are two different types of distributors (drawing is same with Fig. 2-13): the breaker point (mechanical) type and the pickup coil (electronic switching circuit) type. The breaker point type is used in older cars. It uses mechanical breaker points to interrupt the flow of primary current. The pickup coil type is used on many modern cars. It has a trigger wheel, a pickup coil and an ECM (electronic control module) to perform the same function as the breaker point type.

breaker point: 继电器触点

trigger wheel: 信号转子
pickup coil: 点火信号传感器

The spark plug uses a high voltage (10~30kV) to ignite the air and fuel mixture. The temperature of the electrode in the spark plug will be 900℃ in the combustion stroke. Therefore, the spark plug must be able to maintain ignition performance when the engine is running. Fig. 2-14 shows the basic parts of a spark plug which includes the nut, the insulator, the center electrode, the powder seal, the resistor, the threads and the spark plug gap.

combustion stroke: 压缩冲程
insulator: 绝缘子
electrode: 电极
powder seal: 粉末密封层

The electronic distributorless ignition system is the most recent advancement made in modern cars (see Fig. 2-15). In this system, a computer receives input signals from some sensors to control timing adjustment and to allow up to a 3 to 4 degrees of additional spark advance.

distributorless: 无分电器的

The sensors are the engine speed sensor, the crankshaft position sensor, the intake pressure sensor, the intake temperature sensor, the engine coolant temperature sensor, the cam sensor, the knock sensor and the throttle position sensor.

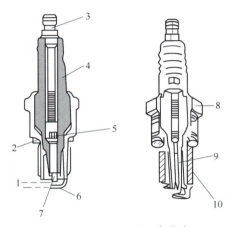

Fig. 2-14 Spark plug 火花塞
1—Gap 间隙；2—Gasket 垫圈；3—Terminal 端子；4—Insulator 绝缘陶瓷；5—Resistor 电阻；
6—Ground electrode 搭铁电极；7—Center electrode 中央电极；8—Nut 螺母；
9—Copper core 铜芯；10—Threads 螺纹

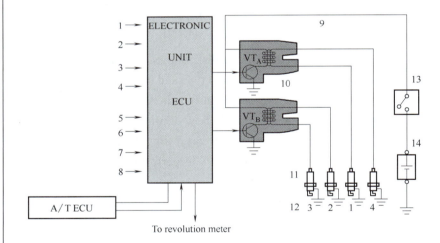

Fig. 2-15 Electronic distributorless ignition system 无分电器式电子点火系统
1—Engine speed sensor 发动机速度传感器；2—Crank shaft position sensor 曲轴位置传感器；
3—Intake pressure sensor 进气压力传感器；4—Intake temperature sensor 进气温度传感器；
5—Engine coolant temperature sensor 发动机水温传感器；6—Cam sensor 凸轮轴传感器；
7—Knock sensor 爆震传感器；8—Throttle position sensor 节气门位置传感器；
9—Ignition coil A 点火线圈 A；10—Ignition coil B 点火线圈 B；11—Spark plug 火花塞；
12—Cylinder 气缸；13—Ignition switch 点火开关；14—Battery 蓄电池

As previously mentioned, according to the structure style, the ignition system could be divided into the conventional breaker point type ignition system (in use since the early 1900s), the electronic ignition system (popular since the mid 1970s, see Fig. 2-16), and the distributorless ignition system (introduced in the mid 1980s, see Fig. 2-17). At present, the conventional breaker point type ignition system has become obsolete, while the electronic ignition system and the distributorless ignition system are widely used in the modern vehicle.

obsolete: 废弃

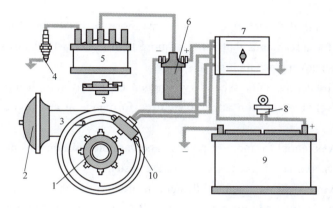

Fig. 2-16　A typical electronic ignition system　一种典型的点火系统
1—Reluctor or armature 磁阻转子或电枢；2—Vacuum advance 真空提前装置；
3—Rotor 分火头；4—Spark plug 火花塞；5—Distributor cap 分电器盖；
6—Ignition coil 点火线圈；7—Electronic control module 电子控制模块；
8—Ignition switch 点火开关；9—Battery 蓄电池；10—Magnetic pick-up 电磁拾波器

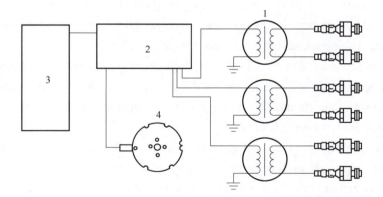

Fig. 2-17　A typical distributorless ignition system　一种典型的无分电器点火系统
1—Coils 线圈；2—Ignition module 点火组件；3—Engine control module 发动机控制组件；
4—Magnetic triggering device 电磁触发装置

(2) Electronic ignition system

The function of the ignition system is to ignite the compressed air and fuel mixture at the correct time, and initiate its combustion. In the spark ignition engine, this is achieved by means of brief electrical arc discharge

electrical arc: 电弧

Sidebar glossary:

electrode：电极

emission control standard：废气排放控制标准

centrifugal：离心

vacuum-advance：真空提前

eliminate：淘汰

secondary voltage：次级电压；二次电压

maintenance cost：维修费

magnetic field：磁场

primary coil：初级线圈

requirement for：需要

solid-state：固态

---

between the electrodes of the sparking plug. At present, electronic ignition system is used mostly, this action was necessary not only to meet stricter emission control standards but to increase the fuel economy of the vehicle. All the function that used to be done mechanically can now be done through electronics. Centrifugal and vacuum-advance mechanisms in the distributor have been eliminated, and ignition timing is controlled by the engine computer.

Although the electronic system costs more to install than the standard system, the advantages that it offers more than the drawbacks of increased cost. These advantages include：

① Greater available secondary voltage, especially at high engine rpm.

② Reliable and consistent system performance at any and all engine speeds.

③ A potential for more responsive and variable ignition advance curves.

④ Decreased maintenance cost of the system.

However, in the standard system in order for a coil in the secondary system to produce adequate voltage at all times, the contact points must remain closed for a given period of time—the dwell period. As vehicle speed increases, the points open and close much faster, and this reduces the effective time the points remain closed. Consequently, there is a reduction in the buildup time of the magnetic field around the primary coil, which is responsible for producing secondary voltage. This characteristic of the standard system permits it to produce a substantially large secondary voltage at lower engine speeds but a reduced voltage at high rpm.

In addition, due to the fact that the contact points mechanically close and open, there is some arcing as the points open. This occurs despite a condenser in the circuit. This arcing results in point wear and the requirement for periodic point replacement.

In summary, standard ignition systems fail at high engine rpm to produce sufficient voltage in order to prevent misfires. These misfires cause negative exhaust emissions and decreased economy. In addition, the standard system requires frequent service on its spark plugs, due to less available secondary voltage at high rpm, especially as the plug's air gap grows larger due to high mileage. This, of course, increases emissions and reduces fuel economy.

The electronic ignition system does not use the contact points as a switching device to open and close, the primary circuit. Instead, the system uses an electronic switch in the form of one or more transistors to control primary current flow. These transistors and other parts of the solid-state control circuitry are inside a sealed control unit.

Since the early 1970s, a number of different types of electronic ignition systems have been designed and produced by the automotive industry (see Fig. 2-18). Many add-on and some of the early factories installed solid-state electronic ignition systems adapted the control unit to the existing triggering device the ignition contact points. With this arrangement, the system uses a conventional distributor with the original contact points, but the unit does not require a condenser.

add-on: 附加装置

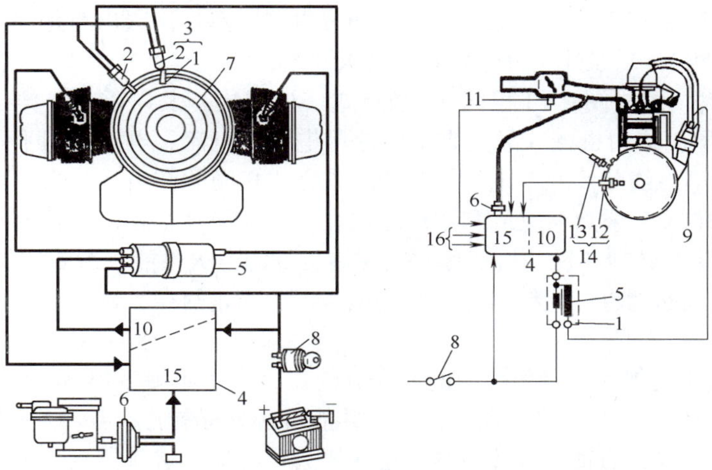

Fig. 2-18 Electronic ignition systems 电子点火系统
1—Magnetic plug 磁堵; 2—Magnetic sensor 磁性传感器; 3—Magnetic pulse generator 磁脉冲发生器; 4—Electronic control unit 电子控制器; 5—Ignition coil 点火线圈; 6—Vacuum sensor 真空传感器; 7—Flywheel rim 飞轮轮辋; 8—Ignition lock 点火开关; 9—High-tension distributor 高压分电盘; 10—Amplifier 放大器; 11—Throttle valve switch 节流阀开关; 12—Reference-speed sensor 基准车速传感器; 13—Rotational-speed sensor 旋转速度传感器; 14—Proximity sensor 接近传感器; 15—Microprocessor 微处理器; 16—Supplementary sensor input 附加传感器输入

In this contact, controlled system, a transistor assembly within the switching unit (the amplifier) takes over the traditional task of the contact points in controlling primary circuit current flow. In other words, the contact points in this electronic system act as an on-off switch for the emitter-base circuit of the transistor. The emitter collector circuit of the transistor handles the current flow of the primary-coil windings to ground while the contact points carry only about 1 ampere, depending on the make and model of the system.

emitter-base circuit: 发射极-集电极回路

An electronic ignition system using a magnetic-pulse triggering device is similar to the contact controlled type. However, when a magnetic pulse triggering is in the distributor, it switches the transistor on or off by means of an electrical charge induced through magnetism. Since this system has no contact points at all, it is known as a breakerless electronic ignition system.

magnetic-pulse: 磁脉冲
triggering device: 触发装置

breakerless: 无触点

Reference Version 参考译文

（1）发动机点火系统

发动机点火系统是发动机的重要组成部分，其功能就是把蓄电池的低压电转化为高压电，并按发动机气缸工作顺序适时地引入气缸，形成电火花点燃混合气，从而使发动机正常工作，如图2-12所示。

点火系统的两个主要组成部分为初级电路及次级电路（如图2-13所示）。初级电路包括蓄电池、点火开关、附加电阻、点火线圈（低压绕组）和分电器触点。次级电路是高压电部分，包括点火线圈（高压绕组）、高压线、分电器转子及火花塞。

分电器有以下两种形式（图与图2-13相同）：触点式（机械式）及电磁式（电子开关式）。触点式使用于老旧车型，使用机械式触点来中断低压电路的电流。电磁式用于现代车型，由一个信号转子、一个电磁线圈及一个电子控制模块来完成相同的作用及功能。

火花塞以高压电（10~30kV）来点燃空气和燃料之混合气。在做功行程，火花塞电极的温度可高达900℃，因此火花塞必须在发动机工作时仍保持良好的点火性能。图2-14所示为火花塞的基本组成部分，它包括螺母、绝缘部分、中心电极、粉末密封层、螺纹和火花塞间隙。

无分电器式电子点火系统是现代车辆所使用的最先进的点火系（如图2-15所示），计算机能从各个传感器接收输入信号，进而控制点火正时，并能再额外提前点火约3°～4°。这些传感器包括发动机转速传感器、曲轴位置传感器、进气压力传感器、进气温度传感器、水温传感器、凸轮轴位置传感器、爆震传感器和节气门位置传感器。

如前所述，点火系统按结构形式分为传统的触点式点火系统（从20世纪初开始使用）、电子点火系统（于20世纪70年代中期起开始受欢迎，见图2-16）和无分电器的点火系统（于20世纪80年代中期起开始引入，见图2-17）。目前，传统的触电式点火系统已被淘汰，现代汽车普遍采用电子点火系统和无分电器的点火系统。

（2）电子点火系统

点火系统的功能就是将压缩空气与燃料的混合物在正确的时间予以点燃并立即燃烧。

电火花点燃式发动机是依靠火花塞电极之间短暂的电弧放电来完成的。目前，大多使用电子点火系统，其功能的必要性在于，不仅可以满足严格的废气排放控制标准，而且还大大提高车辆的燃油经济性。机械方式完成的所有功能都可以由电子产品来实现。分电盘上的离心和真空提前等机械装置已经被淘汰，点火正时已由发动机电脑控制。

虽然电子点火系统的成本比标准体系要高一些，但它的优势远大于增加成本这一弊端。
① 可产生更高的次级电压，特别在发动机转速高时。
② 系统性能在发动机任何转速下都可靠、恒定。
③ 点火提前曲线响应更敏捷而且可改变。
④ 系统的维修费用低。

然而，在标准点火系统中，为了在次级电路中始终产生充足的电压，在延迟期接触点必须在一定时间内保持闭合。当车辆速度增大时，接触点打开、关闭速度加快，这将减少触点闭合的有效时间。因而初级线圈建立磁场的时间减少，导致次级电压降低。标准点火系统的这种特性使其在发动机低速时可以产生大幅度的次级电压，但在高转速时电压会降低。

另外，由于接触点机械地开合，触点断开时会产生电弧，即使有电容器仍会发生放电。电弧放电将会导致触点烧蚀，必须定期更换触点。

总而言之，在发动机高转速时，标准点火系统缺乏产生足够的电压以预防打不着火的能力。这种打不着火的故障会导致废气排放增加和燃油经济性下降。此外，在标准体系中，需要频繁维修火花塞。由于缺少可用的次级电压，特别是随着汽车里程数的增加，火花塞的气隙也会随之增大。

电子点火系统在开关装置进行通断、初级电路中都不用触点。系统使用电子开关取而代之，以一个或多个晶体管的形式控制一次涌流。这些晶体管和其他固态控制电路部件在内部组成密封的控制单元。

20世纪70年代初，一些不同类型的电子点火系统已经由汽车制造业设计和制作出来（见图2-18）。许多附加设备和一些早期安装固态电子点火系统的工厂想使控制单元适应现行触发装置的点火触点。按照这种思路，该系统用一个传统的带经典接触点的分电盘，但该单元不用电容器。

采用这种接触，受控系统、晶体管装配在内部开关单元（放大器），在控制初级电路电流方面取得超过接触点的传统作业效果。换句话说，这种电子系统的接触点相当于一个晶体管发射极-集电极通断开关。晶体管的发射极、集电极电路控制着初级线圈绕组的电流，根据系统的构造和型号，当接触点只带有1A电流时即接地。

用磁脉冲触发装置的电子点火系统相当于一种受控连接类型。不管怎样，当磁脉冲触发时则处于分电中，它依靠磁力诱发电荷改变晶体管的通断。因为这种系统已经完全没有触点，所以被称为无触点电子点火系统。

Section 2.5
Engine Starting System
发动机起动系统

（1）Engine starting system

Automobile engines are not self-start. In order to start them, the engine crankshaft must be turned on. The vehicle's starting system is depend on outside force to turn crank and make it automatically into working cycle. This outside force comes from starter motor. To do this, the starter motor receives electrical power from the storage battery. The starter motor then converts this energy into mechanical energy, which transmits through the drive mechanism to the engine crankshaft flywheel. Fig. 2-19 shows the component of the typical starting system, it consists of several basic assemblies, such as battery, starting switch, magnetic switch, starter motor, etc. The starter motor provides the torque to start the engine at low temperatures. The magnetic switch makes the low-resistance connection between the battery and

self-start：自起动的
working cycle：工作循环
starter motor：起动马达
storage battery：蓄电池
drive mechanism：传动装置
magnetic switch：电磁开关
low-resistance：低电阻

the starting motor.

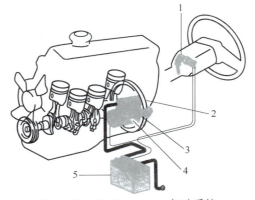

Fig. 2-19 Starting system 起动系统
1—Ignition switch 点火开关；2—Flywheel 飞轮；3—Drive pinion gear 驱动齿轮；
4—Starter motor 起动电机；5—Battery 蓄电池

armature：电枢

field coils：励磁线圈
mesh with：紧密配合
flywheel：飞轮

overrunning clutch：
超越离合器
disengage：松开

The operating principle of the starter motor is shown in Fig. 2-20. When the starting circuit is closed, the starter motor armature will begin to turn by the electromagnetic force created between the field coils. As the armature turns, the starter drive pinion gear rotates in mesh with the teeth on the flywheel ring, then spins the engine over so that the piston can draw in blended fuel which is then ignited to start the engine. When the engine speed is faster than the starter, the overrunning clutch automatically disengages the starter gear from the engine gear. The starter is a powerful motor that can crank the engine fast enough to start the car at 200 rpm.

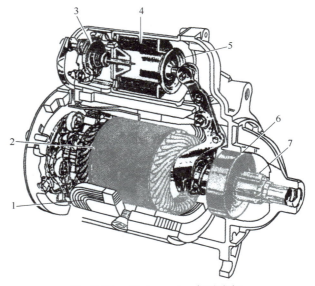

Fig. 2-20 Starter motor 起动电机
1—Field coil 磁场线圈；2—Armature 电枢；3—Plunger contact disk 柱塞接触盘；
4—Solenoid windings 电磁线圈；5—Plunger 柱塞；6—Overrunning clutch 超速离合器；
7—Drive pinion gear 驱动小齿轮

Fig. 2-21 shows a magnetic switch, allows the control circuit to open or close the starter circuit. The magnetic switch connects the starter to the battery through the battery cables for the short period that engine is being cranked. The switch is mounted near the battery or the starter to keep the cables as short as possible. When the ignition switch activates the coil of magnetic switch, the movable plunger is drawn into contact with the internal contacts of the battery and starter terminals. It permits the full battery current to flow to the starter motor.

battery cable: 电池连线
short period: 短周期的
activate: 活化
terminal: 端子

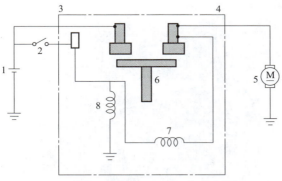

Fig. 2-21　Magnetic switch 电磁开关

1—Battery 蓄电池；2—Ignition switch 点火开关；3—Battery terminal 蓄电池端子；
4—Starter terminal 起动电机端子；5—Starter motor 起动电机；6—Plunger 柱塞；
7—Pull-in coil 吸入线圈；8—Hold-in coil 电磁线圈

Cars equipped with automatic transmissions require a means of preventing the engine from being started in gear. The neutral safety switch is in series with starter magnetic switch (see Fig. 2-22). When the transmission is in D, 1, 2 or R position, the neutral safety switch is disconnected. It keeps current from the magnetic switch and starter when the ignition switch is starting. When the transmission is in N or P position, the starter will be activated because of the neutral safety switch being connected.

automatic transmission: 自动变速箱
in gear: 处于正常状态
neutral safety switch: 空挡安全开关
in series with: 串联

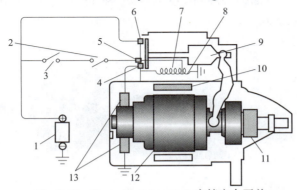

Fig. 2-22　Neutral safety switch 空挡安全开关

1—Battery 蓄电池；2—Neutral safety switch 空挡安全开关；3—Ignition switch 点火开关；
4—M-terminal M 起动电机端子；5—S-terminal S 起动电机端子；6—B-terminal B 电瓶端子；
7—Pull-in coil 吸入线圈；8—Hold-in coil 吸住线圈；9—Plunger 柱塞；10—Field coil 磁场线圈；
11—Drive pinion gear 驱动小齿轮；12—Armature 电枢；13—Brush 电刷

(2) Starter construction

A starter is a high-torque electric motor that converts electrical energy from the battery into mechanical energy to crank the engine. See Fig. 2-23. Advances in technology have changed the construction of some starters. Their new design makes them smaller, lighter, and more powerful. They require less current by using permanent magnets instead of field coils. They use internal gear reduction to increase cranking torque.

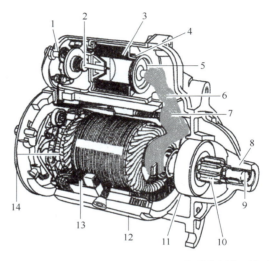

Fig. 2-23　Cutaway view of a solenoid starter 电磁线圈起动机的剖面图
1—Motor-feed terminal 发动机进线接头；2—Plunger contact disk 柱塞连接盘；
3—Solenoid windings 电磁线圈绕组；4—Return spring 回位弹簧；5—Plunger 柱塞；
6—Shift lever 变速杆；7—Pivot pin 枢轴销；8—Bushing 衬套；9—Armature shaft 电枢轴；
10—Drive pinion 传动小齿轮；11—Overrunning clutch 超越离合器；12—Pole shoe 极靴；
13—Field coils 励磁线圈；14—Brush assembly 电刷总成

1) Armature and field coils

A field coil starter contains two basic assemblies: an armature and field coils. See Fig. 2-24.

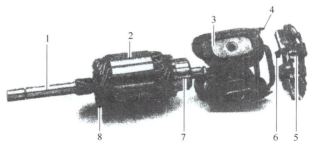

Fig. 2-24　Components of the field coil starter 励磁线圈起动机的部件
1—Armature shaft 电枢轴；2—Armature core 电枢铁芯；3—Pole shoes 极靴；
4—Field coils 励磁线圈；5—Brush hold 电刷柄；6—Carbon brushes 碳刷；
7—Commutator 整流器；8—Armature winding 电枢绕组

The field coils are mounted on the starter housing. An electromagnet consists of a soft iron and a pole shoe (core) wrapped with a coil of copper wire. The field coil is an electromagnet that produces a stationary magnetic field. The pole shoe guides and intensifies the magnetic field so that it reacts strongly with the armature. Field coil starters contain either four or six field coils.

soft iron: 软铁
pole shoe: 极靴

The armature is the part of the starter that rotates. It contains many individual windings (coils). A non-conducting material electrically separates the coils. Current flowing through the coils creates magnetic fields. A laminated iron core increases the strength of the magnetic fields in the armature.

non-conducting: 绝缘的；不导电的
laminated iron core: 叠片铁芯

The armature mounts on a shaft located inside the starter housing. Bearings support the armature at each end. The smaller the space between die armature and the field magnets, the stronger the magnetic reaction. However, the armature must be able to rotate freely without touching the field magnets.

The commutator is a series of copper segments placed side by side to form a ring around the armature shaft. Non-conducting material separates each segment. Two segments, appropriately placed, connect to each end of a coil in the armature. As the armature rotates, carbon brushes ride against the commutator segments and supply current to the armature coils.

commutator: 整流器；换向器

carbon brushes: 碳刷
commutator segment: 换向片

2) Starter operation

Electric motors work on the principle of electromagnetism. Electromagnetism occurs when current flowing through a conductor creates an electromagnetic field. An electromagnetic field is the space around an electromagnet that is filled with invisible lines of force. The strength of the field depends on the amount of current flow and the number of wires in the coil. Placing an iron core inside the coil also increases field strength.

electromagnetism: 电磁学

In a field coil starter, current passing through the field coils creates an electromagnetic field. The same current passes through one brush, into the commutator segment, through the armature coil, out through the other segment, and through another brush to ground. See Fig. 2-25.

Current passing through the armature coils creates another electromagnetic field. As the armature rotates, the brushes and the commutator reverse the direction of the current flow in the armature coils. Reversing the direction of current in each coil reverses the direction of the magnetic field. The magnetic fields in the armature are attracted and repelled by the magnetic field created by the field coils. The action of the magnetic fields makes the armature rotate.

commutator: 换向器
reverse: 颠倒；倒换
attract: 吸引
repel: 排斥

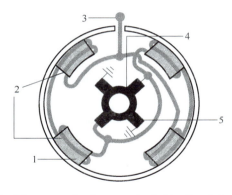

Fig. 2-25　The connection between the field coil and the armature
励磁线圈和电枢的连接

1—Pole shoes 极靴；2—Field coils 励磁线圈；3—Motor terminal 发动机端子；
4—Commutator 整流器；5—Brush 电刷

In a permanent magnet starter, current flows only through the armature windings. The permanent magnets provide the stationary magnetic field. The magnetic fields in the armature are attracted and repelled by the magnetic fields created by the permanent magnets.

High current flows to the starter only when the ignition switch is in the START position. As long as current flow exists, the armature continues to rotate. When the ignition switch returns to the run position, the contacts of the starter relay or solenoid open. No current flows to the starter. Without current flow, the starter armature stops rotating. The starter stops cranking the engine.

3) Relay and solenoid starters

Some manufacturers use both a relay and a solenoid. Low-current applied to the relay coil pulls the relay plunger into the center of the coil. Contacts on the relay plunger connect low-current to the solenoid coil.

Low-current applied to the solenoid coil energizes the solenoid. The energized coil pulls the solenoid plunger into the center of the solenoid coil. Electrical contacts connected to the base of the solenoid plunger close when the pinion and ring gear mesh. The closed contacts provide a high current path between the battery and the starter.

Typical service problems with relays and solenoids may include burned or pitted contacts and binding of the plunger assembly. Defective relays and solenoids are replaced. A chattering or buzzing from a relay, solenoid, or starter is an indication of low battery current or high resistance in the circuit.

4) Starter drive assembly

The starter drive assembly engages and disengages the pinion gear and the ring gear.

The pinion gear is the smallest gear in a gear set. The pinion gear on the armature shaft meshes with the larger ring gear on the flywheel or drive plate of the engine. The ring gear has about fifteen times as many teeth as the pinion gear. The pinion gear must rotate fifteen times to rotate the ring gear one time. If the starter operates at 3000 rpm, it will crank the engine at 200 rpm.

The overrunning clutch prevents the engine from driving the starter. See Fig. 2-26. As the engine starts. its speed may rapidly increase to 2000 rpm or higher. If the pinion gear remained engaged with the ring gear, the starter's armature would rotate at 30000 rpm. The armature would break apart at such speed. The overrunning clutch transmits torque only in one direction. It rotates freely in the opposite direction, preventing armature damage.

overrunning clutch：单向离合器；超速离合器

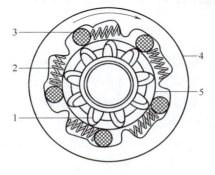

Fig. 2-26　A cutaway view of an overrunning clutch with pinion gear
带小齿轮的超越离合器剖面图
1—Pinion gear 小齿轮；2—Roller spring 滚轴弹簧；3—Roller 滚轴；
4—Shell 壳体；5—Pinion collar 小齿轮套环

During starter operation, rotation of the armature forces the rollers into the small end of the notches in the clutch shell. This action locks the clutch to transmit cranking torque to the engine. As the engine starts, ring gear rotation turns the pinion and clutch shell faster than the armature. The roller springs force the rollers into the large end of the shell notches. The overrunning clutch unlocks, removing cranking torque, allowing the pinion gear to spin freely.

small end：发动机活塞连杆的一端
notch：换极触点

5）Gear reduction and cranking torque

The forces of friction and compression require high torque to crank the engine. Torque is affected by starter design and by the gear ratio between the pinion and the ring gear. A gear ratio expresses the number of rotations one gear must make to rotate a driven gear one time. If the starter connects directly to the crankshaft, the gear ratio is 1∶1. A direct connection does not supply enough torque to crank.

gear ratio：齿轮齿数比

Gear reduction increases starter torque by increasing the gear ratio. In

gear reduction：齿轮减速

reduction gear set：减速装置

our example starter, the pinion gear and ring gear form an external reduction gear set. The pinion gear must rotate fifteen times to rotate the ring gear one time, for a ratio of 15∶1.

Some starters use a combination of internal and external gear reduction to increase torque. Internal gear reduction is supplied by planetary gears. External gear reduction is supplied by the starter pinion gear and the engine ring gear. The combination of internal and external gear reduction provides a much higher gear ratio, for example 45∶1. The pinion gear must rotate forty-five times to rotate the ring gear one revolution.

Reference Version 参考译文

（1）汽车起动系统

汽车发动机是不能自动起动的。为了起动发动机，曲轴必须先运转起来。起动系统是依靠外力转动发动机曲轴使之自动进入工作循环。这个外力来自起动电机。为了起动，起动电机接受来自蓄电池的电能，并把它转换成机械能，通过驱动机构传给发动机飞轮。图2-19所示为典型的起动系组件，由蓄电池、起动开关、电磁开关、起动电机等几个基本部分组成。起动电机在发动机冷车时提供扭力来起动发动机。电磁开关使蓄电池和起动机以低电阻连接。

起动电机作用原理如图2-20所示。当起动电路接通时，起动电机电枢会被电枢及磁场线圈间交互产生的磁力线所带动而转动。当电枢转动时，驱动小齿轮转动，并与飞轮上的齿圈啮合，使发动机旋转，以便活塞吸入混合燃料，被点燃后驱动发动机。当发动机转速超过起动机转速时，超速离合器自动断开起动机齿轮和发动机齿轮的啮合。起动电机为一个强有力的电机，能带动发动机以高达200r/min的速度来起动车辆。

图2-21所示为电磁开关，用来控制电路断开或接通起动电机电路，它是在发动机起动的短暂时间中，经由蓄电池线直接连接起动电机和蓄电池。电磁开关安装于靠近蓄电池或起动电机的位置，以尽可能缩短导线的距离。当点火开关触动电磁开关的线圈时，活动柱塞会被吸入而接触电磁开关内的蓄电池及起动电机接头的接点，这样便可让全部蓄电池电流流至起动电机。

配备自动变速器的小汽车，需要以某种方法来避免发动机在挂挡状态下被起动。空挡安全开关是以串联方式来与起动电机电磁开关连接的，如图2-22所示。当自动变速器在D、1、2或R挡位置时，空挡安全开关是不导通的，因此当点火开关在起动位置时可避免电流流入电磁开关。当自动变速器在N或P挡位置时，起动电机就可动作，因为此时空挡安全开关已导通。

（2）起动机结构

起动机是一个由电池的电能转换为机械能的大转矩电动机，它通过曲轴带动发动机，见图2-23。科技的进步改变了起动机的一些结构，它们的新式样更小、更轻、更强有力，现在要求用以替代励磁线圈的永磁体用量也更少，还把内齿轮简化为增强的由曲轴转动的转矩。

1）电枢和励磁线圈

励磁线圈起动机包括两个基本组件：电枢和励磁线圈，见图2-24。

励磁线圈安装在起动机的壳体上。电磁体由软铁、铜线线圈覆盖的极靴组成。励磁线圈是一个产生固定磁场的电磁体。由极靴支配和强化磁场，以便让电枢的作用更加强有力。励磁线圈起动机包含四个或六个励磁线圈。

电枢是一个让起动机旋转的部件。它包含许多独立的绕组（电磁线圈），绝缘材料从电学上将电磁线圈分离开来，电流流经电磁线圈则产生磁场。叠片铁芯增加了电枢磁场的强度。

电枢安装在起动机壳体内部的一根轴上，两端的轴承支撑着电枢。电枢上下和磁体之间空间越小，磁场的作用就越强。然而，电枢必须能够脱离磁体接触而自由旋转。

整流器是一系列铜块放置在一起形成一个环形围绕着电枢轴。绝缘材料将每一个铜块分隔开，合理配置的两段被分别连接到电枢线圈的两端。当电枢旋转时，碳刷紧靠在换向片上，并且提供电流到电枢线圈。

2）起动机的运行

电动机的工作原理依赖于电磁学。电磁的产生是由于电流流过导体形成电磁场，电磁场是一个周身布满隐线的电磁铁周围的空间。磁场的强度取决于电流量和线圈电线数，在内部放置一个铁芯，线圈磁场强度还会增加。

励磁线圈的起动机里，电流流经励磁线圈时产生磁场，这一电流经过电刷进入整流器，流经电枢线圈，从另一线段流出，然后经过另一个电刷再接地，见图2-25。

电流流经电枢线圈产生不同的磁场。当电枢旋转时，电刷和整流器倒换电枢电流的方向，倒换电流方向后，在另一个线圈里的磁场方向也随之倒换。电枢里的磁场是吸引还是排斥由励磁线圈产生的磁场决定。磁场的作用迫使电枢旋转。

在永磁起动机中，电流仅流经电枢绕组，永磁体提供固定的磁场，电枢里的磁场是吸引还是排斥由磁体的磁场决定。

强电流仅在点火开关的初始位置进入起动机。只要电流存在，电枢就连续旋转。当点火开关置于运行位置时，起动继电器或者螺线管就接通。没有电流进入起动机。没有电流，起动机电枢就停止旋转，起动机也就让曲轴带动的发动机停转。

3）继电器和螺线管起动机

一些制造商使用继电器和螺线管。弱电流加到结晶器线圈，将结晶器柱塞拖到线圈中心，继电器柱塞上的连接点将弱电流连接到螺线管线圈。

加到螺线管的弱电流激励螺线管。被激励的线圈将继电器柱塞拖到螺线管中心，当小齿轮和内齿轮啮合时，连接到结晶器柱塞基点关闭，关闭的连接点在电池和起动机之间提供一个强电流通道。

使用继电器和螺线管的典型维修故障包括继电器柱塞总成烧坏、柱塞烧起凹坑和柱塞的固定等问题。有缺陷的继电器和螺线管应换下。颤振和蜂鸣来自继电器、螺线管或起动机，这是电池电量不足或者电路中电阻高的迹象。

4）起动机传动部件

起动机传动部件能够啮合或脱开小齿轮和内齿轮圈。

小齿轮是齿轮组中最小的齿轮。电枢轴上的小齿轮与飞轮或发动机驱动盘上较大的内齿圈啮合，内齿圈齿数大约有小齿轮的15倍之多，如果起动机运行3000r/min，那么曲轴带动的发动机运行200r/min。

超越离合器可防止起动机突然猛烈驱动发动机，见图2-26。当发动机起动时，它的速度可以迅速地增加到 2000r/min 甚至更高，如果这时小齿轮同内齿圈保持啮合，那起动机电枢将会以 30000r/min 旋转，电枢在这种速度下将会解体。超越离合器传递转矩只在一个方向，它向相反方向自由旋转，以防止损坏电枢。

起动机运行期间，在关键时刻电枢的转动使滚轴滚向换级触点的发动机连杆一端，该动作锁住离合器，不让其传递转动曲轴的转矩。当发动机起动时，内齿圈的旋转带动小齿轮和离合壳体倒转的速度比电枢更快，滚轴弹簧使滚轴滚向壳体换极触点的大端，超越离合器开启，抵消转动曲轴的转矩，允许小齿轮自由地旋转。

5）齿轮减速和曲轴转矩

摩擦和压缩的力量需要高转矩以让曲轴带动发动机旋转。转矩受小齿轮和内齿圈的齿数比影响。齿数比表明在某个时刻一个齿轮让从动轮旋转的比率。如果起动机直接连接到曲轴，那齿数比就是 1∶1。直接连接不能提供足够的转矩给曲轴。

齿轮减速由增大齿数比来增大起动机的转矩。以本起动机为例，小齿轮和内齿圈形成一个外部减速装置。在同一时刻，小齿轮的转数必须是内齿圈的 15 倍，即齿轮齿数比为 15∶1。

一些起动机内外齿轮兼用以增大转矩。内齿轮减速是由行星齿轮来实现，外齿轮减速由起动机的小齿轮和发动机的内齿圈实现，内外兼用减速要提供更大的齿数比，例如 45∶1。这时小齿轮转速必须 45 倍于内齿圈转速。

Section 2.6
Engine Cooling and Lubricating Systems
发动机冷却与润滑系统

engine cooling system：
发动机冷却系
efficient operating：
有效操作
driving condition：
驾驶条件；驾驶状态
exhaust gas：
排放气体；废气
overheating：过热
additional heat：余热

fluid：流体；液体
passageway：通道
heat exchanger：热交换器
radiator：散热器

（1）Engine cooling system

The purpose of the cooling system is to keep the engine at its most efficient operating temperature at all engine speeds and all driving conditions.

A great deal of heat is produced in the engine by the burning of the air-fuel mixture. Some of this heat escapes from the engine through the exhaust gases to keep the engine from overheating. But enough remains in the engine to cause serious trouble, the cooling system takes care of this additional heat. Another important job of the cooling system is to allow the engine to heat up as quickly as possible, and then to keep the engine at a constant temperature.

There are two types of cooling systems found on cars: liquid-cooled and air-cooled.

The cooling system on liquid-cooled cars circulates a fluid through pipes and passageways in the engine. As this liquid passes through the hot engine it absorbs heat, cooling the engine. After the fluid leaves the engine, it passes through a heat exchanger, or radiator, which transfers the heat from the fluid to the air blowing through the exchanger.

Some older cars, and very few modern cars, are air-cooled. Since most cars are liquid-cooled, we will focus on that system in this article.

The liquid cooling system consists of water pumps, water jackets, engine fan, radiator, coolant reservoir tank, radiator cap, thermostat, hoses and so on, as is shown in Fig. 2-27. The cooling system is built into the engine. There are hollow spaces around each engine cylinder and combustion chamber. These hollow spaces are called water jackets, since they are filled with water. When the engine is running, the water takes heat from the engine, becoming hot in the process. A water pump pumps the hot water from the engine water jackets into the radiator. The radiator has two sets of passages. One set carries water. The other set carries air (pulled through by car motion and the engine fan). As the hot water passes through, it gives up its heat to the air passing through. The cooled water then reenters the engine, where it can pick up more heat. In operation, water continuously circulates between the engine and radiator, carrying heat from the engine to the radiator. By this means, excessive engine temperatures are prevented.

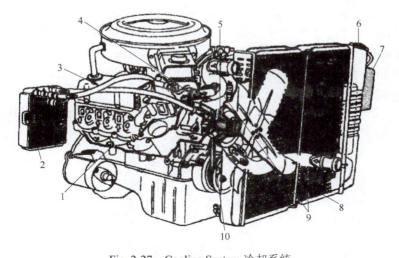

Fig. 2-27　Cooling System 冷却系统
1—Water jacket 水套；2—Heater 暖气水箱；3—Heater hose 暖气水管；4—Thermostat 节温器；
5—Water pump 水泵；6—Pressure cap 压力式水箱盖；7—Coolant reservoir tank 副水箱；
8—Radiator core 散热器芯；9—Hoses 水管；10—Fan belt 风扇皮带

The water pump is a simple centrifugal pump. The water pump, driven by a belt from the engine crankshaft, circulates the cooling liquid between the radiator and engine water jackets. The cooling liquid is water. Antifreeze compounds are added to the water during the winter. The water jacket are cast into the cylinder blocks and heads. The engine fan is usually mounted on the water pump shaft and is driven by the same belt that drives the pump and the generator, see Fig.2-28. The purpose of the fan is to provide a powerful draft of air through the radiator. The radiator is a device for holding a large volume of water in close contact with a large volume of air so that heat will transfer from the water to the air. The radiator core is divided into two separate and intricate compartments; water passes through one, and air passes through the other.

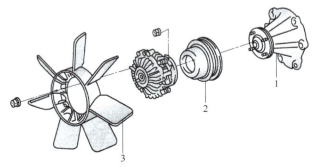

Fig. 2-28　Water pump and fan 水泵和风扇
1—Water pump 水泵；2—Pulley 带盘；3—Cooling fan 冷却风扇

The radiator is the largest part of the cooling system, most of the heat from the engine is transferred from the coolant to the surrounding air, as is shown in Fig. 2-29. The reservoir tank is connected to the overflow hose. When the hot coolant expands in the radiator, the reservoir tank allows coolant to flow in. As the system cools, the coolant will be drawn back into the radiator.

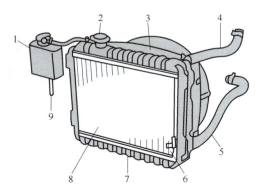

Fig. 2-29　Radiator and reservoir tank 水箱（散热器）和副水箱
1—Reservoir tank 副水箱；2—Pressure cap 压力式水箱盖；3—Upper tank 上水箱；4—Upper hose 上水管；5—Lower hose 下水管；6—Drain 放水塞；7—Lower tank 下水箱；
8—Radiator core 水箱芯子；9—Overflow hose 溢流管

The radiator is normally equipped with a pressure cap or radiator cap that tightly seals the radiator, as is shown in Fig. 2-30. This allows the coolant to rise above 100℃ in temperature without boiling. The thermostat is an important component that controls coolant flow and engine temperature. It is operated by a wax capsule or pellet. If you see a thermostat marked 82℃, it means the thermostat will begin to open at 82℃.

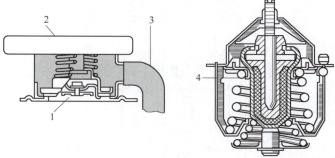

Fig. 2-30　Pressure cap and thermostat 压力水箱盖和节温器
1—Vacuum valve 真空阀；2—Pressure cap 压力式水箱盖；3—Overflow tube 溢流管；
4—Wax 蜡丸

A radiator is a type of heat exchanger. It is designed to transfer heat from the hot coolant that flows through it to the air blown through it by the fan.

The thermostat's main job is to allow the engine to heat up quickly, and then to keep the engine at a constant temperature. It does this by regulating the amount of water that goes through the radiator.

Like the thermostat, the cooling fan has to be controlled so that it allows the engine to maintain a constant temperature.

（2）Engine lubricating system

The main components of engine lubrication system are the oil pan, oil pump, engine oil passages and oil filter, as is shown in Fig. 2-31 and Fig. 2-32.

engine lubricating system：发动机润滑系统
oil pan：油底壳
oil filter：机油滤油器

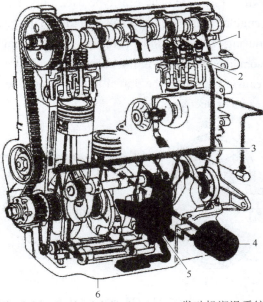

Fig. 2-31　Engine lubrication system 发动机润滑系统
1—Cylinder head oil gallery 气缸盖油道；2—Hydraulic valve lifter 液压阀挺杆；
3—Main oil gallery 主油道；4—Oil filter 滤油器；5—Oil pump 油泵；6—Oil pan 油底壳

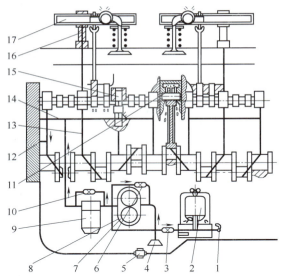

Fig. 2-32 Constitution of lubrication System 润滑系统的组成
1—Valve of oil radiator passage 通机油散热器的阀门；2—Centrifugal oil fine filter 离心式机油细滤器；3—Oiled relief valve of fine Filter 细滤器进油限压阀；4—Oil strainer 机油集滤器；5—Magnetism purge cock 磁性放油螺塞；6—Oil relief valve 机油限压阀；7—Oil pump 机油泵；8—Oil tube 油管；9—Oil first filter 机油粗滤器；10—Oil bypass-valve 机油旁通阀；11—Oil passage of connecting rod small end 连杆小头油道；12—Injector to lubricate timing gear 润滑正时齿轮喷油嘴；13—Tabula oil passage 横隔油道；14—Main oil gallery 主油道；15—Transmission shaft of oil pump 油泵传动轴；16—Oil passage lead to rockshaft 通摇臂轴油道；17—Arm shaft 臂轴

gear type：齿轮式
rotor type：转子式

The most common types of oil pumps are the gear type and the rotor type, as is shown in Fig. 2-33. The gear type uses a drive gear and a driven gear. When the engine starts, oil is pushed into the small spaces between the gears and the housing. The oil, under pressure, will be sent to the oil filter. The rotor type contains two rotors in the pump body. The rotors rotate in the same direction causing the oil to be drawn into or out of the oil pump when the volume increases or decreases.

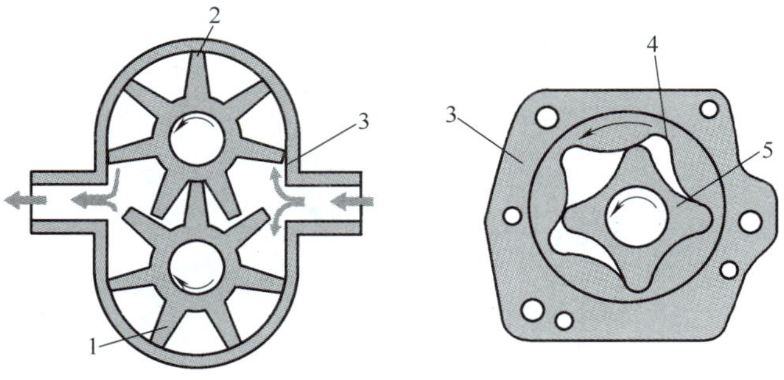

be drawn into or out: 被吸入或排出

(a) Gear type 齿轮式   (b) Rotor type 转子式

Fig. 2-33 Oil pump 油泵
1—Drive gear 主动齿轮；2—Driven dear 从动齿轮；3—Housing 外壳；4—Driven rotor 从动转子；5—Drive rotor 主动转子

The oil pan contains oil and transfer heat from the hot oil to the surrounding air. The oil pump supplies oil under pressure to the moving parts of the engine.

The engine oil filter is designed to remove minute panicles of metal and dirt from the engine oil. When the filter is restricted, the oil can't reach the bearings and damage will occur. At this point, the pressure relief valve will open and the unfiltered oil can flow to lubricate the engine, see Fig. 2-34.

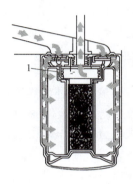 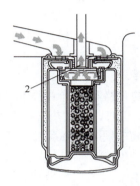

Fig. 2-34　Oil filter and pressure relief valve 机油滤清器和减压阀
1—Pressure relief valve 泄压阀；2—Pressure relief valve open 泄压阀开

The lubricant is used to protect the automotive component. In some cases this protection is in the form of a fluid film that keeps opposing surfaces separated. In other cases, the lubricant provides wear protection by forming a chemical film on a surface, to generate boundary lubrication protection. Automotive lubricants protect against corrosion by virtue of alkaline agents to neutralize acids that form in hot spots.

Under highly loaded and high temperature conditions, fluid film lubrication may not be sufficient to provide complete wear protection, the lubricant must contain additives so that interact with rubbing surfaces to form antiwear films.

The engine lubrication system must perform many direct function, but how successful the lubrication system is in performing all these functions depends on a number of factors and conditions. For example, there must be an adequate supply of good-quality lubricant delivered to all moving engine parts under sufficient pressure to provide hydrodynamic lubrication for rotating parts and oil adhesion to surfaces subject to sliding friction. In addition:

① The oil and filter must be changed at regular intervals.
② The engine must operate at its most efficient temperature.
③ Engine oil temperatures must not be excessively hot or cold.

Reference Version 参考译文

(1) 发动机冷却系统

冷却系统的作用是控制发动机的温度，使发动机在各种转速和各种行驶状态下都能有效地工作。

混合气的燃烧在发动机中产生大量的热，其中部分热量通过废气被排出以防止发动机过热。但是，残留在发动机中的余热仍足以使发动机受到严重损坏，冷却系统就是专门用来消除余热的。冷却系统还有一个重要任务，就是让发动机迅速预热，然后使发动机保持恒定的温度。

冷却系统有两种：液冷和风冷。

液冷系统的流体在发动机中的管路和通道中循环流动。当液体流过发热的发动机时，就吸收了大量热量。当液体流出发动机时，通过热交换器或散热器，将液体变为气体吹走。

有些老式的汽车和少数现代汽车采用风冷系统。因为大部分的汽车采用液体冷却，所以我们主要讨论液冷系统。

液体冷却系由水泵、水套、发动机风扇、散热器（水箱）、副水箱、压力式水箱盖、节温器、水管等组成，如图2-27所示。冷却系统就设置在发动机中。每个气缸体和燃烧室周围都留有空腔，这些空腔装满了水，称之为水套。在发动机运行过程中水被加热，并以水循环方式把热量从发动机中带走。水泵从发动机水套中把热水抽到散热器中，散热器有两条通道：一条是水道，另一条是气道（空气是通过汽车行驶和发动机的风扇抽入的）。当热水流过水道时，气道中流通的空气使热水冷却，冷却后的水又重新进入发动机，再把发动机中的热量传导出去。在这一过程中，水不断地在发动机与散热器之间循环，水携带着热量从发动机流到散热器再散发出去。通过这个方法可避免发动机温度过高。

水泵就是一个简单的离心泵。水泵由发动机曲轴上的带驱动，使冷却液在散热器与发动机水套之间循环流动。冷却液是水，冬季在水中须加入防冻剂。水套被铸入气缸体和气缸盖内部。发动机风扇通常安装在水泵轴上，由驱动水泵和发电机的同一条带驱动，见图2-28。风扇的作用是向散热器提供强大的空气流，与大量空气密切接触的散热器内可以容纳大量的水，这样热量可以通过水散发到空气中。散热器芯为分离和间隔交错的两部分。冷却水在其中一部分中流过，空气在另一部分中通过。

水箱是冷却系最大的零件，大部分发动机的热量由冷却液散发至周围的空气中，如图2-29所示。副水箱连接溢流管，当热冷却液在水箱内膨胀时，冷却液便流入副水箱；当冷却系温度下降后，冷却液又再从副水箱流回水箱。

水箱通常配有压力式水箱盖（压力盖或水箱盖）以紧紧密封水箱，如图2-30所示。如此可让冷却液温度升高至100℃以上而不沸腾。节温器是控制冷却液流量及发动机温度的重要元件，它由石蜡制小容器或石蜡丸来动作，如果节温器上标有82℃，它表示节温器将在82℃时打开。

散热器（水箱）是热交换器的一种。散热器将发热的冷却液的热量传递给空气，然后用风扇吹入大气。

节温器的主要任务是使发动机迅速预热，然后使发动机保持一个恒定的温度。这是通过调节流过散热器的水流量来调节的。

就像节温器一样，冷却风扇能使发动机维持在一个恒定的温度。

（2）发动机润滑系统

发动机润滑系统主要元件有油底壳、机油泵、发动机油道和机油滤清器，如图2-31、图2-32所示。

机油泵最常见的是齿轮式和转子式，如图2-33所示。齿轮式机油泵利用一个主动齿轮和一个被动齿轮，只要发动机一起动，机油便被挤入介于齿轮与外壳间的小空间中，接着被压送至机油滤清器。转子式机油泵在泵体内有两个转子，转子以相同方向旋转并改变两者间的容积，当容积增加或减少时，机油则流入或流出机油泵。

油底壳能保存机油并将机油的热量传递到周围的空气中，机油泵再将机油压送至发动机的旋转元件。

机油滤清器的作用是滤除机油中细小的金属微粒和污物。当机油滤清器堵塞，机油无法到达轴承时，发动机会损坏，此时减压阀将会开启，未经过滤的机油就能流出以润滑发动机，见图2-34。

润滑剂是用来保护汽车零件的。有时候通过在零件表面形成油膜使相接触表面分开来保护零件，有时候通过提供化学膜而增加零件表面抗磨性来保护零件。汽车润滑剂通过利用其碱性中和酸起到对高温零件表面的防腐作用。

在高负荷、高温条件下，油膜润滑不能完全有效地提供摩擦保护，润滑油必须含有添加剂，从而在摩擦表面起作用，形成耐磨层。

润滑系统必须执行很多功能，但是否能成功地实现所有这些功能与很多因素和条件有关。例如，必须要有足够的质量好的润滑剂输送到所有的发动机运动零件上，为运动零件提供液力润滑，同时也为受滑动摩擦影响的表面提供液力润滑。此外：

① 在规定的时间间隔内更换机油和过滤器。
② 发动机必须在有效的温度下工作。
③ 发动机机油温度不许过热或过冷。

Section 2.7
Engine Valve Train
发动机配气机构

The engine valve train on time opens or closes the intake valve or exhaust valve according to operational need of engine，provides timely admission of the fresh gas mixture（gasoline engine）or air（diesel engine）charge into the cylinders and exhaust of spent gases from them. For this purpose the valves at definite moments open and close the intake and exhaust ports in the cylinder head，through which the cylinders communicate with the intake and exhaust manifold，as is shown in Fig. 2-35. Fig. 2-36 shows a DOHC（double over head camshaft）valve train.

valve train：配气机构
intake valve：进气门
exhaust valve：排气门
charge into：冲进
cylinder head：气缸头
double over head camshaft：双顶置凸轮轴

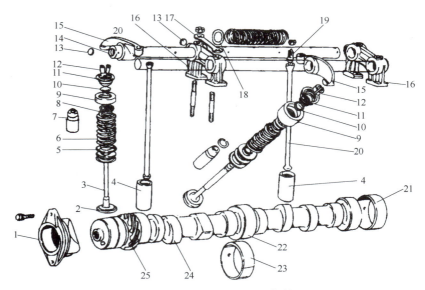

Fig. 2-35　Valve train 配气机构

1—Camshaft front bearing 凸轮轴前轴承；2—Valve head 气门头；3—Valve stem 阀杆；4—Tappet 挺柱；5—Lower valve spring collar 下气门弹簧挡圈；6—Outer valve spring 外气门弹簧；7—Valve guide 气门导管；8—Inner valve spring 气门芯弹簧；9—Shielding cap 防护罩；10—Oil flinger 甩油环；11—Upper valve spring collar 上置气门弹簧挡圈；12—Valve split cone 裂阀锥体；13—Closer 闭合器；14—Rocker shaft 摇杆轴；15—Rocker arm 摇臂；16—Rocker bracket 摇杆支架；17—Retaining washer 弹簧垫圈；18—Thrust washer 止推垫圈；19—Rocker adjusting screw 摇杆调整螺钉；20—Push rod 推杆；21—Camshaft rear bush 凸轮轴后衬套；22—Camshaft 凸轮轴；23—Camshaft center bush 凸轮轴中心衬套；24—Cam 凸轮；25—Oil pump driving gear 油泵主动轮

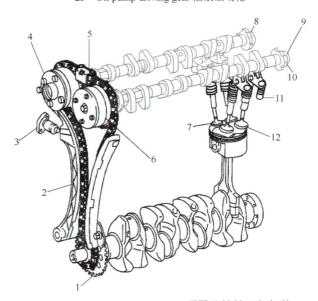

Fig. 2-36　DOHC valve train 双顶置凸轮轴配气机构

1，10—Timing rotor 正时转子；2—Chain slipper 链条导板；3—Chain-tensioner 链条张紧器；4—Exhaust VVT-i controller 智能型排气门可变正时调节器；5—Chain damper 链条减振器；6—Intake VVT-i controller 智能型进气门可变正时调节器；7—Exhaust valve 排气门；8—Exhaust camshaft 排气凸轮轴；9—Intake camshaft 进气凸轮轴；11—Hydraulic lash adjuster 液压式间隙调节器；12—Intake valve 进气门

The valve train is composed of timing gears, a camshaft, tappets, valves, spring with fasteners and valve guides. The basic composed parts of conventional engine valve train are shown in Fig. 2-37.

timing gear: 正时齿轮
tappet: 挺柱
valve guide: 气门导管

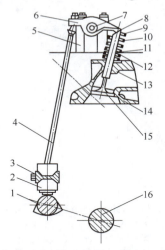

Fig. 2-37 The basic composed parts of conventional engine valve train
传统发动机配气机构的基本组成零件
1—Camshaft 凸轮轴; 2—Valve tappet 气门挺柱; 3—Tappet guiding barrel 挺柱导向体; 4—Push rod 推杆; 5—Rocker bearing block 摇臂轴承座; 6—Rocker 摇臂; 7—Rocker shaft 摇臂轴; 8—Valve-spring retainer 气门弹簧座; 9—Rocker play 气门间隙; 10—Valve key 气门锁片; 11—Valve seal 气门油封; 12—Valve-spring 气门弹簧; 13—Valve guide 气门导管; 14—Valve seat 气门座; 15—Valve 气门; 16—Crankshaft 曲轴

As is shown in Fig. 2-38, the basic composition of engine valve train is divided into two types, i.e. valve group [see Fig. 2-38（a）] and valve transmission group [see Fig. 2-38（b）].

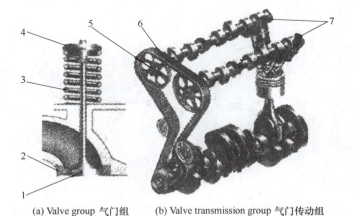

(a) Valve group 气门组   (b) Valve transmission group 气门传动组

Fig. 2-38 The type of valve train 配气机构的类型
1—Valve 气门; 2—Valve seat 气门座; 3—Valve spring 气门弹簧; 4—Valve-spring retainer 气门弹簧座; 5—Timing pulley 正时带轮; 6—Timing belt 正时齿带; 7—Camshaft 凸轮轴

overall structure: 整体结构
valve seat: 气门座
valve key: 气门锁片

① Overall structure of valve group. Valve group parts main include valve, valve seat, valve guide, valve key, and valve spring etc., as is shown in Fig. 2-39.

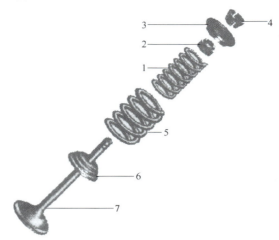

Fig. 2-39 Valve group parts 气门组零件

1—Inner valve-spring 内气门弹簧；2—Valve oil seal 气门油封；3—Upper valve-spring retainer 上气门弹簧座；4—Valve key 气门锁片；5—Outer valve-spring 外气门弹簧；6—lower valve-spring retainer 下气门弹簧座；7—Valve 气门

② Overall structure of valve transmission group. Valve transmission group parts include camshaft, timing transmission, tappet, push rod, rocker arm assembly etc., as is shown in Fig. 2-40.

timing transmission：正时传动装置
push rod：推杆
rocker arm：摇臂

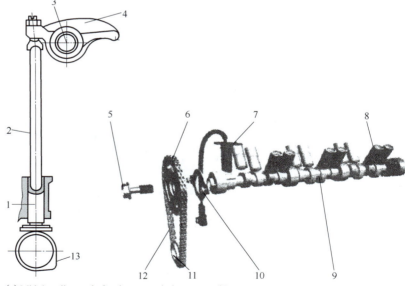

(a) Mid-install camshaft valve transmission group 中置凸轮轴气门传动组

(b) Overhead camshaft valve transmission group 顶置凸轮轴气门传动组

Fig. 2-40 Valve transmission group parts 气门传动组零件

1—Tappet 挺柱；2—Push rod 推杆；3—Rockshaft 摇臂轴；4—Rocker arm 摇臂；5—Camshaft chain wheel bolt 凸轮轴链轮螺栓；6—Camshaft chain wheel 凸轮轴链轮；7—Camshaft position sensor 凸轮轴位置传感器；8—Valve lifter 气门挺杆；9—Camshaft 凸轮轴；10—Camshaft thrust plate 凸轮轴止推板；11—Crankshaft sprocket 曲轴链轮；12—Timing chain 正时链条；13—Cam 凸轮

Engine valve train must use timing gear to transmit rotation from the crankshaft to the camshaft, fuel injection pump shaft, and to oil pump and other mechanisms. The timing gears in most engines are housed in a special case fired at the front end of the engine.

Camshaft's function is to open the engine valves positively and timely, in a definite sequence, and to control their closing against the return action of the valve springs. The shaft is made integral with its cams and bearing journals. Each cam controls a single valve, either intake or exhaust.

The tappets serve to transmit the force from the camshaft to the push rods. The push rods transmits the force from the tappets to the rocker. The rockers transmit the force from the push rod to the valve.

An engine valve is a device designed to open a passage when moving in one direction and to close it when moving in the opposite direction. Each cylinder of a four-stroke-cycle diesel or gasoline engine is commonly equipped with an intake valve and an exhaust valve.

A valve consists of a head and stem. The valve head has a narrow chamfer of 45° or 30° referred to as valve face. The valve face fits tightly against the seat, which is achieved by grinding.

The valve spring provides the force necessary to close the valve and hold it tightly against its seat.

Valve guide supports the valve stem and guides its movement so that the valve face remains perfectly concentric with the valve seat and fits it without any skewing.

are housed in：被安放在……

definite sequence：特定程序

serve to：有助于

designed to：旨在

referred to as：被称为

concentric：同轴的
skewing：偏移

Reference Version　参考译文

发动机配气机构按照发动机的工作需要，定时地开启或关闭进气门、排气门，保证新鲜混合气（汽油机）或空气（柴油机）可以适时进入气缸，同时燃烧后的废气可以及时排出。为实现这一目的，气门在一定的时刻打开并关闭气缸盖上的进排气道，气缸和进排气歧管通过进排气道相沟通，如图 2-35 所示。如图 2-36 所示为双顶置凸轮轴配气机构。

配气机构由正时齿轮、凸轮轴、挺柱、气门、带有锁紧装置的弹簧和气门导管组成。传统发动机配气机构的基本组成零件如图 2-37 所示。

如图 2-38 所示，发动机配气机构的基本组成可分为气门组［图 2-38（a）］和气门传动组［图 2-38（b）］两部分。

① 气门组的总体结构。气门组零件主要包括气门、气门座、气门导管、气门锁片（锁夹）和气门弹簧等，如图 2-39 所示。

② 气门传动组的总体结构。气门传动组零件包括凸轮轴、正时传动装置、挺柱（杆）、推杆、摇臂总成等，如图 2-40 所示。

发动机配气机构必须使用正时齿轮将曲轴的旋转传递到凸轮轴，驱动喷油泵轴、机油泵和其他装置。大多数发动机的正时齿轮安装在专门的壳体内，正时齿轮壳体位于发动机前端。

凸轮轴的功用是按特定的顺序准确适时地打开气门，并通过气门弹簧的回位作用控制气门的关闭。凸轮轴与凸轮、轴颈连成一体。每个凸轮控制一个气门，即进气门或排气门。

挺柱用来将凸轮轴的作用力传递给推杆。推杆将挺柱传来的推力传给摇臂。摇臂将推杆的作用力传递到气门。

发动机气门向某一方向运动时开启一通道，而它向相反方向移动时则关闭此通道。四冲程汽油机或柴油机的每缸一般都装有进气门和排气门。

气门由头部和杆身组成。气门头部相对于气门平面之间存在45°或30°的锥角。通过研磨可使气门平面与气门座紧密贴合。

气门弹簧提供气门关闭时所需要的作用力，保证气门与气门座之间紧密贴合。

气门导管支撑气门杆身，对其运动起导向作用，以保证气门关闭时能准确与气门座贴合而不产生偏移。

Unit 3

Automotive Chassis

汽车底盘

The automotive chassis is a framework used to assemble auto components on it, it is composed of power train system, running gear, steering system and braking system. Its function is to accept motive power of engine, and to make vehicle move and can normally run according to driver manipulate. Fig. 3-1 shows common chassis structure of truck, Fig. 3-2 shows arrangement of major components of car chassis.

automotive chassis：车架
framework：框架
power train system：动力传动系
running gear：行驶系
steering system：转向系
braking system：制动系
manipulate：操纵
truck：货车

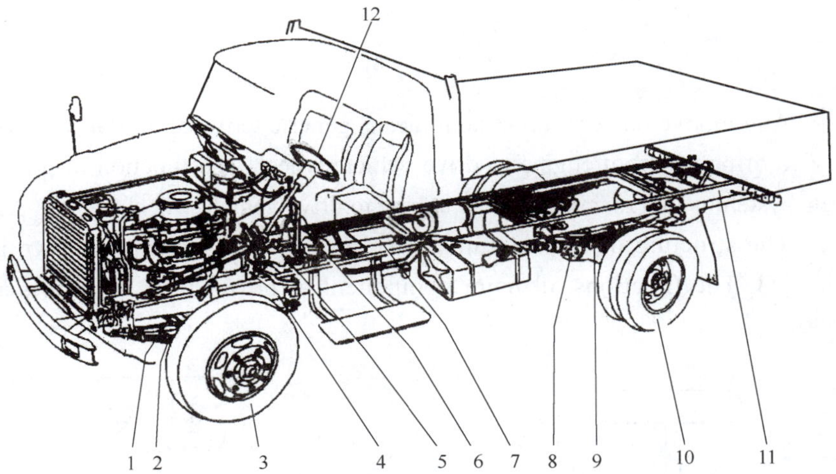

Fig. 3-1　Common chassis structure of truck
常见货车的底盘结构
1—Front axle 前轴；2—Front suspension 前悬架；3—Front wheel 前轮；
4—Clutch 离合器；5—Transmission 变速器；6—Parking brake 驻车制动器；
7—Driveshaft 传动轴；8—Drive axle 驱动桥；9—Rear suspension 后悬架；10—Rear wheel 后轮；11—Frame 车架；
12—Steering wheel 转向盘

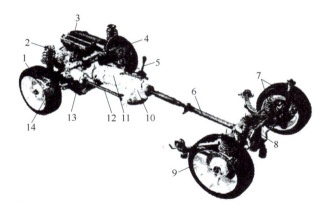

Fig. 3-2 Arrangement of major components of car chassis 轿车的底盘主要部件布置
1—Tire 轮胎；2—Front suspension 前悬架；3—Engine 发动机；4—Steering wheel 转向盘；5—Gear shaft lever 变速杆；6，12—Driveshaft 传动轴；7—Rear suspension 后悬架；8—Rear drive axle 后驱动桥；9—Hub 轮毂；10—Transfer case 分动器；11—Transmission 变速器；13—Front drive axle 前驱动桥；14—Brake 制动器

Section 3.1
Power Train System 传动系统

transmission device：传动装置

Automotive power train system means generic terms of all transmission device of power from engine to drive vehicle wheel. The function of power train system is to transmit power of engine to drive vehicle wheel.

The structure of typical automotive power train system is shown in Fig. 3-3. The functions of major component of power train system is as follow：

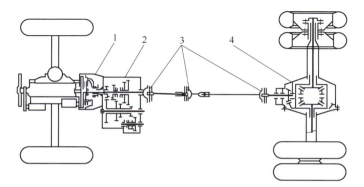

Fig. 3-3 Structure of power train system 传动系统的结构
1—Clutch 离合器；2—Trasmission 变速器；3—Universal gearing 万向传动装置；
4—Drive axle 驱动桥

① Clutch. A clutch is a subcomponent of power train system. It is a friction device used to connect and disconnect a driving force from a driven member. The clutch is used in conjunction with an engine flywheel to provide smooth engagement and disengagement of the engine and manual transmission. The clutch structure is shown in Fig.3-4. Fig.3-5 shows hydraulic control system of clutch.

subcomponent: 基础部件

friction device: 摩擦装置

disconnect: 分离；拆开

driven member: 从动件

in conjunction with: 配合

manual transmission: 手动换挡

hydraulic control system: 液压控制系统

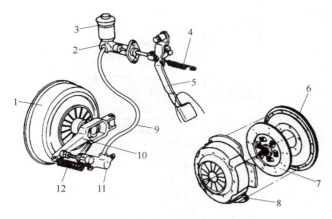

Fig. 3-4　The clutch structure 离合器结构
1—Clutch cover 离合器盖；2—Clutch master cylinder 离合器主缸；3—Reservoir 储液罐；4—Return spring 回位弹簧；5—Clutch pedal 离合器踏板；6—Engine flywheel 发动机飞轮；7—Clutch disk 离合器片；8—Pressure plate 压盘；9—Hydraulic line 液压管路；10—Release fork 分离叉；11—Release cylinder 分离缸；12—Return spring 回位弹簧

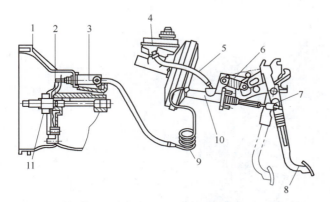

Fig. 3-5　Hydraulic control system of clutch 离合器液压操纵系统
1—Gearbox housing 变速器壳体；2—Release yoke 分离叉；3—Working cylinder 工作缸；4—Liquid storage pot 储液罐；5—Oil-taking tube 进油软管；6—Auxiliary spring 助力弹簧；7—Pushrod joint 推杆接头；8—Clutch pedal 离合器踏板；9—Oil tube assembly 油管总成；10—Main cylinder 主缸；11—Release bearing 分离轴承

② Transmission. A transmission is a speed and power changing device installed at some point between the engine and driving wheels of the vehicle. It provides a means for changing the ratio between engine rpm (revolutions per minute) and driving wheels rpm to best meet each particular

transmission: 传动装置

variable speed：无级变速

driving situation. It is used to variable speed，bending moment，turning，break off transmission of power from engine to drive vehicle wheel. Fig. 3-6 shows manual transmission. Fig. 3-7 shows automatic transmission（A/T）. Fig. 3-8 shows automatic transmission 6T70/6T75（GM）. Fig. 3-9 shows Continuously Variable Transmission（CVT）.Fig. 3-10 shows component install relation of manual transmission（no-included 5 clutch）.

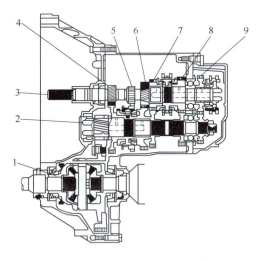

Fig. 3-6　Manual transmission 手动变速器
1—Differential 差速器；2—Output shaft 输出轴；3—Input shaft 输入轴；4—1st gear 1 挡齿轮；5—Reverse gear 倒挡齿轮；6—2nd gear 2 挡齿轮；7—3rd gear 3 挡齿轮；8—4th gear 4 挡齿轮；9—5th gear 5 挡齿轮

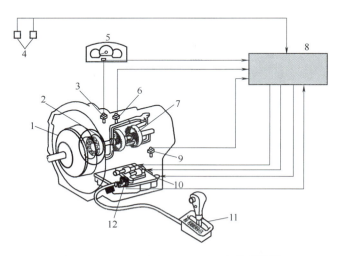

Fig. 3-7　Automatic transmission 自动变速器
1—Torque converter 液力变矩器；2—Oil pump 油泵；3—Vehicle speed sensor 车速传感器；4—Sensors 传感器；5—Combination meter 组合仪表；6—Output shaft speed sensor 输出轴转速传感器；7—Planetary gear 行星轮机构；8—Engine and ECT ECU 发动机和自动变速器 ECU；9—Input turbine speed sensor 输入涡轮转速传感器；10—Solenoids 电磁阀；11—Shift lever 变速杆；12—Hydraulic control 液压控制装置

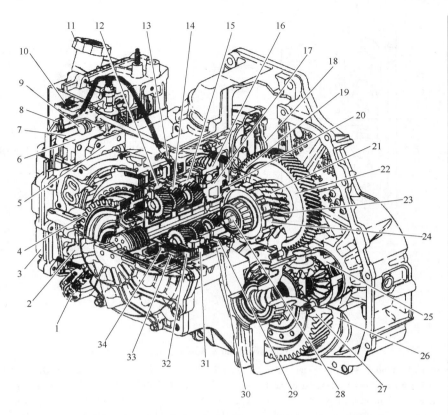

Fig. 3-8　Automatic transmission 6T70/6T75（GM）6T70/6T75
自动变速器（通用汽车公司）

1—Input speed sensor 输入轴转速传感器；2—Case cover assembly 壳盖总成；3—Control valve body cover 控制阀体；4—Input shaft speed sensor reluctance wheel 输入轴转速传感器磁阻转子；5—Control valve lower body assembly 下控制阀体总成；6—Control valve upper body assembly 上控制阀体总成；7—Control valve channel plate assembly 控制阀体油道盖板总成；8—Control solenoid valve assembly 电磁控制阀总成；9—Manual valve 手动阀；10—Manual shift gears maltese crose rod assembly 手动换挡掣子杆总成；11—Trans fluid level indicator 变速器液面指示器；12—Reaction carrier assembly 反作用托架总成；13—Output speed sensor 输出轴转速传感器；14—Input carrier assembly 输入轴托架总成；15—Output carrier assembly 输出轴托架总成；16—Front differential transfer drive gear 前差速器分动器传动齿轮；17—Front differential transfer drive gear support assembly 前差速器分动器驱动齿轮支架总成；18—Torque converter assembly 液力变矩器总成；19—Park pawl actuator assembly 驻车掣爪执行器总成；20—Fluid pump drive link assembly 油泵传动链总成；21—Park pawl 驻车掣爪；22—Front differential transfer driven gear 前差速器分动器从动齿轮；23—Front differential drive pinion gear 前差速器主动齿轮；24—Park gear 驻车挡齿轮；25—Front differential carrier assembly 前差速器架总成；26—Front differential carrier baffle 前差速器架挡板；27—Front differential ring gear 前差速器齿圈；28—Front differential drive pinion gear lube tube 前差速器主动齿轮润滑油管；29—1-2-3-4 Clutch assembly 1-2-3-4 挡离合器总成；30—Low and reverse clutch assembly 低速挡和倒挡离合器总成；31—Low and reverse clutch 低速挡和倒挡离合器；32—2-6 Clutch assembly 2-6 挡离合器总成；33—3-5 Reverse clutch assembly 3-5 挡倒挡离合器总成；34—4-5-6 Clutch assembly 4-5-6 挡离合器总成

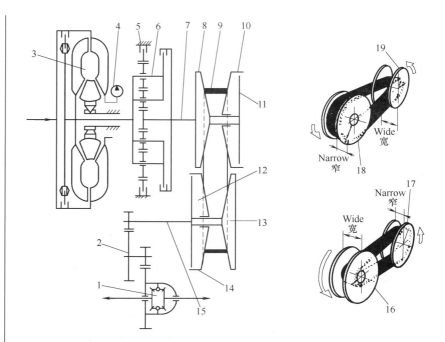

Fig. 3-9　Continuously variable transmission 无级变速器

1—Differential 差速器；2—Final drive 主减速器；3—Torque converter 液力变矩器；4—Oil pump 油泵；5—FWD/REV change-over mechanism 前进/倒车转换机构；6—Planetary (gear) set 行星轮系；7—Input shaft 输入轴；8—Fixed taper disc 固定锥盘；9—Steel belt 钢带；10—Movable taper disc 活动锥盘；11—Oil pressure chamber 油压室；12—Oil pressure chamber 油压室；13—Fixed taper disc in output shaft 输出轴固定锥盘；14—Movable taper disc 活动锥盘；15—Driven pulley shaft 从动带轮轴；16, 18—Driven pulley 从动带轮；17, 19—Drive pulley 主动带轮；

Fig. 3-10　Component install relation of manual transmission
手动变速传动机构的零件安装关系

1—Input axle 输入轴；2—3-4 Clutch synchronizer 3、4挡同步器；3—Output axle 输出轴；4—Helical gear 斜齿轮；5—1-2 Clutch synchronizer 1、2挡同步器；
6—Reverse clutch axle 倒挡轴

③ Universal Gearing. The universal gearing is used to realize transmission of power among two-axle which is of frequent occurrence of included angle change and relative position change, main includes cardan joint and transmission shaft. Fig. 3-11 shows a drive half-shaft and CVJ (constant velocity joint) of FF (front-engine front-wheel-drive) passenger car. For sectional type transmission shaft which transmission distance is further, in order to improve rigidity of transmission shaft, intermediate support is also installed as is shown in Fig. 3-12.

universal gearing：万向传动装置

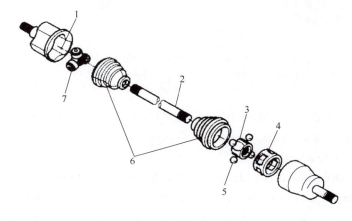

Fig. 3-11 Drive half-shaft and CVJ of FF passenger car
前驱乘用车传动轴和等速万向节
1—Inboard CV-joint housing 内侧等速万向节传动轴罩；2—Interconnecting shaft 内连接轴；
3—Inner race 内座圈；4—Cage 球笼；5—Ball 球；6—Front wheel driveshaft joint boot
前轮驱动轴防尘罩；7—Tripod assembly 三销架总成

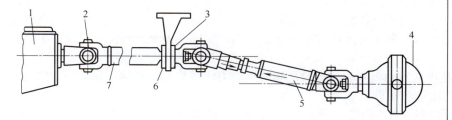

Fig. 3-12 Universal gearing with intermediate support 带中间支承的万向传动装置
1—Transmission 变速器；2—Cardan joint 万向节；3—Intermediate support 中间支承；4—Drive axle 驱动桥；5—Transmission shaft 传动轴；6—Ball bearing 球轴承；
7—Intermediate support 传动轴

Fig. 3-13 shows a rear-drive axle assembly, is contained in a one-piece housing supported by the rear suspension. The assembly includes: differential carder, final drive, differential; right and left axle shafts; right and left axle flanges.

rear-drive axle：后驱动桥
one-piece housing：独立机座
rear suspension：后悬架
differential carder：差速器壳体
final drive：主减速器
axle shaft：半轴
flange：法兰

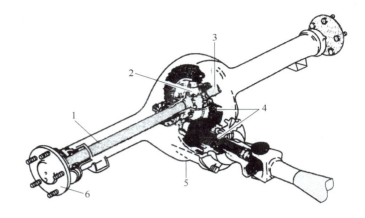

Fig. 3-13　A rear-drive axle assembly 后驱动桥总成
1—Right axle shaft 右半轴；2—Differential 差速器；3—Left axle shaft 左半轴；
4—Final drive 主减速器；5—Differential carrier 差速器壳体；6—Axle flange 车轴法兰

reduction of speed：
降速

increase in torque：
增（加力）矩

④ Final drive. The function of final drive is transfer power to differential，and realize reduction of speed and increase in torque，change transmittal direction.

⑤ Differential. The function of differential is transfer power to axle shaft，and allows right and left axle shafts rotate with different speed.

⑥ Axle Shafts. The function of axle shafts is transfer power of transmittal to drive wheel.

Reference Version　参考译文

汽车底盘是一个用以总装汽车部件的框架，它由传动系统、行驶系统、转向系统和制动系统四大系统组成，其功用为接收发动机的动力，使汽车运动并保证汽车能够按照驾驶员的操纵而正常行驶。如图3-1所示为常见货车的底盘结构，如图3-2所示为轿车的底盘主要部件布置。

汽车传动系统是指从发动机到驱动车轮之间所有动力传递装置的总称。传动系统的功用是将发动机的动力传给驱动车轮。

典型汽车传动系统的结构如图3-3所示。传动系主要部件的功用如下。

① 离合器。离合器是传动系统的基础部件，是用来结合和分离从动部件的摩擦装置。离合器与飞轮协作，为发动机和人力操纵传动提供平稳的结合和分离。离合器的结构如图3-4所示。图3-5所示为离合器液压操纵系统。

② 变速器。变速器是一个速度与动力的转换装置，安装在车辆的发动机和驱动轮之间。它通过改变发动机转速和驱动轮转速间的比率关系，以适应各种行驶状况，用来变速、变矩、变向、中断发动机传给驱动车轮的动力传递。图3-6所示为手动变速器，图3-7所示为自动变速器，图3-8所示为通用汽车公司的6T70/6T75自动变速器，图3-9所示为无级变速器，图3-10表示了手动变速传动机构的零件安装关系（未包括五挡）。

③ 万向传动装置。万向传动装置用来实现有夹角和相对位置经常发生变化的两轴之间的

动力传递。主要包括万向节和传动轴，图 3-11 所示为前驱乘用车传动轴和等速万向节。对于传动距离较远的分段式传动轴，为了提高传动轴的刚度，还设置有中间支承，如图 3-12 所示。

图 3-13 所示为后驱动桥总成，相当于由后悬挂装置支撑的独立机座。后驱动桥总成包括差速器壳体，主减速器，差速器；左、右半轴；左、右车轴法兰。

④ 主减速器。主减速器的功能是将动力传给差速器，并实现降速增矩、改变传动方向。

⑤ 差速器。差速器的功能是将动力传给半轴，并允许左右半轴以不同的转速旋转。

⑥ 半轴。半轴的功能是将差速器的动力传给驱动车轮。

Section 3.2
Vehicle Clutch
汽车离合器

A basic component of all drive trains is a clutch. It is a friction device used to connect and disconnect a driving force from a driven member. In automotive applications，the clutch is used in conjunction with an engine flywheel to provide smooth engagement and disengagement of the engine and manual transmission.

In a vehicle with a manual transmission，we need a clutch because the engine spins all the time and the vehicle wheels don't. In order for a vehicle to stop without killing the engine，the wheels need to be disconnected from the engine somehow. The clutch allows us to smoothly engage a spinning engine to a non-spinning transmission by controlling the slippage between them.

The clutch includes the flywheel，clutch disk，pressure plate，pressure plate cover and the linkage necessary to operate the clutch. See Fig. 3-14.

in conjunction with：共同；与……协力
engine flywheel：发动机飞轮
engagement：结合
disengagement：分离
manual transmission：手动变速器
spin：旋转
kill：伤及
slippage：滑动；滑移
pressure plate：压盘
pressure plate cover：压盘盖
linkage：联动装置

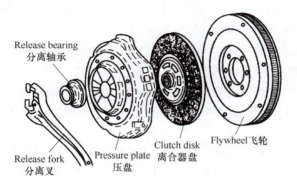

Fig. 3-14 Constitute of clutch 离合器的组成

be bolted to：固定于
torque：扭矩
steel plate：钢板
frictional material：摩擦材料
sheet metal cover：金属盖
release spring：分离弹簧
metal pressure ring：金属压环
clutch disk：离合器盘
release beating：分离轴承
clutch pedal：离合器踏板

The flywheel is bolted to the crankshaft of the engine.Its main function is to transfer engine torque from the engine to the transmission.

The clutch disk is basically a steel plate, covered with a frictional material that goes between the flywheel and the pressure plate.

A pressure plate is bolted to the flywheel. It includes a sheet metal cover, heavy release springs, a metal pressure ring that provides a friction surface for the clutch disk.

The release bearing is the heart of clutch operation. When the clutch pedal is depressed, the release bearing moves toward the flywheel, pushing in the pressure plate's release fingers and moving the pressure plate fingers or levers against pressure plate spring force. See Fig. 3-15.

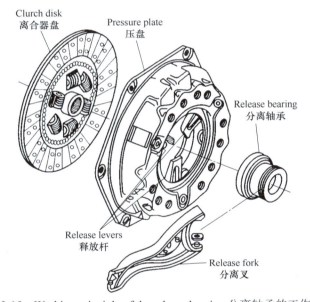

transmit：传递
multipliy：增加
hydraulic clutch：液压离合器
clutch master cylinder：离合器主缸
reservoir：蓄水池
hydraulic line：液压管路
slave cylinder：从动缸
diaphragm spring clutch：膜片弹簧离合器
pressure plate：压盘

Fig. 3-15 Working principle of the release bearing 分离轴承的工作原理

The linkage transmits and multiplies the driver's leg force to the fork of the clutch pressure plate. A mechanical clutch linkage usually consists of the clutch pedal, a series of linkage rods and arms, or a cable. A hydraulic clutch linkage typically includes a clutch master cylinder and reservoir, a hydraulic line and a slave cylinder.

In the diaphragm spring clutch as shown as Fig. 3-16, the flywheel is connected to the engine, and the clutch plate is connected to the transmission.

When your foot is off the pedal, the springs will push the pressure plate against the clutcb disc, which in turn presses against the flywheel. This locks the engine to the transmission input shaft, causing them to spin at the same speed.

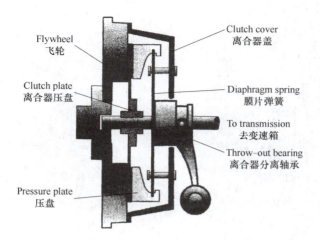

Fig. 3-16 Diaphragm spring clutch 膜片弹簧离合器

The amount of force the clutch can hold depends on the friction between the clutch plate and the flywheel, and how much force the spring puts on the pressure plate. The friction force in the clutch works just like the blocks in the friction section of brake, except that the spring presses on the clutch plate instead of weight pressing the block into the ground.

When the clutch pedal is pressed, a cable or hydraulic piston pushes on the release fork, which presses the throw-out bearing against the middle of the diaphragm spring. As the middle of the diaphragm spring is pushed in, a series of pins near the outside of the spring causes the spring to pull the pressure plate away from the clutch disc. This releases the clutch from the spinning engine.

Note the springs in the clutch plate. These springs help to isolate the transmission from the shock of the clutch engaging.

Although there are many types of clutch, the dry single plate type of friction clutch is used almost exclusively in passenger cars. That Fig. 3-17 shows a typical clutch that has been taken apart. The clutch shaft is mounted on two ball bearings, its front end resting in the flywheel opening and the rear end in the front wall of the transmission box. Housing is attached to engine flywheel. The pressure on driven disk fitted onto the splined portion of shaft is provided by springs installed between the housing and pressure driving disks. The release levers are mounted on spindles attached to housing. The pressure disk, rotating together with the housing and flywheel, can be shifted axially by depressing pedal. The linings are made from anti-friction material, are riveted to either side of the driven disk to increase the force of friction between the driving and driven disks.

depends on：取决于
friction force：摩擦力
cable：缆绳
release fork：分离叉
throw-out bearing：离合器分离轴承
spinning：旋转的
isolate：隔离
shock：冲击
engaging：接合
the dry single plate type of friction clutch：单片干摩擦式离合器
almost exclusively：运用最广泛
rest in：依赖于
transmission box：变速箱
housing：壳体
splined：花键的
release lever：分离杆
spindle：主轴
pressure disk：压盘
lining：衬片
anti-friction material：耐磨材料
rivet：铆接

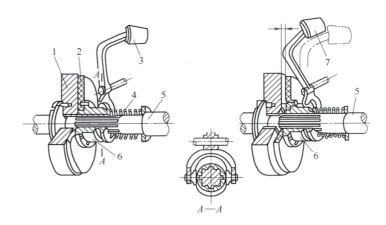

Fig. 3-17　Clutch 离合器

1—Flywheel 飞轮；2—pressure plate 压盘；3，7—Pedal 踏板；4—Spring 弹簧；
5—The clutch shaft 离合器轴；6—Sleeve 套筒

The clutch release mechanism operates as follow.

When sleeve moves towards the flywheel, thrust bearing presses against the ends of the release levers which thereby turn on their axle and separate the pressure driving disk from the flywheel, releasing the driven disk from the action of the spring. The sleeve is shifted by fork, connected with pedal through a system of arms and rods. When the pedal is released, sleeve returns to its initial position and the pressure disk is shifted by the springs towards the flywheel.

In vehicles it is operated by the left-most pedal. No pressure on the pedal means that the clutch plates are engaged（driving）, while depressing the pedal will disengage the clutch plates, allowing the driver to shift gears. When the right-most pedal（the accelerator）is pressed while the clutch pedal is being let out.

In some vehicles, the power train incorporates a turbo clutch, where the hydrodynamic effect of circulating fluid is utilized to transmit torque. This prevents the clutch from heating and wearing as a result of continuous slipping and makes it possible to reduce the number of switching over operations in the transmission box.

Vehicles equipped with automatic transmissions normally do not have a clutch.On these vehicles, the transmission operates automatically so that the driver is not required to use a clutch to shift gears.

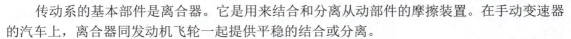

传动系的基本部件是离合器。它是用来结合和分离从动部件的摩擦装置。在手动变速器的汽车上，离合器同发动机飞轮一起提供平稳的结合或分离。

手动变速器汽车需要离合器，因为发动机始终在运转而车轮却不是。要使汽车停下来而不伤及发动机，必须设法让车轮与发动机脱离。离合器通过控制在两者之间生产的滑动，使旋转的发动机与非旋转的变速器平顺啮合。

离合器包括飞轮、离合器盘、离合器压盘、离合器盘盖及离合器运转所需的联动装置。如图 3-14 所示。

飞轮用螺栓固定在发动机曲轴上。它的主要作用是将发动机扭矩从发动机传递到变速器中。

离合器盘基本上是个钢制的盘，上有摩擦材料，在飞轮和压盘之间运行。

压盘固定在飞轮上。它包括一个金属盖、重的分离弹簧、一个为离合器盘产生摩擦的金属压环。

分离轴承是离合器运转的心脏。踩踏离合器踏板时，分离轴承朝飞轮方向移动，推入到压盘分离指中，使压盘分离指抵住压盘弹簧力。如图 3-15 所示。

离合器联动机构增大驾驶者的腿部力量并将其传递到离合器压盘上。机械离合器联动机构包括离合器踏板、一系列连杆臂或拉索。液压离合器联动机构包括离合器主气缸和储液罐、液压管路和从动缸。

在如图 3-16 所示的膜片弹簧离合器中，飞轮与发动机连接，离合器盘与传动系连接。

松开踏板时，膜片弹簧将压盘逐渐压紧在离合器盘上，压力依次传到飞轮。这样使发动机和传动系输入轴可靠地接合，使它们以相同的转速运转。

离合器能传递的力的大小取决于离合器盘和飞轮之间的摩擦系数，以及弹簧对压盘的压紧力大小。离合器的摩擦力和制动器的摩擦力起一样的作用，不同的是压在地面上的重压力变成了离合器中弹簧压在离合器盘上的压力。

当踩下离合器踏板时，在分离叉上的绳索或液压活塞压着分离轴承顶住膜片弹簧的中心。当膜片弹簧的中心被推凹进去时，在弹簧周围的一圈铆钉将压盘后拉，使压盘与离合器盘分离。这样，离合器也就切断了发动机的传动。

注意离合器盘内的弹簧组，这些弹簧帮助隔离离合器接合时的冲击，避免冲击传给传动系统。

虽然有许多类型的离合器，但是单片干摩擦式离合器在车辆上运用最广泛。图 3-17 所示为典型的离合器的零件图。离合器轴（变速器第一轴）安装在两个球轴承上，前端由飞轮中心孔支撑，后端安装在变速箱壳体上。壳体与发动机飞轮连接。花键轴上从动盘的压力是由安装在壳体和压盘之间的弹簧提供的。分离杠杆安装在离合器盖的主轴上。松开离合器踏板，压盘、离合器盖及飞轮一起旋转。衬片是由耐摩擦材料制成的，被铆钉固定到从动盘两侧以增加驱动盘和从动盘之间的摩擦力。

离合器分离机构是按照以下步骤工作的。

当分离套筒向飞轮移动时，止推轴承压住轮轴上转动的分离杠杆，将压盘与飞轮分开，通过弹簧放松从动盘，拨叉拨动分离套筒，通过一系列的杆件与离合器踏板连接；当松开踏板时，分离套筒回到初始位置，压盘被弹簧压向飞轮。

在车上，离合器是由最左的踏板控制的。如果踏板上没有压力，离合器就接合（行驶），而踩下离合器，则可以让驾驶员换挡。当最右的踏板（加速）踩下时，离合器踏板将在同时脱开。

在一些车辆中，传动系统合并成液力变矩器，利用循环液体的液力作用来传递转矩。这样可以避免连续滑动造成的离合器过热和磨损，减少变速器工作的挡位设置。

装有自动变速器的汽车一般不需要离合器。在这些汽车上，变速器自动操作，因此驾驶员不必使用离合器来换挡。

Section 3.3
Automobile Running Gear 行驶系统

running gear：驱动装置
frame（automobile body）：车架（汽车车身）
comfortable ride：乘车舒适性
"sprung" weight：弹簧承重
leaf spring：钢板弹簧
flexibility：弹性

Automobile running gear is an assembly to bear and install various parts, transmits and supports various loads in and below vehicle, so that guarantees normal running of vehicle. The running gear is constituted by frame（automobile body）, axle, suspension, vehicle wheel, etc., as is shown in Fig. 3-18.

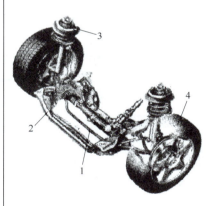
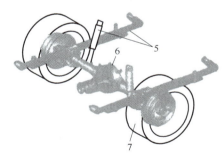

(a) Car running gear 小汽车行驶系统　　(b) Truck running gear 货车行驶系统

Fig. 3-18 Constitution of running gear 行驶系统的组成
1—Anti-roll bar 横向稳定杆；2, 6—Axle 车桥；3, 5—Suspension 悬架；
4, 7—Cart wheel 车轮

Automobile suspension system has two basic functions, to keep car's wheels in firm contact with the road and to provide comfortable ride for the passengers. Automobile suspension refers to the use of the front and rear springs to suspend a vehicle's "sprung" weight. Fig. 3-19 shows leaf spring suspension. The leaf springs most commonly used in automobiles is made up of several long plates, or leaves. Because the leaf spring consists of a series of thin leaves, one on top of another, it does not break when bent. When the spring is bent, the individual leaves bend and slip over one another. This provides a spring with great flexibility and strength. The suspension also includes shocks or struts and sway bars, as is shown in Fig. 3-20. Fig. 3-21 shows S. L. A.（short arm / long arm）suspension. Fig. 3-22 shows all kinds of frame.

shocks or struts and sway bars：减振器杆和稳定器杆

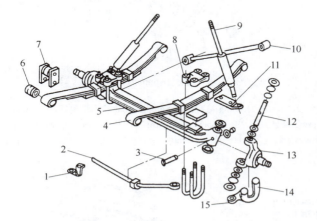

Fig. 3-19 Leaf spring suspension 钢板弹簧悬架

1—Clamp 螺钉钳；2—Locking pin 防松栓；3—Stabilizer bar 平衡杆；4—Leaf spring 钢板弹簧，弹簧片；5—I-Beam 工字梁；6—Bushing 衬套，套管；7—Shackle 卸扣，钩环铁；8，11—Bracket 支架，托架；9—Shock absorber 减振器；10—Tie rod 横拉杆；12—Steering knuckle pin 转向节销；13—Steering knuckle 转向节；14—Steering arm 转向臂，转向摇臂；15—U-bolt 骑马螺栓，U 形螺栓

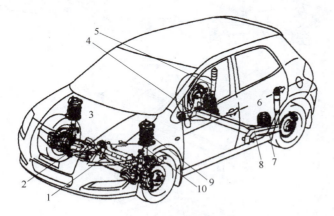

Fig. 3-20 Typical suspension of passenger car 典型的乘用车悬架

1—Stabilizer bar 横向稳定杆；2—Lower arm 下横臂；3—Front suspension 前悬架；4—Trailing arm 纵臂；5—Shock absorber 减振器；6—Rear suspension 后悬架；7—Spring insulator 弹簧隔垫；8—Twist beam 扭转梁；9—Coil spring 螺旋弹簧；10—Strut assembly 滑柱总成

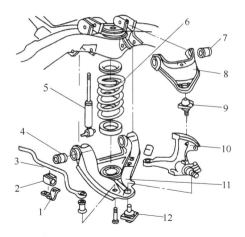

Fig. 3-21 S. L. A. suspension 长短臂悬架

1—Clamp 夹板；2，4，7—Bushing 衬套；3—Stabilizer bar 横向稳定杆；5—Shock absorber 减振器；6—Coil spring 螺旋弹簧；8—Upper control arm 上控制臂；9—Upper ball joint 上球节；10—Steering knuckle 转向节；11—Lower control arm 下控制臂；12—Lower ball joint 下球节

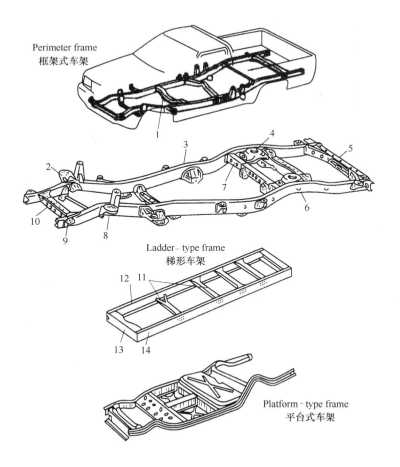

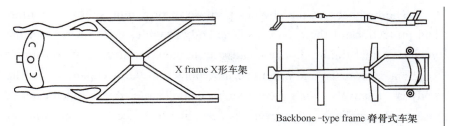

Fig. 3-22 Frame 车架

1，5，7，10，12，14—Cross member 横梁；2，4—Support bracket 支撑架；3，11，13—Side member 纵梁；6，8—Kick-up 上弯处；9—Cab mounting bracket 驾驶室安装支架

There are two basic types of axle: dead axle and live axle. The dead axle does not rotate, the wheel rotates on it. Fig. 3-23 shows dead axle suspension drive axle and axle shaft. Live axles are attached to the wheel so that both the wheel and the axle rotate together. Live axles are classified according to the manner in which they are supported: semi-floating, three-quarter-floating, and full-floating. With live axle suspension, each wheel is free to move up and down with minimum (least attainable) effect on the other wheel. There is also far less twisting motion imposed on the flame.

dead axle：静轴
live axle：活轴
drive axle：传动轴
axle shaft：半轴
semi-floating：半浮动
far less：远不及

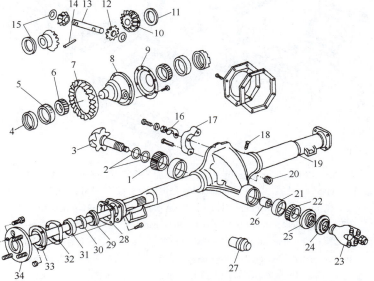

Fig. 3-23 Dead axle suspension drive axle and axle shaft 静轴式悬架驱动桥和半轴

1—Inner bearing 内轴承；2—Locating shim 调整垫圈；3—Drive pinion 主动小齿轮；4—Adjusting nut 调整螺母；5—Bearing cup 轴承座圈；6—Differential bearing 差速器轴承；7—Ring gear 齿圈；8—Differential case 差速器壳；9—Cover 盖；10—Side gear 半轴齿轮；11—Thrust washer 止推垫圈；12—Planet pinion 行星轮；13—Pinion shaft 行星轮轴；14—Shaft retainer 轴锁销；15—Thrust washer 止推垫圈；16—Adjusting nut lock 调整螺母锁片；17—Bearing cap 轴承盖；18—Vent 通风器；19—Axle housing 桥壳；20—Filler plug 加注塞；21—Bearing cup 轴承座圈；22—Outer bearing 外轴承；23—Pinion flange 主动齿轮法兰；24—Dust deflector 防尘罩；25—Seal 油封；26—Spacer 隔套；27—Collapsible spacer 可伸缩隔套；28—Gasket 衬垫；29—Axle shaft seal 半轴油封；30—Bearing retainer ring 轴承固定圈；31—Wheel bearing 车轮轴承；32—Gasket 衬垫；33—Bearing retainer 轴承固定板；34—Axle shaft 半轴

shelter：保护
occupant：乘员（客）
bending：弯曲
torsion：扭曲
collision：冲撞
rigid structure with a compliant interior：外钢内柔的结构
acceleration：加速度
underbody：底部
hood：发动机盖板
fender：挡泥板
roof panel：顶板
instrument panel：仪表板
bumpers：保险杠
luggage compartment：行李厢

The body serves the obvious purpose of providing shelter, comfort and protection for the occupants. The body provides three-quarters of the vehicle's total rigidity in bending and in torsion. In the case of collision it is intended to resist and minimize intrusions into the occupant space. The body is a relatively rigid structure with a compliant interior. Limited exterior structural compliance, however, is desirable to reduce the acceleration of collision experienced by the body. The body is generally divided into four sections: the front, the fear, the top and the underbody. These sections can be further divided into a lot of assemblies and parts, such as the hood, the fenders, the roof panels, the door, the instrument panel, the bumpers and the luggage compartment. Fig. 3-24 shows 4 door passenger car unit body. Fig. 3-25 shows separate frame construction.

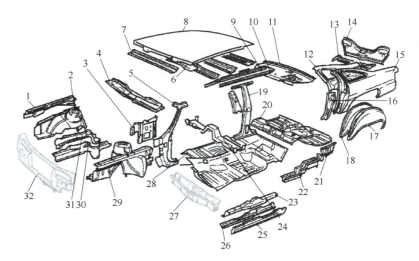

Fig. 3-24 4 door passenger car unit body 四门乘用车承载式车身
1—Upper rail 上梁；2—Apron assembly 挡泥板分总成；3—Hinge pillar, inner 内铰链柱；4—Cowl panel 前围上盖板；5—A pillar A 柱；6—Roof bow 顶盖横梁；7—Windshield header 风窗上框；8—Roof panel 顶盖；9—Side rail, inner 内边梁；10—Side rail, outer 外边梁；11—Package tray 后窗台板；12—Inner panel, upper 上内板；13—Rear cross member 后横梁；14—Rear body panel 后围板；15—Quarter panel 后侧围外板；16—C pillar C 柱；17—Outer wheelhouse 外轮口；18—Inner wheelhouse 内轮口；19—B pillar B 柱；20—Rear floor pan 后地板；21—Floor extension 地板接板；22—Side rail 纵梁；23—Rocker reinforcement 门框下边梁加强件；24—Floor cross member 地板横梁；25—Outer rocker panel 门框外下边梁；26—Inner rocker 门框内下边梁；27—Front cross member 前横梁；28—Front floor pan 前地板；29—Apron assembly 挡泥板分总成；30—Lower rail 下梁；31—Rail reinforcement 加强梁；32—Radiator support 散热器固定框

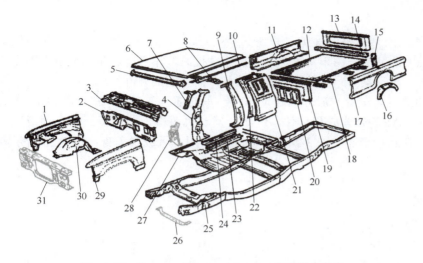

Fig. 3-25　Separate frame construction 非承载式车身

1—Wing fender 翼子板；2—Dash panel 前围板；3—Cowl panel 前围上盖板；4—A pillar A 柱；
5—Windshield header 风窗上框；6—Roof panel 顶盖；7—Hinge pillar, inner 内铰链柱；
8—Roof bow 顶盖横梁；9—Pillar reinforcement 门柱加强件；10—Side rail 边梁；
11—Side bed panel 底板侧板；12—Floor 底板；13—Tail gate 后栏板；14—Rear cross member 后横梁；15—Rear corner pillar 后角撑板；16—Wheelhouse 轮口；
17—Side bed panel 底板侧板；18—Cross rail 横梁；19—Front bed panel 前底板；
20—Rear cab panel 后围板；21—Cab side panel, outer 驾驶室外侧围；
22—Cab side panel, inner 驾驶室内侧围板；23—Outer rocker panel 门框外下边梁；24—Inner rocker 门框内下边梁；25—Frame assembly 车架总成；26—Front cross member 前横梁；27—Front floor pan 前地板；
28—Hinge pillar, inner, lower 内下铰链柱；29—Wing fender 翼子板；
30—Wheelhouse 轮口；31—Radiator support 散热器固定框

Reference Version 参考译文

汽车行驶系统是支承、安装汽车各零部件的总成，传递和承受车上、车下各种载荷，以保证汽车的正常行驶。行驶系主要由车架（车身）、车桥、悬架、车轮等组成，如图 3-18 所示。

汽车悬挂系统有两个作用：保持汽车车轮与路面的良好接触，为乘客提供乘坐舒适性。汽车悬挂是指前后弹簧用来悬挂的汽车重量。图 3-19 所示为钢板弹簧悬架。汽车中运用最广泛的弹簧钢板是由几片长的钢片构成的。由于钢板弹簧是由一组薄的钢片组成，一片叠加在另一片上，在弯曲的时候不会折断。每一片独立的钢片弯曲时，钢片之间会产生相对移动，这样会使得弹簧有很强的韧性和强度。悬挂系统也包括减振器杆和稳定器杆，如图 3-20 所示。图 3-21 所示为长短臂悬架。图 3-22 所示为各种类型的车架。

车桥有两种基本形式：静轴式和活轴式。静轴式车桥不转动，而车轮在车桥上转动。图 3-23 所示为静轴式悬架驱动桥和半轴。活轴式车桥与车轮相连，这样两者一起转动。活轴式车桥根据其承载方式可分为：半浮动、四分之三浮动和全浮动。使用活轴悬架，每个车轮都可以自由地上下运动，几乎不受另一车轮的影响，而且车架的扭动也会大大减少。

车身的基本功能就是向乘客提供保护，并使其乘坐舒适与保证安全。产生弯曲和扭矩时，汽车的整体坚固性的四分之三由车身承担。在发生冲撞时，车身能够阻挡或最大限度地减少对承载空间的冲击。车身具有一种外刚内柔的结构，而特别的外部结构的随变性使车身受到冲击时可降低其加速度。车身一般分为四个部分：车前部、车后部、车顶部和车下部。这些部分可以进一步分为许多分总成和部件。例如：发动机盖板、挡泥板、车身顶板、车门、仪表板、汽车保险杠和行李厢。图 3-24 所示为四门乘用车承载式车身；图 3-25 所示为非承载式车身。

Section 3.4
Differential 差速器

ring gear and cage：冠状齿轮和壳体

depend on：依赖

rear-axle-housing assembly：后桥壳总成

rear axle：后桥

bevel side gear：半轴锥齿轮

differentia-pinion gear：行星齿轮

drive pinion：传动小齿轮

open differential：开式差速器

additional traction：额外的牵引力

off-road：越野的

power-transfer：分动器

spider-gear：十字轴

When a car is driving straight down the road, both drive wheels are spinning at the same speed. The input pinion is turning the ring gear and cage, and none of the pinions within the cage are rotating-both side gears are effectively locked to the cage. When a car makes a turn, the wheels must spin at different speeds. The solution to this problem is depend on a part called differential.

The differential is a part of the vehicle rear-axle-housing assembly, which includes the differential, rear axles wheels and bearings.

The rear axles are attached to the wheels and have bevel side gears on their inner ends. The differential case is assembled on the left axle but can rotate on a bearing independently of the axle. The differential case support the differentia-pinion gear on a shaft, and this gear meshes with the two bevel gears. The ring gear is attached to the differential case so that the case rotates with the ring gear when the latter is driven by the drive pinion.

Most vehicles are sold with open differentials, which do not offer any additional traction off-road. Power-transfer in an open differential follows the path of least resistance, supplying power through the spider-gears to the wheel with the least amount of traction.

Fig. 3-26 shows the components of an open differential.

In Fig. 3-26, the pinions in the cage start to spin as the car begins to turn, allowing the wheels to move at different speeds. The inside wheel spins slower than the cage, while the outside wheel spins faster.

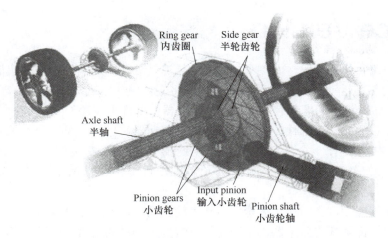

Fig. 3-26　The components of an open differentia
开式差速器的部件

The open differential always applies the same amount of torque to each wheel. There are two factors that determine how much torque can be applied to the wheels: equipment and traction. In dry conditions, when there is plenty of traction, the amount of torque applied to the wheels is limited by the engine and gearing; in a low traction situation, such as when driving on ice, the amount of torque is limited to the greatest amount that will not cause a wheel to slip under those conditions. So, even though a car may be able to produce more torque, there needs to be enough traction to transmit that torque to the ground.

Now if one of the drive wheels has good traction, and the other one is on ice, that the open differential always applies the same torque to both wheels, and the maximum amount of torque is limited to the greatest amount that will not make the wheels slip.It doesn't take much torque to make a tire slip on ice. And when the wheel with good traction is only getting the very small amount of torque that can be applied to the wheel with less traction, your car isn't going to move very much. When you are driving off-road, if one of the front tires and one of the back tires comes off the ground, they will just spin helplessly in the air, and you won't be able to move at all.

The solution to these problems is the limited sup differential（LSD）, sometimes called positraction. Limited slip differentials use various mechanisms to allow normal differential action when going around turns. When a wheel slips, they allow mole torque to be transferred to the non-slipping wheel.

dry conditions：干燥的环境

plenty：足够

torque：转矩

slip：滑动；打滑

maximum amount：最高数额

come off the ground：陷入地中

limited sup differential（LSD）：防滑式差速器

Reference Version 参考译文

当一辆轿车沿着一条路直线行驶时，两侧车轮以同一转速转动。主动齿轮带动冠状齿轮和壳体，壳体内的小齿轮都不转动——两边的齿都有效地将壳体锁住。当一辆汽车转弯时，车轮必须以不同的转速旋转。这个问题就有赖于被称为差速器的部件来解决。

差速器是汽车后桥壳总成的一个部件，后桥壳总成包括差速器、后桥、车轮和轴承。

后桥与车轮相连，内端装有一个半轴锥齿轮。差速器壳支承在左侧车桥上，而且能够在轴承上做独立转动。差速器壳支承在行星齿轮轴上，行星齿轮与两个半轴齿轮相啮合。

冠状齿轮与差速器壳相连，这样当冠状齿轮由传动齿轮驱动时，差速器壳也转动。

大部分市场上的差速器都是开式差速器，不能在越野时提供额外的附着力。开式差速器的分动器在小阻力的道路上，通过十字轴，将动力按最小附着力分配给车轮。

图3-26标出了开式差速器的各部分名称。

图3-26中，壳体内的小齿轮在车辆转向时开始转动，以此实现两侧车轮以不同的转速旋转。内侧车轮要比壳体转得慢，但外侧车轮就要转得相对快点。

开式差速器一般都是将相同大小的扭矩分配到两侧车轮上。有两个因素决定分配到车轮的扭矩多少：设备和牵引力。在干燥的环境，有充足牵引力的情况下，分配到车轮的扭矩受到发动机及齿轮的限制；在牵引力较小的时候，如在冰面上行驶，这种情况下，扭矩的大小限制在车轮不至于打滑的最大值。所以，即使一辆车可以产生更大的扭矩，同样需要足够的牵引力用以将这些扭转力矩传输到地面上。

当汽车的一个驱动轮在附着系数较高的路面上，而另一个驱动轮却在冰面上时，开式差速器总是分配两轮相等的转矩，且最大扭矩受限于最大防滑系数的限制。它并不会给在冰面上的车轮以更大的扭矩，而且牵引力好的那个车轮仅获得和差的车轮一样的很少量的扭矩，此时，你的车就不能正常运行。在你越野驾驶的时候，如果一侧前轮及一侧后轮都陷入地中，那么其他两轮只能在空中无用地旋转，汽车根本无法移动。

这类问题只能通过防滑式差速器（LSD）来解决，有时也叫做"正牵引（positraction）"。防滑差速器使用多种机械技术来实现常规差速器使车辆转弯的行为。当一侧车轮打滑时，它提供更多的扭矩给不打滑的轮子。

Section 3.5

Automobile Steering System
转向系统

traveling：行进

steering wheel：方向盘；转向盘

During the traveling of the car, steering movement is the most basic movement. We manipulate and control the vehicle's rotating direction by using the steering wheel in order to realize our intentions. Automobile steering system is shown in Fig. 3-27. Its function is just to assure automobile travel according to selected direction by driver.

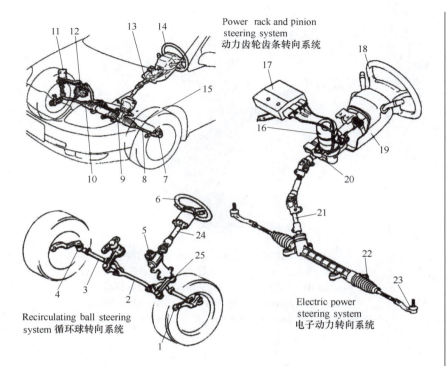

Fig.3-27 Automobile steering system 汽车转向系统
1，7—Steering knuckle arm 转向节臂；2—Relay rod 中继杆；3—Adjusting sleeve 调节管；
4—Ball joint 球节；5，9—Steering gear 转向器；6，14，18—Steering wheel 转向盘；
8—Tie rod 横拉杆；10，22—Boot 防尘罩；11—Reservoir tank 储液罐；
12—Steering pump 转向油泵；13，24—Steering column 转向管柱；
15—Steering linkage 转向传动机构；16—DC motor 直流电动机；
17—Power steering ECU 动力转向 ECU；19—Column cover 管柱罩；
20—Torque sensor 扭矩传感器；21—Pinion shaft 小齿轮轴；
23—Tie rod end 横拉杆接头；25—Pitman arm 转向摇臂

Automobile steering system can be divided into the manual steering system and the power steering system by different energy of steering. The manual steering system relies on the driver's steering power to steer the wheel. It mainly consists of steering control mechanism（include steering wheel, steering column, etc.）, steering gear, steering linkage mechanism（include steering tie rod, steering knuckle arm, steering knuckle, steering vehicle wheel, etc.）, as Fig. 3-28 shown. Under the control of the driver, the power steering system can steer the wheel through the use of liquid pressure produced by the engine or motor driving force. Power steering systems add a hydraulic pump, fluid reservoir, hoses, lines, and either a power assist unit mounted on, or integral with, a steering wheel gear assembly in basic of manual steering system（see Fig. 3-29）. The power steering system is used in general in current automobile.

manual steering system：手控转向系统
power steering system：动力转向系统
steering control mechanism：转向控制机构
steering column：驾驶杆
steering gear：转向齿轮
steering linkage mechanism：转向连杆机构
steering tie rod：转向横拉杆
steering knuckle arm：转向节臂
steering vehicle wheel：转向（车）轮
fluid reservoir：储液罐
steering wheel gear assembly：方向盘齿轮传动装置

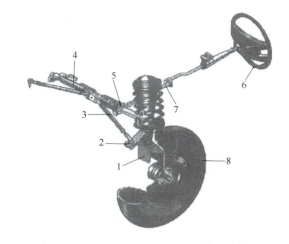

Fig. 3-28　Manual steering system 手动转向系统
1—Steering knuckle 转向节；2—Steering knuckle arm 转向节臂；
3—Steering tie rod 转向横拉杆；4—Steering damper 转向减振器；
5—Manual steering gear 机械转向器；6—Steering wheel 转向盘；
7—Safety steering column 安全转向轴；8—Steering vehicle wheel 转向轮

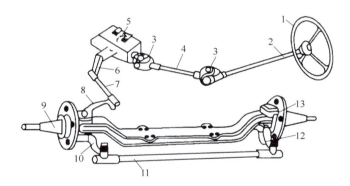

Fig. 3-29　Power steering system 动力转向系统
1—Steering wheel 方向盘；2—Steering column 转向臂柱；3—Universal joint 万向节；
4—Steering shaft 转向轴；5—Steering gear 转向器；6—Pitman arm 转向摇臂；
7—Drag link 直拉杆；8—Steering knuckle 转向节；9—Left steering knuckle 左转向节；
10，12—Steering arms 转向节臂；11—Tie rod 横拉杆；
13—Right steering knuckle 右转向节

The electronic power steering system（EPS，see Fig. 3-30）could make steering wheel convenient and flexible at low speeds；steering in the region to high-speed，the EPS also promises to provide optimal power magnification and stability to handle，thus enhancing the stability of the control during high-speed traveling. So it has been commonly used in car manufacturing in every country.

optimal：最佳的
magnification：放大率；放大倍数
enhance：优化

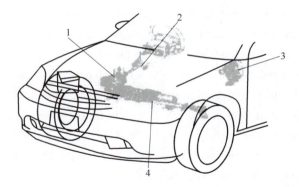

Fig. 3-30　Electronic control power steering system 电子控制动力转向系统
1—Motor 电动机；2—Steering column 转向柱；3—Control computer 控制计算机；
4—Steering gearbox 转向齿轮箱

There are several manual steering system gears in current use. The "rack and pinion" type is the choice of most manufacturers. The "recirculating ball" type is past favorite because the balls act as a rolling thread between the worm shaft and the ball nut. Another manual steering gear once popular in imported cars is the "worm and sector" type. Other manual gears are "worm and tapered pin steering gear" and "worm and roller steering gear".

In automobile steering system，the steering wheel and steering column in steering control mechanism are key parts. The constitute of steering wheel and steering column is shown as Fig. 3-31.

rack and pinion：齿轮齿条副

recirculating ball：循环球（式）

worm and sector：蜗杆齿扇（式）

worm and tapered pin steering gear：蜗杆指销式转向器

worm and roller steering gear：蜗轮蜗杆式转向器

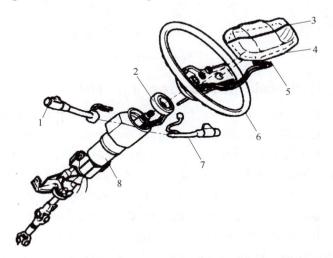

Fig. 3-31　Steering wheel and steering column 转向盘和转向柱
1—Turn indicator/speed control lever 转向指示灯 / 车速控制杆；2—Air bag coil assembly 安全气囊螺旋电缆总成；3—Trim cover 装饰盖；4—Air bag 安全气囊；5—Inflator module（安全气囊）充气模块；6—Steering wheel assembly 转向盘总成；7—Windshield wiper/windshield washer control lever 前窗刮水器 / 前窗清洗器操纵杆；8—Steering column assembly 转向柱总成

The function of steering gear is that converts the rotational motion of the steering wheel into the linear motion needed to turn the wheels, and provides a gear reduction, making it easier to turn the wheels.

On most cars, it takes three to four complete revolutions of the steering wheel to make the wheels turn from lock to lock. The steering ratio is the ratio of how far you turn the steering wheel to how far the wheels turn. Less effort is required because of the higher gear ratio. Generally, lighter, sportier cars have lower steering ratios than larger cars and trucks. The lower ratio gives the steering a quicker response. These smaller cars are light enough that even with the lower ratio, the effort required to turn the steering wheel is not excessive.

Automobiles generally have power steering systems that reduce the input force required to turn or steer an automobile. Power steering is classified into hydraulic power steering (HPS), and electric power steering (EPS). See Fig. 3-32.

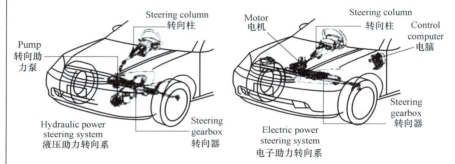

Fig.3-32　Power steering system

（1）Hydraulic power steering（HPS）

A hydraulic power steering uses the engine's power as a drive source, applying hydraulic pressure supplied by all engine-driven pump to assist the motion of turning the steering wheel. As the speed of the engine increases, the pressure in the hydraulic fluid also increases, hence a relief valve is incorporated into the system to allow excess pressure to be bled away. While the power steering is not being used, such as driving in a straight line, twin hydraulic lines provide equal pressure to both sides of the steering wheel gear. When torque is applied to the steering wheel, the hydraulic lines provide unequal pressures and hence assist in turning the wheels in the intended direction.

The system contains a hydraulic booster, which operates when the engine is running and supplies most of the necessary force when the driver turns the wheel. As a safety feature in many modern cars the column on which the steering wheel is mounted will collapse if the driver is thrown against the wheel in a collision. See Fig. 3-33.

collapse: 伸缩；折叠
collision: 碰撞

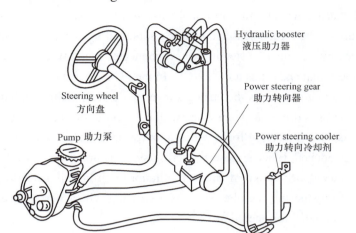

Fig. 3-33　Hydraulic power steering 液压助力转向系统

（2）Electric power steering（EPS）

More and more cars are now fitted with fully electric power steering. Electric power steering using the automobile's battery is more efficient than the hydraulic power steering, since the electric power steering assists only at the time of steering, whereas the hydraulic pump must run constantly. Therefore, EPS is expected to grow for this type in the near future.

Typically, an electric power steering system consists of a powerful electric motor geared to the steering shaft; torque sensor that detects how much effort is being put into the steering; an electric power steering system electronic control unit（ECU）and a road speed input to the ECU. See Fig. 3-34.

fully electric power steering: 全电动动力转向

torque sensor: 扭矩传感器

road speed: 路面速度

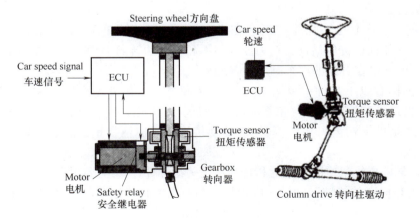

Fig. 3-34　Electric power steering 电动动力转向系统

The electric power steering system has a steering mechanism which is

analog signal：模拟信号

digital：数字的

converter circuit：变换器电路

output rotation：输出旋转

according to：根据

connected with a steering wheel via a steering shaft. The steering mechanism is provided with a torque sensor for detecting a steering torque applied to the steering wheel and a motor for assisting operations of the steering mechanism. The torque sensor converts a torsional torque of a steering shaft generated by steering of a steering wheel connected to the steering shaft, into an analog signal and sends it to an ECU. In the ECU, an analog to digital (AD) converter circuit converts the analog signal to a corresponding digital value. As the motor is driven in accordance with the steering torque detected by the torque sensor, a steering force which a driver needs to apply to the steering wheel is reduced. Electric power steering systems are generally adopted to control the output rotation of an electric motor according to a steering torque applied to a steering member such as a steering wheel when the steering member is rotated for operation.

Reference Version 参考译文

　　在汽车行驶中，转向运动是最基本的运动。我们通过方向盘来操纵和控制汽车的行驶方向，从而实现自己的行驶意图。汽车转向系统如图 3-27 所示。其功用就是保证汽车能够按照驾驶员选定的方向行驶。

　　汽车转向系统可按转向的动力来源不同分为手动转向系统和动力转向系统两类。手动转向系统是依靠驾驶员操纵转向盘的转向力来实现车轮转向的，主要由转向操纵机构（包括转向盘、转向轴等）、转向器、转向传动机构（包括转向横拉杆、转向节臂、转向节、转向轮等）组成，如图 3-28 所示。动力转向系统则是在驾驶员的控制下，借助于汽车发动机产生的液体压力或电动机驱动力实现车轮转向的。动力转向系统在手动转向系统的基础上增加了液压泵、油缸、管、线，还有安装或集成在转向机构上的动力辅助装置（见图 3-29）。现在的汽车普遍采用动力转向装置。

　　电动动力转向系统（简称 EPS，见图 3-30），在低速行驶时可使转向轻便、灵活；当汽车在高速区域转向时，又能保证提供最优的动力放大倍率和稳定的转向手感，从而提高了高速行驶的操纵稳定性，因此已在各国的汽车制造中普遍采用。

　　目前使用的转向机构有以下几种："齿轮齿条式"转向器是大部分生产厂家采用的形式；"循环球式"是过去最受欢迎的形式，依靠循环球在蜗杆和滚道之间滚动；另一种在进口车中曾经流行的形式是"蜗轮齿扇式"；其他的传动机构有"曲柄指销式"和"蜗轮蜗杆式"。

　　汽车转向系统中，转向操纵机构的转向盘和转向柱是关键部件，其组成如图 3-31 所示。

　　转向器的作用是把转向盘的旋转运动转变成车轮转向所需的直线运动，并且减速增力，使转向更方便容易。

　　在大多数情况下，转向盘转三到四周方能使车轮从一个极限位置转到另一个极限位置。转向盘的转角与车轮偏转角的比值，称为转向系的角传动比。高的角传动比可以使转向更轻便。一般来说，轻型车、赛车的转向系角传动比较低，而重型车和卡车角传动比较高。传动系角传动比低，则转向灵敏。而且，这些轻便型和小型车不必过多地考虑其转向轻便问题。

汽车通常拥有助力转向系统：减小汽车转向需要施加的操作力。助力转向系统分为液压助力转向系统（HPS）和电动动力转向系统（EPS）。如图 3-32 所示。

（1）液压助力转向

液压助力转向使用发动机的能量作为驱动源，使用发动机驱动泵提供的液压帮助方向盘转向。随着发动机转速加快，液压油的压力就加大，因此，泄压阀并入到系统中，使过多的压力排泄掉。不使用助力转向，例如直线行车时，双液压管路向转向盘提供相等的压力。转矩施加到转向盘时，液压管路压力不等，从而帮助车轮向预想的方向转动。如图 3-10 所示。

液压助力转向系统包括液压增压机。它在发动机起动后运行，并在驾驶员转动方向盘时提供大部分必须的操作力。作为许多现代汽车的安全特点，在车辆碰撞中如果驾驶员惯性撞到转向盘时，安装在转向盘上的转向柱就会伸缩。如图 3-33 所示。

（2）电动动力转向系统

现今越来越多的汽车安装了全电动动力转向系统。电动动力转向使用汽车蓄电池，要比液压动力转向更有效，因为电动动力转向只是在转向时助力，而液压动力转向时，泵就必须始终运行。因此，这种类型的电动助力转向的应用在不久的将来有望增长。

一般来说，电动动力转向系统的组成是：与转向轴啮合的电动机；扭矩传感器，检测出转向所施加的转向力；电控单元（ECU）和传递到 ECU 的路面速度信号输入。如图 3-34 所示。

电动助力转向系统有一个通过转向轴与方向盘连接的转向部件。这个转向部件为扭矩传感器提供了检测适用于方向盘和帮助转向部件运转的电动机的转向扭矩。扭矩传感器将转向盘转向产生的转向轴扭转扭矩转变成模拟信号，发送到 ECU。在 ECU 中，数模转换器把模拟信号转化成相应的数码值。根据扭矩传感器检测出来的转向扭矩来驱动电动机，这就减轻了驾驶员需要用在转向盘上的转向操作力。根据施加在转向元件的转向扭矩，如转向盘操作时转动的转向元件，一般采用电动动力转向系来控制电动机的输出旋转。

Section 3.6
Four-wheel Steering
四轮转向

Four-wheel steering （4WS）changes the way of the car handles by allowing the driver to steer the rear wheel as well as the front wheels during turns. It adds a steering unit and linkage to the rear axle, requiring rear wheels equipped with steering adds a steering arms and sometimes using a shaft running from the front steering gear to the rear unit. It is one of the most important steering innovations in many years.

Four-wheel steering first became available on mass-market automobile

four-wheel steering：	四轮转向
handle：	操纵
rear wheel：	后轮
front wheel：	前轮
turn：	转弯
linkage：	连接机构

in the late 1980s, and by 1990 three manufacturers offered 4WS on their automobile. Those three were Honda Motor Company, Mazda Motor Company, and Nissan Motor Company. In 1991, Chrysler and Mitsubishi also introduced a 4WS system.

In the 4WS, rear wheels adopt traditional steering system, front wheels adopt direct assist electric power steering system.

At steering, the signals of sensor of front wheel steering angle, speed of a motor, yaw velocity etc., are fed into ECU (electronic control unit) to proceed analytical calculation. ECU determines steering angle of rear wheels and outputs driving signal to stepping motor. By means of that rear wheel steering gear drives rear wheel deflection to front-wheel steering, so that the 4WS is realized. The structure of the 4WS is shown as Fig. 3-35.

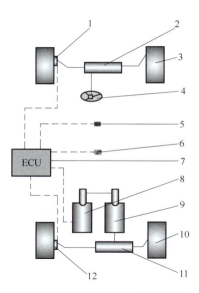

Fig. 3-35　The stucture of the 4WS 四轮转向系统结构

1—Sensor of front wheel steering angle 前轮转角传感器；2—Front wheel steering gear 前轮转向机构；3—Front wheel 前车轮；4—Steering wheel 转向盘；5—Speed sensor of a motor 车速传感器；6—Sensor of yaw velocity 横摆角速度传感器；7—Electronic control unit 电控单元；8—Stepping motor 步进电机；9—Retarding mechanism 减速机构；10—Rear wheel 后车轮；11—Sensor of rear wheel steering angle 后轮转角传感器；12—Rear wheel steering gear 后轮转向机构

There are three ways that 4WS can work: ① opposite-phase operation; ② same-phase operation; ③ phase-reverse operation.

During opposite-phase operation, the rear wheel turns in the opposite direction of the front wheel, and in same-phase direction as the front wheels. The Honda and Mazda 4WS systems operate in the opposite at low speed and for sharp turns, and in same phase at higher speeds and for wider turns or lane changes. Phase-reverse operation, used in the Nissan system, is really a combination of the other two operational modes in which the rear wheels steer opposite the front wheels very quickly before turning in the same direction. The Nissan 4WS system uses phase-reverse operation at low speeds and during sharper, quicker turns, and it operates in the same phase at high speeds and for wider, more gradual turns. Each operational mode provides a unique advantage over ordinary two-wheel steering. Opposite phase occurs during sharp turns and low vehicle speeds. This mode allows tighter turns than when only the front wheels turn, improving maneuverability during sharp, slow turns, for example, during parking. Honda and Mazda use this mode, but Nissan does not. Same-phase operation is used for smaller directional changes and at high speeds, such as during lane changes. It provides better handling and stability when changing direction at high speeds by reducing the tires side-slip angle. As a result, the car's rear end yaws or swings back and forth, less and for a short period of time than with 2WS. The Honda, Mazda and Nissan 4WS systems all use this mode.

Honda uses a completely mechanically operated 4WS system, in which the front steering gear operates a center shaft, which in turn operates the rear steering gear. In the rear steering gear, a gear train transmits rotary motion to a slider and guide mechanism that directs the rear wheels through a stroke rod and tie rods. The Mazda 4WS system is both mechanically and hydraulically operation and uses electronic controls. The front steering gear operates a steering angle transfer shaft, which provides input motion to the rear steering gear. An electronic control unit sends a speed-based signal to a stepper motor at the rear steering gear and monitors steering gear operation. Inside the rear steering gear, a complex system of gears and rods responds to transfer shaft movement and stepper motor input to operate a control valve. The control valve hydraulically actuates an output rod that moves the tie rods to turn the rear wheel. The Nissan use an electronically controlled, hydraulically operated 4WS system. The electronic control unit monitors vehicle speed and steering wheel movement through sensors, and controls the hydraulic system accordingly. The signal from the control valves to apply hydraulic pressure to one side or the other side of the rear power cylinder. The rear cylinder operates the rear steering linkage to turn the rear wheels.

---

lane change: 变换车道

side-slip angle: 侧滑角度

rear steering gear: 后转向器

guide mechanism: 导轨机构

mechanically and hydraulically operation: 机械和液力操作

monitor: 监测

Reference Version   参考译文

　　四轮转向改变了汽车的操纵方式，在汽车转弯时允许后轮和前轮一样可以转向。它增加了转向单元和与后轴的连接，需要后轮安装转向机构，增加转向臂和从前转向器到后轴转向单元的转向轴。这是多年来汽车转向的一项最重要发明。

　　四轮转向在汽车大众市场第一次出现是在20世纪80年代末期，到1990年有三家汽车制造公司在他们的车上装备了四轮转向装置。这三家公司是日本的本田汽车公司、马自达汽车公司和日产汽车公司。在1991年，美国的克莱斯勒和日本的三菱汽车公司也引进了四轮转向系统。

　　在四轮转向中，后轮采取传统的转向系统，前轮采取电子助力式转向系统。

　　转向时，前轮转角、车速、横摆角速度等的传感器信号送入电子控制单元进行分析计算，ECU确定后轮转角并向步进电动机输出驱动信号，通过后轮转向机构驱动后轮偏转以适应前轮转向，实现四轮转向。四轮转向系统结构如图3-35所示。

　　四轮转向有三种工作方式：① 反向工作方式；② 同向工作方式；③ 异向工作方式。

　　在反向工作过程中，后轮与前轮的偏转方向相反；在同向工作过程中，后轮与前轮的偏转方向相同。本田和马自达公司的四轮转向系统在车速较低、转弯很急时工作处于反向工作，在高速和转弯很缓或变换车道时为同向工作。异向工作主要用于日产系统，这实际上是将其他两种操作方式结合在一起的工作方式，在前后车轮同向运动之前，后轮相对于前轮有一个很快的反向运动。日产的四轮转向系统在低速急转弯时异向工作，在高速转弯缓时采用同向工作。每一种工作模式都比普通两轮转向更具优势。反向工作是在汽车急转向过程中，车速较低时使用。这种工作模式比只有前轮转向的汽车允许有更急的转向，提高了在低速急转弯的操作性，比如在汽车停车时。本田和马自达使用这种方式，而日产不同。同向工作是用来在高速行驶过程中进行很小的方向改变，如变换车道。它可以在高速改变方向时有比较好的操作性和稳定性，减少轮胎的侧滑移角度。因此，汽车尾部的前后摆动量要比两轮转向的车小。本田、马自达和日产的四轮转向系统都采用这种方式。

　　本田使用一套完整的机械操作四轮转向系统，前面的转向器驱动一根中心轴，通过中心轴来驱动后转向器。在后转向器中，齿轮传递旋转运动给拖板，导向机构通过拉杆和连杆带动后轮。马自达的四轮转向系统中机械和液力工作都采用电子控制。前轮转向器带动转向传动轴，传动轴为后转向器提供输入运动。电子控制单元发送速度基准信号给在后转向器的步进电动机监控后转向器工作。在后转向器内部，复杂的齿轮和杆件系统响应传动轴的运动和步进电动机的输入使得控制阀工作。液压控制阀驱动推杆带动连杆使得后轮偏转。日产使用电子控制液压操作的四轮转向系统。电子控制单元通过传感器检测汽车的速度和转向轮的运动，进而控制液压系统。控制阀的信号使液压施加到一边或另一边的后助力油缸。后助力油缸推动后转向杆件使后轮偏转。

Section 3.7
Braking System
制动系统

Modern cars can run very fast, so good brakes are essential for safety. If the brakes fail, the result can be disastrous. Two complete independent braking systems are used on the car. They are the service brake mechanism and the parking brake mechanism. The service brake mechanism refers to the brakes that function to slow and stop the motion of a driving vehicle while the parking brake mechanism serves to prevent a parked vehicle from sliding or moving mechanism. Now, the car's service brake mechanism also is generally equipped with anti-lock braking system (ABS). The brake system arrangement is shown in Fig. 3-36. The brake system components is shown in Fig. 3-37.

essential: 必不可少的
disastrous: 灾难性的
service brake mechanism: 行车制动机构
parking brake mechanism: 停车制动机构
anti-lock braking system (ABS): 制动防抱死系统
arrangement: 布置

Fig. 3-36　Brake system arrangement 制动系统的布置
1—Brake hoses/lines 制动器软管；2—Master cylinder 主缸；
3—Power brake booster 制动助力器；4—Rear brakes 后制动器；
5—Parking brake lever 驻车制动操纵杆；6—Brake pedal 制动踏板；
7—Front brakes 前制动器

In terms of power source, automotive brakes are basically of two types: the mechanical actuated brakes and the hydraulic (or air-operated) brakes. The mechanical brake has already been out-of-date, but the hydraulic brake has enjoyed the universal adoption around the world on cars. Practically all cars use hydraulics brakes (which operate by applying pressure to a fluid). The constitute fluid-pressure-type brake gearing is shown in Fig. 3-38.

mechanical actuated brake: 机械制动系统（器）
hydraulic: 液压的
applying pressure: 施压
fluid-pressure-type: 液压型

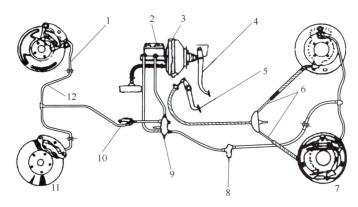

Fig. 3-37　Brake system components 制动系统的组成

1—Brake hose 制动软管；2—Master cylinder 主缸；3—Power brake 动力制动器；
4—Brake pedal 制动踏板；5—Parking brake 驻车制动器；6—Parking brake cable 手制动拉索；
7—Brake drum 制动鼓；8—Proportioning valve 比例调节阀；
9—Brake warning light switch 制动报警灯开关；10—Metering valve 限流阀；
11—Disc brake 盘式制动器；12—Brake line 制动油管

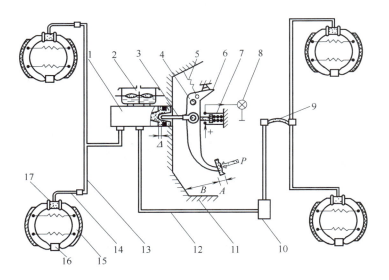

Fig. 3-38　Fluid-pressure-type brake gearing components 液压式制动传动装置的组成

1—Master cylinder 制动主缸；2—Fluid reservoir 储油罐；3—Push rod 推杆；
4—Rest pin 支承销；5—Reset spring 复位弹簧；6—Brake pedal 制动踏板；
7—Stop lamp switch 制动灯开关；8—Indicator light 指示灯；9，14—Hose 软管；
10—Proportional valve 比例阀；11—Floor 地板；12—Rear axle line 后桥油管；
13—Front axle line 前桥油管；15—Brake shoe 制动蹄；16—Support seat 支承座；
17—Wheel cylinder 轮缸；Δ—Liberty gap 自由间隙；A—Liberty stroke 自由行程；
B—Effective stroke 有效行程

master cylinder：制动主缸

separate sections：独立部分

brake pedal：刹车踏板

In most modern brake systems, there is a fluid-filled cylinder, called master cylinder, which contains two separate sections, there is a piston in each section and both pistons are connected to a brake pedal in the driver's compartment. When the brake is pushed down, brake fluid is sent from the master cylinder to the wheels. At the wheels, the fluid pushes shoes, or pads, against revolving drums or discs. The friction between the stationary shoes, or pads, and the revolving drums or discs slows and stops them. This slows or stops the revolving wheels, which, in turn, slow or stop the car.

In structure of brake, automotive brakes are basically of two types: disc brakes and drum brakes. In practical application, most modern cars have disc brakes on the front wheels, and drum brakes on the rear wheels.

The main components of a disc brake are: brake pads; caliper, which contains a piston; rotor, which is mounted to the hub. As is shown in Fig. 3-39.

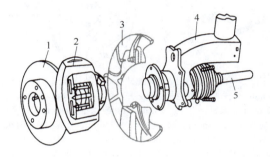

Fig. 3-39　Disc brake components 盘式制动器的组成
1—Brake disc 制动盘；2—Brake caliper 制动钳；3—Braking plate 制动底板；
4—Wheel support cover assembly 车轮支承壳总成；5—Drive shaft 传动轴

The disc brake is a lot like the brakes on a bicycle. Bicycle brakes have a caliper, which squeezes the brake pads against the wheel. In a disc brake, the brake pads squeeze the rotor instead of the wheel, and the force is transmitted hydraulically instead of through a cable. Friction between the pads and the disc slows the disc down.

The most common type of disc brake on modern cars is the single-piston floating caliper.

Drum brakes, as is shown in Fig. 3-40, work on the same principle as disc brakes: shoes press against a spinning surface (in this system, that surface is called a drum). Fig. 3-41 shows a drum-type parking brake.

In the drum-and-shoe type, there is a wheel brake cylinder with two pistons. When brake pedal is pushed by the driver, brake fluid is forced into the brake cylinder by the action at the master cylinder, and the two pistons are forced outward. This causes the curved brake shoes to move into contact with the brake drum. The brake shoes apply friction to the brake drum, forcing it and the wheel to slow or stop.

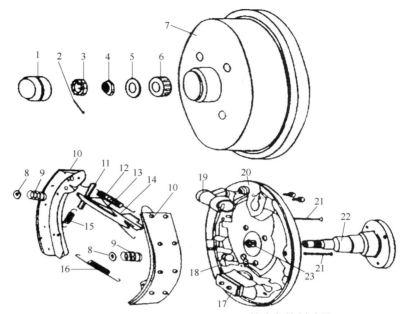

Fig. 3-40　Drum-type wheel brake 鼓式车轮制动器

1—Wheel hub cover 轮毂盖；2—Cotter 开口销；3—Slotting gasket 开槽垫圈；
4—Adjusting nut 调整螺母；5—Thrust washer 止推垫圈；6—Bearing 轴承；
7—Brake drum 制动鼓；8—Spring seat 弹簧座；9—Spring 弹簧；10—Brake shoe 制动蹄；
11—Wedge-shape part 楔形件；12—Return spring 回位弹簧；13—Upper return spring 上回位弹簧；
14—Pressure rod 压力杆；15—Return spring for wedge-shape part 用于楔形件的回位弹簧；
16—Down return spring 下回位弹簧；17—Dead plate 固定板；
18—Bolt（tightening torque 60N·m）螺栓（拧紧力矩 60N·m）；
19—Rear brake cylinder 后制动轮缸；20—Braking plate 制动底板；
21—Locating pin 定位销；22—Rear axle wheel support short axis 后桥车轮支承短轴；
23—Peep door rubber plug 观察孔橡胶塞

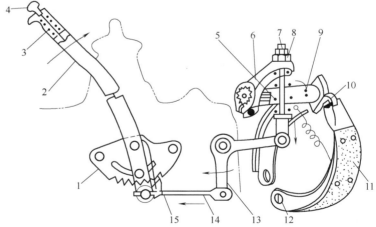

Fig. 3-41　Drum-type parking brake 鼓式驻车制动器

1—Sector gear 齿扇；2—Parking brake lever 驻车制动杆；3—Pull-rod spring 拉杆弹簧；
4—Press-button 按钮；5—Holddown spring 压紧弹簧；6，13—Rocker 摆臂；
7—Pull-rod 拉杆；8—Adjusting nut 调整螺母；9—Camshaft 凸轮轴；10—Idler wheel 滚轮；
11—Brake shoe 制动蹄；12—Decentration rest pin hole 偏心支承销孔；
14—Transfer bar 传动杆；15—Lock pawl 锁止棘爪

Back in the day, when most cars had drum brakes, power brakes were not really necessary, drum brakes naturally provide some of their own power assist. Since most cars today have disc brakes, at least on the front wheels, they need power brakes. Without this device, a lot of drivers would have very tired legs. The brake booster uses vacuum from the engine to multiply the force that your foot applies to the master cylinder. The Fig.3-42 shows the structure of a vacuum booster.

back in the day：目前
power brake：动力制动

vacuum booster：真空助力器

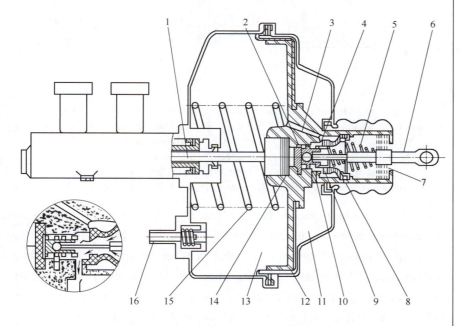

图 3-42 Structure of a vacuum booster 真空助力器结构
1—Push rod 推杆；2—Air valve 空气阀；3—Vacuum passage 真空通道；
4—Vacuum valve seat 真空阀座；5—Return spring 回位弹簧；
6—Brake pedal push rod 制动踏板推杆；7—Air filtration chip 空气滤芯；
8—Rubber valve 橡胶阀门；9—Air valve seat 空气阀座；
10—Air passage 通气道；11—Afterburning air-chamber rear-chamber 加力气室后腔；
12—Diaphragm seat 膜片座；13—Afterburning air-chamber anter-chamber 加力气室前腔；
14—Rubber reaction disc 橡胶反作用盘；15—Diaphragm return sping 膜片回位弹簧；
16—Vacuum port and check valve 真空口和单向阀

Anti-lock braking system（ABS）is designed to provide best deceleration and stability during hard braking by adjusting the hydraulic pressure at each wheel to prevent wheel lock. There are many different variations and control algorithms for ABS. Regardless of the type, all work in a similar manner. Fig. 3-43 shows the constitution of ABS.

hard braking：急制动
wheel lock：车轮抱死；制动跑偏

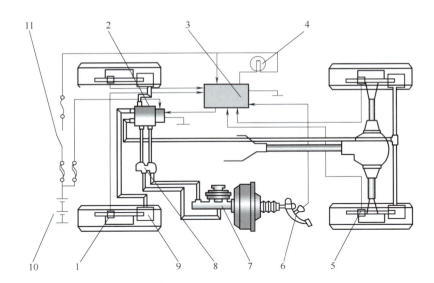

Fig. 3-43　The constitution of ABS braking system　ABS 制动系统的组成
1—Front wheel velocity sensor 前轮速度传感器；2—Brake pressure regulator 制动压力调节装置；
3—ABS electronic control unit ABS 电控单元；4—ABS warning light ABS 警告灯；
5—Rear wheel velocity sensor 后轮速度传感器；6—Stop light switch 停车灯开关；
7—Brake master cylinder 制动主缸；8—Proportion selector valve 比例分配阀；
9—Brake cylinder 制动轮缸；10—Battery 蓄电池；11—Ignition lock 点火开关

speed sensor：速度传感器

out of the ordinary：不寻常的

　　The controller monitors the speed sensors at all times. It is looking for decelerations in the wheel that are out of the ordinary. Fig. 3-44 shows the wheel speed sensor. Right before a wheel locks up, it will experience a rapid deceleration. If left unchecked, the wheel would stop much more quickly than any car could. It might take a car five seconds to stop from 60 mph（96.6 kph）under ideal conditions，but a wheel that locks up could stop spinning in less than a second.

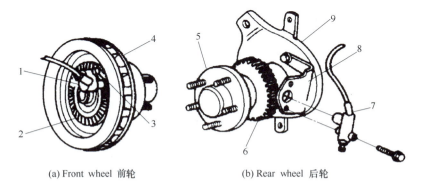

(a) Front wheel　前轮　　　(b) Rear wheel　后轮

Fig. 3-44　Wheel speed sensor　车轮转速传感器
1，7—Sensor 传感器；2，6—Sensor gear ring 传感器齿圈；3—Positioning screw 定位螺钉；
4—Hub and components 轮毂和组件；5—Axle shaft 半轴；8—Sensor support 传感器支架；
9—Rear brake connecting device 后制动器连接装置

Reference Version 参考译文

　　现代汽车速度很快，良好的制动系统是安全的基本保证。如果制动失效，后果可能是灾难性的。汽车上使用两套完全独立的制动系统：行车制动和驻车制动。行车制动机构用来减慢车速、停止行驶车辆。驻车制动机构指的是用来防止已停车辆滑行或移动的制动器。现在汽车的行车制动系还普遍装有制动防抱死系统（ABS）。制动系的布置如图 3-36 所示，其基本组成如图 3-37 所示。

　　就动力源而论，汽车制动器基本上有两种类型：机械制动器与液压（或气动）制动器。机械制动器已过时，而液压制动器已在汽车上获得全球使用。实际上所有的汽车都使用液压制动（通过向液体加压来完成的）。液压式制动传动装置的组成如图 3-38 所示。

　　现代车辆的制动系统中，有一个充满液体的油缸叫制动主缸，它分为独立的两部分，每部分里面都有一个活塞，两个活塞都和驾驶室内的制动踏板连接。当制动踏板被踩下时，制动液从主缸被送到车轮上。在车轮上，液体推动制动蹄片或制动块阻止制动鼓和制动盘的转动。在固定的制动蹄片或制动块和转动的制动鼓或制动盘之间产生摩擦力，这样可以降低车速或制动汽车。按顺序降低或制动转动的车轮，就可以把汽车的速度降下来，或使车辆停止。

　　就制动器的结构而言，汽车制动器基本上有两种类型：盘式制动器与鼓式制动器。实际应用中，大多数汽车的前轮采用盘式制动，后轮采用鼓式制动。

　　盘式制动器包括以下主要的零件：制动摩擦片；制动钳，内有活塞；制动盘，安装在轮毂上。如图 3-39 所示。

　　盘式制动器和自行车上的刹车很像。自行车的刹车有一个夹钳，夹钳夹紧摩擦片，使它紧紧地夹紧车轮。在盘式制动器中，摩擦片夹住的是制动盘而不是车轮，夹紧力不是通过刹车带提供的，而是由液压系统提供的制动力。制动摩擦片和盘之间的摩擦力使制动盘速度降下来。

　　现代汽车中常见的盘式制动器是浮钳盘式制动器。

　　鼓式制动器如图 3-40 所示，其工作原理与盘式制动器是一样的：制动蹄压在旋转表面上（在鼓式制动中，这个表面被称为鼓）。图 3-41 所示为鼓式驻车制动器。

　　在蹄-鼓制动器中，有一个带有两个活塞的制动轮缸。当驾驶员踩下制动踏板时，制动液由于主缸的作用进入轮缸，推动两个活塞向外侧移动。这使得圆弧状的制动蹄张开与制动鼓相接触。制动蹄对制动鼓所产生的摩擦力迫使制动鼓和车轮减速或停车。

　　目前，后轮大部分采用鼓式制动，不一定需要动力制动——鼓式制动可以自己提供助力。因为现在大多数汽车采用盘式制动，至少前轮采用盘式制动，那就需要动力制动了。若没有制动助力器，那么司机的腿会非常疲劳。制动助力器采用真空泵把司机的脚作用在主缸上的力放大。图 3-42 所示为真空助力器结构。

　　防抱死制动系统（ABS）是为汽车急刹车时提供最佳减速度和稳定性而设计的，它通过调节每个车轮的制动液压来防止车轮抱死。目前有各种各样的 ABS 系统以及控制算法。不考虑其类型，所有系统的工作原理是相似的。图 3-43 所示为 ABS 制动系统的组成。

　　控制系统始终监视着速度传感器。它随时检测车轮的减速度是否异常。图 3-44 所示为车轮转速传感器。当车轮即将抱死前，ABS 系统迅速检测到车轮减速异常。假如没有 ABS 系统的检测，那么抱死比车轮普通制动更迅速。在理想条件下，当车速为 60mile/h（96.6km/h）行驶时，完全停车需 5s，但是车轮抱死在不到 1s 的时间内就可能发生了。

Unit 4

Auto Electrical Equipment
汽车电气设备

Section 4.1
Auto Electric Appliance
汽车电气

(1) The composition of auto electric appliance

The function of auto electric system is to ensure reliability, safety and comfort of automobile in travel. The auto electric system is shown in Fig. 4-1, is divided into following part.

reliability: 可靠性
comfort: 舒适

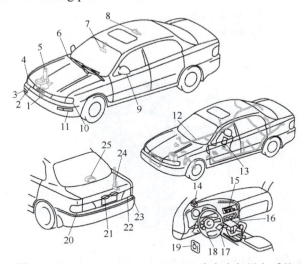

图 4-1　Automotive electrical system 汽车电气设备系统
1—Horn 喇叭；2—Headlight 前照灯；3—Front turn signal lamp 前转向信号灯；
4，10—Width lamp 示宽灯；5—Windshield washer 前窗洗涤器；
6—Wiper 刮水器；7，9—Mirror 后视镜；8—Interior lamp 顶灯；
11—Side turn signal lamp, fog light 侧转向信号灯，雾灯；12—Wiring 线路；
13—Seat heater 座椅加热器；14—Automatic light control system 照明自动控制装置；
15—Compact disc player CD 播放机；16—Air bag ECM 安全气囊电子控制模块；
17—Cruise control 巡航控制器；18—Combination switch 组合开关；19—Speaker 扬声器；
20，23—Reverse lamp 倒车灯；21—License plate lamp 牌照灯；
22—Rear combination lamp 后组合灯；24—Antenna 天线；25—Center stop lamp 中间制动灯

charging system：充电系统
alternator：交流发电机

1）Power system

Including battery, charging system, alternator and its regulator. Fig. 4-2 shows conventional battery. Fig. 4-3 shows maintenance-free battery. Fig. 4-4 shows charging system. Fig. 4-5 shows an alternator.

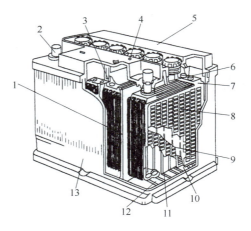

Fig. 4-2　Conventional battery 传统蓄电池
1—Cell partition 单体电池隔板；2—Terminal post 极桩；
3—Cell connecting bar 单体电池连接条；4—Vent plug 通气孔塞；
5—One-piece cover 整件式盖；6—Electrolyte level mark 电解液面标记；
7—Plate bridge 极板连接条；8—Negative plate 负极板；9—Positive plate 正极板；
10—Sediment space 沉淀室；11—Separator 隔板；
12—Element rest 元件支承台；13—Battery box 蓄电池壳体

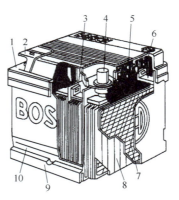

Fig. 4-3　Maintenance-free battery（MF battery）免维护蓄电池
1—One-piece cover 整件式盖；2—Terminal-post cover 接头盖；
3—Cell connecting bar 单体电池连接条；4—Terminal post 极柱；5—Frit 玻璃纤维滤网；
6—Plate bridge 极板连接条；7—Negative plate 负极板；8—Separator envelope 隔板套；
9—Bottom mounting rail 底部安装导轨；10—Battery box 蓄电池壳体

2）Start-up system

start-up system：起动系统

Including starter, starter relay, starting safety switch, etc.
Fig. 4-6 shows a start-up system. Automobile engines are not self-starts.

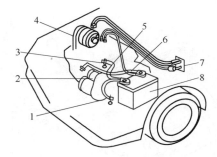

Fig. 4-4 Charging system 充电系统
1—Sheet metal ground 金属板式搭铁；2—Starter solenoid switch 起动机电磁开关；
3—Engine ground 发动机搭铁；4—Alternator 发电机；
5—Negative battery cable 蓄电池负极电缆；6—Positive battery cable 蓄电池正极电缆；
7—Fuse panel 烙丝板；8—Battery 蓄电池

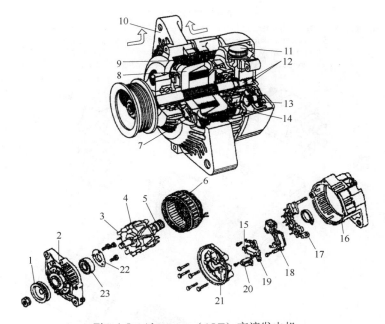

Fig. 4-5 Alternator（ALT）交流发电机
1—Pulley 带轮；2，10—Drive end frame 前端盖；3，7，14—Internal fan 内装式风扇；
4，8—Rotor 转子；5—Collector ring 集电环；6，9—Stator 定子；
11，18—Voltage regulator 电压调节器；12—Collector ring 集电环；13—Diode 二极管；
15—Brush 电刷；16—Slip ring end frame 后端盖；17—Diode assy 二极管总成；
19—Brush holder 电刷架；20—Suppression capacitor 静噪电容器；
21—Fan leader 风扇导向器；22—Bearing retainer 轴承保持板；
23—Front bearing 前轴承

In order to start them, it is necessary that equips a starter. The starter is shown in Fig. 4-7. the starter motor receives electrical power form the storage battery. The starter motor then converts this energy into mechanical energy, which it transmits through the drive mechanism to the engine's flywheel.

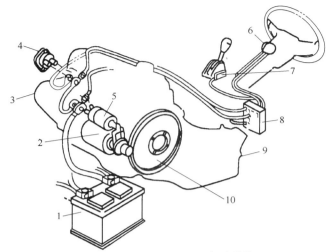

Fig. 4-6　Start-up system 起动系统

1—Battery 蓄电池；2—Starter 起动机；3—Engine 发动机；4—Starter relay 起动继电器；
5—Solenoid switch 电磁开关；6—Ignition switch 点火开关；
7—Neutral safety switch 空挡安全开关；8—Fuse panel 熔丝板；
9—Transaxle 变速驱动桥；10—Engine flywheel 发动机飞轮

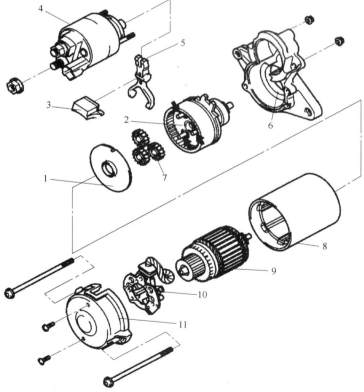

Fig. 4-7　Starter 起动机

1—Armature plate 电枢板；2—Center bearing clutch assy 中间轴承离合器总成；
3—Rubber seal 橡胶密封件；4—Magnet switch assy 电磁开关总成；
5—Pinion drive level 小齿轮驱动杆；6—Drive housing assy 驱动壳总成；
7—Planetary gear 行星轮；8—Yoke assy 磁轭总成；9—Armature assy 电枢总成；
10—Brush holder assy 电刷架总成；11—Commutator end frame assy 换向器端盖总成

The starter motor draws a great deal of electrical current from the battery. The driver controls the flow of this current using the starting switch. Fig. 4-8 shows outline of solenoid switch for starter. The starting system is designed with two connected circuits: the starter circuit and the control circuit.

Fig. 4-8　Outline of solenoid switch for starter 汽车用起动电磁开关外形

The starting safety switch, is also called a neutral start switch. It is a normally open switch that prevents the starting system from operating when the automobile's transmission is in gear.

A magnetic switch (relays and solenoids) in the starting system allows the control circuit to open and close the starter circuit.

The starter motor converts electrical energy from the battery into mechanical energy to turn the engine. It does this through the interaction of magnetic fields. An automotive starter motor has many conductors and uses a lot of current to create enough rotational force to crank the engine.

3）Ignition system

Including ignition lock, ignition coil, distributor (has been canceled on some vehicle), electronic control unit (ECU), signal generator, ignition controller, spark plug, high voltage wire, etc., as is shown in Fig. 4-9.

The ignition system on an internal combustion engine provides the spark that ignites the combustible air/fuel mixture in the combustion chamber. The spark consists of an electric arc produced by applying a high voltage (from approximately 6~40kV) between the center electrode and ground across the electrodes of a spark plug.

The ignition system is divided into two circuits: the primary and the secondary. The primary circuit is the low-voltage side of the system and controls the secondary circuit, which is the high-voltage side of the system.

The basic operations of the ignition system with the ignition switch closed and the engine started, are as follows:

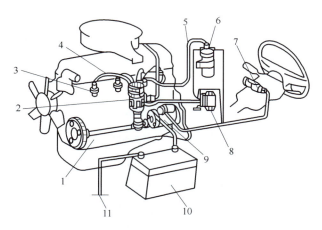

Fig. 4-9　Composition of ignition system 点火系统的组成
1—Jack shaft 中间轴；2—Distributor 分电器；3—Spark plug 火花塞；
4—Branched high-tension cable 分高压线；5—Central high-tension cable 中央高压线；
6—Ignition coil 点火线圈；7—Ignition switch 点火开关；8—Ignition controller 点火控制器；
9—Starter 起动机；10—Battery 蓄电池；11—Ground end 搭铁端

① The trigger wheel rotates with engine RPMs and causes the speed sensor, or pickup coil, to produce triggering voltage pulses that correspond to engine speed and piston position.

② The electronic control unit allows current to flow through the ignition coil primary winding until it senses a triggering voltage pulse from the speed sensor, or pickup coil.

③ Each triggering voltage pulse actuates the electronic control module to open the circuit to the ignition coil primary winding, causing the magnetic field to collapse quickly and induce a high voltage in the secondary winding.

④ The high secondary voltage travels from the coil wire to the distributor rotor and cap and then on to fire the spark plug of the cylinder that is on the proper stroke for igniting the air/fuel mixture.

4）Illuminating system

Including headlight, fog light, license plate lamp, interior lamp, reading lamp, dash board floodlight, trunk lamp, door lamp, engine nacelle floodlight, etc.

The main lighting switch（sometimes called the headlight switch）is the heart of the lighting system. It controls the headlights, parking lights, side marker lights, taillights, license plate light, instrument panel lights, and interior lights.

trigger：触发器
pickup coil：拾波线圈
triggering voltage pulses：触发电压脉冲
primary winding：初级绕组
secondary winding：二次绕组
headlight：前大灯；前照灯
license plate lamp：牌照灯
interior lamp：车内灯
dash board floodlight：仪表盘照明灯
trunk lamp：行李厢灯
engine nacelle floodlight：发动机舱照明灯
parking light：停车灯
taillight：尾灯

① Headlight and taillight system（see Fig. 4-10）.

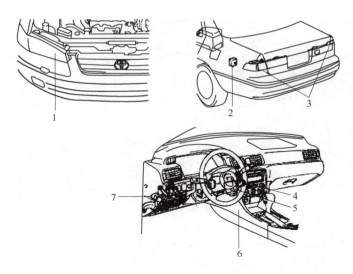

Fig. 4-10 Headlight and taillight system 前照灯和尾灯系统
1—Headlight 前照灯；2—Light failure sensor 照明故障传感器；3—Taillight 尾灯；
4—Ignition switch 点火开关；5—D.R.L relay 日间行车灯继电器；
6—Combination switch 组合开关；7—Instrument panel J/B 仪表板接线盒

② Turn signal and hazard warning light system（see Fig. 4-11）.

turn signal：转变灯
hazard warning light：危险警告灯

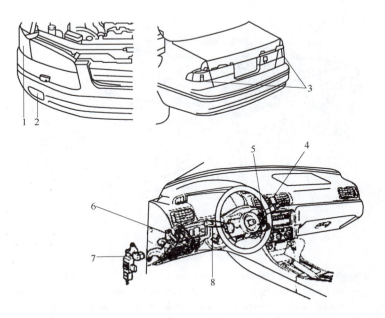

Fig. 4-11 Turn signal and hazard warning light system 转弯灯和危险警告灯系统
1，3，7—Turn signal light 转弯灯；2—Front fog light 前雾灯；4—Hazard warning switch 危险警告开关；5—Ignition switch 点火开关；6—Instrument panel J/B 仪表板接线盒；8—Combination switch 组合开关

stop light：停车灯
back up light：倒车灯

③ Stop light and back up light（see Fig. 4-12）.

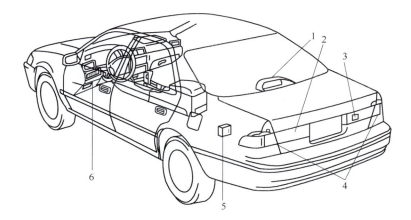

Fig. 4-12　Stop light and back up light　停车灯和倒车系统
1—Hi-mounted stop light 高位停车灯；2—Rear fog light 后雾灯；
3—Back up light 倒车灯；4—Stop light 停车灯；
5—Light failure sensor 灯光故障传感器；
6—Instrument panel J/B 仪表板接线盒

④ Interior light system（see Fig. 4-13）.

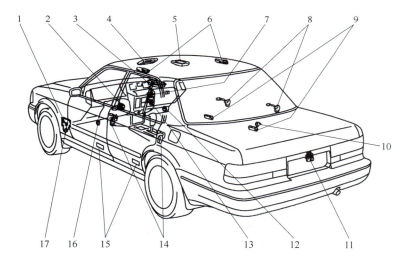

Fig. 4-13　Interior light system 客厢顶灯系统
1—Integration relay 继电器总成；2—Ignition switch 点火开关；3—R/B No.3 三号防滚杆；
4—Map light assembly 导航灯总成；5—Interior light assembly 客厢顶灯总成；
6—Rear room light assemblies 后车厢总成；7—Glove box light 后备厢灯；
8，14—Door courtesy switches 锁门开关；9，15—Door courtesy lights 锁门提示灯；
10—Luggage compartment light 行李舱灯；11—Luggage door courtesy switch 行李舱开关；
12，16—Step lights 踏板灯；13—Glove box light switch 后备厢开关；
17—R/B cassette No.1，No.2 and J/B No.1 一号、二号防滚杆和一号仪表板接线盒

5) Instrument system

Including speedometer, fuel meter, water-thermometer, engine tachometer, etc. Fig. 4-14 shows a integrated instrument panel of typical car.

fuel meter：油量表
water-thermometer：水温表
engine tachometer：发动机转速表

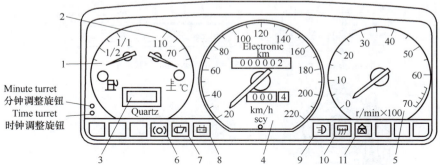

Fig. 4-14　Integrated instrument panel of typical car 典型轿车组合仪表板
1—Fuel meter 燃油表；2—Coolant temperature gauge 冷却液温度表；
3—Liquid crystal electronic clock 液晶电子时钟；4—Speedometer 车速里程表；
5—Engine tachometer 发动机转速表；6—Parking braking caution light 驻车制动装置警示灯；
7—Oil pressure caution light 机油压力警示灯；8—Charge lamp 充电指示灯；
9—Distance light pilot lamp 远光指示灯；
10—Rear window heater pilot lamp 后窗加热器指示灯；
11—Cooling liquid caution light 冷却液液面警告灯

audible signal：音响信号
braking signal lamp：刹车信号灯
turn signal lamp：转向灯
reverse signal lamp：倒车信号灯
alarm lamp：报警灯
high-mounted stop lamp：高位刹车灯

6) Signaling system

Including audible signal and light signaling device, braking signal lamp, turn signal lamp, reverse signal lamp and all kinds of alarm lamp, etc.

The directional signal switch is installed just below the hub of the steering wheel. A manually controlled lever projecting from the switch permits the driver to signal the direction in which he wants to turn.

In order to signal a stop, a brake pedal operated "stoplight switch" is provided to operate the vehicle's stop lamps. In addition to lighting the conventional rear lights, the switch also operates the center high-mounted stop lamp.

warm braw：暖风
dehumidification：除湿
power-driven window regulator：电动（车窗）升降器
central locking：中控锁
air window wiper：刮水器
syringe：洗涤器
klaxon：汽车喇叭；电喇叭
cigarette lighter：点烟器
power sunroof：电动天窗
cruise control system：巡航控制系统
power seat：电动座椅

7) Air conditioning system

Including warm braw, refrigeration and dehumidification device, etc.

8) Else assist electric equipments

Including power-driven window regulator, central locking, power mirror, air window wiper, syringe, klaxon, cigarette lighter and power sunroof, cruise control system, Supplementary Restraint System (SRS), power seat, etc. Fig. 4-15 shows central locking. Fig. 4-16 shows supplemental restraint system (SRS).

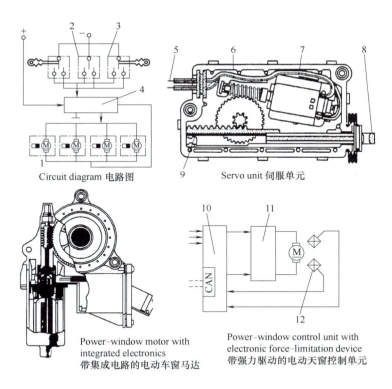

Fig. 4-15　Central locking 中控门锁
1—Door lock motor 门锁电动机；2—Central switch 中控开关；3—Door lock switch 门锁开关；4—Control unit 控制模块；5—Wiring 线束；6—Gear unit 齿轮机构；7—Door lock motor 门锁电动机；8—Actuating lever 执行杆；9—Flexible end-position coupling 柔性终端位置接合器；10—Microcomputer 微处理器；11—Relay output stage 输出延迟级；12—Hall effect sensor 霍尔效应传感器

(2) The Characteristic of auto electric appliance

① Low tension. The nominal voltage of auto electric equipment is 12V and 24V. Most of gasoline motor car uses 12V power voltage，while most of large-scale diesel vehicle uses 24V power voltage.

② Direct current. It mainly think about charging of battery. Because battery must use direct current，so auto power voltage must be direct current.

③ Single wire system. All of auto electric equipment is multiple on automobile. From power to electric equipment is connected only by one wire，while metal portion of engine body instead of other wire，as common circuit. This connection type is called single wire system. Single wire system may save wire，change wire into simple and distinct，convenient for installation and service，and the auto electric equipment does not insulate the body，so modern car uses single wire system generally.

single wire system：单线系统

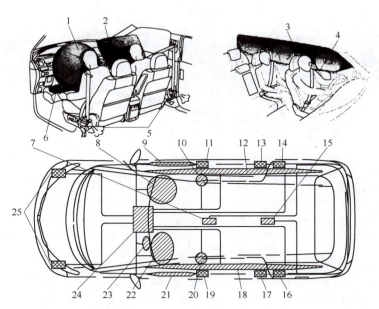

Fig. 4-16　Supplemental restraint system 辅助约束系统（安全气囊）

1，22—Driver airbag 驾驶员安全气囊；2，8—Front passenger airbag 前排乘客安全气囊；
3，12，18—Curtain shield airbag 窗帘式安全气囊；4，9，21—Side airbag 侧安全气囊；
5，10，20—Seat belt pretensioner 安全带预收紧器；6，23—Knee airbag 膝部安全气囊；
7—Center floor airbag sensor 中地板安全气囊传感器；
11，19—Side airbag sensor for front side 侧安全气囊前传感器；
13，17—Side airbag sensor for rear side 侧安全气囊后传感器；
14，16—Rear airbag sensor 安全气囊后传感器；
15—Rear floor airbag sensor 后地板安全气囊传感器；
24—SRS unit 辅助约束系统模块；25—Front airbag sensors 安全气囊前传感器

④ Negative earth. As single wire system is used, the one pole of battery must be connected with metal portion of car body or engine body, it is commonly called "Ground". If the negative pole of battery is connected with metal portion of car body or engine body, it is called "negative earth". At present, automobile made in every country all use mainly "negative earth".

car body：车身
engine body：发动机机体
negative earth：负极搭铁

（3）The arrangement of auto electric appliance

The installation site of auto electric appliance may mainly refer to Fig. 4-17. Therein, most components of power system, starting system, ignition system, air-conditioning system all are installed in engine room. Instrument system is installed in cab. Illuminating system and signaling system are installed in front and rear of car body. Power-driven window regulator, central locking, power mirror, air window wiper, and power sunroof are installed on car body.

Fig. 4-17　Installation site of auto electric appliance 汽车电气设备安装位置

1—Two-tone horn 双音喇叭；2—Air condition compressor 空调压缩机；
3—Alternator 交流发电机；4—Fog-light 雾灯；5—Headlight 前照灯；
6—Direction indicator lamp 转向指示灯；7—Air condition receiver-drier 空调储液干燥器；
8—Intermediate relay 中间继电器；
9—Electric fan double speed thermoswitch 电动风扇双速热敏开关；
10—Fan motor 风扇电机；11—Intake electric preheater 进气电预热器；
12—Carburetor cut-off electromagnetic valve for idle speed 风窗清洗液电动泵；
13—Thermoswitch 热敏开关；14—Oil pressure switch 机油油压开关；15—Starter 起动机；
16—Spark plug 火花塞；17—Electric pump of leaner for air window 风窗清洗液电动泵；
18—Liquid level sensor of coolant 冷却液液面传感器；19—Distributor 分电器；
20—Ignition coil 点火线圈；21—Battery 蓄电池；
22—Liquid level sensor of brake fluid 制动液液面传感器；
23—Back-up lamp switch 倒车灯开关；
24—Blower for air-condition，heater 空调、暖风用鼓风机；
25—Door touch switch 车门接触开关；26—Loudspeaker 扬声器；
27—Ignition controller 点火控制器；28—Air window wiper motor 风窗刮水器电动机；
29—Central connecting box 中央接线盒；30—Headlamp dimmer switch 前照灯变光开关；
31—Switch group 组合开关；32—Knob of air condition and air volume 空调及风量旋钮；
33—Fog lamp switch 雾灯开关；34—Rear window electric heater switch 后窗电加热器开关；
35—Danger warning light switch 危急报警灯开关；36—Radio-cassette player 收放机；
37—Interior lamp 顶灯；38—Liquid level sensor of fuel tank 油箱油面传感器；
39—Rear window electric heater 后窗电加热器；40—Combination tail lamp 组合后灯；
41—License lamp 牌照灯；42—Power antenna 电动天线；43—Power mirror 电动后视镜；
44—Central locking 中央控制门锁；45—Power rocker of window 电动摇窗机；
46—Power sunroof switch 电动天窗开关；47—Rear centralized control lock 后盖集控锁；
48—Trunk lamp 行李厢灯

Reference Version　参考译文

（1）汽车电气的组成

汽车电气系统的功能是保证车辆在行驶过程中的可靠性、安全性和舒适性。汽车电气系统如图 4-1 所示，可分为以下几部分。

1）电源系统

包括蓄电池、充电系统、交流发电机及其调节器。图 4-2 所示为传统蓄电池；图 4-3 所示为免维护蓄电池；图 4-4 所示为充电系统；图 4-5 所示为交流发电机。

2）起动系统

包括起动机、起动继电器、起动安全开关等。

图 4-6 所示为汽车起动系统。汽车发动机是不能自动起动的。为了起动发动机，必须配备起动机，起动机如图 4-7 所示。起动机必须从蓄电池得到足够的电能。接着起动机将这部分电能转化成机械能，通过驱动机构传到发动机曲轴飞轮上。

起动机需要蓄电池提供大量的电流。驾驶员通过起动开关来控制这个电流。图 4-8 为汽车用电磁开关外形。起动系统设计有两套电路：起动机电路与控制电路。

起动安全开关又称为空挡起动开关。它是一个常开开关，用来防止在汽车挂挡后起动系统工作。

起动系统的电磁开关用于控制控制电路断开或接通起动机电路。

起动机将蓄电池的电能转化为驱动发动机起动的机械能。它是利用电磁互感的原理制成的。当大电流流过汽车起动机的线圈时，可以产生足以让发动机曲轴转动的力矩。

3）点火系统

包括点火开关、点火线圈、分电器（有的车型已取消）、电控单元（ECU）、信号发生器、点火控制器、火花塞、高压导线等，如图 4-9 所示。

内燃机的点火系统产生电火花，点燃燃烧室内的可燃混合气体。火花由电弧产生，是由经过火花塞电极由在中心电极和旁电极之间的高电压（大约 6～40kV）形成的。

点火系统分为两条回路：初级和次级。初级回路是系统的低压端，并控制着次级回路，而次级回路是系统的高压端。

点火系统以及发动机起动的基本工作过程如下。

① 触发叶轮随发动机转速而旋转，使得转速传感器或拾波线圈产生与发动机转速和活塞位置相对应的触发电压脉冲。

② 电子控制单元使电流通过初级绕组直到感知到一个从转速传感器或拾波线圈产生的触发电压脉冲。

③ 每个触发电压脉冲促使电子控制单元断开点火线圈初级绕组的电流，使得电磁场迅速消失，在次级绕组中产生一个高电压。

④ 次级的高电压从线圈里，经过分火头和分电器盖，到达处于合适行程的气缸的火花塞，点火，点燃混合气。

4）照明系统

包括前照灯、雾灯、牌照灯、顶灯、阅读灯、仪表板照明灯、行李厢灯、门灯、发动机舱照明灯等。

灯光总开关（有时叫做前照灯开关）是照明系统的心脏。它控制前照灯、停车灯、轮廓灯、尾灯、牌照灯、仪表板灯和车内灯。

① 前照灯和尾灯系统（见图 4-10）。

② 转弯灯和危险警告灯系统（见图 4-11）。
③ 停车灯和倒车灯系统（见图 4-12）。
④ 客厢顶灯系统（见图 4-13）。

5) 仪表系统

包括车速里程表、燃油表、水温表、发动机转速表等。图 4-14 所示为典型轿车组合仪表板。

6) 信号系统

包括音响信号和灯光信号装置，制动信号灯、转向信号灯、倒车信号灯以及各种报警指示灯等。

转向开关就安装在转向柱毂的下面。开关上有一个凸出的用手控制的杠杆，使驾驶员能根据所转的方向显示转向信号。

为了发出停车信号，由刹车踏板操纵"制动灯开关"控制汽车的制动灯。除了传统照明的后灯，开关也控制中央高位刹车灯。

7) 空调系统

包括暖风、制冷与除湿装置等。

8) 其他辅助用电设备

包括电动玻璃升降器、中央控制门锁、电动后视镜、风窗刮水器、洗涤器、电喇叭、点烟器及电动天窗、巡航控制系统、安全气囊、电动座椅等。图 4-15 所示为中控门锁；图 4-16 所示为辅助约束系统（安全气囊）。

（2）汽车电气的特点

① 低压。汽车用电设备的额定电压有 12V、24V 两种。汽油车多采用 12V 电源电压，而大型柴油车多采用 24V 电源电压。

② 直流。主要从蓄电池的充电来考虑。因为蓄电池充电时必须用直流电，所以汽车电源必须是直流电。

③ 单线制。汽车上所有用电设备都是并联的，电源到用电设备只用一根导线连接，而另一根导线则用汽车车体或发动机机体的金属部分代替，作为公共回路，这种连接方式称为单线制。单线制可节省导线，使线路简化、清晰，便于安装与检修，并且用电设备无需与车体绝缘，因此现代汽车广泛采用单线制。

④ 负极搭铁。采用单线制时，蓄电池的一个电极需要接到汽车车体或发动机机体的金属部分，俗称"搭铁"。若将蓄电池的负极接到汽车车体或发动机机体的金属部分，便称为"负极搭铁"。目前各国生产的汽车基本上都采用"负极搭铁"。

（3）汽车电气的布置

汽车电气设备的安装位置基本上可参照图 4-17。其中，电源系统、启动系统、点火系统、空调系统的大部分部件都安装在发动机舱内。仪表系统安装在驾驶室内。照明系统、信号系统安装在车身的前后部位。电动玻璃升降器、中央控制门锁、电动后视镜、风窗刮水器、电动天窗等安装在车身上。

Section 4.2
Vehicle Air Conditioning
汽车空调

Not only do we depend on our cars to get us where we want to go, we also depend on them to get us there without discomfort. We expect the heater to keep us warm when it's cold outside, and the air conditioning system to keep us cool when it's hot. Fig. 4-18 shows the basic composition of vehicle air conditioning (A/C) system.

discomfort: 不舒适
heater: 加热器
air conditioning system: 空调系统

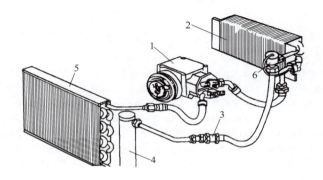

Fig. 4-18　Basic composition of vehicle air conditioning system
汽车空调系统的基本组成
1—Compressor 压缩机；2—Evaporator 蒸发器；
3—Sight window for liquid level 视液窗；
4—Receiver-dryer 储液干燥器；5—Condenser 冷凝器；
6—Thermostatic expansion valve 热力膨胀阀

In hot weather, your car's air conditioner cleans and dehumidifies (removes excess moisture), the outside air entering your car. It also has the task of keeping the air at the temperature that you select. The job of the air conditioning system is really to "remove" the heat that makes us uncomfortable, and return the air to the car's interior in an "unheated" condition. Fig. 4-19 shows typical A/C and controls. Fig. 4-20 shows schematic of air conditioner electronic control.

hot weather: 炎热天气
dehumidify: 除湿
moisture: 湿气

Being caught in a long traffic jam on a hot day can be purgatory with all the exhaust fumes coming straight into your open windows, particularly if you are dressed for business—wet under the arms and hot under the collar—probably the time when you most wished that you had bought a car with AC.

be caught in: 陷于
traffic jam: 交通堵塞
purgatory: 炼狱，苦难
exhaust fume: 废气
be dressed for: 穿着……

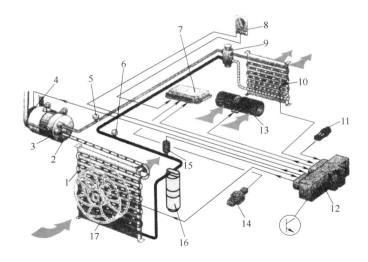

Fig. 4-19 Typical A/C and controls 典型空调及控制装置

1—Condenser 冷凝器；2—Relief valve 压缩机；3—Compressor 压缩机；
4—Magnetic clutch 电磁离合器；5—Low-side service port 低压侧维修口；
6—High-side service port 高压侧维修口；7—Engine control module 发动机控制模块；
8—A/C controls 空调控制装置；9—H-expansion valve H 形膨胀阀；
10—Evaporator temperature switch 蒸发器温度开关；
11—Ambient temperature sensor 环境温度传感器；12—A/C control module 空调控制模块；
13—Blower 鼓风机；14—Coolant temperature switch 冷却液温度开关；
15—Three function switch 三功能开关；16—Receiver-drier 储液干燥器；17—Fan 风扇

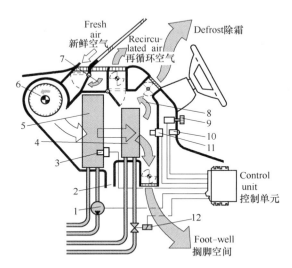

Fig. 4-20 Schematic of air conditioner electronic control 空调电子控制原理图

1—Compressor 压缩机；2—Condensation drain 冷凝滴水；
3—Evaporator temperature sensor 蒸发器温度传感器；4—Heater core 取暖器芯体；
5—Evaporator 蒸发器；6—Blower 鼓风机；7—A/C bypass 空调旁通空气；
8—Ventilation 通风；9—Set-point control 定点控制；10—Interior sensor 车内温度传感器；
11—Air exit-temperature sensor 出风口温度传感器；12—Electric controlled water valve 电控水阀

Reference Version 参考译文

我们不仅靠汽车去我们想去的地方，而且还要让汽车将我们舒适地送达。当外界寒冷的时候，我们希望车内温暖；当外界炎热的时候，我们希望空调系统使我们凉爽。图 4-18 所示为汽车空调系统的基本组成。

在炎热的天气里，你轿车里的空调起到清洁和除湿（带走多余的水汽）的作用，把外面的空气带进你的轿车里。它也承担着使空气处于你所选择的温度这一工作。空调系统的作用是将令人不舒服的热量"带走"，同时在寒冷的时候将热量返送到轿车内部。图 4-19 所示为典型空调及其控制装置；图 4-20 所示为空调电子控制原理图。

在热天，若遇到长时间的交通拥堵，排出的废气直逼开着的车窗，会让你感到炼狱般的痛苦，尤其是当你因公着装时——手臂下潮湿、衣领冒热气——也许这时你最想购买的是带空调的汽车。

Section 4.3
Safeguard System
安全保护系统

(1) Air bag system

The air bag system is designed to work in concert with the seat belts to further prevent personal injury during a head-on collision with another object. The air bag system utilizes an air bag module, front impact sensors, a clock spring (or spiral cable), and control module.

With the battery cables connected, the air bag system is energized and monitoring the front impact sensors and the safing sensor for collision confirmation messages. When the vehicle strikes, or is struck by, another object, the front impact sensors and safing sensor send impulses to the control module, which determines the force and direction of the impact. Based on this information the control module either deploys or does not deploy the air bag. Inflation happens when there is a collision force equal to running into a brick wall at 10 to 15 miles per hour (16 to 24 km per hour). The airbag's inflation system reacts sodium azide (NaN$_3$) with potassium nitrate (KNO$_3$) produce nitrogen gas (see Fig.4-21). Hot blasts of the nitrogen gas inflate the air bag. The air bags are fully deployed within 50 milliseconds of impact.

air bag system：安全气囊系统
be designed to：旨在
seat belts：安全带
prevent：预防
personal injury：人身伤害
head-on collision：正面相撞
front impact sensor：正面碰撞传感器
clock spring (or spiral cable)：螺旋电缆
control module：控制模块
safing sensor：紧急状态保护传感器
deploy：部署

inflation：膨胀
collision force：撞击力
brick wall：砖墙
sodium azide（NaN_3）：叠氮化钠
potassium nitrate（KNO_3）：硝酸钾
nitrogen gas：氮气
millisecond：毫秒

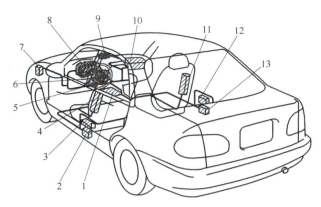

Fig. 4-21　Air bag system 安全气囊系统

1—Airbag sensor assembly 安全气囊传感器总成；2—Side airbag sensor assembly（LH）侧面安全气囊传感器总成（左侧）；3—Seat belt pretensioner（LH）座位安全带预紧装置（左侧）；4—Side airbag assembly（LH）侧面安全气囊总成（左侧）；5—Steering wheel pad 方向盘护垫；6—Spiral cable 螺旋电缆；7—Front airbag sensor assembly（LH）前安全气囊传感器总成（左侧）；8—Combination meter 组合仪表；9—Front airbag sensor assembly（RH）前安全气囊传感器总成（右侧）；10—Passenger airbag assembly 乘客安全气囊总成；11—Side airbag assembly（RH）侧面安全气囊总成（右侧）；12—Seat belt pretensioner（RH）座位安全带预紧装置（右侧）；13—Side airbag sensor assembly（RH）侧面安全气囊传感器总成（右侧）

（2）Anti-theft system

1）Central locking system

central locking system：中央门锁系统
boot lid/tailgate：行李厢/后挡板
fuel filler door：装油车门
electric and electric-pneumatic system：电子和电-气系统
electric central locking system：电子中控锁系统
electric actuators-door lock motors or solenoids：电子制动门锁电机或电磁阀
vacuum：真空
dual-pressure pump：双重压力泵

The central locking system is used to lock and unlock all doors，boot lid/tailgate and fuel filler door. This systems are divided into electric and electric-pneumatic system. Electric central locking system uses electric actuators-door lock motors（Fig. 4-22）or solenoids. In the electric-pneumatic central locking system，locking and unlocking the doors is performed by electric-pneumatic actuators（Fig. 4-23）which are supplied with vacuum or pressure by a dual-pressure pump（contained in a pneumatic control unit）.

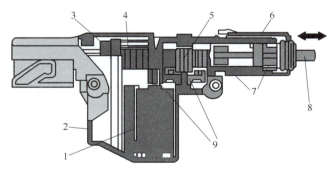

Fig. 4-22　A electric actuator 电动装置

1—Servo-motor with pinion 带小齿轮的伺服电机；2—Housing 壳体；3—Pin contacts 连接端子；4—Toothed rack 齿条；5—Drive pinion for toothed rack 齿条的驱动小齿轮；6—Rubber cover 橡胶保护层；7—Rubber damper 橡胶减振器；8—Pull/push rod 拉/推杆；9—Gearbox 齿轮箱

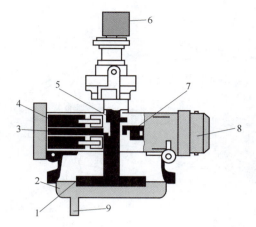

Fig. 4-23 A electric-pneumatic actuator 电-气装置
1—Diaphragm 膜片，隔膜；2—Vacuum/pressure chamber 真空/压力室；3—Pin 端子；4—Safe coil 保险线圈；5—Pull/push rod 拉/推杆；6—Locator for lock linkage 车锁连接探测器；7—Microswitch 微动开关；8—Housing 壳体；9—Connection for electro-pneumatic control unit 电-气控制单元的连接

The components of the electric central locking systems is shown in Fig. 4-24.

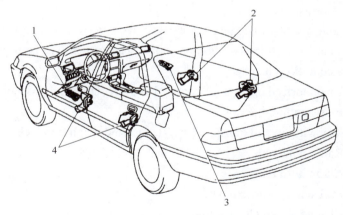

Fig. 4-24 An electric central locking system 电子中控门锁系统
1—Power window master switch 电动车窗总开关；2，4—Door lock assembly 门锁总成；3—Door lock control switch 门锁控制开关

2) **Engine immobilizer**

Engine immobilizer is an electronic system that prevents <u>unauthorized</u> persons from bringing the engine into operation. This system consists of a control unit and，depending on the manufacture，either a <u>handheld transmitter</u> or a <u>transponder</u>. The transponder can <u>be integrated in</u> a <u>electronic key</u> or <u>chipcard</u>. Part location of a common engine immobilizer is shown in Fig. 4-25.

engine immobilizer：发动机防盗器
unauthorized：未获授权的
handheld transmitter：手持发送器
transponder：应答机
be integrated in：归并到
electronic key：电子钥匙
chipcard：芯片卡

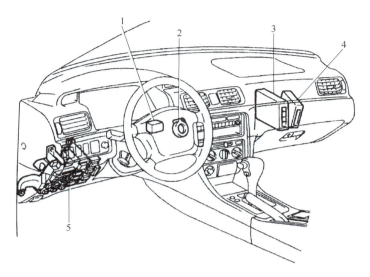

Fig. 4-25 Part location of a common engine immobilizer
普通发动机防盗器零件的位置

1—Transponder key amplifier 应答器钥匙放大器；2—Transponder key coil 应答器钥匙线圈；
3—Engine ECU（M/T）发动机电控单元（手动变速器），Engine and ECT ECU（A/T）
发动机和电子控制、电控单元（自动变速器）；4—Transponder ECU 应答器电控单元；
5—Instrument panel J/B 仪表接线盒

3）Alarm system

An alarm system triggers optical and acoustic warning signals in the event of unauthorized intervention or impact. The system will be triggered at following conditions happen.

① Unauthorized opening of doors，boot lid，tailgate or bonnet；
② Intrusion into interior；
③ Key with invalid transponder code inserted in ignition lock；
④ Radio removed；
⑤ Alarm horn removed；
⑥ Intrusion sensor removed；
⑦ Change to vehicle position.

alarm system：报警系统
optical and acoustic warning signals：光学和声学报警信号
in the event of：万一
impact：撞击
interior：内部

Reference Version 参考译文

（1）安全气囊系统

安全气囊系统和安全带一样，是为了进一步预防汽车与其他物体发生正面碰撞时造成人身伤害。安全气囊系统包括气囊组件、正面碰撞传感器、螺旋电缆和控制模块。

一接上电池连线，安全气囊系统就被激活并开始监视正面碰撞传感器和紧急状态保护传感器发来的有关正面碰撞的确切信息。当车辆撞击其他物体或被其他物体撞击，正面碰撞传感器和紧急状态保护传感器便会判断撞击的力和方位并发送到控制模块。根据这些信息，控制模块决定是否启用气囊。当撞击力超过 10～15mile/h（16～24km/h）撞击砖墙的力量时气囊便会充气。气囊的膨胀系统使叠氮化钠和硝酸钾发生化学反应生成氮气（见图 4-21）。氮气的热爆炸使气囊充气，该气囊将在 50ms 内充分展开。

（2）防盗系统

1）中央门锁系统

中央门锁系统用于所有门、行李厢 / 后挡板和装油车门的锁定和开锁。中央门锁系统分为电子和电 - 气系统。电子中控锁系统使用电动门锁电机（见图 4-22），或者使用电子制动门锁电机或电磁阀。在电 - 气中控锁系统中，门的锁定或者开锁都由电气制动器执行（见图 4-23），电气制动器由双重压力泵（包括气压操纵单元）提供真空或压力。

电子中控门锁系统的部件如图 4-24 所示。

2）发动机防盗器

发动机防盗器是一种阻止未经授权的人操作发动机的电子控制系统。该系统由控制单元和手持发送器或应答机（二者选一，取决于制造厂家）组成。应答机可以整合到电子钥匙或芯片卡。普通发动机防盗器的零件位置见图 4-25。

3）报警系统

万一有未经许可的人闯入或者被什么东西撞击，报警系统就会触发光学和声学报警信号。当发生以下情况时，该系统就会被触发。

① 未经许可，门、行李厢、后挡板或发动机罩被打开；

② 有人闯入汽车内部；

③ 插入点火开关的应答机钥匙密码有误；

④ 收音机被拆卸；

⑤ 报警喇叭被拆卸；

⑥ 闯入传感器被拆卸；

⑦ 更改车辆定位。

Part II

Automobile Service and Maintenance

汽车维修与保养

Unit 5

Summarize of Auto Maintenance
汽车保养概述

Section 5.1
Factors Influencing the Stability and Control of Vehicle
影响车辆稳定性和操作性的因素

（1）Steering behavior of vehicle

The most important factors which influence steering action and therefore stability are：

① The stiffness of the tyres in the sideways direction，and therefore the sideways "creep" of the wheel when a side force is applied；

② The position of the center of gravity；

③ The moment of inertia of the vehicle about the vertical axis through the center of gravity （the moment in yaw）；

④ The role of moment of inertia.

1）Oversteer

Stiff tyres at the front and soft ones at the rear or a center of gravity too far to the rear can result in "oversteer"，so that the rear tends to swing round in cornering，with possible instability in cornering or manoeuvring. The effect of oversteer in producing instability increases with speed. An oversteering car，although stable at low speed，becomes increasingly responsive to steering wheel movement as speed increases，until，at a critical speed，the vehicle becomes uncontrollable.

2）Understeer

Soft tyres at the front，combined with stiff ones at the rear. Produce "understeer"，when the front tyres creep sideways more than the rear ones in cornering. As speed around comers increases，the steering wheel has to be

---

steering behavior of vehicle：车辆转向性能

sideways direction：侧向
moment of inertia：转动惯量
center of gravity：重心

stiff：僵硬的
soft：柔软的
oversteer：转向过度
swing round：突然掉头
cornering：转弯
critical speed：临界转速；极限转速
uncontrollable：无法控制的
understeer：操作失灵

rotated further and further to get around a particular corner, until, finally, if understeering is very pronounced, the vehicle refuses to take the corner at all, and, if the wheel is rotated still further, the front wheels skid and the vehicle goes straight on.

(2) Friction cause

1) Tyre/road adhesion

Adhesion has been confined to circumstances in which the vehicle has not begun to skid out of control, although this may well be end result of cornering or manoeuvring at too high a speed, whether the vehicle oversteers or understeers, or indeed has neutral steering (that is, the front wheels and rear wheels have the same cornering stiffness).

Tyre/road adhesion, as measured by the coefficient of friction between tyre and road surface at the relevant speed, has an even greater influence on whether control is lost than the steering characteristics of the vehicle. When driver age and other characteristics are considered, the national statistics of car accidents reveal very little evidence of differences in the risk of having accidents attributable to differences in the steering characteristics of cars but large differences attributable to differences in tyre/road adhesion.

2) Friction coefficient on dry roads

On dry roads it for car tyres is always high and does not vary appreciably with speed, except when a locked wheel skids along a road at high speed and melting of the rubber or of the road surface takes place in the tyre track.

The coefficient of friction μ is equal to the maximum force in the plane of the roads which the tyre can exert divided by the vertical load at the tyre/road interface $\mu=F/W$ where F is tyre force and W the load. When the coefficient may decrease below the normal value of 0.8 to 1.0. The coefficient is independent of tread pattern; indeed, smooth treads give better adhesion on dry roads than patterned ones. Even with such high coefficients, loss of control and skidding can occur although the probability of it occurring is much less than on wet roads. For heavy goods vehicles the coefficient of friction on dry surfaces has been found to decrease with increased load.

3) Wet roads

Wet roads may have coefficients of friction between 0.05 and 0.8 depending upon the texture of the road surface, the tyre tread pattern, the thickness of the layer of water on the road, the speed of the vehicle and whether its wheel are rolling or skidding.

---

go straight on: 一直向前

friction cause: 摩擦因素

adhesion: 黏附

neutral steering: 不稳定转向

cornering stiffness: 转向刚性

attributable to: 由……造成

melting: 熔融

coefficient of friction: 摩擦系数

tread pattern: 胎面花纹

A road may be considered wet when it has more than a thickness of approximately one-fiftieth inch of water on it—a very small thickness. An important property of all wet roads is that the coefficients of friction between tyre and road decrease with increased speed. The main reason is that as speed increases there is less time to displace the water which acts as a lubricant between tyre and road, and so to establish the intimate contact between tyre and road which is necessary good adhesion.

On wet roads there are two coefficients of friction; the first comes into operation when the vehicle is actually skidding, either forwards with locked wheels, or sideways; the second, when the wheels are rolling and pointing in the direction of travel, is a higher coefficient, sometimes twice as great as the sliding coefficient, and is produced in the direction of travel, when the brakes are applied progressively until the wheel is almost skidding, and approximately at right angles to the direction of travel to oppose the outward centrifugal force in cornering, and to prevent sideways sliding.

This peak friction is therefore available for both steering and braking and is probably the reason why comparatively few vehicles lose control on wet slippery roads. Once the vehicle starts to skid, the much lower skidding coefficient makes the recovery of control difficult even at moderate speeds, and almost impossible at high speeds. One should also recognize that it is almost impossible to use the peak coefficient in forward braking unless the vehicle is fitted with automatically operated nonlocking brakes.

(3) Wear cause

1) Road surface wear

It is not surprising that wear of both road surface and tyre reduces performance in wet weather. On roads which carry a large amount of heavy traffic, all road surfacing materials with a bituminous base gradually consolidate and polish, so that a surface may change eventually into a smooth surface, the aggregate having been pushed down into the matrix and its edges worn smooth. The effect on concrete surfaces is not quite as drastic since it is confined to polishing the aggregate.

2) Tyre wear

Similarly, as the pattern on a tyre is reduced in depth, it also provides poorer drainage. When tyre patterns have been worn down to their legal limit of 0.04in (1mm) depth, their wet weather performance is considerably reduced.

Reference Version 参考译文

（1）车辆的转向性能

影响转向动作和稳定性的重要因素有以下几点：

① 在弯道中的轮胎稳定性，在侧向力作用时车轮的侧向滑移；
② 重心的位置；
③ 垂直方向的车辆重心的运动惯性（转弯）；
④ 惯性运动的作用。

1）转向过度

前轮偏硬和后轮偏软或者重心离后桥较远都会导致转向过度，所以这样在转弯时后轮也会旋转，会带来转向和控制的不稳定性。随着转速的上升，转向过度的效果会增强。对转向过度的汽车，低速时还能保持稳定，但当转速提高时，车辆的不稳定性就增强了，车速增加到某一极限车速时车辆将变得无法控制。

2）转向不足

前轮偏软，同时后轮偏硬，转向时，前轮侧移比后轮多，会造成转向不足。随着转弯速度的提高，转向盘转角越来越大以转过给定的弯道，直到最后，如果转向不足非常明显，则车辆根本不能转弯，此时若仍过多转动转向盘，前轮会打滑而使车辆直行。

（2）摩擦因素

1）轮胎与地面的附着能力

附着能力受到地面条件的约束，即使在高速行驶时，不论是转向过度或者不足，或者不稳定的转向（也就是说前后轮转向稳定性相似），车辆的转向和操控都受到限制，因而不会失控。

轮胎与地面的附着能力是由相应轮胎和地面的摩擦系数确定的，也易受到环境温度的影响。在考虑了驾驶员年龄和其他因素后，关于车辆事故的全国统计显示，转向特性的差别没有轮胎与地面附着性能的差别对事故形成的作用大。

2）干燥路面的摩擦系数

干燥路面上，（轮胎与地面间的）摩擦系数会保持较高数值且变化不大，除非是高速时车轮抱死、轮胎胎面过热熔化或轮胎陷入路面。

摩擦系数等于在轮胎上能获得的最大切向力除以轮胎与地面间的法向作用力，即 $\mu = F/W$，此处 F 指轮胎切向力，而 W 指法向正压力。当摩擦系数低于正常数值 $0.8 \sim 1.0$ 时，摩擦系数的大小与轮胎花纹形式无关，事实上在干地上，与有花纹的胎面相比，光滑的胎面能产生更大的摩擦系数。即使有这样高的摩擦系数，车辆失控和打滑仍会产生，只是发生概率要比湿滑道路小得多。对于重型货车而言，提高摩擦系数的最好方法是减少载荷。

3）潮湿路面

根据路面结构、轮胎花纹、路面水层厚度、车速和车轮是否打滑等因素，轮胎与潮湿路面间的摩擦系数为 $0.05 \sim 0.8$。

当路面水层厚度大概超过 1/50in（厚度非常小，1in=25.4mm）时，就可以认为路面湿滑。所有潮湿路面的重要特点是摩擦系数随车速提高而降低。其主要原因是当车速提高时，车轮与地面间的水层无法立即排除，而水层此时相当于轮胎与路面间的润滑剂，所以保持轮胎与路面的密切接触对提高附着能力很有帮助。

在湿路面上，有两个摩擦系数。第一个在车轮抱死后车辆向前滑移或侧滑时起作用；车轮朝行驶方向滚动时，第二个摩擦系数较大，有时为滑动摩擦系数的 2 倍。当逐渐施以制动直至车轮快要滑移时，该系数在运行方向上产生；而转弯时，该系数几乎与运行方向成直角，抵消向外的离心力，从而防止侧向滑移。

最大摩擦在转向和制动时产生，这就是为什么车辆在湿地上不易失控的原因。当车辆开始打滑时，较小的滑动摩擦系数会导致车辆中速时难以控制，高速时失去控制。另一点要注意的是，除非车辆使用自动控制防抱死制动系统，否则在车辆向前制动时不会获得最大摩擦系数。

（3）磨损因素

1）道路磨损

在潮湿环境中，道路和轮胎的磨损会导致性能下降是很正常的。当道路交通流量过大时，路面材料中的沥青基表面会逐渐变硬、消磨，这样，路面最终会变得光滑，表面结构会变化，材料表面会脱落。混凝土路面由于本身就打磨过，就不会磨损得那么严重。

2）轮胎磨损

与道路磨损相似的是，当轮胎花纹的深度变浅，其排水性能会降低。当轮胎花纹磨损到只有 0.04in（1mm）的极限深度时，轮胎的湿地工作性能就显著降低。

Section 5.2
Maintenance Technique of Car Exterior
汽车外表保养技巧

wash car regularly：定期洗车
once a month：一月一次
dirt：尘埃；污垢
salt：盐类物
accumulated：积聚的
corrosion：腐蚀
once in a while：偶然
paint：油漆
wax：上蜡

（1）Wash your car regularly

Wash your car regularly—at least once a month.

Make sure to wash off all the places where the dirt and salt may be accumulated—the moisture accumulates in dirty areas causing corrosion.

Use pressure wash at least once in a while—removes the dirt from difficult to reach areas, particularly helpful after winter.

Have the car waxed in car wash stations—make the car shiny and protect the paint.

（2）How to wax your car

Wax your car after washing—wax helps to protect the paint,

minimizing harm of chemicals and protecting the paint from fading; plus the car looks shiny.

Wax your car once in a three or four months—the often, the better.

Wax a whole car with high quality car wax—it takes about 30 minutes.

(3) Rustproofing your vehicle

Rustproofing will be helpful for many reasons.

It protects a car body from the rust. It protects electrical connectors and wires from the moisture. It protects the brake lines from corrosion (which is very important for safety reasons).

(4) How to repair stone chips

The stone chips will cause corrosion if not repaired in time.

First, buy the matching spray paint from a dealer and find a toothpick.

Second, shake the spray paint very well (for a few minutes).

Third, spray very small amount into the cap.

Last, deep the end of the toothpick into the paint in the cap to feel up damage.

Note: Be very carefully, don't let the paint to come out.

Now it looks much better and it will not be corroded later.

(5) How to remove residue marks (paint) left by other objects

If there is a mark on the bumper was made in the underground parking. If you look very closely, it's actually white paint residue over original clear coat. The clear coat itself seems to be damaged only slightly. Now, try to remove it.

Step 1: buy ultra-fine 1500-grit or 2000-grit waterproof sandpaper (the higher number stays for the finest abrasive: the 60-grit sandpaper is very rough, while the 2000-grit sandpaper is ultra-fine).

Step 2: find polishing compound containing mild abrasives (you can use one from Turtle Wax).

Step 3: find a car wax (you can use Turtle Wax liquid car wax with Carnauba).

Step 4: try on some tiny spot to see how it works.

Step 5: sand the marks with wet sandpaper until they all gone (but the clear coat has lost its shine).

Step 6: put small amount of the polishing compound onto the damp sponge and rub well until the clear coat becomes shiny.

Last step, buff the area with the car wax.

---

fading: 褪色

rustproofing: 防锈

moisture: 潮湿
brake line: 刹车线路
repair stone chips: 修补碎片
toothpick: 牙签

remove residue marks: 清除残渣漆斑
bumper: 保险杠
underground parking: 地下停车场
ultra-fine: 超细
waterproof sandpaper: 防水砂纸
polishing compound: 抛光膏
abrasive: 研磨材料

scratch：划痕

matching：相配的
thoroughly：彻底地

（6）How to remove deep scratches

Some the deep scratches may be repainted.
Step 1：buy matching spray paint.
Step 2：wash the area thoroughly and let it dry completely.
Step 3：shake the spray paint very well（at least 2～3 minutes）.
Step 4：spray a little amount into the cap. Don't spray directly onto the scratch—it won't look good.

Now，apply the paint over the scratch very carefully with a wooden toothpick. Only cover the scratch without letting the paint to pour down. If the painting pours down，wipe it off immediately with the clean tissue.

minor scratches：
小划痕

（7）How to remove minor scratches

If there are minor scratches on the trunk were made by the tree branches. It's not a big problem，but...

I will remove these scratches in two steps.

First，I use polishing compound to polish the scratches. It contains mild abrasive and removes very thin coat of painting. When you will shop for this kind of product，there are few grades available. You need the one that contains the finest abrasive.

overdo：做得过分

Second，I put a little amount of polishing compound onto a damp sponge and buff the scratched area in a circular motion until scratches disappear. But don't overdo it. I'd suggest trying a small area first，to get use to the process. Then I wash off the area completely.

evenly：均匀地

Now it's time to use a liquid wax. I squeeze a little amount of wax onto a sponge and spread evenly on the scratched area. I wait a little allowing product to haze，then，using a soft towel，I buff the wax.

Reference Version　参考译文

（1）定期清洗你的车

要定期地清洗车辆——至少每月一次。

保证把所有可能积聚污垢和盐类物的地方都要清洗干净——（车子不干净的话）潮气会藏垢积尘而引起锈蚀。

至少过一段时间就必须用高压水冲洗——去除难清洗部位的污垢，尤其在冬季过后更有好处。

到清洗站上蜡——使车子光亮如新，而且也保护漆面。

（2）如何上蜡

清洗后上一次蜡——蜡可以保护油漆、减少化学腐蚀并防止油漆褪色，因此，能使汽车亮丽如新。

每隔三四个月上蜡——上蜡的次数越多越好。

对整个车身上高质量的车蜡——需要约 30min 的时间。

（3）车辆防锈

防锈对汽车是很有好处的。

防锈可以保护车身不生锈，可以保护电接头和电线不受潮，还可以保护制动管路不锈蚀（这是重要的安全因素）。

（4）如何修补碎片剥落

碎片剥落如果不及时修补，就会导致锈蚀。

第一步，从商店购一罐合适的喷漆，找一根牙签。

第二步，把喷罐充分摇匀（大约数分钟）。

第三步，把少量油漆喷到盖子里。

最后，用牙签挑一点油漆，补好破损处。

注意：仔细一点，别把油漆弄得多出来。

现在看起来好多了，而且也不会再锈蚀了。

（5）如何去除其他物质留下的残渣（漆斑）

如果在保险杠上有个斑点是地下室停车时留下的。假如你凑近一点看的话，实际上，这个斑点是在原涂层上有一点白色的漆斑。漆面本身好像只是轻微受损。现在，来清除它。

第一步，购买超细的 1500 号或 2000 号的防水砂纸（砂纸标号越高，代表磨料越细：60号砂纸是很粗的，而 2000 号砂纸是超细型的）。

第二步，取含有细磨料的抛光混合物（可以从龟牌车蜡中取一点）。

第三步，取少量车蜡（带棕相树脂的液体龟牌车蜡）。

第四步，在一小处地方试擦看看是否可行。

第五步，用潮湿的砂纸来擦抹斑点直到斑点全部擦去（原来的漆面也失去了光泽）。

第六步，在湿海绵上放一点抛光混合物，并仔细擦拭直至漆面重新光亮为止。

最后，用软布给这个区域打上车蜡。

（6）如何去掉较深的划痕

划痕是可以修补的。

第一步，购买颜色相配的喷漆。

第二步，把车子这个地方彻底清洗一遍。等它完全干透。

第三步，把喷漆瓶充分摇匀（至少 2～3min）。

第四步，在盖子里喷一点油漆。不要直接喷在划痕上——这样不会好看的。

现在，用一个牙签把一点点油漆小心地涂抹在划痕上。只要盖住划痕，别让油漆滴下来即可。如果油漆滴下来了，立刻用干净毛巾把它擦掉。

（7）如何清除细小划痕

如果卡车上的这些划痕是树枝刮的，这没什么大不了的，但是……

分两步把这些划痕清除掉。

第一步：用抛光混合物把划痕擦亮。混合物中含有细小磨料因而磨掉了一点点漆面。商店销售的这种混合物会有几种级别，要挑选最细的那种磨料。

第二步：在湿海绵上放一点混合物然后用软皮打圈圈般地涂抹这些划痕直至划痕消失。别涂抹得太厉害。建议先在小一点的地方试一试，熟悉这个步骤。然后把这个地方清洗干净。

现在，该是上液体蜡的时间了。挤出少许车蜡放在海绵上，然后均匀地涂在划痕处。等一会儿，当它变得朦胧混浊后，再用软毛巾擦亮。

Section 5.3
Paint Your Car at Home
自己漆车

reward：值得欣赏
hassle：令人头疼
crafting：手工工艺
daunting challenge：令人气馁
primer：底漆
blocking：补土
detailing：细部装饰
taken as a whole：总体来看
insurmountable：无法逾越的
a couple of days：一两天
grille：护栅
wipe-down：揩干净
sanding down：打磨光
dual-action：双重的
orbital air sander：轨道空气喷砂器
hammer-and-dolly：钣金整形
seamless repair：无裂缝修复
plastic filler：塑料填料
be tempted to：敷衍了事
cut-off wheel：切割轮
focus：对准
skim：刮平
plastic spreader：塑料板
coarse texture：质地粗糙

Having a car with nice paint is both the biggest reward and the biggest hassle in car crafting. The most daunting challenge for the first-time painter is understanding the various steps of the process: prep, primer, blocking, and the final spray job and detailing. Taken as a whole, it seems like an insurmountable hurdle, but each step by itself takes no more than a couple of days.

(1) Preparation

① Strip a car of all its trim, bumpers, mirrors, grille, and other items that need to be removed.

② After thoroughly cleaning the car with detergents followed by a wipe-down with wax and grease remove, the work starts by sanding down the old paint with a dual-action (DA) orbital air sander.

(2) Primer, blocking

① After grinding the weld and some hammer-and-dolly work, the result was a solid, seamless repair. This area will get just a very thin coat of plastic filler to get the surface perfect.

② The small rust areas exhibits only minor pinhole through the surface. These pinhole areas will blow out paint or filler in a short time, so don't be tempted to just cover them up with body filler.

③ A cut-off wheel is useful for grinding back any excess welding buildup at the tacks. The thin cutting wheel can be focused precisely on the weld beads to avoid unnecessary thinning of the sheet metal.

④ Minor surface flaws are easily fixed with a skim of filler. Apply the filler smoothly with a plastic spreader.

⑤ Regular filler has a fairly coarse texture, and is subject to leaving pinhole-size bubbles. The final step of the filling process is to use acrylic glazing compound to fill minor surface flaws.

⑥ Masking is an important step in getting a quality job. We bought a 1000-foot roll of 3-foot-wide masking paper and enough auto body masking tape to do the job right. The under chassis is also vulnerable to overspray, and the only way to avoid a mess below is to build a curtain all the way around the underside of the car, taping it to the backside of various panels. A good masking job takes six to eight hours, and will need to be redone before the final paint is applied.

bubble：气泡
acrylic glazing：丙烯酸釉
masking：遮蔽
overspray：喷涂过量

（3）Spray

① For the first primer coat, we used Valspar epoxy primer. We could have used other types of primer, but epoxy provided the best sealing and stability.

② Sanding the primer is critical to a distortion-free finish. Coarse paper quickly whittles down the high spots without riding into the low areas.

③ Once the final detail repairs were complete, we sprayed on a second coat of primer/sealer. This blended and filled the detail repairs as well as the 220-grit surface left in the epoxy primer coat by the blocking process. The second primer layer will be sanded to a much finer 600-grit surface for the base coat and clear coat.

④ The final paint needs to cure for at least a few days before it is ready for the final sanding and buffing process, wrapping up the project.

epoxy primer：环氧底漆

critical：关键
distortion-free：不变形的；无失真的
sealer：密封

wrapping up the project：大功告成

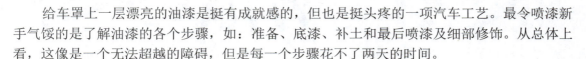

给车罩上一层漂亮的油漆是挺有成就感的，但也是挺头疼的一项汽车工艺。最令喷漆新手气馁的是了解油漆的各个步骤，如：准备、底漆、补土和最后喷漆及细部修饰。从总体上看，这像是一个无法超越的障碍，但是每一个步骤花不了两天的时间。

（1）准备工作

① 拆下车上所有的饰品、保险杠、反光镜、车身护栅和其他在喷漆时需要拆下的东西。

② 在使用洗涤剂和蜡油混合的油漆清洗剂清理完车身之后，先用 DA（双重轨道空气喷沙器）来清理车身上残留的旧漆。

（2）底漆、补土

① 在打磨焊缝和钣金整形后，应该形成一个毫无裂缝的车身。再罩上一层薄薄的树脂系油灰更使车身表面完美无瑕。

② 一些很小的锈迹仅仅只有针眼大小，但是这些针眼往往很快使油漆或补土起泡，因此不能仅仅用补土盖住针眼了事。

③ 可用切割轮打磨掉突出的粗大焊缝。用切割砂轮对准焊缝打磨，但要避免磨得太薄。
④ 表面上的小瑕疵只要刮平就可以轻易修复。再用一块塑料板把补土涂抹均匀。
⑤ 一般的补土质地粗糙，会使漆面上起泡。最后的步骤是用丙烯酸釉填充表面的裂缝。
⑥ 遮蔽是一项很重要的工作。我们用 1000ft（1ft=0.3048m）长，3ft 宽的遮蔽纸和足够用于整车的遮蔽带来将遮蔽工作做好。底盘下面很容易喷得过多，唯一的方法是用帘子遮住，防止喷涂得一塌糊涂，同时，各个板上也要贴上遮蔽带。认真做一次遮蔽工作需要 6～8h，并且在最后一道漆喷漆前，需要再一次遮蔽。

（3）喷漆

① 用 Valspar 环氧树脂底漆刷第一层底漆。也可以用其他底漆，但是环氧树脂密封良好，性能稳定。
② 打磨底漆是表面处理不变形的关键。粗砂纸能很快地把表面上的凹凸点磨平。
③ 完成精修后，开始上第二遍底漆的保护层/密封层。在环氧树脂底漆上经过补土程序，添加辅料、填补凹陷后用 220 号砂纸打磨。这层中漆用 600 号砂纸精磨成干净的底涂层。
④ 最后的喷漆涂层至少需要固化几天，然后再进行最后的研磨和抛光，就大功告成了。

Section 5.4

Auto Repair Equipment
汽车维修装备

（1）Auto repair tools 汽车维修工具（Fig. 5-1）

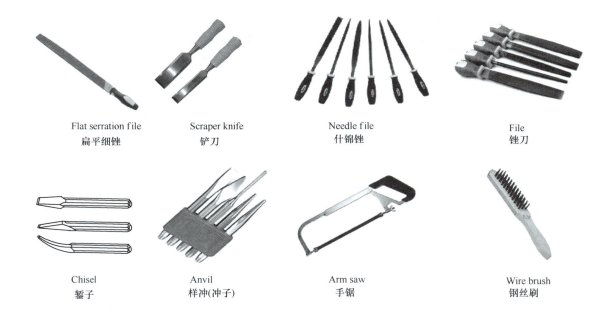

Part II Automobile Service and Maintenance 汽车维修与保养

Fig. 5-1

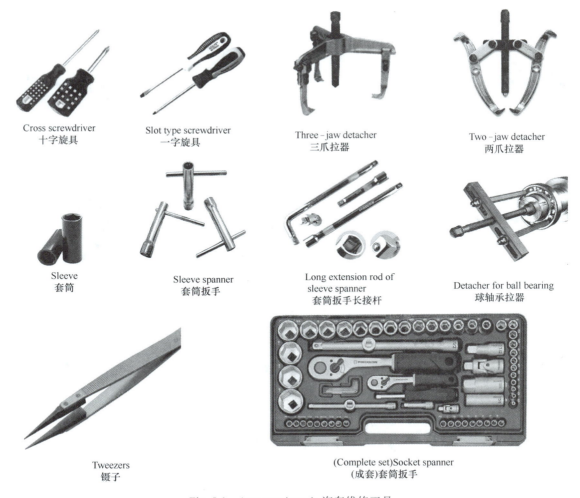

Fig. 5-1　Auto repair tools　汽车维修工具

（2）Auto repair measuring tools　汽车维修量具（Fig. 5-2）

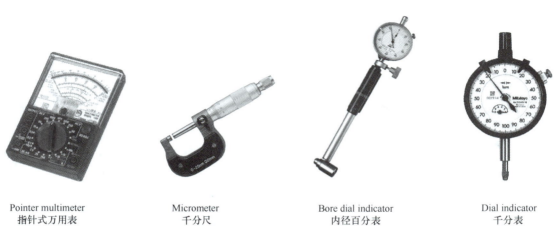

Automobile Service and Maintenance 汽车维修与保养 Part II 125

Ⅰ-type vernier caliper
Ⅰ型游标卡尺

Ⅲ-type vernier caliper
Ⅲ型游标卡尺

Vernier caliper with meter
带表游标卡尺

Digital readout vernier depth gauge
数显深度游标卡尺

Fig. 5-2 Auto repair measuring tools 汽车维修量具

（3）Auto repair testing equipments 汽车维修检测设备（Fig. 5-3)

  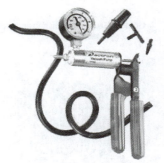

(Single)Infusion-bottle-type avoid-cleaning machine for fuel oil
(单)吊瓶式燃油免清洗机

(Double)Infusion-bottle-type avoid-cleaning machine for fuel oil
(双)吊瓶式燃油免清洗机

Manual operation vacuum pump
手动真空泵

431ME E-eye fault diagnosis tester
431ME电眼睛故障诊断仪

XP-STAR dedicated fault diagnosis tester for Benz
奔驰专用故障诊断仪XP-STAR

Bosch KT660 fault diagnosis tester
博世KT660故障诊断仪

Fig. 5-3

Golden-Gallop chellona star III fault diagnosis tester
金奔腾神州星-III故障诊断仪

IT2 dedicated fault diagnosis tester for Toyota
丰田专用故障诊断仪IT2

MT2500 US fault diagnosis tester
美国MT2500故障诊断仪

Golden-Gallop fault diagnosis tester
金奔腾故障诊断仪

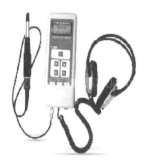
Bearing fault diagnosis tester
轴承故障检测仪

Cable fault diagnosis tester
电缆故障检测仪

Oil atomizer cleanout detector
喷油器清洗检测仪

Comprehensive detector for Yuanzhen EA-2000 engine
元征EA-2000发动机综合检测仪

Portable CO detector
便携式CO检测仪

Test lamp
测试灯

Jumper wire
跨接线

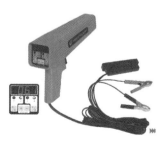
Auto timing lamp
汽车正时灯

Automobile Service and Maintenance 汽车维修与保养

OTC3850 four channels oscilloscope
OTC3850四通道示波器

Auto dedicated oscilloscope
汽车专用示波器

Fuel pressure gauge
燃油压力表

Fig. 5-3　Auto repair testing equipments 汽车维修检测设备

（4）Auto repair processing equipments 汽车加工设备

1）Machining equipments 机加工设备（Fig. 5-4）

Vertical driller
立式钻床

Bench drilling machine
台式钻床

Grinding machine
砂轮机

Electric hand drill
手电钻

Fig. 5-4　Machining equipments 机加工设备

2）Repair lifting equipment 维修起重设备（Fig. 5-5）

Single-arm type hanging bracket
单臂式吊架

Endless chain lever block
环链手扳葫芦

Hydraulic jack
液压千斤顶

Fig. 5-5　Repair lifting equipments 维修起重设备

3）Repair Assembling Equipments 装配设备（Fig. 5-6）

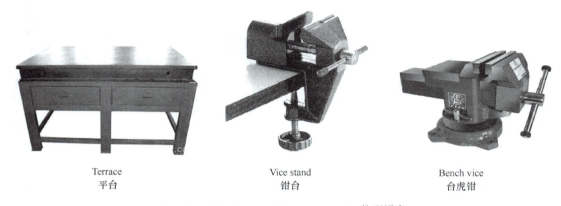

Terrace
平台

Vice stand
钳台

Bench vice
台虎钳

Fig. 5-6　Repair assembling equipments 装配设备

Unit 6

Engine Maintenance
发动机的维修

Section 6.1
Fuel-system Service and Maintenance
燃油系统的维修与保养

Fuel-system troubles usually show up in engine operation, causing such troubles as poor acceleration, missing, loss of power, failure to start, backfiring, stalling, and so on. Fuel-pump and fuel-mileage testers can be used to check the pump action and the kilometers per kilowatt that the engine is delivering. These and other checking devices will help track down trouble causes. An engine tune-up will disclose malfunctioning fuel-system components, since the carburetor and fuel pump are checked during the tune-up job.

A number of quick checks can be made that will give a rough idea of whether the various carburetor circuits are functioning satisfactorily. The results of these checks should not be considered final. Accurate analysis of carburetor operation requires the use of an exhaust-gas analyzer and an intake manifold vacuum gauge.

The following cautions should be carefully observed in fuel-system work.

① Remember that even a trace of dirt in a carburetor or fuel pump can cause fuel-system and engine trouble. Be very careful about dirt when repairing these units. Your hands, the workbench, and the tools should be clean.

② Gasoline vapor is very explosive. Wipe up spilled gasoline at once, and put cloths outside to dry. Never bring an open flame near gasoline!

---

poor acceleration: 加速不良
missing: 缺少
failure to: 不能做某事
backfiring: 回火
stalling: 失速
tune-up: 调整
malfunctioning: 故障
carburetor: 化油器
satisfactorily: 令人满意地
vacuum gauge: 真空计

open flame: 明火

air cleaner：空气过滤器

overrich：过浓的

③ When air-drying parts with the air hose，handle the hose with care.

Air cleaners should be removed periodically and the filter element washed，the usual recommendation is that this should be done every time the engine oil is changed.

Fuel-pump pressure and capacity can be checked with special gauges. Low pump pressure will cause fuel starvation and poor engine performance. High pressure will cause an overrich mixture，excessive fuel consumption，

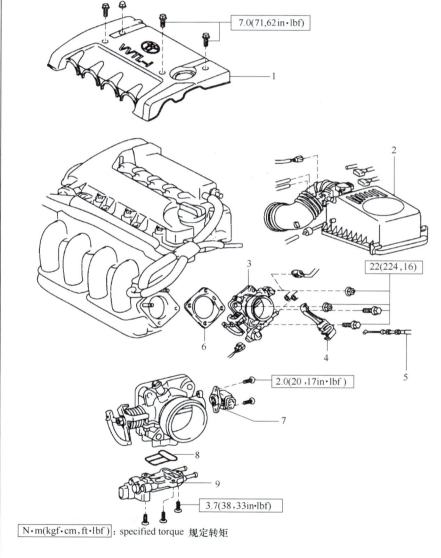

Fig. 6-1　Throttle body assembly components 节气门体总成零部件
1—Cylinder head cover No.2　2#气缸盖罩；2—Air cleaner cap sub-assy 空气过滤器盖分总成；3—Throttle body assy 节气门体总成；4—Accelerator control cable bracket sub-assy 油门控制电缆架分总成；5—Accelerator control cable assy 油门控制电缆总成；6,8—Gasket 衬垫；7—Throttle position sensor 节气门位置传感器；9—Idle speed control valve assy 怠速控制阀总成

and such troubles as fouled spark plugs, rings, and valves (from excessive carbon deposits).

Fuel filters require no service except periodic checks to make sure that they are not clogged, and replacement of the filter element or cleaning of the filter, according to type.

There are different types of gasoline fuel injection systems used in automobiles. The two basic arrangements in EFI systems are the port fuel injection and the throttle body injection (TBI). Here, throttle body assembly inspection mainly is discussed.

Throttle body assembly components shows in Fig. 6-1.

The main job of throttle body assembly inspection is following:

① Inspect the throttle body idle speed control valve assembly;
② Inspect the throttle body assembly;
③ Inspect EFI throttle position sensor resistance;
④ Inspect EFI engine coolant temperature sensor resistance.

carbon deposit: 积炭

fuel injection system: 燃油喷射系统

throttle body assembly: 节气门体总成

engine coolant temperature: 发动机冷却液温度

Reference Version 参考译文

燃油系统的故障经常发生在发动机运行过程中，引起加速不良、发动不起、动力损失、无法起动、回火、失速等故障。燃油泵和燃油里程故障诊断仪可以用来检查泵的动作和发动机输出的每千瓦公里数，它们和其他检查设备可以帮助找出故障原因。发动机的调整将揭示出故障的燃油系统部件，因为在调整过程中化油器和燃油泵会得到检查。

一些快速检查可以粗略地判断出各种化油器是否能有效地发挥作用，但这些检查结果不能作为最终的结论。化油器运行的精密分析需要使用一种废气分析仪和进气歧管真空计。

以下是维修燃油系统时必须注意的事项。

① 化油器和燃油泵上的一丝丝污垢都能引起燃油系统和发动机故障，当修复这些部件时要非常小心污垢，手、工作台和工具必须清洁。

② 汽油蒸汽爆炸力很强，溢出的汽油应立即擦干净，并且将布拿到外面弄干，绝不能让明火靠近汽油。

③ 风干部件带空气软管时，要小心处理软管。

空气过滤器必须定期拆下来清洗过滤器滤芯，建议每当此时换一次发动机润滑油。

燃油泵的压力和容量可以用专门的计量表检查。压力过低会引起燃料不足和发动机性能变差；压力过高会引起混合气过浓，耗油量过大，以及火花塞、活塞环、阀门污染（因过分积炭）等故障。

燃油滤清器除了定期检查，确保其没有阻塞，并且根据型号更换滤芯或者清除滤芯污垢之外，不用修理。

汽车上使用几种不同的燃油喷射系统。电子燃油喷射系统的两种基本类型是进气口燃油喷射和节气门体燃油喷射。这里主要讨论节气门体总成的检查。

节气门体总成零件如图 6-1 所示。

节气门体总成的检查主要有如下几项工作：

① 检查节气门体怠速控制阀总成；

② 检查节气门体总成；

③ 检查 EFI 节气门位置传感器电阻；

④ 检查 EFI 发动机冷却液温度传感器电阻。

Section 6.2

Cooling-system and Lubricating-system Service and Maintenance
冷却系统与润滑系统的维修与保养

（1）Cooling-system service and maintenance

heat transfer：热传递

The cooling system controls temperature through heat transfer. The temperature control and heat transfer are based on the pressure of the system and coolant circulation （see Fig. 6-2）.

coolant circulation：冷却液循环

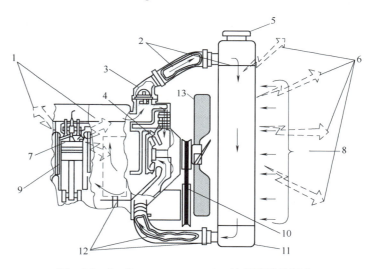

Fig. 6-2　Cooling system operation 冷却系统的运作
1—Heat transfer from combustion chamber to colder coolant 从燃烧室到冷却剂的热传递；2—Hot coolant 热的冷却剂；3—Thermostat 节温器；4—Water pump 水泵；5—Pressure cap 压力水箱盖；6—Heat transfer from coolant to airflow 从冷却剂到空气流的热传递；7—Combustion chamber 燃烧室；8—Airflow through radiator 通过散热器的空气流；9—Water jacket 水套；10—Drive belt 传动带；11—Radiator 散热器；12—Cooled coolant 冷的冷却剂；13—Fan 风扇

rust：铁锈

water jacket：冷却管；水套

Over a period of time, rust and scale accumulate in the radiator and engine water jackets; the rust and scale restrict the circulation of water, and the engine tends to overheat. In addition, the hose and connections between the radiator and the engine may deteriorate, causing leakage or inadequate passage of water. The thermostat, if stuck or distorted, may not close and open properly, thus reducing the effectiveness of the cooling system. A number of tests of the cooling system and its components can be made to determine the condition of these parts. In addition, the strength of the antifreeze solution can be tested.

Before servicing the cooling system, you need to pay particular attention to: to avoid the danger of being burned, do not remove the reservoir cap while the engine and the radiator are still hot, as fluid and steam can be blown out under pressure. In addition, be sure that the engine is turned off. More than one person has injured his hand seriously by placing it in an engine fan when the engine was running.

The main job of cooling system inspection is following.

① Inspect the cooling system for leaks.

② Check engine coolant level at reservoir. The engine coolant level should be between the "LOW" and "FULL" line. Fig. 6-3 shows the mark of coolant liquid level position

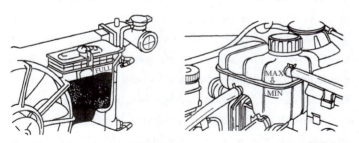

(a) Mark of FULL and LOW 满位、低位记号　　(b) Mark of MAX and MIN 最大、最小记号

Fig. 6-3　The mark of coolant liquid level position 冷却液水平位置记号

③ Check engine coolant quality. Check if there are any excessive deposits of rust or scale around the radiator cap and radiator filler holes. The coolant should be free from oil. If excessively dirty, replace the coolant.

④ Inspect the thermostat. There are three ways to check the thermostat. If the valve opening temperature is not as specified, replace the thermostat. If the valve lift is not as specified, replace the thermostat. When the thermostat is at low temperatures (below 77℃), if the valve is not closed, replace the thermostat.

⑤ Inspect the radiator cap sub-assembly. If the reservoir cap has contaminations, always rinse it with water.

⑥ Coolant replacement. A coolant change should be performed at every two years or 36000 km.

⑦ Pressure-testing the system and pressure-testing the pressure cap.

⑧ The cooling system should be cleaned at periodic intervals to prevent the accumulation of excessive rusts and scale.

(2) Lubricating-system service and maintenance

Few troubles occur in the lubrication system that are not intimately related to engine troubles. We have already discussed causes of excessive oil consumption, oil dilution, and water-sludge formation and why it is necessary to change oil periodically. In the engine, the places where oil may be lost will cause high oil consumption. Using the bearing oil-leak detector to check for excessive bearing wear has also been described. Other lubrication-system troubles that may require checking into include low oil pressure and high oil pressure.

① Low oil pressure. Low oil pressure can result from a weak relief-valve spring, a worn oil pump, a broken or cracked oil line, obstructions in the oil lines, insufficient or excessively thin oil, or beatings that are so badly worn that they can pass more oil than the oil pump is capable of delivering. A defective oil-pressure indicator may be recording low.

② Excessive oil pressure. This may result from a stuck relief valve, an excessively strong valve spring, a clogged oil line, or excessively heavy oil. A defective oil-pressure indicator may read high.

There are certain lubrication-system jobs that are done more or less when engine is repaired. For example, the oil pan is removed and cleaned during such engine, overhaul jobs as replacing bearings. When the crankshaft is removed, it is the usual to clean out the oil passages in the crankshaft. The oil passages in the cylinder block should be cleaned out as part of the engine block service and maintenance jobs. Also, lubricating-system service and maintenance jobs include changing oil, servicing the oil-pressure relief valve and the crankcase ventilator valve, changing the oil filter, and servicing the oil pump and the oil, pressure indicator.

In general, with operating conditions, the specified interval for oil changes on some automobiles is every 2 months or 6000/10000 km, whichever occurs first. Oil should be changed more frequently for such conditions as start-and-stop, cold weather, low-mileage, or dusty driving. Most manufacturers specify that, change recommendations, the oil filter should be changed every time the engine oil is changed. Fig. 6-4 shows disassembly of oil filter.

---

oil consumption：（润滑油）耗油量
dilution：稀释
water-sludge：水污泥
bearing oil-leak detector：轴承漏油检测器
weak relief-valve spring：疲软的减压阀弹簧
obstruction：障碍
delivering：提供；交付

overhaul：大修

crankcase ventilator valve：曲轴箱通风阀

low-mileage：短途运输
dusty driving：沙尘中驾驶

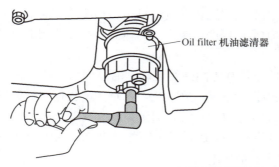

Fig. 6-4　Disassembly of oil filter 机油滤清器的拆卸

Reference Version　参考译文

（1）冷却系统的维修与保养

冷却系统通过热传递控制温度。温度控制和热传递是基于系统的压力和冷却液循环的（如图6-2所示）。

经过一段时间，铁锈和水垢就在散热器和发动机水箱里沉积，它们限制了水的流通，进而发动机趋向过热。另外，软管和散热器与发动机间的连接也可能恶化。引起水的泄漏或者流动不畅。如果节温器被撞击或者变形，可能不能正确地关闭和打开，因此降低了冷却系统的效力。一些冷却系统及其部件的测试可以判断这些部件的状态。此外，防冻剂的强度也可以测试。

在检修冷却系统之前，需要特别注意：为避免烫伤，当发动机和散热器仍然处于高温状态时，不要打开储液罐盖，因为在压力下，冷却液和蒸汽会喷出。此外，要确认发动机已经关闭。不止一个人因为发动机正在运行时让手伸进发动机风扇而严重受伤。

冷却系统的检查主要有如下几项工作。

① 检查冷却系统有无泄漏。

② 检查储液罐中的发动机冷却液液位。发动机冷却液的液位应在"LOW"和"FULL"标线之间。图6-3所示为冷却液液面位置标记。

③ 检查发动机冷却液品质。检查散热器加水口帽盖和加水口周围是否有过量的锈及水垢的沉积物，冷却液中应无机油。如果过脏，则更换冷却液。

④ 检查节温器。有3种方法可以对节温器的工作状况进行检查。如果阀开启温度不符合规定，则更换节温器；如果阀门升程不符合规定，则更换节温器；当节温器在低温（低于77℃）时，如果阀门未关闭，则更换节温器。

⑤ 检查散热器加水口帽盖分总成。如果储液罐盖有污物，则必须用水冲洗。

⑥ 冷却液的更换。冷却液应该每两年或行驶36000km更换一次。

⑦ 系统的压力测试和压力水箱盖的压力测试。

⑧ 冷却系统应定期清洗以免铁锈和水垢的过度沉积。

（2）润滑系统的维修与保养

几乎所有润滑系统的故障都与人们熟悉的发动机故障有关。我们已知润滑油过浓、过稀和水污泥形成以及为什么需要定期换油的原因。在发动机中，那些缺油的地方会引起油耗过高。用轴承漏油检测器可以检查到轴承已经严重磨损。其他需要检查的润滑系统的故障包括机油压力高和机油压力低。

① 机油压力低。机油压力低可能是减压阀弹簧疲软、油泵磨损、油管折断或破裂、油管中有障碍物、油不足或过稀、敲击振动引起，换言之，严重的磨损使它们能够流过比油泵可能提供的更多的油，油压故障指示器可以记录的（油压）低。

② 机油压力过高。这可能是减压阀被卡住、安全阀弹簧过强、油管阻塞或者过分的重质油引起。油压故障指示器可以记录（油压）高。

修理发动机时，或多或少就可以确定润滑系统的工作了。例如，大修工作在更换轴承时，要拆除或清洗发动机油盘；当拆除曲轴时，通常要清洗干净曲轴的油道；清理气缸体的油道是发动机体维修和保养工作的一部分。而且润滑系统的维修与保养保养还包括换油、维修机油减压阀和曲轴箱通气阀、更换机油滤清器，以及维修油泵、压力指示器。

一般来说，根据工作状况，按规定的时间间隔更换机油，一些汽车每两个月或者每6000～10000km 更换一次（两种方式任取一种）。对于有些起停频繁、寒冷天气、短途运输或者沙尘中驾驶的情形，更换机油应更多些。大多数制造商都要求按每次更换机油滤清器所推荐的的机油更换。图 6-4 所示为机油滤清器的拆卸。

Section 6.3

Ignition-system and Starting-system Service and Maintenance
点火系统和起动系统的维修与保养

ignition control unit:
点火控制单元
engine control unit:
发动机控制单元
distributorless ignition system：无分电器点火系统
inspect the ignition coil：检查点火线圈

(1) Ignition-system service and maintenance

Now, most of car adopts the distributorless ignition system. The spark plugs are fired directly from the coils. The ignition timing is controlled by an ignition control unit (ICU) and the engine control unit (ECU). The distributorless ignition system may have one coil per cylinder, or one coil for each pair of cylinders. Now, we introduce the service procedures of the ignition system.

1) Inspect the ignition coil

When malfunctions occur in the ignition coils and their circuit, check that the spark occurs. If the spark does not occur, go to the four steps as follows.

① Check the wirings and the connectors between the engine ignition coils and the ECU.

② Check the engine ECU.

③ Check the wirings and the connectors between the engine ignition coil and the ECU.

④ Check the wirings and the connectors of all ignition coils.

2）Inspect the crankshaft position sensor

① Using an ohmmeter, measure the resistance between CPS terminals. In the cold state (the temperatures of the coils is from −10℃ to 50℃), the resistor is 1630～2740Ω; but if in the hot state (the temperatures of the coils is from 50℃ to 100℃), the resistor is 2065～3225Ω. If the resistance is not as specified, the crankshaft position sensor should be replaced.

② Check the wirings and the connectors between crank position sensors and the ECU.

③ Check whether the crankshaft position sensor has been installed firmly, or whether the signals gear is intact; if it is abnormal, replace the crankshaft position sensor.

3）Inspect the camshaft position sensor

① Using an ohmmeter, measure the resistance between CPS terminals. In the cold state, the resistor is 835～1400Ω; but if in the hot state, the resistor is 1060～1645Ω. If the resistance is not as specified, the camshaft position sensor should be replaced.

② Check the wirings and the connectors between cam shaft position sensors and the ECU.

③ Check whether the camshaft position sensor has been installed firmly.

inspect the crankshaft position sensor：检查曲轴位置传感器

ohmmeter：欧姆表

crankshaft position sensor：曲轴相位传感器

inspect the camshaft position sensor：检查凸轮轴传感器

（2）Starting-system service and maintenance

The starting system is the heart of the electrical system in your car, begins with the battery. When you turn the ignition key to the "Start" position, the battery voltage goes through the starter control circuit and activates the starter solenoid, which in turn energizes the starter motor. The starter motor cranks the engine.

Many starting system problems are the result of neglect. Following will show you which problems you can fix yourself and which require professional service.

Problems 1 The engine does not crank　故障1　发动机不转
（The solenoid or relay does not click　电磁开关或继电器没滴答声）

Causes 原因	What to do 解决办法
Dead battery　蓄电池没电	Charge or replace battery　再充电或更换蓄电池
Loose, corroded or broken connections　连接松动、腐蚀或损坏	Clean or repair connections　清洁或修理连接
Corroded battery terminals（Lights will always light）　蓄电池端子腐蚀（灯一直亮）	Clean terminals　清洁端子

Causes 原因	What to do 解决办法
Faulty ignition switch　点火开关坏了	Have the ignition switch checked/replaced　检查或更换点火开关
Faulty neutral safety switch or clutch switch（to test: push on brake pedal, hold key in "Start" position and move the shift lever or clutch pedal）　空挡安全开关或离合器开关损坏	Have neutral safety switch or clutch switch checked or replaced　检查或更换空挡安全开关或离合器开关
Defective starter switch, relay or solenoid　起动开关、继电器或电磁开关损坏	Have the defective components replaced　更换有问题的零件

Problems 2　The engine will not crank　故障 2　发动机不转
（The solenoid or relay clicks　电磁开关或继电器有滴答声）

Causes 原因	What to do 解决办法
Low or "dead" battery　蓄电池电量低或没电	Charge or replace the battery　再充电或更换蓄电池
Corroded bakery terminals or cables　蓄电池端子或电缆腐蚀	Clean or replace the terminals or cables　清洁或更换蓄电池端子或电缆
Defective starter solenoid or relay　起动电磁开关或继电器有问题	Have defective components replaced　更换有问题的零件
Defective starter motor（if current is passed through the relay or solenoid）（如果电磁开关或继电器有电，则是）起动电动机有问题	Have the starter replaced or overhauled　更换或彻底检修起动电动机

Problems 3　The starter motor cranks slowly　故障 3　起动电机转动慢

Causes 原因	What to do 解决办法
Low battery　蓄电池电量低	Charge or replace the battery　再充电或更换蓄电池
Loose, corroded or broken connections　连接松动、腐蚀或损坏	Clean, repair or replace the connections　清洁或修理或更换连接
Cable size too small　电缆尺寸太小	Replace with proper size cables　更换为合适尺寸的电缆
Internal starter motor problems　内部起动电动机出现故障	Have the starter replaced or overhauled　更换或彻底检修起动电动机
Engine oil too heavy　发动机油太稠	Use proper oil viscosity for temperature　根据温度选择适当黏度的油
Ignition timing too far advanced　点火提前角太大	Set timing to the specifications　按照说明设定点火时间

Part II Automobile Service and Maintenance 汽车维修与保养

Problems 4 Starter spins, but will not crank the engine 故障 4 起动机转，但发动机不转

Causes 原因	What to do 解决办法
Broken starter drive gear 起动机驱动齿轮磨损	Have the drive gear replaced 更换驱动齿轮
Broken flywheel teeth 飞轮齿磨损	Have the flywheel checked 检查飞轮

Problems 5 Noisy starter motor 故障 5 起动电动机噪声大

Causes 原因	What to do 解决办法
Starter mounting loose 起动机安装松动	Tighten the mounting bolts 拧紧安装螺栓
Worn starter drive gear or flywheel teeth 起动机驱动齿轮或飞轮磨损	Have the starter or flywheel checked 检查起动机或飞轮
Worn starter bushings 起动轴套磨损	Have the starter replaced or overhauled 更换或彻底检修起动机

Reference Version 参考译文

（1）点火系统的维修与保养

现在的轿车绝大多数都采用无分电器点火系统。火花塞直接由点火线圈点燃。ICU（点火控制单元）和 ECU（发动机控制单元）共同来控制点火时间。无分电器点火系统中每缸分配一个点火线圈，或两个气缸共用一个点火线圈。下面介绍该点火系统的检测过程。

1）检测点火线圈

当点火线圈及其点火器线路有故障时，检查电火花，如没有电火花发生，则进行以下四个步骤检查。

① 检查点火线圈与发动机 ECU 之间的配线和连接器。

② 检查发动机 ECU。

③ 检查发动机 ECU 与点火线圈之间的配线和连接器。

④ 检查各点火线圈的连接器和配线。

2）曲轴位置传感器的检测

① 使用欧姆表，测量曲轴位置传感器端子间的电阻。冷态（指点火线圈的温度是 $-10 \sim 50℃$）时应为 $1630 \sim 2740 \Omega$，而热态（指点火线圈的温度是 $50 \sim 100℃$）时应为 $2065 \sim 3225 \Omega$，如果电阻不符合规定，则应更换曲轴位置传感器。

② 检查发动机 ECU 与曲轴位置传感器间的配线和连接器。

③ 检查曲轴位置传感器是否安装牢固，信号齿盘是否完好，若不正常，就应更换曲轴位置传感器。

3）凸轮轴位置传感器的检测

① 使用欧姆表，检查凸轮轴位置传感器端子间的电阻。冷态时应为 $835 \sim 1400 \Omega$，而热态时应为 $1060 \sim 1645 \Omega$，否则应更换凸轮轴位置传感器。

② 检查发动机 ECU 与凸轮轴位置传感器间的配线和连接器。

③检查凸轮轴位置传感器是否安装牢固。

（2）起动系统的维修与保养

起动系统是车内电子系统的核心，始于电池。当把点火钥匙转到起动位置时，蓄电池电压经过起动控制电路，激活起动机电磁开关，电磁开关依次将能量传给起动电动机，从而使发动机起动。

许多起动问题都是由于疏忽造成的，以下展示了哪些问题可以自己修理，哪些问题需要专业维修。

Unit 7

Chassis Maintenance
底盘的维修

Section 7.1
Clutch System and Transmission Troubleshooting
离合器与变速箱的检修

(1) Clutch system service and maintenance

1) How to check clutch fluid level and add brake fluid to the clutch master cylinder?

Cars with manual transmissions use either a clutch cable or a hydraulic system. If your car has a hydraulic clutch, you must check the fluid level in the clutch reservoir regularly and add brake fluid to the clutch master cylinder when you check all the other fluids. See your car owner's manual to find out what grade of brake fluid your car requires (DOT 3 or 4).

Things you'll need: extra brake fluid, heavy-duty gloves, funnel, rag.

① Turn the engine off before opening the hood.

② Find the clutch master cylinder's fluid reservoir. It looks like the brake master cylinder's reservoir, but it's smaller and usually closer to the driver's side fender and close to the back of the engine, near the brake fluid reservoir.

③ Clean the top of the reservoir with a rag so debris won't fall in when you open the cap.

④ Remove the cap and check the fluid level. The cap may screw off counterclockwise or may pop off. There may be low and full indicators. If not, the full level should reach the top of the reservoir. If it is not filled to the top, you will need to add brake fluid.

---

clutch fluid: 离合器液压操纵系统用油
brake fluid: 刹车油
manual transmissions: 手动变速器
hydraulic clutch: 液压（力）离合器
clutch master cylinder: 离合器主油缸
heavy-duty gloves: 耐受力强的手套
fluid reservoir: 储液室
fender: 挡泥板

⑤ Add brake fluid if the reservoir is low, using a funnel to avoid any spills.

⑥ Replace the cap tightly.

⑦ If the fluid was low, recheck it weekly for a few weeks to make sure your car doesn't have a leak.

Tips & warnings:

① Before you start looking for the clutch reservoir, make sure your car has a hydraulic clutch in the first place. Cars with cable clutches do not use fluid.

② Be careful when working with brake fluid. It's very corrosive. Don't let it go on the car's paint or any part of your body.

③ If you keep finding a low clutch fluid level, you might have a leak, which can render your clutch pedal useless. See your mechanic to have this problem fixed.

2) Tips for adjusting the clutch

The clutch on a manual transmission car usually lasts anywhere from four to seven years, depending on where you drive (in the city, on hills, etc.) and your personal driving habits.

A clutch that needs an adjustment will create the same symptoms as a clutch that needs replacing. Replacing the clutch is typically a 5 to 6 hour job (pricey!), while a clutch adjustment takes less than 5 minutes.

Make sure the handbrake works well and be prepared to move your foot quickly to the foot brake in case the car starts moving or lurches forward.

For safety, you should really understand, any clutch adjustment should be performed with the engine turned off, transmission in neutral, and the parking brake firmly set. If you want the clutch to adjust back to normal, just use the method described in the owner's manual.

(2) How to keep the transmission alive

If you are able to relate various automatic transmission malfunctions to the condition that cause them, you can save a great deal of time and effort to find what is causing the trouble.

Most of the transmission troubles start after overheating. Under heavy load, such as towing a heavy trailer, rocking the vehicle from the snow, having continuous stop and go traffic in hot weather, racing, etc., transmission overheats.

At higher temperature the transmission fluid bums losing its lubricating qualifies and becomes oxidized leaving deposits all over inside the transmission. Exposed to the heat the rubber seals and gaskets inside the

---

recheck：复查；再核对

render：使得；给予

pricey：高代价的
handbrake：手刹
lurch forward：突然前冲

overheating：过热
trailer：拖车

oxidized：氧化的
all over：遍及

transmission become hardened causing leaks. The metal parts warp and lose their strength. All of this, sooner or later, results in transmission failure.

However, this is not the only reason—sometimes transmission break down just because of poor design, or after being rebuilt by inexperienced technician. Few other cases that can cause an automatic transmission damage: bad driving, too low or too high transmission fluid level, wrong transmission fluid type.

The first thing you should do when you suspect any transmission problem is to check the transmission fluid level and condition. The engine should be running with the transmission in "PARK".

If the fluid level is low, fill it to the proper level and test the vehicle. If the abnormal symptoms are gone, the primary problem is a leak. Then continue to monitor the fluid level, add as appropriate, and have the leak source diagnosed before additional problems occur.

There are numerous transmission seals, gaskets, and O-rings that can leak. Therefore, a visual inspection is necessary to determine leak sources before an estimate for repair can be made.

If the fluid level is okay, and you still have a problem: check for any transmission related linkage, vacuum hoses, or electrical connections that may be loose or disconnected. One of the most common problems is corroded battery terminal connections. Clean terminals are particularly important for late model computer controlled transmissions.

Always check your parking space for leaks. Doesn't matter is it the engine oil leak, power steering fluid or transmission fluid—if you discover any, get it fixed before it caused something serious. Once in a while check the transmission fluid level and condition.

If the level is too low, there is a leak somewhere that needs to be fixed.

Note: A slow leak is worse than a big leak! A slow leak will allow the transmission to operate until the level is low enough to subject the unit to low fluid operation which will cause excessive wear! A big leak will certainly get your attention and usually result in little or no internal damage.

Change the fluid as often as it said in your owner's manual or when it becomes too dark (rather brown than red) or dirty.

Also, keep in mind that an automatic transmission cannot be drained completely—there is always some transmission fluid left inside the transmission (the torque converter, in the valve body, etc.) which means you only can change about 60% of the fluid at once. This is one more reason to change it more often.

① Use only the same type of the transmission fluid as specified in the owner's manual or on the dipstick. Some vehicles are very sensitive to fluid type.

② Never shift to the reverse or parking until the car comes to a complete stop.

③ Never shift from the parking mode when engine rpm is higher than normal idle.

④ Always hold a brakes down when shifting from parking.

⑤ The automatic transmission can be damaged if towing with the drive wheels on the road. Always use a dolly or place powered wheels on the towing platform（if the vehicle is front wheel drive—tow it from the front leaving rear wheels on the road）.

If you experience any problems with your transmission such as leaks，noises，problems with shifting，etc.—don't wait until the problem will become worse and car will finally stop somewhere on a highway，visit your trusted local transmission shop. Automatic transmission problems never disappear by themselves. Also，when going for the repair，try to explain to service person more detailed—what exactly problem you experience，when it happens，what does it look like. It will be easier for them to repair the transmission. Before going to the transmission shop for the repair ask them about the warranty—the longer warranty they will give you，the better will be the repair.

towing platform：牵引平台

Reference Version 参考译文

（1）离合器的保养与调整

1）如何检查离合器液位及给离合器主油缸添加制动液？

配备手动变速箱的汽车使用绳索式或液压式的离合器操纵机构。如果汽车使用的是液压离合器，在检查其他油液时，必须定期检查离合器储液罐中制动液的液位，并给离合器主油缸添加制动液。应根据车主手册找出汽车所要求的制动液的等级（DOT 3 或 4）。

需要的东西：足够量的制动液、耐受力强的手套、漏斗、抹布。

① 在打开车盖之前关闭发动机。

② 找到离合器主油缸储液室，它看上去像制动主油缸的储液室，但比它小，通常更靠近驾驶位车轮挡泥板，且靠近发动机后部，在制动储液室附近。

③ 用抹布清洁储液室上部，以便当你打开储液室盖时杂质不会掉进去。

④ 拆下盖子，检查制动液液位，盖子向逆时针方向旋出或弹出，可能有低位和满位的

显示；如果没有，满液位应该到达储液室顶部。如果没填充到顶部，就需要添加制动液。

⑤ 如果液位低，用一个避免油液溢出的漏斗添加制动液。

⑥ 再把盖子盖紧。

⑦ 如果液位低，则应每周检查一次并持续几个星期，以确定车无漏油现象。

建议与警示：

① 在开始寻找离合器储液室之前，应首先确定你的汽车有一个液压式离合器，配备绳索式离合器的汽车不用制动液。

② 使用制动液时要特别小心，因其腐蚀性很强，别让它溅到汽车油漆上或你身体的任何部位。

③ 如果连续发现离合器制动液液位过低，那么汽车可能存在泄漏，这将会使离合器踏板变得不起作用，可以让机修师来修理这个故障。

2）离合器调整要点

手动变速箱汽车的离合器通常能够持续使用 4~7 年，这要取决于在哪里驾驶（城市、山区等）和个人的驾驶习惯。

一个需要调整的离合器将会产生和需要更换离合器一样的征兆。

更换一个离合器需要 5~6 工时（代价太高），但调整离合器不超过 5min。

确信手刹工作正常，并且准备好将脚迅速移到脚刹上，以防汽车开始移动或突然向前冲。

为了安全，必须真正明白：任何离合器的调整都应该在发动机关闭、变速箱处于空挡、驻车制动设置牢固的情况下进行。如果想将汽车的离合器调整到正常位置，只需按照车主手册上所描述的方法去做。

（2）变速器养护之道

如果知道自动变速器的各种故障与引起故障的原因之间的关系，那么在寻找故障原因时，就可以节省大量的时间和精力。

大多数变速器的故障是由于过热造成的。在大载荷下，如用拖车载运、在雪地上车子剧烈摇摆、在炎热的天气下连续刹车、赛车等，变速器就会过热。

在比较高的温度下，自动变速器油燃烧，导致它失去润滑性能并氧化，致使在整个变速器里留下沉积物。变速器里的密封圈和密封垫受热后会发硬，造成漏油。金属零件受热会弯曲变形，强度下降。所有这些都会导致变速器失灵。

然而，过热并不是变速器故障的唯一原因——有时变速器故障是由于设计缺陷、修理技师经验不足造成的，其他原因有：驾驶不当；变速器油的油位过低或过高；变速器油的型号不对。

当怀疑变速器有问题时，第一件应该做的事是检查变速器油液液面和状况。此时，发动机应一直转动而变速器是在"停车"状态。

如果油液液面低，将其填充至合适液面并测试车辆。如果不正常症状消失了，根源问题就是泄漏。然后继续监控油液液面，增加适当油液，并在出现其他故障之前诊断出泄漏源。

有很多种变速器油封、垫圈和 O 形密封圈，它们都可能泄漏，因此在做出维修评估之前，有必要进行视觉检测，以确定漏点。

如果油液液面正常，则仍然有一个故障存在：检查变速器所有的连接、真空软管或者电路连接，它们可能是松了或者是断了。最常见的故障之一是电池端子连接被腐蚀。对新型的电脑控制变速器而言，清洁端子是特别重要的。

应坚持停车查漏油。无论是发动机漏油、动力转向漏油或者是变速器漏油——一经发现，立刻修理，避免进一步恶化。偶尔检查自动变速器油的液面高度及其状况。

如果油位太低，可能某处漏油，需要修理。

注意：小漏比大漏更糟糕！小漏会使变速器直到油液面足够低时才会停止工作，这样会使装置在低油液状态下工作，导致过度磨损。大漏无疑将引起你的注意，通常会导致很小的损伤或者无内部损伤。

按用户手册的要求经常更换变速器油，油的颜色变深了（棕红色）或油变脏了，也要换油。

另外，切记变速器的油不能全部抽干——变速器里应始终留一点油（液力变矩器、阀体等），这就是说一次只能换60%的油。这也使换油更频繁。

① 使用用户手册或量油计指定型号的变速器油。有些汽车对油的品种是十分敏感的。
② 在车子未停稳前，千万别换到倒车挡或驻车挡。
③ 在发动机的转速高于正常空转转速时，千万别换到驻车挡。
④ 换驻车挡一定要刹车。
⑤ 如果驱动轮在公路上拖曳，那么自动变速器可能会损坏。用小车或把驱动轮放在牵引平台上（如果是前驱汽车——牵引前轮，后轮着地）。

如果变速器出现了如漏油、噪声、换挡故障等问题——不要等到问题越来越严重，导致车子在高速公路上抛锚，应立刻去可靠的变速器商店。自动变速器的故障不会自行消失。而且去维修时要尽量向服务人员详细地描述——到底是什么问题，什么时候发生，症状是什么。这样可以便于他们维修变速器。在去变速器维修店前，要向他们要保单——他们给的保单越长，维修会越好。

Section 7.2

Steering System Service
转向系统的维修

steering column：转向柱
pitman arm：转向摇臂
drag link：直拉杆
rotary valve：旋转阀
rack-and-pinion steering：齿轮齿条转向装置
recirculating-ball：循环球
checking the power steering fluid：检查动力转向液

The key components that make up a power steering system are the steering wheel, the steering column, the steering shaft, the steering gear, the pitman arm, the drag link, the pump, the rotary valve, the rack-and-pinion steering, the recirculating-ball steering (Fig. 7-1). If these components could fail, they would require repair or replacement.

The power steering system service typically consists of the following.

(1) Checking the power steering fluid

Basic procedures for checking the level of the power steering fluid are as follows.

① Turn off the engine of your car. With the parking brake set, place the transmission in either PARK or NEUTRAL.

Automobile Service and Maintenance 汽车维修与保养

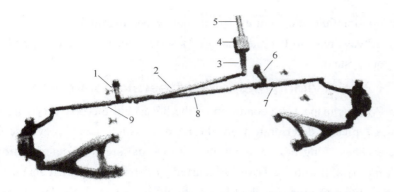

Fig. 7-1 The recirculating-ball steering system 循环球式转向机构
1—Idler arm 空转臂；2—Linkage 连杆；3—Pitman arm 转向摇臂；4—Steering box 转向器；
5—Steering shaft 转向轴；6—Idler arm 空转臂；7, 9—Tie rod 拉杆；8—Track rod 横拉杆

Open the hood and find the reservoir for the power-steering fluid. It will probably be labeled on the cap. If not，look near the belts for a pulley-driven pump with a plastic or metal reservoir on top（many cars today use a semi-transparent reservoir for power steering fluid）.

② Unscrew and remove the cap to the power steering reservoir.

③ Check the fluid level. If the reservoir is made of clear plastic，look for full and low indicator lines on the outside（Fig. 7-2）. The cap will have a small dipstick attached if the reservoir isn't see-through. Wipe the dipstick clean with a rag and put the cap back on. Remove the cap and check the level on the dipstick. Most dipsticks will have HOT and COLD markings.

power-steering fluid：动力转向液

dipstick：（量）油尺
see-through：透明的；透视

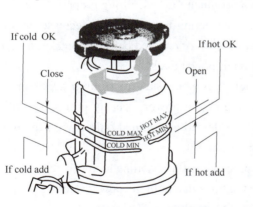

Fig. 7-2 Clear plastic reservoir 透明塑胶储液槽

Note：The fluid level will rise on the dipstick as the steering system warms.

If required，only add enough fluid to reach the correct mark on the dipstick. Automatic transmission fluid is commonly used in a power steering system. Some power steering systems，however，do NOT use automatic

automatic transmission fluid：自动变速箱油

transmission fluid and require a special power steering fluid.

Always refer to the manufacturer's service for the correct type of fluid for your system.

(2) Servicing the power steering hoses and belt

Always inspect the condition of the hoses and the belt very carefully. Hoses typically deteriorate from the inside, which means they lose their effectiveness long before showing any external signs of deterioration or leaking. You'll know a hose has started to deteriorate if it feels soft and spongy. Oil and grease-soaked hoses should be replaced. Replace hard and brittle hoses because these will have lost their ability to expand and contract properly and then crack.

Look for exterior hose wear caused by abrasive contact with metal pans. This can eventually wear a hole in a hose and cause it to burst under pressure. Replace the hose and correct the reason for the damage. Reroute the hose and tighten the brackets using tie downs or rubber sheaths placed over the hose.

Note: Power steering pump pressure can exceed 1000 psi. This is enough to cause serious eye injury. Wear eye protection when working on a power steering system.

If it is necessary to replace a power steering hose, use a flare nut or tubing wrench. This action will prevent you from stripping the nut. When starting a new hose fitting, use your hand. This action will prevent cross threading. Always tighten the hose fitting properly.

A loose power steering belt can slip, decrease pump output and cause erratic operation. A worn or cracked belt may break during operation, which would cause a loss of power assist.

Note: When it is necessary to tighten a power steering belt, do not pry on the side of the power steering pump. The thin housing on the pump can easily be dented and ruined only pry on the reinforce flange or a recommended pry point.

The basic procedures for installing a power steering belt are as follows.

① Loosen the bolts that hold the power steering pump to its brackets.

② Push inward on the pump to release tension on the belt. With the tension removed, slide the belt from the pulley.

③ Obtain a new belt and install it in reverse order. Remember when adjusting belt tension to specifications, only pry on the reinforced flange or a recommended pry point.

(3) Power steering leaks

A common problem with power steering systems is fluid leakage. With pressure over 1000 psi, typical leak points include the reservoir cap, the reservoir-to-pump-body seal, the shaft seal, the bolts, the fittings and the hose connections.

When checking for leaks, wipe the fluid-soaked area(s) with a clean rag. Then have another person start and idle the engine. While watching for leaks, have the steering wheel turned to the right and the left. This action will pressurize all components of the system that might be leaking. After locating the leaking component, repair or replace it.

fluid-soaked: 液体浸透的

pressurize: 增压

A power steering pressure test checks the operation of the power steering pump, the pressure relief valve, the control valve, the hoses and the power piston. Basic procedures for performing a power steering pressure test are as follows.

pressure relief valve: 卸压阀

① Using a steering system pressure tester, connect the pressure gauge and shut off valve to the power steering pump outlet and hose. Torque the hose fitting properly.

pressure gauge: 压力表

② With the system full of fluid, start and idle the engine (with the shutoff valve open) while turning the steering wheel back and forth. This will bring the fluid up to temperature.

idle: 空闲；闲置
shutoff valve: 截止阀

③ Close the shutoff valve to check system pressure. Note and compare the pressure reading with manufacturer's specifications.

Note: Do not close the shutoff valve for more than 5 seconds. If the shutoff value is closed longer, damage will occur to the power steering pump from overheating.

(4) Bleeding a power steering system

Any time you replace or repair a hydraulic component (pump, hoses, and power piston), you should bleed the system. Bleeding the system assures that all of the air is out of the hoses, the pump, and the gearbox. Air can cause the power steering system to make a buzzing sound. The sound will occur as the steering wheel is turned right or left.

bleeding a power steering system: 动力转向系统的排气
bleed: 排气

To bleed out any air, start the engine and turn the steering wheel fully from side to side. Keep checking the fluid and add as needed. This will force the air into the reservoir and out of the system.

Reference Version 参考译文

组成动力转向系统的关键部件有方向盘、转向管柱、转向轴、转向器、转向摇臂、转向直拉杆、泵、旋转阀、齿条小齿轮转向机构、循环滚珠式转向机构（见图7-1）。如果这些部件失效，则需要维修或更换。

动力转向系统的维修一般由以下部分组成。

（1）检查动力转向液

检查动力转向液液位的基本步骤如下。

① 关闭车子的发动机。拉起驻车手刹，将变速器挡位置于驻车挡或空挡。

打开发动机盖并找到助力转向液的储液槽。它一般会标记在盖子上。如果储液槽盖上未标注，则查看皮带的附近，从动轮泵上方有一个塑料或金属储液槽（如今，许多汽车使用半透明的储液槽装动力转向液）。

② 旋松并将盖子拿掉，放置在动力转向液的储液槽上。

③ 检查液位。如果储液槽是透明塑料制成的，在外部检查满标刻线和最低读数标线。见图7-2，如果储液槽不可透视，则在盖子上会附有一个小的量油尺。用抹布擦净量油尺，盖上盖子，再拧下盖子并检查量油尺上的液位。多数量油尺都有热态和冷态标记。

注意：动力转向系统变暖时，量油尺的液位会上升。

如果需要，仅加足够的转向液使量油尺液位达到一个合适的标记处。自动变速箱油液通常被使用在动力转向系统中；然而，一些动力转向系统并没有使用自动变速箱油液，而需要一种特殊的动力转向液。

对您的系统而言，请参照生产商的保养手册，使用正确型号的转向液。

（2）检查动力转向系统的软管和皮带

应经常性地细查软管和皮带的状况。通常软管从内部开始恶化，这意味着在任何外部显示恶化迹象或泄漏之前，软管很久之前就已经失去其效力。如果一根软管很柔软并像海绵一样，该软管就已经开始恶化了。油和浸油软管应该被更换。将坚硬、易碎的软管进行更换，因为它们失去了适当膨胀和收缩的能力容易破裂。

检查由于与金属部件的接触、磨损而引起的软管外部磨损情况。这些磨损处最终能使软管磨出一个洞，在压力的作用下引起爆裂。置换软管，查明导致这种损坏的原因并纠正。重新安装软管，使用置于软管上的栓扣或橡胶鞘将支架拉紧。

注意：动力转向泵的泵压可以超过1000psi（1psi=6.89kPa）。这足够引起严重的眼睛伤害。当检修动力转向系统时，请戴上护眼罩。

如果有必要更换动力转向软管，请使用锥螺母或套筒扳手。这样做可以防止剥脱螺母。用手安装新的软管，有助于防止螺纹交叉。安装软管时要适当地将它拉紧。

动力转向带松弛就易产生滑动，且将会减少泵的排量并导致运转不稳定。在运行过程中，一条磨损或爆裂的皮带可能断裂，这会导致辅助动力的损失。

注意：必须拉紧动力转向带时，禁止撬起动力转向泵的一侧。泵的薄外壳很容易凹进和毁坏。只能撬起加固轮缘或推荐的撬点。

安装动力转向带的基本步骤如下。

① 松动螺钉，保证动力转向泵在其支架上。

② 向内推泵，以释放皮带的张力。随着张力的消失，皮带从滑轮中滑落下来。

③ 取条新的皮带，反方向进行安装。记住当调整皮带张力到规定值时，只能撬起加固轮缘或推荐的撬点。

（3）动力转向的泄漏

动力转向系统的一个普遍问题就是存在转向液泄漏。气压大于6890kPa时，典型的泄漏点包括储液槽盖、储液槽到泵体的密封处、轴封、螺钉、接头及软管连接处。

检查泄漏时，用一块干净的抹布擦拭浸油区域。然后，另一个人起动发动机并使其怠速运转。观察泄漏时，左右旋转方向盘。这个动作将对系统中所有可能出现泄漏的部件增压。确定泄漏部件后，及时修理或更换它。

一个动力转向压力的测试会检查对动力转向泵、泄压阀、控制阀、软管和动力活塞的工作情况。动力转向压力的测试基本步骤如下。

① 使用一台转向系统压力测试仪，将压力表和截止阀与动力转向泵输出和软管连接起来。适当地扭动软管的接头。

② 在系统加满转向液的情况下，一边来回旋转方向盘，一边起动发动机并使其怠速（打开截止阀），这将增加转向液的温度。

③ 关闭截止阀，检查系统压力。阅读制造商的说明书，记录并比较压力读数。

注意：关闭截止阀不要超过5s。如果关闭截止阀时间太长，过热就会损害动力转向泵。

（4）动力转向系统的排气

任何时候，当更换或修理液压部件（泵、软管和动力活塞）时，应该将系统排气。系统排气确保了软管、泵和变速箱中空气的释放。空气可能引起动力转向系统产生"嗡嗡"的声音。当方向盘向右或向左转时，这个声音就会发生。

为了排出空气，起动发动机并将方向盘左右来回满转。继续检查转向液并按需要添加，迫使空气进入储液槽并排出系统。

Section 7.3
Brake System Service
制动系统的维修

The brake system is the most important system in cars. If the brakes fail, the result can be disastrous. Brake problems vary greatly with the manufacturing and model of a car, the age of the car and other variables. Below are some general types of trouble.

① Step on the brakes, with the car's engine turned off. A soft or mushy brake pedal indicates that brake fluid may be low, or may need to exhaust your brakes. Sometimes out-of-adjustment brake shoes could cause this.

② If it is safe, drive the car at low speed, braking as needed. The brake pads need replacing or cleaning, if they squeal.

③ In a clear area, step sharply on the brake pedal. If the brakes do not stop the car effectively, several things may be wrong, including worn pads, contaminated brake fluid or contaminated brake pads.

disastrous：灾难性的

turned off：关闭

soft or mushy：软塌塌的

out-of-adjustment：失调的

squeal：啸叫；尖叫

contaminated：被污染的

pull the car to one side:
（车）跑偏

scored rotor：刹车鼓

brakes drag：制动器拖滞
retract：收缩；退回
brake lining：刹车片

greasy：油腻的
out of adjustment：失调
noisy brake：制动噪声

eliminate：消除

emergency brake：紧急刹车
long periods of time：长时间

④ If the brakes pull the car to one side, this means that more braking pressure is being applied to one side than the other, or insufficient hydraulic pressure in one part of the brake system.

⑤ Begin driving forward slowly. If the brakes bind or drag, it may be due to grease on the pads or scored rotors.

⑥ Bake pedal goes to floor board. When this happens, it means that there is no pedal reserve, since full pedal movement does not provide adequate braking. This would be a very unlikely situation with a dual-brake system. One section might fail (front or rear) but it would be rare for both to fail at the same time. If this happens, chances are the driver has been driving for some time with one section out.

⑦ Brakes drag. When all brakes drag, it may be that the brake pedal does not have sufficient play, so that the piston in the master cylinder does not fully retract.

⑧ Poor braking action requiring excessive pedal pressure. If the brake linings are soaked with oil or brake fluid, they will not hold well, and excessive pedal pressure is required for braking action. Improper brake-shoe adjustment or the use of the wrong brake lining could cause the same trouble.

⑨ Brakes too sensitive. When the brakes are too sensitive, it will brake hard with slight brake-pedal pressure. It may be that the linings have become greasy, that the brake shoes are out of adjustment, that the wrong lining is being used and that drums are scored or rough.

⑩ Noisy brakes. Brakes will become noisy if the brake linings wear so much that the rivets come into contact with the brake drum, if the shoes become warped so that pressure on the drum is not uniform, if shoe rivets become loose so that they contact the drum, or if the drum becomes rough or worn.

⑪ Warning light comes on when braking (dual system). This is a signal that one of the two braking systems has failed. Both systems (rear and front) should be checked so that the trouble can be found and eliminated. It is dangerous to drive with this condition, even though braking can be achieved, because only half the wheels are being braked.

⑫ Some cars have an adjuster that is actuated when the emergency brake is applied. This type of adjuster can come out of adjustment if the emergency brake is not used for long periods of time.

Whenever you encounter a complaint of faulty braking action, always try to analyze it and determine its cause. Sometimes, all that is necessary (in earlier drum-type brakes) is a minor brake adjustment to compensate for lining wear.

Reference Version 参考译文

　　制动系统是汽车上最重要的系统。如果制动失效，后果可能是灾难性的。制动故障是千变万化的，它与汽车的制造、型号、车龄以及其他变化因素有关。以下是一些常见的制动故障。

　　①关掉发动机，踩一下刹车。如果感觉踏板软塌塌的，说明制动液不够了，或者应该从制动系统中排出空气。有时，调整不当的制动蹄片也会发生这种现象。

　　②在安全的情况下，使汽车低速行驶，同时刹车。如果制动发出尖叫声，那么应该更换制动片或者清洗制动器。

　　③在空旷的地方，用力踩下刹车踏板。如果不能有效地把车停下来，可能是部分地方出了问题，如摩擦块的问题、制动液中有杂质或者刹车片脏了。

　　④如果制动时跑偏，这意味着提供的制动力一边比另一边要大，或者可能是制动系统某处油压不足。

　　⑤慢慢地向前开，如果刹车卡住或阻滞，那么就应该给刹车片和刹车盘加润滑油了。

　　⑥制动踏板移至汽车底板。发生这种情况时，由于整个踏板位移，不能提供满意的制动效果，意味着没有踏板行程余量。这对于装有双管路的制动系来说，是极不可能发生的事。（前轮或后轮）一套管路可能损坏，但两套管路同时损坏是极少见的。如果发生这种情况，驾驶员很可能在一套管路失灵的情况下已行驶了一段时间。

　　⑦ 制动器拖滞。如果所有的制动器都咬死，可能是由于踏板未能充分地起作用，致使制动总泵中的活塞不能完全退回。

　　⑧ 制动作用不佳，需加大踏板压力。如果制动衬片被油或制动液浸渍，就会失去作用，必须用力踩踏板才能使制动起作用。调整不当的制动衬片或是使用的制动衬片有毛病均会引起同样的问题。

　　⑨ 制动器反应过于灵敏。制动器过于灵敏，轻轻踏下制动踏板就会猛然刹车。可能是衬片被油浸渍、制动蹄调节不当、衬片缺陷以及制动鼓工作面擦伤或凹凸不平所致。

　　⑩ 制动噪声。下列情况都会使制动器产生噪声：制动器衬片磨损严重，致使铆钉直接与制动鼓接触；制动蹄翘曲，使得制动鼓上的压力不均；制动蹄上的铆钉松动，使其直接触及制动鼓；制动鼓凹凸不平或磨损。

　　⑪ 制动时（双管路系统）警示灯亮。这是两路制动系统之一发生故障的信号。检查（前后）两个系统以便发现并排除故障。带着这类故障行车是非常危险的，即使还可实现制动，也仅仅是因为半数车轮还能够实现制动。

　　⑫ 有些汽车在紧急制动时会用自激励调节器。假如长时间不使用紧急制动的话，这种调节器会调节失灵。

　　无论何时制动出现故障，总要尽力去分析并确定其原因。有时所要做的仅仅是对制动器稍做调整，以减少衬片磨损。

Unit 8

Vehicle Electric Maintenance
汽车电气的维修

Section 8.1
Vehicle Information Displaying System Service
汽车信息显示系统的检修

The vehicle information displaying system is one of the important systems of the automobile. By it, the driver can know whether the cars, especially the various operating parameters of the engine are normal or not in order to take timely measures to prevent the occurrence of physical accident and mechanical accident.

The vehicle information displaying system is comprised in some instruments. The instruments commonly used include speedometer, engine tachometer, oil pressure gauge, water temperature gauge, fuel gauge, ammeter, etc. Changes of the monitored object's status are directly shown in most instruments through the sensors.

(1) Speedometers

The speedometer shows your speed in kilometers per hour (km/h) and/or miles per hour (mph) depending on type.

Inspect speedometer: ① Using a speedometer tester, inspect the speedometer for allowable indication error and check the operation of the odometer. ② Check the deflection width of the speed meter indicator: below 0.5km/h.

Note: Tire wear and tire over or under inflation will increase the indication error.

(2) Tachometer

The tachometer shows the engine speed in revolutions per minute (rpm).

---

physical accident and mechanical accident: 人身事故和机械故障

fuel gauge: 燃油表

allowable: 容许的

inflation: 充气；膨胀

To protect the engine from damage, never drive with the tachometer needle in the red zone.

Inspect tachometer: ① Connect a tune-up test tachometer, and start the engine. ② Compare the test with tachometer indications: DC 13.5V, 25℃.

If it is normal, replace the combination instrument panel; otherwise, repair or replace the wirings and connectors.

wiring: 接线；线路

(3) Fuel gauge

The fuel gauge displays approximately how much fuel you have in the fuel tank.

approximately: 大约

Note: For proper fuel gauge operation, the ignition switch must be in the OFF position before you add fuel to the fuel tank. The fuel gauge indicator may vary slightly while the vehicle is in motion. This is the result of fuel movement within the tank. An accurate reading may be obtained with the vehicle on the smooth, level ground.

Inspect the fuel gauge: ① Disconnect the connector from the sender gauge. ② While turning the ignition switch ON, check the position of the receiver gauge needle which should be in "empty" status. ③ Connect two terminals on the wire harness side connector and turn the ignition switch ON, then check the position of the receiver gauge needle which should be in "full" status.

empty: 空（箱）

Inspect fuel level warning: ① Disconnect the connector from the sender gauge. ② Turn the ignition switch ON. Check the fuel level needle indicates EMPTY and fuel level warning lights light on.

(4) Temperature gauge

This shows the temperature of the engine's coolant. During normal operation. the pointer should rise from the bottom blue mark to about the middle of the gauge. In severe driving conditions, such as very hot weather or a long period of uphill driving the pointer may rise to the upper white mark. If it reaches the red (hot) mark, the engine is overheated and may be damaged.

overheated: 过热的

If your engine overheats: ① Pull off the road as soon as it is safely possible. ② Turn off the engine. ③ Let the engine cool. ④ Check the coolant level and adding coolant to your engine following the instructions on checking.

Inspect the water temperature receiver gauge warning light: ① Disconnect the connector from the sender gauge. ② Turn the ignition switch ON, and check the position of the water temperature receiver gauge needle which should indicate "cool". ③ While ground terminal is on the wire harness side, check the water temperature receiver gauge needle which should indicate "hot".

(5) Engine oil pressure warning light

This light indicates the engine oil pressure, not the oil level. However, if your engine oil level is low, it could affect the oil pressure. The light should come on every time your ignition key is turned to ON or START and go out when the engine starts.

If the light stays on or turns on while the engine is running, you have lost oil pressure and continued operation will cause severe engine damage.

If you lose oil pressure: ① Pull off the road as soon as it is safely possible. ② Shut off the engine immediately. If you do not stop the engine as soon as possible, severe engine damage could occur. ③ Check the engine oil level, following the instructions under checking and adding engine oil in the owner guide. To ensure an accurate reading, your car should be on level ground. ④ If the level is low, add only as much oil as necessary before you start the engine again. Do not overfill. Do not operate the engine again, if the light is on, regardless of the oil level.

Inspect the oil pressure warning light: ① Disconnect the connector from the low oil pressure switch. ② Turn the ignition switch ON. ③ While connecting the terminal of wire harness side connector and ground. Check the low oil pressure warning light.

(6) Inspect the brake warning light

Inspect the parking brake warning light: disconnect the connector from the parking brake switch and ground terminal on the wire harness side connector. Turn the ignition switch ON and check that the warning light lights up.

Inspect the brake fluid level warning light: disconnect the connector from the brake fluid level warning switch and connect terminals on the wire harness side connector. Turn the ignition swish ON and check that the warning light lights up.

(7) Inspect the key unlock warning buzzer

Check the operation: While the driver side door is open, insert the ignition key, set the ignition switch to OFF and check for the buzzer sound whether it is intermittent.

Check the function: Remove the combination meter. Connect the positive (+) lead from the battery to corresponding terminal and the negative (−) lead to corresponding two terminals. Connect the negative (−) lead to other corresponding two terminals, and check whether the buzzer sound is intermittent. While the buzzer is sounding, connect the battery positive terminal to corresponding terminal and check that the buzzer sound is stopped.

Note: When the key unlock warning and light auto turn off warning are output simultaneously, the key unlock warning precedes the other.

simultaneously：同时地

(8) Inspect the light auto turn off buzzer

Check the operation: remove the ignition key with the tail light switch ON and the driver side door open and check whether the buzzer sound is continuous. While the buzzer is sounding, perform any of the following: ① Turn the tail light switch OFF. ② Close the driver side door. ③ Insert the ignition key into the key cylinder.

If the buzzer sound is stopped, replace the combination instrument panel.

Check the function: remove the combination meter. Connect the positive (+) lead from the battery to corresponding terminal and the negative (-) lead to corresponding two terminals. Connect the positive (+) lead from the battery to corresponding terminal and the negative (-) lead to other corresponding two terminals. Check that the buzzer sound is continuous. While the buzzer is sounding, connect the battery positive terminal to corresponding terminal and check that the buzzer sound is stopped.

Reference Version 参考译文

汽车信息显示系统是汽车系统中一个重要的系统。通过它，司机能够了解汽车，特别是发动机的各种工作参数是否正常，以便适时采取措施来防止人身事故和机械故障的发生。

汽车信息显示系统由若干仪表组成。常用的仪表有速度表、发动机转速表、机油压力表、水温表、燃油表、电流表等。大部分仪表通过传感装置获得被监测对象的状态变化而直接表述出来。

(1) 速度表

速度表根据汽车类型显示每小时行驶的千米数或每小时的英里数。

检查速度表：①用车速表测试仪，检测车速表的允许指示误差，并检查里程表的工作状况。②检查速度表指针的误差范围：低于 0.5km/h。

注意：轮胎磨损和轮胎过分充气或充气不足均会增加示值误差。

（2）转速表

转速表显示发动机每分钟的转速。驾驶时，不要使转速表的指针指向红色区，以免发动机受到损伤。

检测转速表：①连接校准测试转速表，起动发动机。②比较测试值和转速表显示值：直流电压13.5V，25℃。

如果检查数据正常，则替换组合仪表板；否则就修理或替换电线和连接器。

（3）燃油表

燃油表可大约显示油箱中现存的油量。

注意：加油前点火开关须在"关"（OFF）位置，燃油表才可正常显示。行车时燃油表有少许摆动是由于油箱内燃油波动的缘故。当汽车在平坦路面上行驶时，油量读数较精确。

检查燃油表：①从发送仪表上断开连接器。②将点火开关扭至"开"（ON）位置，然后检查接收仪表指针的位置应处于"空"状态。③将线束侧连接器两端子连接，并将点火开关扭至"ON"位置，然后检查接收仪表指针的位置，应处于"满"状态。

检查燃油液位警告灯：①从发送仪表上断开连接器。②将点火开关扭至"ON"位置，检查燃油液位指针是否指示"EMPTY"（空）以及燃油液位警告灯是否点亮。

（4）温度表

这个表显示发动机冷却剂的温度。正常驾驶时，表的长针应从表中蓝色标记下端指到大约中间的位置上。在恶劣的驾驶条件，例如非常炎热或长时间爬坡过程中，表的指针会指向上面的白色范围内。如果指针指向红色（热）范围内，则发动机已过热，可能会损坏发动机。

若发动机过热：①尽快安全地停在路边。②关闭发动机。③让发动机冷却。④根据有关说明，检查冷却剂液面并给发动机加注冷却剂。

检查水温表警告灯：①从发送仪表上断开连接器。②将点火开关扭至"ON"位置，检查水温表指针的位置，应指示"冷态"。③将线束侧一端子接地，然后检查水温表指针的位置，应指示"热态"。

（5）发动机油压警告灯

油压警告灯显示发动机油压，而不是机油液位，然而若发动机机油液位低，就会影响油压。每次点火钥匙扭至"ON"或"START"位置时，油压警告灯亮，发动机起动时应该熄灭。如果警告灯持续亮或发动机运转时仍亮着，则表明汽车油压过低，如果继续工作将会给发动机带来严重的损害。

如果油压过低：①尽快安全地停在路边。②立即关闭发动机。如果未尽快停止发动机，则发动机可能会发生严重损伤。③依照用户指南中检查和添加发动机机油的说明，检查发动机机油液面。为了获得精确读数，请将汽车停在平坦路面。④如果液面过低，在再次起动发动机之前，请按需求添加机油。不要溢出。油压警告灯亮时，无论液面怎样，都不要再次起动发动机。

检查油压警告灯：①从油压过低警告灯开关上断开连接器。②将点火开关扭至"ON"

位置。③将线束侧连接器端子接地，然后检查油压过低警告灯。

（6）检查制动警告灯

检查驻车制动警告灯：从驻车制动开关上断开连接器，并将线束侧连接器端子接地。将点火开关扭至"ON"位置，检查警告灯能否点亮。

检查制动液液位警告灯：断开制动液液位警告灯开关上的连接器，并连接线束侧连接器端子。将点火开关扭至"ON"位置，检查警告灯能否点亮。

（7）检查钥匙开锁警告蜂鸣器

检查工作情况：当驾驶员侧门开时，插入点火钥匙，将点火开关扭至"OFF"位置，并且检查蜂鸣器声音是否间歇。

检查功能：拆下组合仪表。将蓄电池正极（+）导线连接至端子，负极（-）导线连接至相应两端子。将负极（-）导线连接至另外相应两端子，检查蜂鸣器声音是否间歇。蜂鸣器发出响声时，将蓄电池正极端子与相应的端子相连，并检查蜂鸣器声音是否停止。

注意：当未锁警告和灯自动关闭报警同时输出时，未锁警告优先。

（8）检查灯自动关闭蜂鸣器

检查工作情况：将尾灯开关位于"ON"并且驾驶员侧门开时，取下点火钥匙，检查蜂鸣器声音是否连续。当蜂鸣器发出声音时，执行下列操作：①将尾灯开关扭至"OFF"位置。②关闭驾驶员侧门。③将点火钥匙插入锁芯。

如果没有蜂鸣器声音，则更换组合仪表板。

检查功能：拆下组合仪表。将蓄电池正极（+）导线连接至端子，负极（-）导线连接至相应两端子。将蓄电池正极（+）导线连接至相应的端子，负极（-）导线连接至端子另外的相应两端子，检查蜂鸣器声音是否连续。当蜂鸣器发出声音时，将蓄电池正极导线连接至相应的端子，检查蜂鸣器声音是否停止。

Section 8.2
Lighting System Service
照明系统的维修

The automotive lamp assembly is the basic component of the group lighting, which comprises three parts: light (bulb), the mirror reflector and light transmittance.

Automotive lamps with different functions can be divided into two categories: lighting and signal lamps (see Fig. 8-1). Lighting includes: the headlamp (low beams and high beams), the fore-fog-lamp, the reversing light and the side marker light. Signal lights include: the location fight, the turn signal, the brake light, the rear-fog-lamp, the license plate lamp and the retroreflector.

mirror reflector：反光镜
light transmittance：透光度
fore-fog-lamp：前雾灯
side marker light：轮廓灯；边灯
license plate lamp：牌照灯
retroreflector：反光镜

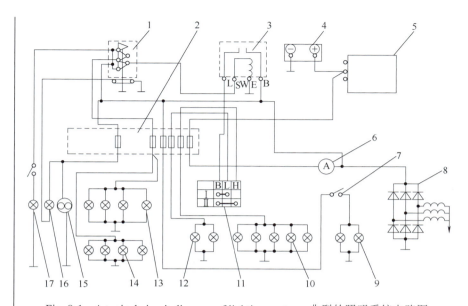

Fig. 8-1　A typical circuit diagram of lighting systems 典型的照明系统电路图
1—Light switch 灯开关；2—Fuse box 保险丝盒；3—Light relay 光继电器；
4—Storage battery 蓄电池组；5—Starter 起动机；6—Current meter 电流计；
7—Fog-lamp switch 雾灯开关；8—Generator 发电机；9—Fog-lamp 雾灯；
10—High beam 远光灯；11—Antidazzle switch（dimmer switch）变光开关（前照灯变光开关）；
12—Low beam（dipped headlight）车头灯短焦距光（近光灯）；13—Width light 示宽灯；
14—Dash lamp 仪表板照明灯；15—Working lamp socket 工作灯座；
16—Ceiling lamp（dome lamp）吸顶灯（车顶灯）；17—Working lamp 工作灯

Repair Manual

（1）Headlamps

1）Bulb replacement

Removal：① Remove the headlamp assembly（as shown in Fig. 8-2）.
② Turn the high/low beam bulb socket counterclockwise to remove.

repair manual：修理手册
headlamp：前照灯

counterclockwise：逆时针方向

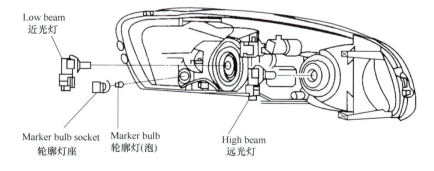

Fig. 8-2　The frame of headlamp bulbs 前照灯总成框架

clockwise：顺时针方向

Installation：① Turn the high/low beam bulb socket clockwise to install.
② Install the headlamp assembly.

2) Headlamp assemblies (the park, turn, cornering and side marker lamp)

Removal: ① Rotate the headlamp assembly retainer pins and pull up to remove. ② Remove the mounting bolts. ③ Disconnect the harness connectors.

Installation: ① Connect the harness connectors. ② Position the headlamp assembly on the panel. ③ Rotate the retainer pins and push down to lock in place. ④ Install and secure the mounting bolts.

Aiming: when adjusted properly, the lights should not glare on oncoming traffic's windshields, nor should they illuminate the passenger compartment of vehicles driving in front of you.

Caution: when headlights are replaced or any time front-end work is performed on the vehicle, the headlights should be aimed using the proper equipment. Headlights not properly aimed can make it virtually impossible to see and may blind other drivers on the road, causing injury or death.

glare: 眩光
oncoming: 迎面而来
windshield: 挡风玻璃
passenger compartment: 乘客舱

(2) Dome lamps

Removal: ① Remove the dome lamp lens from the dome lamp. ② Remove the mounting screw and remove the dome lamp from the headliner.

Installation: ① Install and secure the dome lamp to the headliner with the mounting screw. ② Install the dome lamp lens on the dome lamp.

dome lamps: 车顶灯

(3) High mounted stop lamp assemblies

Removal: ① Remove the mounting screws from the high mounted stop lamp. ② Remove the high-mounted stop lamp from the tailgate door. ③ Disconnect the electrical harness connector.

Installation: ① Connect the electrical harness connector to the high-mounted stop lamp. ② Install and secure the high-mounted stop lamp to the tailgate door with the mounting screws.

high mounted stop lamp assemblies: 高位刹车灯总成

(4) Taillight assemblies (the turn signal, side-marker stop and back up lamp)

Removal: ① Open the tailgate. ② Remove the mounting screws from the taillight assembly. ③ Pull the taillight assembly rearward to release the retainers from the body panel. ④ Disconnect the electrical harness connector. ⑤ Remove the bulb sockets by pressing the lock tab down and turning the sockets counterclockwise.

Installation: ① Install the bulb sockets by turning the sockets clockwise until the lock tab engages. ② Connect the electrical harness connector. ③ Position the taillight retainers to align with the body panel. ④ Seat the taillight into the body cavity. ⑤ Install and secure the tail lamp mounting screws. ⑥ Close the tailgate.

tailgate door: 后挡板
taillight assemblies: 尾灯总成

license plate lights：
车牌灯

（5）License plate lights

Removal：① Remove the mounting screws from the license light lens. ② Remove the license light lens from the tailgate. ③ Remove the bulb from the license light socket.

Installation：① Insert the bulb into the socket. ② Install and secure the license light lens on the tailgate with the mounting screws.

Reference Version 参考译文

汽车车灯装置是组合照明设备的基本元素，一般由3部分构成：灯泡、反光镜和透光度。

具有不同功能的汽车车灯可分为两大类：照明灯和信号灯，如图8-1所示。照明设备包括：前照灯（近光和远光）、前雾灯、倒车灯和轮廓灯；信号灯包括：方位灯、转向灯、刹车灯、后雾灯、牌照灯和回射器。

维修手册

（1）前照灯

1）更换灯泡

拆卸：①拆卸前照灯总成，如图8-2所示。②逆时针旋转远/近光灯泡座以便拆下。

安装：①顺时针旋转并安装远/近光灯泡座。②安装前照灯总成。

2）前照灯总成（驻车灯、转向灯、轮廓灯）

拆卸：①旋转前照灯总成固定销，拉出大灯。②拆卸安装螺栓。③断开线束连接器。

安装：①连接线束连接器。②将前照灯总成装配在嵌板上。③旋转固定销，按下大灯将其锁止在固定位置上。④安装并紧固安装螺栓。

校准：当调整好后，在会车时灯光不应该在对面车辆的挡风玻璃上形成眩光；在跟车时，灯光也不应该照射在你前方车辆的乘客舱。

注意：当前照灯被更换或者是维修工作涉及汽车头部的时候，必须使用合适的设备校准前照灯，前照灯校准不正确将造成视野不清晰，并可能使公路上其他司机致盲，造成伤害或死亡。

（2）车顶灯

拆卸：①拆卸车顶灯镜头。②拆卸安装螺钉，从导向线拆下车顶灯。

安装：①用安装螺钉将车顶灯安装并紧固到导向线处。②将车顶灯镜头安装到车顶灯上。

（3）高位刹车灯总成

拆卸：①拆卸高位刹车灯安装螺钉。②从后挡板拆下高位刹车灯。③断开电气线束连接器。

安装：①将电气线束连接器连接到高位刹车灯。②用安装螺钉将高位刹车灯安装并紧固到后挡板上。

（4）尾灯总成（转向信号灯、侧灯、停车灯和倒车灯）

拆卸：①打开汽车后挡板。②拆卸尾灯总成安装螺钉。③向后拉动尾灯总成以解除车身面板上的锁销。④断开电气线束连接器。⑤下按锁环并逆时针旋转灯座,以便拆下灯泡座。

安装:①顺时针方向旋转灯座直到锁环锁定,以便装上灯泡座。②连接接线盒。③将尾灯锁销与车身面板连接。④将尾灯安装进车身。⑤安装和固定尾灯安装螺钉。⑥关上后挡板。

(5)车牌灯

拆卸:①拆卸车牌灯镜头的安装螺钉。②从车后挡板拆下车牌灯镜头。③拆下车牌灯座的灯泡。

安装:①将车牌灯灯泡插进灯座。②用安装螺钉把车牌灯镜头安装并紧固到车的后挡板上。

Section 8.3

Air Conditioning System Detection and Services 空调系统的检测与维修

The A/C system has two major parts:the high side <u>starts at the compressor</u> and <u>ends at the expansion device</u>. The low side starts at the expansion device and ends at the compressor,as shown in Fig. 8-3.

start at the compressor:始于压缩机
end at the expansion device:结束于膨胀装置

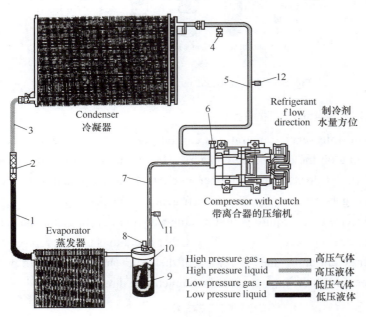

Fig. 8-3　The A/C system 空调系统

1,3—Liquid line 液体管路；2—Orifice tube 节流管；4—High pressure cut off switch 高压切断开关；5—Discharge line 排放管；6—High pressure relief valve 高压减压阀；7—Suction line 吸入管；8—Clutch cycling pressure switch 离合器循环压力开关；9—Desiccant bag 干燥剂包；10—Accumulator 蓄电池；11—Low pressure service port 低压维修端子；12—High pressure service port 高压维修端子

The pressure on the liquid R-124a drops as it passes through the orifice

evaporator：蒸发器

tube. The low pressure allows it to boil and absorb heat in the evaporator. Heat transfers from the air passing through the evaporator to the liquid R-124a. This heat boils the refrigerant, causing it to change state to a gas. The heat transfer cools the air.

(1) Gauge sets

gauge set：（歧管）量表装置

Most service operations can be performed using a manifold and gauge set. A gauge set has two gauges, two hand valves, and three service hoses, as shown in Fig. 8-4.

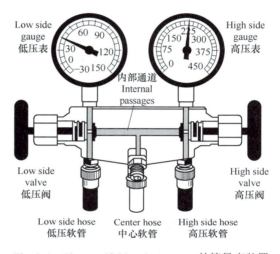

Fig. 8-4　The manifold and gauge set 歧管量表装置

(2) Service units

service unit：维修装置

Multiple service operations can be performed on the service units. Depending on the unit, they contain：① a vacuum pump；② refrigerant and a way of dispensing the proper amount；③ a refrigerant recovery unit；④ a refrigerant recycling unit；⑤ refrigerant oil dispensing unit.

recovery unit：回收装置
recycling unit：再循环装置
replacement：更换
calibration：校准

Service units require periodic maintenance. Recycling units have a filter that must be replaced when it is dirty. Other operations include replacement of the refrigerant tank, the calibration of the scale, and the vacuum pump oil changes. Check the manufacturer's maintenance directions.

(3) A/C service procedures

A/C service procedure：空调维修检测
identification：鉴别
contaminated：污染
expensive：昂贵的
take a chance：冒险一试
ingredient：成分

1) Refrigerant identification

The refrigerant in a system should be identified before recovery. Recovery of contaminated refrigerant can cause very expensive results. In our modern world, there are too many possibilities for contamination to take a chance. Identifiers sample the refrigerant in a system. Then they determine what it is composed of and print out or display the ingredients.

2) Sealant detection

One source of contamination is from stop leaks sealants. These can be put into a system and are designed to close refrigerant leaks. There are two general types: a seal conditioning type that causes O-rings and gaskets to swell and a sealant that is designed to close small holes. The second type hardens when it contacts moisture from air. Sealants can damage A/C service equipment. A quick detect sealant detector can be connected to a system to determine if the refrigerant contains sealant. Special service procedures are necessary if a sealant is detected.

detection: 检测

3) Recovery Procedures

Most recovery units will shut off when the pressure drops to zero. Watch the pressure. If it rises after a few minutes, continue the recovery process. After recovery, check the amount of refrigerant and oil that were recovered.

Tips: If you are recovering refrigerant from a system that has a leak, you will probably begin with a system that has low pressures. After this small amount of refrigerant has been recovered, there is a probability that the recovery unit will pull air through the leak. This air will be added to the refrigerant already recovered. Operate the recovery unit in a normal manner, but watch the operation. Recovery will probably take less time than normal. If the pressure drops to a low value yet does not continue to drop, the machine is probably pulling air from the outside. Stop the recovery.

4) Recycling

A recycle guard (special filter) can be connected into the hose entering the recovery machine. It will trap and filter out sealant, oil, and dye from the recovered refrigerant. The trapped materials should be drained out after each recovery.

trapped material: 滤渣
drain out: 排尽

The recycling operation depends on the service unit. The unit has a display screen to show the machine operations and a key pad for the technician to enter the job to be done.

5) Services by using a manifold and gauge set

The center hose of the manifold is connected to a vacuum pump during the evacuation process. It is connected to a refrigerant source while charging a system. Note that the manifold valves are open or closed as needed, see Fig. 8-5.

evacuation: 排放

6) Evacuation

① During evacuation using a manifold, the center hose is connected to the vacuum pump. Both hand valves are opened, and the pump is operated to pull all of the air and water out of a system. Air is removed with any other gas. If the pressure drops to 29.9 inHg, there will be no gas left in the system.

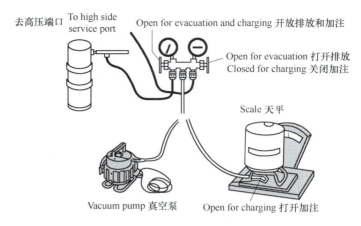

Fig. 8-5　Evacuation or charging using a manifold 使用歧管排放或填料

② Evacuation using a service unit is essentially the same as using a manifold and vacuum pump，as shown in Fig. 8-6.

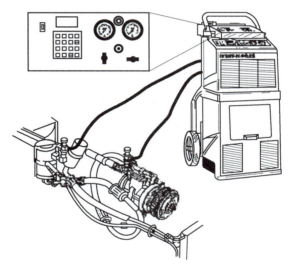

Fig. 8-6　Evacuating using a service unit 使用维修装置排放

drop：降低
boil：沸腾

Water is removed from a system by dropping the pressure to cause it to boil. The boiling point of water at 29.2 inHg is 70°F.

7）Vacuum Leak Check

When evacuation process reaches full vacuum，shut off both high and low valves，and observe the vacuum reading. This vacuum should hold for several minutes. A leak in the system is indicated if the pressure rises.

8）Charging

This is the process of putting the correct amount of refrigerant into the system. A manifold（shown）or service unit can be used to charge. In this case，gas will be leaving the refrigerant container and entering the low side with the system running (see Fig. 8-7).

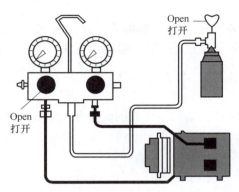

Fig. 8-7　Charging by using a manifold　使用多歧管加注

Charging from a large container while using a manifold requires a means to measure the refrigerant. A scale or a dial-a-charge can be used. The scale can be programmed to shut after the correct charge has left the container. A service unit is programmed with the correct charge amount, and the process is begun. Refrigerant is then transferred from the machine to the system.

dial-a-charge：数码灌装机

9）Leak detection & system check

It is always a good practice to check any fittings that were disturbed to make sure there are no leaks. The system should be operated to make sure that the operating pressure is correct, the air discharge from the ducts is a cool temperature, and the compressor and drive belts are running properly and quietly.

fitting：配件

Reference Version　参考译文

　　空调系统可以分为两大部分：高压侧始于压缩机，结束于膨胀装置（节流管或膨胀阀）；低压侧始于膨胀装置，结束于压缩机，如图8-3所示。

　　当制冷剂 R-124a 通过节流管后，其压力下降，低压下的液态 R-124a 吸收蒸发器内的热量而汽化。当空气流经蒸发器时，其热量传递给制冷剂 R-124a，使制冷剂汽化，正是这种热量转移使空气得以冷却。

　　（1）歧管量表装置

　　大多数维修操作可以用歧管量表装置完成。歧管量表装置由2块压力表、2个手动阀和3个软管接头组成，如图8-4所示。

　　（2）维修装置

　　维修装置可以进行多项维修操作，根据该装置的情况，主要包括：①真空泵；②制冷剂和充注方式（分配或计量方式）；③制冷剂回收装置；④制冷剂再循环装置；⑤冷冻机油充注设备。

维修装置需要定期保养。再循环装置有一个过滤器，脏的时候需要更换；其他操作包括制冷剂罐的更换、计量器的校准、真空泵油的更换等，根据厂商说明书检查。

（3）空调维修检测

1) 制冷剂鉴别

制冷剂回收之前应予以鉴别，回收被污染的制冷剂的价格非常昂贵。在当今社会，可能发生的污染很多，我们不能掉以轻心，对系统制冷剂取样检测，确定其成分，并将其打印出来（或列出来）。

2) 密封剂检测

一种污染源是来自于防漏密封剂，这些密封剂作用于系统以防止制冷剂泄漏。密封剂有两种基本类型：一种密封类型是使O形环和垫圈膨胀；另一种类型是用密封剂密封小洞。第二种类型的密封剂在接触到潮湿的空气时发生凝固，会对空调维修设备造成损害。可以将一个快速的密封剂检测探测器连接到系统，查看制冷剂里是否含有密封剂。如果检测到密封剂，则需要专业的检测维修。

3) 回收程序

在压力降为0的时候大部分回收装置都会关闭。观察压力，如果几分钟后压力上升，则继续回收。回收完后，检查回收的制冷液和机油的数量。

提示： 如果是从一个有泄漏的系统回收制冷剂，那么开始回收时，压力就可能较低。这一小部分制冷剂被回收后，就会有一部分空气从缝隙中被抽入回收装置，这些空气将会混入已回收的制冷剂中。按正常方法操作回收装置，并进行监测，回收的时间有可能比平时短。如果压力降到一定值后就不再下降，那么回收装置可能在从外面抽进空气，这时（手动）停止回收。

4) 再循环

再循环装置连接到回收系统的软管，它将拦截并从被回收的制冷剂中过滤出密封剂、油和染料，回收后的滤渣应排出。

再循环操作取决于维修装置。该装置有一个显示屏，显示机器操作过程；还有一个键盘，让技术人员完成这项操作。

5) 用歧管量表装置检测

在排放过程中，歧管量表装置的中心软管被连接到真空泵；当加注制冷剂于系统的时候，则与制冷剂罐相连接。要注意的是，歧管量表装置控制阀的关闭视具体情况而定，见图8-5。

6) 排放

①排放时，歧管量表装置的中心软管与真空泵相连接。两个手动阀都是开着的，真空泵把系统内所有的空气和水排出，空气和其他所有气体也均被排出。如果压力降到29.9inHg（$1.01×10^5$Pa），系统中将不会残留气体。

②用维修装置排放和用歧管量表及真空泵排放的效果是完全一样的，见图8-6。可以通过降压使水汽化而排出系统，从而除去水蒸气。在$1.01×10^5$Pa的压强下，水的沸点是70°F

（21.1℃）。

7）真空泄漏检测

当排放达到全真空时，关闭高、低压阀，观察真空读数，这个真空应该持续几分钟。如果压力上升，则表明系统有泄漏。

8）加注制冷剂

这个过程是把正确数量的制冷剂注入系统。一个歧管量表或维修装置可以完成此项工作。在这种情况下，气体会从制冷剂的容器里跑出来，并随着系统的运转进入低压侧，见图8-7。

当用歧管量表装置从大容器向空调系统加注制冷剂时，需要一个计量制冷剂的办法。计量器或数码灌装机会被用到，当大容器加注正确的制冷剂后，计量器会根据程序自动关闭。注入正确的制冷剂后，维修装置便可以工作了，制冷剂将被从维修装置转移到系统中。

9）泄漏检查和系统检查

检查所有被拆装过的部件并确保其没有泄漏是一个很好的习惯。应起动空调系统，检查工作压力是否正常，看排出的空气是否凉爽，压缩机和传动带运转是否平稳、安静。

Unit 9

Car Beauty
汽车美容

Section 9.1
Clean Car Interior
内饰美容

Clean interior not just looks great，it's also better for your health. Below are few tips on how to clean the interior of your car.

（1）Vacuuming

Remove the floor mats. Vacuum the seats and the carpet. Using the proper attachment，reach under the seats，around the pedals and the area between the front seats and the central console. Vacuum floor mats separately.

Use soft brush attachment to vacuum the dashboard and doors. Be careful not to damage knobs，vents and sticking parts. Use the same attachment vacuuming the seats.

（2）Cleaning fabric seats and door upholstery

There are a number of upholstery cleaning agents available. Simply spray evenly on the seat or door upholstery and rub vigorously. Then，wipe it thoroughly with a dry cloth.

If you don't have an upholstery cleaner，simple laundry detergent will work as well. Just mix some detergent with warm water，dip a clean cloth into it，wring out good and then just wipe the seat. Work hard on dirty areas. Then，rub dry with a clean soft cloth.

（3）Cleaning the carpet

Clean the carpet the same way you cleaned the seats and upholstery. Spray evenly with the carpet cleaner and rub vigorously. Then，wipe it

---

vacuuming：真空吸尘

floor mat：地垫；脚垫
carpet：地毯
central console：中（央）控（制）台
sticking part：粘接件

fabric seat：绒布座椅
door upholstery：车门内衬

detergent：清洁剂

spray：喷射
vigorously：大力地

thoroughly with a dry cloth. The laundry detergent will work on the carpet as well. Damp a rag with a little bit of water and detergent, squeeze the excess of water and rub the carpet vigorously. Then, rub dry with a clean dry cloth.

laundry detergent：洗衣粉；洗洁精

(4) Cleaning and polishing the dashboard

Clean a dashboard, central console, and other plastic parts with a slightly damp cloth. Use very small amount of laundry detergent to remove the stains. Dry with a clean soft dry cloth. To make it shiny, spray plastic polish and spread it evenly with soft brush.

polish：抛光；擦亮

Dry-polish gently with clean soft dry cloth. Polish not only makes the dashboard shiny, but also protects the plastic. All you need to do after, is just use a soft duster periodically and your dashboard will look like new for a long time.

(5) How to get rid of musty smell from the air conditioner

It you experience that unpleasant musty smell from the vents when the air conditioner is turned on, you can try one odor treatment. It kills the bacteria and removes that mildew smell. You simply spray into outside air intake vent (check directions on the can).

musty smell：霉烂味

bacteria：细菌

mildew smell：霉味

Clogged air conditioner drain tube and accumulation of leaves and other debris under the cowl cover also may cause damp mildew smell. Ask the mechanic to check it when you do your next oil change.

drain tube：排水管

cowl cover：通风斗罩

Reference Version 参考译文

车内清洁不仅使汽车看起来美观，对健康也很有好处。下面将介绍一些汽车内饰美容的方法。

(1) 真空吸尘

移去地垫，用真空吸尘器清洁座位和地毯。用合适的工具作为辅助，伸到座位下面，除去脚踏板周围及前排座位与中控台之间地垫上的尘土。

用软刷作为辅助工具，清洁仪表板和门，小心不要弄坏门把手、通风孔及粘接件。用同样的辅助工具清洁座位。

(2) 绒布座椅和车门内衬清洁

汽车内饰清洗剂有很多种，将其简单而均匀地喷到绒布座椅或车门内衬上，用力擦。然后，用一块干抹布将其彻底地擦干净。

如果没有汽车内饰清洗剂，洗涤剂也是可以的。将一些洗涤剂与温水混合好，用一块干净的布蘸一下，拧出多余的水分，将座位擦拭干净。对于脏的地方用力些，然后用一块干净的软布擦干。

（3）地毯清洁

清洁地毯和清洁绒布座椅及车门内衬的方法相同。

均匀地喷上地毯清洁剂，用力擦，然后用一块干布彻底地擦干净。洗涤剂也可以用来清洁地毯，用少许的水和洗涤剂弄湿碎布，挤出多余的水分，用力地擦地毯，最后，再用干净的干抹布将其擦干。

（4）清洁并抛光仪表盘

用一块微湿的软布清洁仪表盘、中控台和其他塑料部件。如有污渍，则要先用极少量的洗涤剂清洗，再用干净的软布擦干。为使仪表盘光亮如新，喷上塑料抛光剂，用软刷涂抹均匀即可。

用干净且柔软的干抹布轻轻地将表面擦干并抛光。抛光不仅仅使仪表板看起来光亮，更重要的是，它可以保护塑料。此后要做的仅仅是定期用软刷掸一下，这样仪表板就可以长期光洁如新了。

（5）除去空调霉味

如果发现当车内空调打开时通风口发出难闻的霉味，可以试一下除臭法，它可以杀死细菌，除去霉味。要做的仅仅是将除臭剂喷入车厢内进风口处（从外壳上查看方向）。

空调的排水管被堵或通风口处积累了叶子和碎片也同样会引起潮湿的霉味。在下次换油的时候，让修理工检查一下就可以了。

Section 9.2
Car Body Care
车身美容

corrosion：腐蚀

To keep a car shiny and protect it from corrosion, please take care of car body.

（1）Wash the car

limestone：石灰岩

moisture：湿气；潮湿
accumulate：积聚

Wash the car regularly—we'd recommend to do this at least once a month. Things like bugs, bird's dropping, or limestone dripping damage the paint leaving permanent stains if not washed off in time. When the car is clean, all the moisture dries up quickly, but when it's dirty, the moisture accumulates in dirty areas causing corrosion. At least once in a while use pressure wash—it removes the dirt difficult to reach. Wash off all the places where the dirt and salt could be accumulated; for example, behind moldings, inside wheel arches, under the bumpers, etc. It's particularly helpful after winter season—to wash out all the salt accumulations that speed up the corrosion process.

salt accumulation：积盐

（2）Wax the car

minimizing：极小化

Wax the car regularly. Wax helps to protect the paint, minimizing harm from chemicals and protecting the paint from fading; plus the car looks shiny. It takes only about 30 minutes to wax a whole car and high quality car wax stays on the car for three to four months. In order to maintain protective coat, any product needs to be reapplied periodically.

fading：褪色

(3) Undercoat and rustproof the vehicle

If you live in an area with high humidity, or where the salt is common in winter months, undercoating and rustproofing your car can be very helpful. Properly-done undercoating and rustproofing can protect important components of the car from corrosion.

undercoat：涂底漆
rustproof：防锈；防锈处理

(4) Repair stone chips

The stone chips if not repaired in time will cause corrosion. That's why it's a good idea to repair stone chips as soon as they appear.

If this position is not corroded yet, we'll try to repair it. The car is clean and dry and we have all we need—the matching spray paint and a toothpick.

After shaking the spray paint very well (for a few minutes), spray very small amount into the cap. Now, slightly dip the end of the toothpick into the paint in the cap. Very carefully, try to barely fill up the damage with the paint without letting it to come out.

Now it looks much better and it won't be corroded later.

toothpick：牙签
shake：摇晃

(5) Remove residue marks (paint) left by other objects

This mark on the bumper, if you look very closely, it's actually white paint residue over original clearcoat. The clearcoat itself seems to be damaged only slightly. We'll try to remove this mark.

All we need for this is ultra-fine 1900-grit or 2000-grit waterproof sandpaper (the higher number stands for the finest abrasive), polishing compound containing mild abrasive and car wax.

Very carefully (don't remove the clearcoat), We sand the marks with wet sandpaper (use only ultra-fine waterproof sandpaper) until all marks are gone.

Now there is no mark, but the clearcoat has lost its shine: we will use polishing compound to restore the shine. We put small amount of the polishing compound onto the damp sponge and rub well until the clearcoat becomes shiny.

Last step, we buff the area with the car wax.

residue：残留
clearcoat：清漆
ultra-fine：超精细的
grit：磨粒
waterproof sandpaper：防水打磨砂纸
polish：磨光；抛光

(6) Remove minor scratches

Sometimes, these scratches on the trunk were made by the bushes. It's not a big problem, but we will remove these scratches in two steps.

scratch：划痕

mild abrasive：柔和磨料

liquid wax：上蜡
squeeze：挤压
haze：薄雾
ideal result：理想效果

First, we use polishing compound to polish the scratches. It contains mild abrasive and removes very thin coat of painting. We put a little amount of polishing compound onto a damp sponge and buff the scratched area in a circular motion until the scratches disappear. But don't overdo it. We'd suggest trying a small area first, to get used to the process. Then we wash off the area completely.

Then it's time to use a liquid wax. We squeeze a little amount of wax onto a sponge and spread evenly on the scratched area. We wait a little time allowing product to haze, then, using a soft towel, we buff the wax. You will find an ideal result.

Reference Version　参考译文

想使汽车清洁亮丽且不受腐蚀，需注意车身的美容。

（1）洗车

定期洗车——建议至少一个月洗一次车。像虫子、鸟屎或石灰水可能会破坏漆面，如果不及时清除，将会留下永久的痕迹。当汽车比较干净时，所有水汽会很快蒸发；相反，当汽车比较脏时，水汽会积聚在较脏的地方进而引起腐蚀。至少偶尔用高压水枪冲洗一次——它会将难以接触到部分的脏物予以清除。要清洗所有脏物和盐分可以积聚的地方，例如，翼子板、挡泥板的内部及保险杠的下面等。在冬季结束之后，这样做特别有好处——可以清除所有加剧腐蚀的盐分积聚物。

（2）打蜡

定期打蜡。打蜡不仅可以保护漆面，使化学作用的伤害最小化，而且可以防止漆面褪色，使车看起来亮丽、有光泽。整车打蜡仅仅需要 30min 的时间，而且高质量的车蜡能保持 3~4 个月之久。为了持续保护漆面，任何产品（车蜡）都应定期重新施涂。

（3）涂底漆和车身防锈

如果你居住的地方高度潮湿，或者冬季盐分较多，对你的爱车来说，涂底漆和防锈是非常有益的。恰当地涂底漆和防锈将会防止汽车的重要部件受到腐蚀。

（4）修复片状破损

如果片状破损没有被及时修复，也会引起腐蚀，这就是一旦出现片状破损就要及时修复的原因。

如果破损位置还没有腐蚀，我们可以试着去修复它。（如果）这辆车干净且干燥，我们所需要的只是匹配的喷漆和牙签。

将喷漆摇晃均匀后喷到盒盖里少许。然后，用牙签的一端轻轻蘸一下盒盖里的喷漆，小心用漆填满破损处，不要使其流出来。

现在车看起来美观多了，以后也不会被腐蚀了。

（5）除去其他物体留下的擦痕

对于保险杠上的擦痕，如果靠近观察就会发现，在原来的清漆层上面其实是白色的喷漆残渣，而清漆层本身只是受了点轻微的损害。可以试着除去这个擦痕。

这项工作所需要的是极细的1900#或2000#防水打磨砂纸。砂粒的数目越多，表示研磨剂越细，抛光剂包含少许的研磨剂和车蜡。

小心（不要破坏清漆层）地用湿砂纸（仅用极细的防水砂纸）打磨擦痕，直到其消失。

现在虽然没有了擦痕，但清漆层已经失去了它的光泽；用抛光剂便可恢复它的光泽。挤少许抛光剂到湿海绵上，认真地擦拭，直到清漆层恢复光泽。

最后一步，在这块区域打上车蜡。

（6）除去小的划痕

有时候，汽车尾部行李厢的那些划痕是树枝刮的。这不是一个大问题，但是需要两步来完成：首先，用抛光剂抛光这些刮痕，抛光剂包含少许研磨剂，可以除去薄的清漆层。

将少量的抛光剂挤到湿海绵上，以画圈的方式，均匀擦拭划痕，直到消失，但是不要太过用力了。建议从一小部分开始，习惯操作后，再将划痕彻底地清除掉。

然后要打液体蜡。把少量车蜡挤到海绵上，在刮痕部分涂抹均匀。等车蜡模糊后，用软毛巾对其进行抛光处理，最后将会得到理想的效果。

Section 9.3
Car's Accessorizing
汽车装饰

Making your car stand out from the crowd is not hard to accomplish with all of the different accessories available today. From wheels and tires to music and DVD players，you can customize your ride to your style. Learn how to accessorize a ride by following the text.

stand out from：脱颖而出

customize：量身定制

（1）How to install a sunroof

how to install a sunroof：如何安装天窗

Just about everyone dreams of driving down scenic roads with the wind in their hair. Of course，this dream isn't always attainable or very practical，but there's always the option to install a sunroof for the next best thing to a true convertible.

convertible：敞篷车

① The sunroof comes complete with everything that you'll need（except tools）to make quick work of the installation. Before beginning，check the completeness of the sunroof package using the provided parts list.

② Then，locate，mark and tape the proper position for the roof cutout template.

cutout：剪贴

③ Position the template flat against the roof and tape it making sure it's straight and there are no creases.

single-edge blade：
单刃刀片

bit stop：钻深触止器

④ Using a single-edge blade, carefully cut out the area of the paper template for the roof cut and draw the cut outline on the roof metal with a marking pen.

⑤ Drill the six holes as marked on the front of the template for the wind deflector, making sure not to damage the inside roof lining.

Note：A "bit stop" can be used for safety.

⑥ Drill a "pilot hole" for the nibbler (or heavy duty sabre saw) inside the outline on the roof.

⑦ Using a nibbler or sabre saw, carefully cut out the metal roof along the outline.

Note：A die grinder can also be used to cut out the metal roof.

⑧ Carefully peel the roof metal away from the roof ribs and properly discard it.

⑨ This is what the roof looks like with the metal cut out. No turning back now!

⑩ Next the roof ribs must be cut out along the edge of the roof metal and removed.

unplug：拆除
interior light：客厢顶灯
razor knife：剃刀

⑪ Unplug and remove the interior light next.

⑫ Mark the hard headliner using the roof metal as a guide.

⑬ Using a razor knife, carefully cut out the hard headliner to match the roof cutout.

⑭ On the inside, lay 3/4-inch tape around the edge of the hard headlineras a guide and cut out the headliner along the outer edge of the tape, thus makingthe inside headliner cutout 3/4-inch larger than the roof metal cutout.

⑮ Use the die grinder or sabre saw to cut the ribs 3/4-inch smaller man the roof cutout as well.

⑯ Then grind off the edges of the roof cutout to remove any burrs.

⑰ Apply the protective foil strips, without creases, flush with the cutout edge of the roof, starting with the front strip. Then place the side strips flush with the cutout edge, overlapping with the front edge of the strip that has already been applied.

wind deflector：挡风板
sealing washer：密封垫圈

⑱ Place the wind deflector in the holes drilled earlier.

⑲ Using the special sealing washers and nuts provided, attach the wind deflector but do not tighten the nuts yet.

⑳ Carefully drop the sunroof into the cutout being careful not to dent the roof metal. Also make sure that the sealing rubber is correctly seated on the flame edge as this cannot be corrected after fitting.

㉑ Remove the "A" pillar cap and route sunroof motor wiring down the pillar and under the dash board. Later, you will connect the wires to a verified constant 12-volt source.

㉒ Remove the two retaining screws from the motor unit on the frame and make sure that the motor can be slid in between the outer roof skin and the inside lining.

Caution: Don't kink the black end tubes for the drive cables.

㉓ Push the front clamp frame part in place and put the motor fastening screws in.

㉔ Put the rear clamp frame part on and screw in the enclosed nuts onto the stay bolts. Then push the frame sides on. Attach with screws provided all the way around.

Note: Do not place any screws into holes with labels stuck on them because the supports for the trim frame are fastened in those holes.

㉕ Place the supports in position with the upwardly flanged nose of the support engaging the gap between the mainframe and the clamping frame, attach with the fastening screws and tighten equally.

㉖ Connect the operating switch to the wiring loom and make sure that it works. Close the roof, adjust the wind deflector as needed and tighten the wind deflector nuts.

㉗ Fit the front trim cover, guiding the wire for the operating switch through the opening provided.

㉘ With the roof fully open, fit the side and rear trim covers in place and attach them with the push-in fasteners provided.

㉙ Beginning in the middle at the rear, attach the edge protection all the way around and trim the excess with wire cutting pliers.

㉚ The finished installation looks almost factory and opens up to let the sunshine in.

(2) Replacing old carpet

If the carpet in your vehicle has become so worn, damaged faded or stained that a cleaning or detailing won't do much good, you may want to simply replace the entire carpet. The job may be easier than you think, particularly if you purchase a replacement carpet made specifically to fit your vehicle.

Materials: ① Replacement carpet; ② Cordless drill with screwdriver attachments; ③ Socket wrench.

Steps:

① Remove the seats from the vehicle. The seats are held in place by bolts underneath the bench. Use a ratchet wrench to remove the bolts and

---

drive cable：电动机电源线

clamp frame：夹钳

fasten：固定

replace old carpet：更换旧地毯

door-sill：门槛

hand-lay：手工铺设
glue：粘贴

ultraviolet resistance：
抗紫外线

seatbelt：座位安全带

carefully remove the seats.

② Remove the door-sill plates that hold the sides of the carpet in place. You'll also need to remove the seat belts and any other items that are attached to the floor, such as a center console.

③ With the seats and other items removed, pull the old carpet up from the floorboard and remove it from the passenger compartment. The difficulty of this procedure depends on the vehicle and the type of carpet. Molded, custom-fit carpets do not require glue. So they lift out easily. If the carpet was hand-laid and glued, or if heat has caused the carpet backing to adhere to the floor of the vehicle, it may take more time.

④ Installation is much easier, if you purchase a molded carpet made specifically for the model of your vehicle. For larger vehicles, they may be installed in two pieces. In smaller vehicles, there is usually only a single piece. They already have trim around the edges and padding attached to the underside. They are available in a wide range of colors to match most vehicle interiors. Vehicle carpeting is required to meet certain specifications for flame and ultraviolet resistance.

⑤ Before installing your new carpet, take advantage of the opportunity to clean the interior surface of the cab floor. A brush or broom will help with this job. Check the floorboard for leaks or rust spots. If you find rust, you may want to sand the spot and apply a sealer. Leaks should be patched.

⑥ Once you've cleaned away any debris from the interior, lay the new carpet in place and position it properly.

⑦ Reinstall the seats, center console, seatbelts, doorsills and anything else you removed for the installation.

Important note：Any time that you reinstall seatbelts, it's necessary to torque the bolts to the proper specifications. This is a safety issue, and the torque specs should be in your vehicle's owner's manual or service manual.

Reference Version 参考译文

要想使汽车与众不同并非难事，因为目前有很多装饰件可供选择。从车轮轮胎到各种影音设备，可以按自己的风格装饰你的爱车。下面来学习如何装饰汽车。

（1）如何安装天窗

几乎每个人都梦想驾车驰骋在景色秀美的道路上，微风轻拂着秀发。当然了，这种梦想不一定能够实现或符合现实，但是安装一个天窗是除敞篷车外最好的选择。

① 准备好天窗及将用到的（除工具外）所有配件，这样可以保证快速地完成安装工作。

开始安装前，根据提供的零件单检查包装盒里的零件是否配备齐全。

② 在恰当的位置定位，标记剪切模板，并预留边缘。

③ 平靠车顶定位剪切模板，并用胶带粘贴好，确保它是直的并且没有折痕。

④ 用一个单刃刀片，小心地剪下要开天窗部分的纸模板，并用画线笔在顶棚蒙皮上画出轮廓线。

⑤ 在模板的前部按照所做标记钻 6 个孔来安装挡风板，确保不要触及内顶板。

注意：为了安全，可以用钻深触止器。

⑥ 钻一个"导向孔"，以便板料切割机（或重型电锯）沿轮廓线切割顶棚。

⑦ 用板料切据机（或重型电锯）沿轮廓线小心地剪下顶棚蒙皮。

注意：打磨机同样也可以用来剪切顶棚蒙皮。

⑧ 小心地将顶棚蒙皮从顶棚加强筋上揭下，恰当地予以处理。

⑨ 这就是顶棚蒙皮揭下后看到的顶棚形状，现在不要翻起。

⑩ 下一步应该将顶棚加强筋沿着顶棚蒙皮的边缘剪下并移开。

⑪ 再将客厢顶灯拆除并移去。

⑫ 沿顶棚蒙皮在顶棚内衬板上做好标记。

⑬ 用剃刀小心地裁下顶棚内衬板，使其与剪下的顶棚蒙皮相匹配。

⑭ 在内部，在硬的顶棚内衬板的周围预留 3/4in（1in=25.4mm）的边缘作为指引，沿着外部预留边缘剪切顶棚内衬板，使剪下的内部顶棚内衬板比剪下的顶棚蒙皮大 3/4in）。

⑮ 用打磨机或电锯剪切顶棚加强筋，同样比顶棚蒙皮小 3/4in。

⑯ 然后打磨剪下的顶棚蒙皮的边缘，除掉所有毛刺。

⑰ 首先，从前部开始粘贴保护性胶带，要没有折痕，并使其与剪下的顶板边缘在同一平面内；然后沿侧边一直粘贴过来，同样也要使其与剪下的顶棚边缘在同一平面内；最后与已贴好的前部胶带重叠。

⑱ 放置挡风板，使其上面的孔与先前所钻的孔相对齐。

⑲ 用所提供的专用密封垫圈和螺母固定挡风板，但不要把螺母拧紧。

⑳ 把天窗小心地放置到剪好的切口位置，轻轻落座，不要使顶棚蒙皮凹陷。同样还要保证密封胶条正确地落座于框架边缘上，因为一旦安装好天窗后将不能更改。

㉑ 移去 A 柱内饰板，沿柱在仪表盘下部布置好天窗的电动机电源线，然后将其连接到 12V 的直流电源上。

㉒ 移去电动机在边框上的两个固定螺栓，保证电动机可以在顶棚蒙皮和顶棚内衬之间滑动。

警告：不要把黑色管子的尾部拧在一起作为电动机电源线。

㉓ 把前边框推入，放上电动机固定螺栓。

㉔ 放置好后边框，将各个长螺栓上的螺母拧紧，然后放置好侧边框，将周围提供的全部螺栓固定好。

注意：不要把粘着标签的螺栓放到孔里，因为剪切边框的支撑件被固定在这些孔里。

㉕ 把支撑件放在顶框和侧框间，用支撑件向上的法兰凸缘来消除它们之间的间隙，装上紧固螺钉并均衡地将其拧紧。

㉖ 将操控开关和接线器连接起来，保证其能正常工作，然后关上天窗，根据需要调整

好挡风板,将其螺钉拧紧。

㉗ 安装前衬罩,将电源线通过预留的开口部分接到操控开关。

㉘ 将天窗完全打开,再安装侧装饰罩和后装饰罩,最后用推入式卡扣将其固定。

㉙ 从后部的中间开始,在四周贴上防护条,然后用剪线钳将多余的部分剪掉。

㉚ 安装好后的天窗看起来非常令人满意。打开它,让明媚的阳光照进来吧!

(2) 更换旧地毯

如果汽车中的地毯已变得十分破旧,并且严重褪色,以致仔细清洁保养也很难达到一个好的效果,那么就应该考虑更换整个地毯了。这项工作可能比想象的容易,尤其是当选购了一个根据自己的爱车而定做的成型地毯时。

所需材料: ①新地毯;②带螺丝刀的无线钻;③管钳。

步骤:

① 移去车内座椅。座位被下部的螺栓固定,用棘轮扳手拧下螺母,将座椅移出车内。

② 将固定地毯边缘的门槛压板移去,同样还要移去安全带及其他固定在车底板上的物体,比如中控板。

③ 将座位和其他东西移出后,将旧地毯揭起,并移出驾驶室。这个程序的困难程度取决于车辆和地毯的类型。成型的、定做的地毯未经粘贴,因此较容易移出。如果地毯是手工放置并粘贴的,或者由于受热而使地毯背部粘到车辆底板上,那么就会需要一些时间。

④ 如果购买的是根据车型配备的成型地毯,安装就比较容易。对大型车来说,需要安装两块地毯,对小型车来说,一块就足够了。这些地毯周围和衬垫都有镶边用来固定到车的底板上。对汽车地毯来说,有一系列的颜色可选择,使其与车的内部相匹配。车内地毯要求满足一定的耐火性和耐紫外线性。

⑤ 在安装新地毯之前,好好利用这次机会,把驾驶室底板内部清扫干净,一个刷子或一把扫帚可以帮你完成这项工作。检查一下底板是否有漏洞或锈斑。如果有锈斑的话,应先磨光,再涂上密封保护层;如果是漏洞的话,则必须修补。

⑥ 一旦你已将车内清扫干净,便可铺上新地毯,并布置妥当。

⑦ 然后安装好座椅、中控台、安全带、门槛压板及所有你移出的物体。

重要提示: 无论何时,只要重新安装安全带,就必须按照说明书的力矩要求拧紧其上的螺栓。这是一个安全问题,可以在汽车的使用手册或服务手册上找到力矩说明。

Appendix

附录

Appendix I

Common Terminology on Automobile
常用汽车专业术语

专业术语	中文含义	专业术语	中文含义
A		annual production volume	年产量
ABS actuator checker	ABS 执行器检查仪	antifreeze fluid	防冻液
accelerator-pedal	加速踏板	antifreeze solution	防冻液
accumulator piston	蓄能器活塞	arc welding	弧焊
active safety system	主动安全系统	atmospheric pressure	大气压力
active suspension	主动悬架	auto shut down relay	自动关闭继电器
active test	主动测试,执行元件检测	automated manual transmission (AMT)	机械式自动变速器
adaptive cruise control	自适应巡航控制		
adhesive bonding	粘接	automatic clutch system (ACS)	离合器自动操控系统
air cleaner	空气滤清器		
air cleaner assembly	空气滤清器总成	automatic gearbox	自动变速器
air gap	气隙	automatic transmission	自动变速器
air induction system	进气系统	automatic transmission fluid (ATF)	自动变速器液
air injection	空气喷射		
air pump	空气泵	axle shaft	半轴
air spring	空气弹簧	B	
air valve	空气阀式(翼片式)(空气流量计)	back pressure	背压
air-and-petrol charge	空气与汽油的混合气	backup light	倒车灯
air-cooled engine	风冷发动机	back up value	备用值
airflow sensor	空气流量计	balance shaft	平衡轴
air-fuel ratio	空燃比	ball bearing	球轴承
alignment machine	车轮定位仪	ball joint	球节
alloy steel	合金钢	barometric pressure	大气压力
alternative fuel	替代燃料,代用燃料	barometric pressure sensor	大气压力传感器

续表

专业术语	中文含义	专业术语	中文含义
battery cell	单格电池	central locking system	中央门锁系统
bearing shell	轴瓦	centrifugal advance mechanism	离心式点火提前角调节装置
block ring	（同步器）锁环		
body-on-frame	车身在车架上的设计	cetane number	十六烷值
boost pressure	增压压力	chain sprocket	链轮
boot valve	靴阀	charcoal canister	活性炭罐
bore gauge	孔径量表	charging circuit	充电电路
boxed section	箱型截面	charging system	充电系统
box-end wrench	梅花扳手	check valve	单向阀
brake booster	制动助力器	circuit breaker	电路断电器
brake caliper	制动钳	circuit protection device	电路保护装置
brake drum	制动鼓		
brake fluid	制动液	clock spring	时钟弹簧，盘旋电缆
brake force distribution	制动力分配	closure panel	车身蒙皮
brake hose	制动软管	cluster gear	齿轮组，塔齿轮
brake line	制动管路	clutch disc	离合器从动盘
brake lining	制动器摩擦衬片	clutch housing	离合器壳
brake pedal	制动踏板	clutch linkage	离合器操纵机构
brake shoe	制动蹄	clutch pedal	离合器踏板
break-in	磨合，走合	clutch plate	离合器片，离合器从动盘
break-out box	检测盒	code pulling	故障码读取
C		coil assembly	（安全气囊）盘旋电缆，时钟弹簧
cable clamp	蓄电池接线夹		
cam follower	凸轮随动件，气门挺柱，摇臂	coil spring	螺旋弹簧
		cold start valve	冷起动阀
cam lobe	凸轮的凸起部分	combustible mixture	可燃混合气
camless engine	无凸轮发动机	combustion chamber	燃烧室
canister purge valve	炭罐排污阀，炭罐清空阀	combustion efficiency	燃烧效率
carbon deposit	积炭	combustion mode	燃烧模式
cardan（universal）joint	十字轴式万向节，万向节	commercial vehicle	商用车
cast iron	铸铁	common-rail injection	共轨喷射
catalytic converter	催化转化器	composite material	复合材料
center console	中央控制台	compression gauge	气缸压力表
central fuel injection	中央燃油喷射	compression ratio	压缩比

专业术语	中文含义	专业术语	中文含义
compression ring	压缩环	cylinder bore	气缸孔，气缸直径
compression stroke	压缩行程	cylinder head	气缸盖
compression-ignition engine	压燃式发动机	cylinder head gasket	气缸垫
		cylinder liner	气缸套
connecting rod	连杆	cylinder sleeve	气缸套
connecting rod bearing	连杆轴承	cylinder wall	气缸壁
contact point	触点	D	
continuous fuel injection	连续燃油喷射	dash panel	仪表板
continuously variable transmission（CVT）	无级变速器	data capture mode	数据捕捉模式
		data item	数据项
control arm	悬架摆臂，控制臂	data list	数据列表，数据流
control module	控制模块	data monitor	数据检测
control rack	控制齿条	data stream	数据流
conventional automatic transmission（AT）	传统式自动变速器	dead axle	从动桥，非驱动桥
		delivery truck	送货车
conventional front suspension	传统式前悬架	delivery valve	出油阀
		dependent suspension	非独立悬架
conversion efficiency	转换效率	diagnostic codes	故障码
converter lockup	液力变矩器锁止	diagnostic tester	诊断（检测）仪
converter transmission	带变矩器的变速器	dial caliper	带刻度盘游标卡尺
coolant pump	水泵（water pump）	dial indicator	百分表
crank angle	曲轴转角	diaphragm-spring	膜片弹簧
crank position sensor	曲轴位置传感器	diesel engine	柴油机
crankcase	曲轴箱	diesel fuel injection	柴油机燃油喷射
crankshaft journal	曲轴轴颈	differential pinion shaft	差速器行星齿轮轴
crankshaft throw	曲柄销，连杆轴颈	differential pinion	差速器行星齿轮
cross and roller universal joint	十字轴式万向节	digital storage oscilloscope	数字式存储示波器
		digital volt-ohmmeter	数字式电压欧姆表
cross-hatch pattern	网格线痕迹	dimensional accuracy	尺寸精度
cruise control	巡航控制	diode trio	二极管三件组合
curb height	全装备高度	direct drive gear	直接挡齿轮，直接挡
CV joint	等速万向节	direct fuel injection	燃油直接喷射
cycle time	周期	direct-shift transmission	直接换挡变速器
cylinder block	气缸体	disc brake	盘式制动器

续表

专业术语	中文含义	专业术语	中文含义
distributor injection pump	分配式喷油泵	electronic fuel injection（EFI）	电子控制燃油喷射
distributorless ignition system	无分电器式点火系统	electronic stability control（ESC）	电子稳定性控制
diverter valve	分流阀		
dog tracking	蛇形行驶	end gap	端隙
double overhead camshaft（DOHC）engine	双顶置凸轮轴发动机	end play	轴向间隙
		energy density	能量密度
diesel particular trap（DPT）	柴油机微粒捕集器	energy reserve capacitor	储能电容器
drive line	传动系统	engine block	气缸体
drive pinion	主动小齿轮，驱动小齿轮	engine compartment	发动机室
drive plate	传动板	engine immobilizer	发动机防盗器
drive shaft	传动轴	enigne oil	发动机油
drive train	传动系	engine speed sensor	发动机转速传感器
drive wheel	驱动轮	evaporative emission control（EVAP）	蒸发排放控制
driven member	从动件		
driving license	驾驶执照	exhaust gas recirculation（EGR）	废气再循环
driving member	主动件		
driving program	驾驶程序	exhaust manifold	排气歧管
driving road wheel	驱动轮	exhaust pipe	排气管
driving speed	行驶速度	exhaust stroke	排气行程
drum brake	鼓式制动器	exhaust valve	排气门
dry sleeve	干式气缸套	expansion（overflow）tank	膨胀（溢流）箱
dual mass flywheel	双质量飞轮		
dwell time	闭合时间，初级电路接通时间	expansion tank	膨胀水箱
		exploded view	分解图
E		extension housing	加长壳，后壳
EGR valve	废气再循环阀	external EGR	机外 EGR
EGR valve position（EVP）sensor	废气再循环阀位置传感器	F	
		fan clutch	风扇离合器
electric fuel pump	电动燃油泵	feedback control	反馈控制
electric starting motor	电起动机	feeler gauge	塞尺
electrical device	电气设备	fiber reinforced polymer	纤维增强聚合物
electrical energy	电能	final drive assembly	最终传动总成，主减速器
electro-hydraulic converter	电-液转换器	firing order	点火顺序

续表

专业术语	中文含义	专业术语	中文含义
first gear	1挡	fuel injector	喷油器
five-speed transmission	5挡变速器	fuel inlet line	进油管
flammable mixture	可燃混合气	fuel line	燃油管
flat（horizontal-opposed）engine	水平对置式发动机	fuel mileage	燃油经济性
		fuel pressure gauge	燃油压力表
flexible fuel vehicles（FFV）	灵活燃料汽车	fuel pump	燃油泵
		fuel rail	燃油分配管，油轨
flexible joint	柔性接头	fuel shutoff solenoid	燃油切断阀
flexible tube	柔性管	fuel stratified injection（FSI）	分层喷射
fluid bearing	液体轴承		
fluid reservoir	储液室	fuel tank	燃油箱
forward sensor	前传感器	fuel-saving potential	节油潜力
fossil fuel	矿物燃料	function code	功能码
four valves per cylinder	每缸四气门	functional test	功能测试
four-stroke cycle	四冲程循环	fuse block	熔断器盒
four-stroke-cycle engine	四冲程（循环）发动机	fusible link	易熔线
free travel	自由行程（free play）	G	
friction limited-slip differential	摩擦式限滑差速器	gas cap	汽油箱盖
		gas metal arc welding（GMAW）	金属极气体保护电弧焊
friction lining	摩擦衬片		
friction mechanism	摩擦机构	gas mileage	每加仑燃油所能行驶的里程，燃油经济性
friction stir spot welding（FSSW）	摩擦搅拌点焊		
		gas pump	汽油泵
friction stir welding(FSW)	摩擦搅拌焊	gas tank	汽油箱
front impact sensor	正面碰撞传感器	gas tungsten arc welding（GTAW）	钨极气体保护电弧焊
FTP level	燃油箱压力标准值		
fuel cell	燃料电池	gasoline direct injection	汽油直喷
fuel consumption	燃油消耗，燃油消耗率	gasoline engine	汽油机
fuel delivery system	供油系统	gas-turbine	燃气轮机
fuel distributor	燃油分配器	gear end play	齿轮轴向间隙
fuel economy	燃油经济性	gear ratio	传动比
fuel filter	燃油滤清器	gear shaft	齿轮轴
fuel injection	燃油喷射	gear teeth	齿轮轮齿
fuel injection pump	喷油泵	gearshift lever	变速杆

专业术语	中文含义	专业术语	中文含义
global warming	全球变暖	hot-wire air-mass sensor	热线式空气流量计
glow plug	预热塞	hybrid drive	混合动力装置，混合驱动
governor pressure	调速器压力	hybrid engine	混合动力装置
graphing multimeter	示波万用表	hydraulic actuator	液压执行器
greenhouse effect	温室效应	hydraulic regulating valve	液压调节阀
H		hydraulic unit	液压单元
half shaft	半轴（axle shaft）	hydraulic valve lifter	液力挺柱
Hall-effect switch	霍尔效应开关	hydrodynamic lubrication	流体动力润滑
hand tool	手持工具	hydrodynamic torque converter	液力变矩器
hand-held tester	手持式诊断仪		
hand-operated vacuum pump	手动真空泵	I	
		idle-speed control	怠速控制
hard fault	硬故障	idle-speed stabilizer	怠速稳定器
harmonic balancer	谐波平衡器，谐波减振器	ignition coil	点火线圈
hatchback car	仓背式轿车	ignition module	点火模块
hazard warning light	危险警告灯	ignition scope	点火示波器
head bolt	缸盖螺栓	ignition switch	点火开关
head light	前照灯	ignition timing	点火正时
headway sensor	车距传感器，车距探测装置	impact sensor	碰撞传感器
		impact wrench	冲击扳手
heat element	加热元件	independent ignition system	独立点火系统
heat resistant	耐热的		
heat shield	隔热板	independent suspension	独立悬架
heated oxygen sensor（HO$_2$S）	加热型氧传感器（HO$_2$S）	indicator light	指示灯
		indirect fuel injection	燃油间接喷射
heated wire	热线式（空气流量计）	induction stroke	进气行程
helical gear	斜齿轮	inductive sensor	感应式传感器
hex key	六角扳手	initial timing	初始点火正时
high strength steel	高强度钢	injection molding	注射成型
high tension spark plug wire	高压火花塞线	injection pump	喷油泵
hold-down clamp	固定夹	injection rate	喷油速率
horizontal-opposed engine	水平对置式发动机	injection timing	喷油正时

续表

专业术语	中文含义	专业术语	中文含义
inlet valve	进气门	laser welding	激光焊接
inline engine	直列式发动机	lead-acid (storage) battery	铅酸蓄电池
inline injection pump	直列式喷油泵	leaf spring	叶片弹簧
insert bearing	镶嵌轴承	leak detector	检漏器
insert molding	嵌入成型	LEV	低排放车辆
instrument panel	仪表板	life expectancy	预期寿命,预计使用期限
intake air heater	进气加热器	light emitting diode	发光二极管
intake air temperature (IAT) sensor	进气温度传感器	light truck	轻型货车
		light vehicle	轻型汽车
intake manifold	进气歧管	light-off point	起燃点,起燃温度
intake manifold absolute pressure sensor	进气歧管绝对压力传感器	limited-slip differential	防滑差速器
		line pressure	主油路压力
intake port	进气道	liquid phase welding	液相焊接
intake stroke	进气行程	liquid-cooled engine	水冷发动机
integrated circuit	集成电路	low carbon steel	低碳钢
interior light	车内灯	M	
intermittent misfire	断续性缺火	Macpherson strut front suspension	麦弗逊滑柱式前悬架
intermittent symptom	间歇性故障		
internal combustion engine	内燃机	Mac pherson strat	麦弗逊滑柱
internal EGR	机内 ECR	magnetic pickup	电磁式传感器
inward opening injector	内张式喷油器	main bearing	主轴承
J		maintenance free	免维护
jumper cables	(利用另一辆汽车蓄电池进行起动使用的)跨接电缆	malfunction indicator light (MIL)	故障指示灯
jumper wire	跨接线	manifold absolute pressure (MAP) sensor	进气歧管绝对压力(MAP)传感器
junction block	接线盒		
K		manifold vacuum sensor	进气歧管压力传感器
Karmann vortex	卡曼涡旋式(空气流量计)	manual steering	机械转向,人力转向
		manual transaxle	手动变速驱动桥
knock control regulator	爆燃控制调节器	manual transmission	手动变速器
knock sensor	爆燃传感器	mass airflow sensor (MAF)	质量空气流量计
L			
lab scope	实验室级示波器	mass production	批量生产
lambda closed-loop control	λ闭环控制	master cylinder	主缸

续表

专业术语	中文含义	专业术语	中文含义
master cylinder cut solenoid valve	主缸切断电磁阀，主缸隔离电磁阀	oil control ring	油环
		oil film	油膜
mechanical fuel injection	机械控制燃油喷射	oil pan	油底壳（sump）
		oil pressure gauge	机油压力表
mechanical joining	机械连接	oil pump	机油泵
mechanical valve lifter	机械式气门挺柱	one-way clutch	单向离合器
mini-catalytic converter	小催化转化器，副催化转化器	open circuit	开路，断路
		open-end wrench	呆扳手
model year	年款	operator control	操纵开关
modulator pressure	调压阀压力	optical sensor	光电式传感器
mold cavity	模腔	outsert molding	包容成型
molecular orientation	分子取向	outward opening injector	多张式喷油器
molten pool	熔池	overdrive gear	超速挡齿轮
monolith converter	整体式载体催化转化器	overhead camshaft（OHC）	顶置凸轮轴
motor oil	发动机油	overhead valve（OHV）	顶置气门
motor vehicle	汽车，机动车	overrunning clutch	超越离合器
mounting plate	安装板	oxidation catalyst	氧化催化剂
movie mode	电影模式	oxygen sensor	氧传感器
multilink rear suspension	多连杆式后悬架	P	
multi-piece ring set	组合环	parallel hybrid	并联式混合动力装置，并联混合驱动
multiple channel（trace）capability	多通道功能		
		parallelogram linkage	平行四杆机构
multi-point injection	多点喷射	parking brake	驻车制动器
multi-point system	多点喷射系统	parking brake system	驻车制动系统
multi-port injection	多点喷射	parts order	配件订单
multi-purpose van（MPV）	多用途厢式车	passenger car	乘用车
N		passenger compartment	乘客室，乘客舱
naturally aspirated	自然吸气（发动机）	pellet-type converter	颗粒状载体催化转化器
needle bearing	滚针轴承	petrol engine	汽油机
non-ferrous alloy	有色金属合金	photodiode	光电二极管
non-powered test light	无源试灯	photo sensitive diode	光电二极管，光敏二极管
normally aspirated	自然吸气（发动机）	pickup coil	传感线圈
O		piezoelectric injector	压电式喷油器
octane number	辛烷值	pilot bearing	导向轴承
octane rating	辛烷值（octane number）	pilot injection	预喷射
off-road vehicle	非道路车辆，越野车辆	pin test	端子测试

续表

专业术语	中文含义	专业术语	中文含义
pinion shaft	小齿轮轴，行星齿轮轴	pressure regulator valve	调压电磁阀
pinpoint test	详细检测	pressure-charged engine	增压发动机
piston blow-by	活塞环漏气，窜气	primary circuit	初级电路
piston pin	活塞销	production rate	生产率
piston ring	活塞环	program code	程序代码
piston skirt	活塞裙部	program map	程序图
pitman arm	转向摇臂	programming mode	编程模式
planet carrier	行星架	propeller shaft	传动轴
planetary gear set	行星齿轮机构	proton exchange membrane fuel cell（PEMFC）	质子交换膜燃料电池（PEMFC），PEM 燃料电池
planetary gearbox sun gear	行星齿轮变速器太阳轮		
pneumatic control unit	气动控制单元	prototype engine	发动机样机
port injector	进气道喷油器	pull to one side	跑偏
positive crankcase ventilation（PCV）	曲轴箱强制通风	pulse fuel injection	间歇式燃油喷射
		pulse width	脉冲宽度
positive displacement vane type	叶片容积式	pulse width modulation	脉宽调制
		purge valve	清污阀
power density	功率密度	push rod	推杆
power door lock	电动门锁	PZEV	部分时间零排放车辆
power rear mirror	电动后视镜	R	
power steering	动力转向	rack-and-pinion steering gear	齿轮齿条式转向器
power steering fluid	动力转向液		
power stroke	做功行程	rack-and-pinion steering system	齿轮齿条式转向系统
power tool	动力工具		
power train	传动系，动力装置	radial tire	子午线轮胎
power transistor	功率晶体管	radiator	散热器
power unit	动力装置	radiator cap	散热器盖
power window	电动车窗，电动门窗	rear axle	后桥
powertrain control module（PCM）	动力控制模块（PCM）	rear view mirrors	后视镜
		rear window defogger	后窗除雾器
prechamber	预燃室	reciprocating motion	往复运动
precision machinery	精密机械	recirculating ball steering gear	循环球式转向器
press fit	压入式配合，过盈配合		
pressure gauge	压力表	reducing catalyst	还原催化剂
pressure plate	压盘	reduction gear	减速齿轮，减速挡
pressure regulator	压力调节器	reference voltage	参考电压

续表

专业术语	中文含义	专业术语	中文含义
regenerative braking	再生制动	S	
relay block	继电器盒	safety glass	安全玻璃
relay rod	中间拉杆，继动杆	safing sensor	保险传感器
release bearing	分离轴承	scan tool	诊断仪
release lever	分离杆	scope set	示波器
release switch	解除开关	seat belt	座椅安全带
relief valve	卸压阀，减压阀，调压阀	second gear	2挡
reluctor wheel	磁阻轮	secondary air injection	二次空气喷射
reminder light	提示灯，警告灯	secondary circuit	次级电路
remote keyless-entry system	遥控无钥匙进车系统	secondary/emergency brake	应急制动器
repair shop	维修车间	security system	防盗系统
residual stress	残余应力	selector cylinder	选挡工作缸
resistance spot welding	电阻点焊	selector lever	变速杆，选挡杆
resistive sensor	电阻型传感器	self-powered test light	自备电源试灯
retarder braking system	缓速制动系统	series hybrid	串联式混合动力装置，串联混合驱动
reverse gear	倒挡齿轮，倒挡		
reverse-flow muffler	倒流式消声器	service brake system	行车制动系统
ride quality	乘坐舒适性	service package	修理包
rigid tube	刚性管	service（repair）facility	维修机构，维修厂家
ring gear	齿圈	shift cylinder	换挡工作缸
ring gear pinion shaft	主减速器主动锥齿轮轴	shift lever	变速杆
road vehicle	道路车辆	shift map	换挡程序图
road wheel	车轮	shift paddle	换挡拨片
rocker arm	摇臂	shift point	换挡点
rocker shaft	摇臂轴	shift quality	换挡质量
roller lifter	滚子式挺柱	shift rail	变速轨，拨叉轴
rolling code	滚动码	shift valve	换挡阀
rolling radius	滚动半径	shifting element	换挡元件
rolling resistance	滚动阻力	shifting mechanism	换挡机构
root cause	根本原因，起因	shifting valve	换挡阀
rotary engine	转子发动机	shock absorber	减振器
rotary motion	旋转运动	shutter wheel	遮光轮
rotor plate	遮光板	side gear	半轴齿轮
rubber bumper	（保险杠）缓冲胶条	single-point injection（SPI）	单点喷射

续表

专业术语	中文含义	专业术语	中文含义
sink mark	缩痕，凹痕	spring oscillation	弹簧振荡
slave cylinder	（离合器）工作缸	sprung weight	悬挂重量
slide valve	滑阀	spur gear	直齿圆柱齿轮
sliding friction	滑动摩擦	stabilizer bar	横向稳定杆
sliding gear	滑移齿轮	start injector	起动喷油器，冷起动喷油器
slow-rate charging	低速充电		
smart airbag	智能安全气囊	starter motor	起动机
smart sensor	智能传感器	starter relay	起动继电器
smart valve	智能气门	starting performance	起动性能，起步性能
snap ring	卡环	station wagon	旅行车
sodium hydroxide	氢氧化钠	steel frame	钢梁车架
soft（intermittent）fault	软故障（断续性故障）	steering arm	转向臂
solenoid switch	电磁开关	steering axis inclination	转向轴线内倾角
solenoid valve	电磁阀	steering gear	转向器
solenoid winding	电磁阀线圈	steering knuckle	转向节
solenoid-type injector	电磁式喷油器	steering shaft	转向轴
solid axle	实心轴，整体轴，整体式车轿	steering wheel	转向盘
		Stirling engine	斯特林发动机
solid coupling	刚性连接	stoichiometric ratio	理想配比的空燃比
solid phase welding	固相焊接	storage battery	蓄电池
solid state	固态	straight-ahead driving	直线向前行驶
space frame	空间构架	straight-through muffler	直通式消声器
spark-ignition engine	点燃式发动机	sub-throttle plate	副节气门
spark-ignition（S.I.）engine	点燃式发动机	SULEV	超级低排放车辆
		supplemental inflatable restraint（SIR）	辅助充气保护装置（SIR，通用汽车公司对安全气囊的称谓）
spark-plug	火花塞		
specialist application	专家系统，专门应用软件	supplemental restraint system	乘员约束辅助保护装置（SRS）
speed density	速度密度		
speedometer gear	车速表齿轮	supply pump	供油泵
speed-sensitive power steering	速敏动力转向	surface blemsih	表面缺陷
		surface finish	表面抛光，表面处理
spiral cable	螺旋电缆	synchronized gear	同步器
splined hub	花键毂	synchronizing mechanism	同步机构
spool valve	滑阀	T	
sport utility vehicle（SUV）	多用途轻型运动车	tachometer	转速表

续表

专业术语	中文含义	专业术语	中文含义
tail pipe	排气尾管	torsion beam	扭转梁
telescope gauge	伸缩式内径规	torsional damper	扭转减振器
temperature sensor	温度传感器	torsional vibration	扭转振动
test bench	实验（台）架	TRAC brake actuator	TRAC 制动执行器
thermal efficiency	热效率	traction control system（TCS）	牵引力控制系统
thermo-fuse（circuit breaker）	热熔断器（电路断电器）	tractive effort	驱动力
		tractive force	驱动力
thermostat	节温器	trailing arm	（悬架）纵臂，拖臂
thermostatic air cleaner	恒温式空气滤清器	trammel bar	游标前束测量规
thermo-time switch	温控定时开关	transmission case	变速器壳
three-way catalytic converter（TWC）	三元催化转化器	transmission clutch	变速器换挡离合器
		transmission housing	变速器壳
three-way valve（TWV）	三通阀	trickle charger	微电流充电器
throttle actuator	节气门执行器	trigger wheel	磁阻轮
throttle body	节气门体	trouble spot	出故障处，故障点
throttle body injection（TBI）	节气门体喷射	trunk deck	行李箱盖
throttle opening	节气门开度	tuned intake runners	调谐进气管
throttle position sensor	节气门位置传感器	turbo boost	涡轮增压器增压压力
throttle response	节气门响应	turbo lag	增压滞后
throw-out bearing	分离轴承	turbocharged car	涡轮增压轿车
thrust angle	推力角，推力线	turn signal light	转向信号灯
thrust bearing	推力轴承	twin clutch	双离合器
thrust washer	推力垫圈	tyre chains	轮胎防滑链
timing belt	正时带	U	
timing chain	正时链条	ULEV	极低排放车辆
timing light	正时灯	unit injector	泵喷嘴
timing mark	正时标记	unit pump	单体泵
tipping effect	侧倾效应	unsprung weight	非悬架重量
top speed	最高车速	upshift point	升挡点
torque converter	液力变矩器	V	
torque wrench	扭力扳手	vacuum advance mechanism	真空式点火提前角调节装置
Torsen differential	托森差速器		
torsion bar	扭杆弹簧	vacuum booster	真空助力器

续表

专业术语	中文含义	专业术语	中文含义
vacuum cleaner	真空吸尘器	weld line	焊接线
vacuum gauge	真空表	wet clutch	湿式离合器
vacuum hose	真空软管	wet sleeve	湿式气缸套
valve guide	气门导管	wheel alignment	车轮定位
valve lifter	气门挺柱	wheel cylinder	轮缸
valve overlap	气门叠开，气门重叠	wheel rotation	车轮换位
valve seat	气门座	wheel tracking	（前轮与后轮）同辙行驶
valve spring	气门弹簧	wide-open throttle（WOT）	大节气门开度（WOT）
valve stem	气门杆	wind resistance	空气阻力，风阻
valve timing	气门正时	window defroster	风窗除霜器
valve train	气门机构，气门组	wiper motor	刮水器电动机
vane-type air-flow sensor	叶片式空气流量计	wire brush	钢丝刷
vapor canister	蒸气罐	wire mesh	（金属、钢、塑料）丝网，线网
variable valve timing（VVT）	可变气门定时		
vehicle speed sensor	车速传感器	wire wheel	钢丝轮
vibration damper	减振器	wiring diagram	电路图
viscosity compensator valve	黏度补偿阀	wiring harness	线束
voltage regulator	电压调节器	working cylinder	工作缸
volumetric efficiency	容积效率，充气效率	working plunger	工作活塞
V-type engine	V形发动机	worm and wheel gear	蜗杆蜗轮机构
VVT-i（Variable Valve Timing with intelligent）	智能型可变气门定时	worm gear	蜗轮
W		worm-and-roller steering gerar	蜗杆滚轮式转向器
waste gate	旁通阀	worm-gear pair	蜗杆副
water jacket	水套	wrist pin	曲柄销，连杆轴颈
water pump	水泵		
water separator	（油）水分离器	Z	
wedge chamber	楔形燃烧室	ZEV	零排放车辆

Appendix II
Common English-Chinese Abbreviations on Automobile
常用汽车英语缩略语

英语缩略语	含 义	英语缩略语	含 义
1GR	first gear （第）一挡	ACM	① airbag control module （安全）气囊控制模块
2GR	second gear （第）二挡		② audio control module 音响控制模块
2WD	two wheel drive 两轮（4×2）驱动	ACS	air conditioning system 空调系统
3GR	third gear （第）三挡	ACT	air charge temperature 进气温度
4GR	fourth gear （第）四挡	ADL	automatic door lock 自动门锁
4WD	four wheel drive 四轮（4×4）驱动	AEC	automotive emission control 汽车排放控制
4WS	four wheel steering 四轮转向	AFC	air-fuel control 空燃比调节装置
5GR	fifth gear （第）五挡	AFE	automobile fuel economy 汽车燃油经济性
A		AFL	adaptive forward lighting system 自适应前部灯光系统
A/C，AC	air conditioner, air conditioning 空调	AFS	① air flow sensor 空气流量计
A/F	air fuel ratio 空燃比		② air-fuel ration sensor （丰田公司用语）空燃比传感器
A/T 或 AT	automatic transmission [transaxle] 自动变速器 [变速驱动桥]	AH	active handling 主动操作
A4WD	automatic four-wheel drive 自动四轮驱动	AH，a-h	ampere-hour 安·时（A·h）
AAA	American Automobile Association 美国汽车协会	AI	（secondary）air injection 二次空气喷射
ABDC	after bottom dead center 下止点后	AIP	air injection pump 二次空气喷射泵
ABS	anti-lock brake system 防抱死制动系统	AIR	secondary air injection 二次空气喷射
ACC	① accessory 附件	AIV	air injection valve 空气喷射阀
	② adaption cruise control 自适应巡航控制装置	ALB	anti-lock brake system 防抱死制动系统
	③ air conditioning clutch 空调离合器	ALC	① automatic level control （悬架）高度自动控制，自动调平
ACCEL	accelerator 加速踏板		② automatic lamp control 灯光自动控制
ACCRY	accessory 附件	AM	air management （二次空气喷射）空气管理
ACCS	air conditioning cycling switch 空调循环开关	AM/FM	amplitude modulation/frequency modulation （无线电）调幅/调频
ACCUM	accumulator 蓄压器	AMT	automatic/manual transmission [transaxle] 自动/手动一体式变速器 [变速驱动桥]
ACEA	European Automobile Manufacturers Association 欧洲汽车制造商协会	ANSI	American National Standards Institute 美国国家标准协会
ACIS	acoustic control induction system 声控进气系统	ANT	antenna 天线
ACL	air cleaner 空气滤清器		

续表

英语缩略语	含义	英语缩略语	含义
AP	accelerator pedal 加速踏板	ATX	automatic transmission-front wheel drive 前驱自动变速器（克莱斯勒公司用语）
APCM	accessory power control module 附件电源控制模块	AVM	automatic vehicle monitoring 车辆自动检测
API	American Petroleum Institute 美国石油学会	AWD	all wheel drive 全轮驱动
		AWG	American wire gage 美国线（径）规
APP	accelerator pedal position 加速踏板位置	AWP	awaiting parts 维修备件
APPS	accelerator pedal position sensor 加速踏板位置传感器	B	
		B/L	bi-level （空调出风）分层通风，双向
APS	absolute pressure sensor 绝对压力传感器	BA	brake assist 辅助制动装置
APT	adjustable part throttle 部分可调节气门	BARO	barometric pressure 气压，大气压力
APV	all purpose vehicle 多用途车辆	BAS	brake assist system 制动辅助系统
AQS	air quality sensor 空气品质传感器	BAT，BATT	battery 蓄电池
ARC	active ride control 汽车平顺性自动控制	BBDC	before bottom dead center 下止点前
ASC	acceleration anti-slip control 加速防滑控制，牵引力控制	BBW	brake by wire 汽车电制动系统
		BCM	① body control module 车身控制模块
ASE	Automotive Service Excellence（美国）汽车维修技能鉴定协会		② brake control module 制动控制模块
		BDC	bottom dead center 下止点
ASM	① accelerator and servo control module 加速踏板和伺服控制模块	BHP，b.h.p.	brake horsepower 制动功率
		BLW	blower 鼓风机
	② assembly 总成	BM	breakdown maintenance 故障维修
ASR	① acceleration [anti] slip regulation 防滑调节，牵引力控制	BMW	【德语】Bayerische Motoren Werke 宝马汽车公司
	② acceleration slip regulation 汽车驱动防滑控制系统	BP	① back pressure 背压
			② brake pressure 制动压力
ASSY，ASY.	assembly 总成		③ best power 最佳功率
AT	① automatic transmission 自动变速器	BPP	brake pedal position 制动踏板位置
	② automatic transmission fluid 自动变速器油	BPS	boot pressure sensor 增压压力传感器
		BT	brake/transmission 制动器/变速器（互锁）
ATA	anti-theft alarm 防盗报警（装置）	BTDC	before top dead center 上止点前
ATC	① automatic transfer case 自动分动器	BTM	battery thermal module 蓄电池加热模块
	② automatic temperature control 自动温度	BTSI	brake transmission shih interlock 制动变速器换挡互锁
ATDC	after top dead center 上止点后		
ATF	automatic transmission fluid 自动变速器油[液]	BTU	British Thermal Units 英制热量单位
		BVSV	bimetallic vacuum switching valve 双金属真空开关阀
ATFT	automatic transmission fluid temperature 自动变速器油温度	C	
ATSLC	automatic transmission shift lock control 自动变速器换挡锁止控制	C/Ltr	cigar lighter 点烟器
		C/OPN	circuit open 开路

续表

英语缩略语	含义	英语缩略语	含义
CA	crank angle 曲轴转角	CD	① coefficient of drag （空气）阻力系数，风阻系数
CAC	charge air cooler 进气冷却器，中冷器		② compact disc 光盘
CAD	computer aided design 计算机辅助设计	CDV	car derived van 基于轿车平台的厢式车
CAE	computer aided engineering 计算机辅助工程	CE	commutator end 整流子端
CAFE	corporate average fuel economy 公司平均油耗	CEGR	cooling EGR 冷却式废气再循环
		CEX	cabin exchanger 客厢[驾驶室]热交换器
CAL	calibration 校准	CH	channel 频道，通道
Cam	camshaft 凸轮轴	CHG	charging 充电
CANP	canister purge 炭罐清污[脱附]	CHK ENG	check engine （警告灯）检查发动机
CAP	crank angular position 曲柄相位角	CHMSL	center high mount stop lamp 中置高位制动灯
CARB	California Air Resources Board 加利福尼亚州大气资源局	CHT	cylinder head temperature 气缸盖温度
CAS	crank angle sensor 曲轴位置传感器	CI	compression ignition 压燃
CAT	catalyst 催化剂或催化转化器	CID	① center information display 中央信息显示屏
CB	circuit breaker 电路断路器		
CBE	cab-behind-engine 长头驾驶室（的）		② cubic inch displacement 立方英寸排量
CC	① coast clutch 滑行离合器	CIS	continuous injection system 汽油连续喷射系统
	② climate control （客厢）气候控制		
	③ combustion chamber 燃烧室	CJB	central junction box 中央接[集]线盒
CCC	① computer command control 计算机指令控制	CKD	completely knocked down kits 全散件组装
		CKP	crankshaft position 曲轴位置
	② converter clutch control 变矩器锁止离合器控制	CKPS	crankshaft position sensor 曲轴位置传感器
		CKT	circuit 电路
CCE	command control equipment 指令控制装置	CL	① closed loop 闭环
CCM	① chassis control module 底盘控制模块		② clutch 离合器
	② comprehensive components monitor 部件综合监视器	CLR	① clear 清除，清零；（导线颜色代号）透明的
	③ convenience charge module 便捷充电模块		② colo(u)r 颜色，色彩
			③ cooler 冷却器
	④ coupling control module 离合器控制模块	CLS	coolant level switch 冷却液液面开关
		CLV	calculate load value 计算负荷值
CCOT	cycling clutch orifice tube （空调）循环离合器节流孔管	CMC	compressor motor controller 压缩机电动机控制器
CCP	climate control panel 空调控制板	CMP	camshaft position 凸轮轴位置
CCS	cruise control system 汽车巡航控制系统	CMPS	camshaft position sensor 凸轮轴位置传感器

续表

英语缩略语	含 义	英语缩略语	含 义
CMS	computer monitor system 计算机监视系统	CTD	① content theft deterrent （通用汽车公司）内带防盗
CN	cetane number 十六烷值		
C-NCAP	China New Car Assessment Program 中国新车评价规程		② controlled traction differential 可控制牵引力差速器
CNG	compressed natural gas 压缩天然气	CTO，CTOX	continuous trap oxidizer 连续捕集式氧化器
CO	① carbon monoxide 一氧化碳	CTP	closed throttle position 节气门关闭位置
	② circuit open 电路开路	Ctrl	① control 控制，调节，操纵，管理
Coax	coaxial 同[共]轴的		② controlled （被）控制的
COE	cab over engine 平头驾驶室	CTS	coolant temperature sensor 冷却液温度传感器
COMB	combination 组合（式的）		
COMM	communication 通信	CV	① commercial vehicle 商用车
Conn	connector 插[连]接器		② constant velocity 等速
CONV	converter 变矩器		③ constant velocity joint 等速万向节
COP	coil-on-plug 装在火花塞上的点火线圈，笔式点火线圈	CVJ，CV	joint constant velocity joint 等速万向节
		CVRSS	continuously variable road sensing suspension 连续路感调谐悬架
CP	crankshaft position 曲轴位置		
CPA	connector position assurance 插接器位置保证	CVT	continuously variable transmission 无级变速器
CPE	coupe 双门乘用[轿]车	CW	curb weight （汽车）整备质量
CPP	clutch pedal position 离合器踏板位置	CYL	cylinder 气缸
CPS	① central power supply 中央电源	D	
	② crankshaft position sensor 曲轴位置传感器	D	① drive（自动变速器）前进挡位，D 挡位
			② diagonal（bias）（轮胎）斜交（线的）
CPU	central processing unit 中央处理器	DAB	delayed accessory bus 附件延时总线
CR	① common rail 共轨	DC	① direct current 直流电
	② cream 奶油色（的）		② drag coefficient 风阻系数，空气阻力系数
CRI	common rail injection 共轨喷射		
CRS	① child restraint seat 儿童安全[约束型]座椅		③ duty cycle 占空比
			④ dead center 止点
	② child restraint system 儿童约束（保护）系统	DCI	direct cylinder injection 直接喷入气缸
		DCM	① door control module 车门控制模块
CRT	cathode ray tube 阴极射线管		② display control module 显示器控制模块
CRTC	cathode ray tube controller 阴极射线管控制器	DDE	digital diesel electronics 数字式柴油机电子装置
CS	① charging system 充电系统	DDM	driver-door module 驾驶员车门控制模块
	② crankshaft 曲轴	DE	drive end 驱动端

续表

英语缩略语	含 义	英语缩略语	含 义
DEC	digital electronic controller 数字式电子控制器	DME	digital motor electronics 数字式电动机电子系统
DEF	defogger 除雾器	DMM	① digital multimeter 数字式万用表
DERM	diagnostic energy reserve module 诊断能源储备模块		② damper motor module （空调）风门电动机模块
DFI	① direct fuel injection（柴油机）直接燃油喷射	DMSDS	drive motor speed and direction sensor 驱动电动机转速和方向传感器
	② digital fuel injection 数字燃油喷射（某些制造商对多点燃油喷射的称谓）	DMU	drive motor unit 驱动电动机单元
		DOHC	double overhead camshaft 双顶置凸轮轴
DFI	direct fuel injection 直接燃油喷射	DOT	Department of Transportation （美）交通部
DFL	deflector 导流器[板]	DOT1～DOT5	按美国交通部标准的五种制动液
DI	① distributor ignition 分电器点火	Double-VANOS	双凸轮轴可变气门正时系统
	② direct ignition 直接点火，无分电器点火	DPA	distributor pump assembly 分配泵总成
	③ direct injection 直接燃油喷射，直喷	DPF	① differential pressure feed back 差压反馈
DIAG	diagnostic 诊断		② diesel particulate filter 柴油机微粒过滤器
DIC	① dimming control 变光控制	DPM	driver position module 驾驶员位置模块
	② driver information center 驾驶员信息中心	DRL	daytime running lamps 日间行车灯
		DR，Drvr	driver 驾驶员
DID	direct injection diesel 直喷式柴油机	DS	detonation sensor 爆震传感器
DIFF	differential 差速器	DSC	dynamic stability controller 动态稳定性控制器
DIM	① dash integration module 仪表板集成模块		
	② dimmer 变光器	DSCC	distance sensing cruise control 距离传感式巡航控制
	③ dimming 变光	DSG	direct shift gearbox 直接换挡变速器
DIN	【德语】德国工业标准	DSM	driver seat module 驾驶员座椅控制模块
DIS	① distributorless ignition system 无分电器点火系统	DSO	digital storage oscilloscope 数字式存储示波器
	② direct ignition system 直接点火系统	DSP	digital signal processor 数字信号处理器
DISI	direct injection spark ignition 直喷点火（马自达对其汽油直喷技术的专用术语）	DSPV	deceleration sensing proportioning valve 减速感应比例阀
DISP	display 显示器；显示	DTC，DTCS	diagnostic trouble code 诊断故障码
DLC	data link connector 诊断插座，数据（通信）链路插接器	DTM	diagnostic test mode 诊断测试模式
		DVD	digital video disc 数字（视频）光盘
DLI	distributorless ignition 无分电器点火	D-VVT	dual-VVT 双凸轮轴可变气门正时系统，进、排气门可变正时
DLX，DX	deluxe 豪华的，高级的		
DMCM	drive motor control module 驱动电动机控制模块	E	
		E	earth 搭铁，接地

续表

英语缩略语	含 义	英语缩略语	含 义
E/G	engine 发动机	ECM	① electronic control module 电子控制模块（ECU）
E85	含85%乙醇的混合汽油		② engine control module 发动机控制模块
EAC	engine air control 发动机空气量控制		
EAS	electronic air suspension 电子控制空气悬架	ECON	economy 经济，节约
EATC	electronic automatic temperature control （空调）电子自动温度控制	ECS	① electronic controlled suspension 电子控制悬架
			② emission control system 排放控制系统
EATCM	electronic automatic temperature control module （空调）电子自动温度控制模块		③ engine control system 发动机控制系统
EATX	electronic automatic transaxle 电控自动变速驱动桥	ECT	① electronic controlled transmission 电子控制变速器
			② electronic controlled transaxle 电子控制变速驱动桥
EBA	electronic brake assist 电子控制刹车辅助系统		③ engine coolant temperature 发动机冷却液温度
EBCM	① electronic body control module 车身电子控制模块	ECTS	engine coolant temperature sensor 发动机冷却液温度传感器
	② electronic brake control module 制动电子控制模块	ECU	electronic control unit 电子控制单元
EBD	electronic brake force distribution 电子制动力分配	EDC	electronic damper control 电子控制减振器
		EDF	electro-drive fan 电动风扇
EBTCM	electronic brake and traction control module 制动和牵引力电子控制模块	EDIS	electronic direct ignition system 电子直接点火系统
EBV	【德语】电子制动力分配（EBD）	EEC	engine electronic center 发动机电子控制中心
EC	① electrical center 电气中心		
	② engine control 发动机控制	EECS	evaporative emission control system 蒸发排放物控制系统
EC-AT	electronic controlled automatic transmission [transaxle] 电子控制自动变速器[变速驱动桥]	EEGR	electrically EGR 电动废气再循环
		EEPROM	electrically erasable programmable read only memory 电可擦可编程只读存储器
ECC	① electronic climate control 电子气候控制	EEVIR	evaporator equalized values in receiver （空调）储液器中蒸发器平衡值
	② electronic control clutch 电子控制离合器		
ECCS	electronic concentrated engine control system 发动机电子集中控制系统	EFE	early fuel evaporation 早期燃油蒸发
		EFI	electronic fuel injection 电子控制燃油喷射
ECD	electronic control diesel 电子控制式柴油机	EGAS	电子节气门
ECE，UNECE	United Nations Economic Commission for Europe 联合国欧洲经济委员会	EGR	exhaust gas recirculation 废气再循环
		EGRV	EGR valve 废气再循环阀
ECI-MULTI	electronically controlled injection multiport 电控多点燃油喷射	EGS	electronic gearbox control system 变速器电子控制系统
ECL	engine coolant level 发动机冷却液液面	EHB	electro-hydraulic brake 电动液压制动

续表

英语缩略语	含 义	英语缩略语	含 义
EHC	① electrically heated catalyst 电加热催化器[剂] ②【德语】车辆高度电子控制系统	ESB	expansion spring brake 膨胀弹簧制动器
EHPS	electro-hydraulic power steering 电动液压助力转向	ESC	① electric suspension control 电动悬架控制 ② electronic stabilization control（制动系统）电子稳定性控制
EHV	electric and hybrid vehicle 电动混合动力车	ESD	electrostatic discharge 静电放电
EI	electronic ignition 电子[无分电器]点火	ESI	electronic service information 电子服务信息
EIS	electronic ignition system 电子点火系统	ESN	electronic serial number 电子序列号
ELB	electronically controlled braking system 电控制动系统	ESP	electronic stability program 电子稳定性程序
ELC	electronic level control 电子高度[调平]控制	ESP/【德语】DSC	electronic stability program 电子车身稳定装置
ELR	emergency locking retractor （安全带）紧急锁止式卷收器	ETC	① electronic throttle control 电子节气门控制 ② electronic temperature control 电子温度控制 ③ electronic timing control 电子正时控制
EM	engine modification 发动机修正		
EMC	electromagnetic compatibility 电磁兼容性		
EMI	electromagnetic interference 电磁干扰		
EMR	engine maintenance reminder 发动机维护提醒器	ETCC	electronic touch climate control 触摸式电子气候控制
EMS	electronic modulated suspension 电子调节悬架	ETCS	electronic throttle control system 电子节气门控制装置
EOP	engine oil pressure 发动机机油压力	ETCS-i	electronic throttle control system-intelligent 智能型电子节气门控制装置
EOT	engine oil temperature 发动机机油温度		
EPA	① earth，accelerator pedal position sensor 加速踏板位置传感器搭铁 ② Environmental Protection Agency （美国）环保署	ETR	electronically tuned receiver （空调）电动调谐式储液器
		ETS	① enhanced traction system 加强型牵引力控制系统 ② exhaust-gas turbo supercharge 废气涡轮增压器
EPAS	electrical power assisted steering 电动助力转向		
EPB	electrical park brake 电控驻车制动	Euro III	欧盟第三阶段汽车排放限值标准，欧三排放法规（欧盟2000—2004年间执行，2005年起执行 Euro Ⅳ，我国于2008年1月实行相当于欧三排放法规的国三排放法规）
EPC	① electronic braking-pressure control 电子制动压力控制 ② electronic parts catalog 电子零件目录 ③ electronic power control 电子功率控制（指采用电子加速踏板和电子节气门）		
		Euro Ⅳ	欧盟第四阶段汽车排放限值标准，欧四排放法规（我国于2011年实行相当于欧四排放法规的国四排放法规）
EPM	electric power management 电源管理		
EPR	exhaust pressure regulator 排气压力调节器	EV	① electric vehicle 电动车 ② exhaust valve 排气门
EPROM	erasable programmable read only memory 可擦可编程只读存储器	EVAP	evaporative emission 蒸发排放物
		EVO	electronic variable orifice 电子可变量孔
EPS	electrical power steering 电动助力转向	EVP	exhaust gas recirculation valve position 废气再循环阀位置
ESA	electronic spark advance 电子点火提前		

续表

英语缩略语	含 义	英语缩略语	含 义
EVR	exhaust gas recirculation vacuum regulator 废气再循环真空调节器	FRP	① fuel rail pressure 轨压，燃油轨压力 ② fuel return pipe 燃油回油管 ③ fuel rail pressure 燃油轨油压
EWD	electrical wiring diagram 电路图	FRT	fuel rail temperature 燃油轨温度
EX，EXH	exhaust 排气	FRZ，FRZF	freeze frame 冻结帧，保持帧
F		FSI	fuel stratified injection 燃料分层喷射技术
F/A	fuel-air ratio 燃空比	FT	fuel trim 燃油修整 [正]
F/F	front engine/front wheel drive 发动机前置前驱	FTP	fuel tank pressure 燃油箱压力
F/R	front engine/rear wheel drive 发动机前置后驱	FWD	① forward 前进挡 ② four wheel drive 四轮驱动 ③ front wheel drive 前轮驱动
F4WD	full time four wheel drive 全时四轮驱动		
FBC	feedback control 反馈控制	G	
FC	① family car 家用轿车 ② fan control 风扇控制 ③ fuel cell(s) 燃料电池	G	（丰田 ECU 端子用词）凸轮轴位置传感器信号
		GA	ga(u)ge 仪表
FC IDL	feedback control idle 怠速反馈控制	GAWR	gross axle weight rating 轴额定总质量，额定轴载荷
FCHEV	fuel cell hybrid electric vehicle 燃料电池混合动力车	G-CON	G control G 力控制
FDC	fuel data center 燃油数据中心	GCW	gross combination weight 车辆总重
FE	fuel economy 燃油经济性	GDI	gasoline direct injection 汽油直接喷射
FEAD	front end accessory drive （发动机）前端附件驱动	GDL	gaseous-discharge lamp 气体放电灯
FED	Federal All United States except California （美国）除加州外联邦各州（在汽车法规上）	GDS	Global Diagnostic System （GM）全球诊断系统（2009 年后产品用此系统）
		GE	【德语】黄色
FEDS	fuel enable data stream 燃油启用数据流	GEM	generic electronic module 普通电子模块
FEEPROM	flash electrical erasable programmable read only memory 快存式电可擦除可编程只读存储器	GEN	generator 发电机
		GIS	geographic information system 地理信息系统
FF	① freeze frame 定格，冻结帧 ② flexible fuel 混合燃油（尤指乙醇汽油） ③ front-engine front-wheel-drive 前置发动机前轮驱动	GL	① gear lubricant 齿轮油（美国 API 齿轮油代号，如 GL1~GL5） ② grand luxury 特豪华的
		GM	General Motors （美）通用汽车公司
Fig.	figure 图，插图	GM-LAN	GM-local area network 通用汽车公司局域网
FIPG	formed in place gasket 就位成形密封垫		
FL	fusible link 易熔线	GND，GRD	ground 搭铁，接地
FMVSS	Federal Motor Vehicle Safety Standard （美）联邦汽车安全标准	GPM，gpm	gallons per mile 加仑数每英里
		GPS	global positioning system 全球卫星定位导航系统
FPCM	fuel pump control module 燃油泵控制模块		
FP，F/P	fuel pump 燃油泵	GR	gear ratio 传动比
FR	front-engine rear-wheel-drive 前置发动机后轮驱动	GT	① grand touring （乘用车）高性能（类） ② grand touring car 高性能轿 [乘用] 车

续表

英语缩略语	含　　义	英语缩略语	含　　义
GTDI	gas turbine direct injection　汽油涡轮增压直接喷射	HPS	① hand push steering　手按式转向（盘） ② high performance system　高性能系统
GVW	gross vehicle weight　车辆（最大）总质量	HPV	high pressure vapor　高压蒸气
GVWR	gross vehicle weight rating　车辆（最大）允许总质量	HS	high speed　高速
		HSCAN	high speed CAN　高速CAN
H		HSD	hybrid synergy drive　混合协同驱动
H/B，HB	hand back　（车身）舱背（式）	HT	① hard top　（乘用车）硬顶 ② high tension　高电压
H/CMPR	high compression　高压缩		
H/D	heater/defroster　加热器/除霜器	HTC	hydraulic torque converter　液力变矩器
h/w	height/width　（轮胎）高宽比	HTD，Htd	heated　加热的
H2	high speed，2WD　（分动器）高速挡位、两轮驱动	HTR	heater　（客厢）暖风装置，取暖器；加热器
Harn	harness　线束	HU	hydraulic unit　液压单元
HAS	heated air system　空气加热系统	HUD	head up display　抬头显示
HB	high beam　远光	HV	hybrid vehicle　混合动力车
HBA	hydraulic brake assist　液压制动辅助装置（紧急制动时助力用）	HVAC	heating，ventilation，air conditioning　取暖、通风和空调
HC	hydrocarbon　碳氢化合物	HVACM	heater vent air conditioning module　取暖、通风和空调模块
HCM	① HVAC control module　取暖、通风、空调控制模块 ② hydraulic control module　液压控制模块	HVM	heater vent module　暖风装置通风模块
		I	
		I/P，IP	instrument panel　仪表板
HD	heavy duty　重型的，加强型的	I/C	intercooler　中冷器
HDC	heavy duty cooling　加强型冷却	I/F	interface　接口，界面
HDLP	head lamp　前照灯	I/M，IM	inspection and maintenance　检查和维护
HDP	high pressure pump　高压泵	I/PEC	instrument panel electrical center　仪表板电气中心
HDS	Honda Diagnostic System　本田诊断系统		
HEGO	sensor heated exhaust oxygen sensor　加热型（排气）氧传感器	IA	intake air　进气
		IAC	idle air control　怠速空气控制
HEI	high energy ignition　高能点火	IACV	idle air control valve　怠速控制阀
HEV	hybrid electric vehicle　混合动力电动车	IAT	intake air temperature　进气温度
H-fuse	high current fuse　大电流熔断器	IATS	ntake air temperature sensor　进气温度传感器
Hi Alt	high altitude　高海拔		
HID	high-intensity discharge　高强度放电	IC	① ignition control　点火控制 ② integrated circuit　集成电路
HLA	hydraulic lash adjuster　液压式间隙调节器		
H-LP	head lamp　前照灯	ICCS	integrated chassis control system　底盘集成式控制系统
HO2S 1	heated oxygen sensor 1　1号（加热型）氧传感器		
HOS，HO2S	heated oxygen sensor　（加热型）氧传感器，前氧传感器	ICM	① ignition control module　点火控制模块 ② instrument control module　仪表控制模块
HP，hp	① high pressure　高压 ② horsepower　马力（1hp≈0.746kW）	ICP	injection control pressure　喷射控制压力
		ID	① identification　识别 ② inner diameter　内径
HPL	high pressure liquid　高压液[油]		

续表

英语缩略语	含义	英语缩略语	含义
IDI	① integrated direct ignition 集成式直接点火	ITCM	integrated transmission control module 变速器集成式控制模块
	② indirect（diesel）injection 柴油机间接喷射	IV	intelligent vehicle 智能汽车
IDL	idle 怠速	i-VTEC	intelligent VTEC 智能型可变配气正时和气门升程控制装置
IFI	indirect fuel injection （柴油机）间接燃油喷射	J	
		J/B	junction block （集中式）接线盒
IFS	① independent front suspension 独立式前悬架	J/C	junction connector 中间插接器
		JACV	jet air control valve 空气喷射控制阀
	② inertia fuel shutoff 惯性燃油切断	K	
IG	ignition 点火	KAM	keep alive memory 保持存储器
IGF	ignition reference 点火参考	KD	knock down 散件就地装配
IGN，ign.	ignition 点火	KNKL	（丰田 ECU 端子用词）2 号爆燃传感器信号电压端子
IGT	ignition timing 点火正时		
ILSAC	International Lubricants Standardization and Approval Committee 国际润滑剂标准化及批准委员会	KNKR	（丰田 ECU 端子用词）1 号爆燃传感器信号电压端子
IMA	integrated motor assisted 集成式电动机辅助	KOEO	key on engine off 钥匙在"ON"（接通）位置，但发动机不运转（此术语常用于发动机诊断上），静态测试
IMMO，IMMOBI	immobilizer （发动机）起动阻断器，发动机防盗器		
IMO	immobilizer （发动机）起动阻断器，发动机防盗器	KOER	key on engine running 钥匙在"ON"（接通）位置，但发动机运转（此术语常用于发动机诊断上），动态测试
IMRC	intake manifold runner control 进气歧管调谐控制，可变进气歧管长度控制	KS	knock sensor 爆震传感器
		L	
IMSC	intake manifold swirl control 进气歧管涡流控制	L4	① in line four cylinder engine 四缸直列发动机
IMT RV	intake manifold runner valve 进气歧管调谐阀，可变进气歧管长度控制阀		② low speed, 4WD（分动器）低速挡位、四轮驱动
IMU	inertial measurement unit 惯性测量单元	L6	in line six cylinder engine 六缸直列发动机
IN	① identification number 识别号	LB	low beam （前照灯）近光
	② intake 进气	LC	load cell 负荷传感器
INF，INFO	information 信息	LCD	liquid crystal display 液晶显示器
INJ	① injection 喷射	LCV	light commercial vehicle 轻型商用车
	② injector 喷油器	LD	light-duty 轻型的，轻负载（型）的
INT	intermittent 间歇（的），断续（的）	LDCL	left door closed locking 左门关闭锁止
IPC	instrument panel cluster 组合仪表	LDCM	left door control module 左门控制模块
IPM	① instrument panel module 仪表板模块	LDM	lamp driver module 车灯驱动模块
	② injector pulse width 喷油脉宽	LED	light emitting diode 发光二极管
ISC	idle speed control 怠速控制	LEE	low emission engine 低排放发动机
ISO	International Organization for Standardization 国际标准化组织	LEV	low emission vehicle 低排放汽车（执行美国加州大气资源局排放标准的汽车）
ISS	input shaft speed 输入轴转速		

续表

英语缩略语	含 义	英语缩略语	含 义
LEV II	二代低排放汽车（执行美国加州大气资源局 2004 年排放标准的汽车）	MB	Mercedes-Benz 梅塞德斯-奔驰
LF	left front 左前	MDI	Multiple Diagnostic Interface（GM） 多功能诊断仪
LH	left hand 左手（方，侧）	MDP	manifold differential pressure （进气）歧管压力差
LHD	left hand drive 左侧驾驶		
LLC	long-life coolant 长效冷却液	MDT	中负荷货车
lm	Lumens 流明	MF	maintenance free 免维护（的）
LNG	liquified natural gas 液化天然气	MFD	① multi-functional display 多功能显示器
LO	① lubricating oil 润滑油		② manufacturer 制造商
	② low 低的	MFI	multipoint fuel injection 多点燃油喷射
LP	① line pressure 管路压力	M-fuse	medium fuse 中电流熔断器
	② low pressure 低压	MHDE	中重负荷柴油发动机
	③ lamp 灯	MIL	malfunction indicator lamp 故障指示灯
LPG	liquefied petroleum gas 液化石油气	MIS	maintenance indicator system 保养指示系统
LR	left rear 左后	MIST	雾，（显示器字符）除雾
LSCAN	low speed CAN 低速 CAN	MLPS	manual lever position sensor 手动变速杆位置传感器
LSD	limited slip differential 限［防］滑式差速器		
LT	① long term 长期燃油修正	M-MT	multi-mode manual transmission 多模式手动变速器
	② light truck 轻型货车	MON	① motor octane number 马达法辛烷值
	③ light 浅色的，轻（便）的		② monitor 监视器
	④ left 左边（的）	MOST	media oriented systems transport 媒体定向系统传输
LTPI	low tire pressure indicator 轮胎低压指示器	MP	multipurpose 多用途的
LTPWS	low tire pressure warning system 轮胎低压警告系统	MPI	① multi-point injection 多点燃油喷射
			② multi-port injection 多点燃油喷射
LUS valve	lock up solenoid valve 锁止电磁阀	MPV	multipurpose passenger vehicle 多用途轿车
LWB	long wheel base 长轴距	MS Bus	moderate speed bus 中速总线
LX	luxury 豪华（的）	MSCAN	mid speed CAN 中速 CAN
M		MSDI	multiple-spark discharge ignition 多火花点火
M/C	mixture control 混合气调节		
MAF	mass air flow 质量型空气流量	MSM	memory seat module 座椅记忆模块
MAFS	mass air flow sensor 质量空气流量计［传感器］	MS, M&S	mud and snow （轮胎）泥雪地，全天候
		MTM	manual transmission 手动变速器
MAN.	manual 手动的；手册	MTX	manual transmission-front wheel drive 前驱手动变速器
MAP	manifold absolute pressure （进气）歧管绝对压力		
MAPS	manifold absolute pressure sensor 进气歧管绝对压力传感器	MT, M/T	manual transmission/transaxle 手动变速器/手动变速驱动桥
MAT	manifold air temperature （进气）歧管空气温度	N	
		N	① neutral （变速器）空挡
			② Newton 牛顿
MATS	manifold air temperature sensor 进气温度传感器		③ nitrogen 氮
		NA	naturally aspirated 自然吸气

续表

英语缩略语	含义	英语缩略语	含义
NATS	Nissan anti-theft system 日产汽车防盗系统	ODM	output drive module 驱动输出模块
NAVI	navigation 导航	ODO	odometer 里程表
NA，N/A	not available 不提供（的）	OE	① optional extra 选装件
NC	normally closed 常闭（的）		② original equipment 原装设备
NCAP	New Car Assessment Program 新车评价规程	OEM	original equipment manufacturer 原装设备制造商［厂］
NDS	neutral drive switch 空挡起动开关	OHC	overhead camshaft 顶置凸轮轴
NE	（丰田 ECU 端子用词）曲轴位置传感器信号电压端子	OHV	overhead valve 顶置气门
		OH，O/H	overhaul 大修
NEG	negative 负的	OL，OP	open loop 开环
NHP	nominal horsepower 标定功率	OPT	option 选装件
NHTSA	National Highway Traffic Safety Administration （美）国家公路交通安全署	ORC	oxidation reduction convener catalytic 氧化还原催化转化器
Ni-MH	nickel metal hydride 镍金属氢化物	ORVR	on-board refilling vapor recovery 车载加油蒸汽回收（装置）
NLGI	National Lubricating Grease Institute 全美润滑脂学会	OSC	output status control 输出状态控制
NO	normally open 常开（的）	OSRM，SRVM	out side rear view mirror 车外后视镜
NORM	normal position 通常位置	OSS	output shaft speed 输出轴转速
NOVRAM	non-volatile random access memory 非易失性随机存储器	OS，O2S	oxygen sensor 氧传感器
		Overtemp	over temperature 温度过高
NOX，Nox	nitrogen oxide 氮氧化物	OWC	one way clutch 单向离合器
NT	net tons 净重吨数	P	
NTC	negative temperature coefficient 负温度系数	P	park 驻车;（自动变速器）驻车挡;停车场
NVH	noise，vibrations and harshness 噪声、振动和不平顺性	P/B	power brakes 电动制动器
		PAB	power-assisted brake 助力制动
O		PAIR	pulsed secondary air injection 脉冲二次空气喷射
O/D	overdrive （变速器）超速挡		
O/S	oversize 加大尺寸	PAM	parking assistant module 驻车辅助装置模块
O2S	oxygen sensor 氧传感器		
OBC	on-board computer 车载计算机	PASS	① passenger 乘客
OBD	on-board diagnostic 车载诊断装置		② personal automotive security system 汽车个人防盗系统
OBD II	on-board diagnostics second generation 第二代车载诊断装置	PATS	passive anti-theft system 被动防盗系统
OBD STAT	OBD status （显示器用字符）车载诊断装置状况	PC	① passenger calf 乘用车,小客车
			② pressure control 压力控制
OC	① oxidation catalyst 氧化催化剂	PCB	printed circuit board 印刷电路板
	② oxidation catalytic convener 氧化催化转化器	PCM	powertrain control module 动力系统控制模块
OCV	oil control valve 机油控制阀		
OD	overdrive 超速传动	PCS	pressure control solenoid 压力控制电磁阀
ODD	output drive date 输出驱动器数据		

续表

英语缩略语	含义	英语缩略语	含义
PCSV	purge control solenoid 清污控制电磁阀	PROM	programmable read only memory 可编程只读存储器
PCV	positive crankcase ventilation 曲轴箱强制通风	PSA	Peugeot/Citroen SA 【法语】标致/雪铁龙公司
PDM	passenger door module 乘客车门模块	PSC	Dower steering control 动力转向控制
PEPS	passive entry and passive start 被动进入和被动起动	PSCM	① power steering control module 动力转向控制模块
PFI	port fuel injection（system） 进气口燃油喷射（系统）		② passenger scat control module 乘客座椅控制模块
PGM-FI	programmed fuel injection 程控燃油喷射	PSD	power sliding door 电动滑门
PHV	plug-in hybrid vehicle 插电式混合动力车（可插入市电进行充电的混合动力车）	PSGR	passenger 乘客
		PSP	power steering pressure 动力转向液压
PID	parameter identification 参数识别	PS，P/S	power steering 动力转向
PIHEV	plug-in hybrid electric vehicle 插电式混合动力电动车（可插入市电进行充电的混合动力电动车）	PT	pressure-time （康明斯喷油泵）压力-时间
		PTC	positive temperature coefficient 正温度系数
PIM	power inverter module 电源逆变器模块	PTO	power take-off 取力器
PIN	personal identification number 个人识别号	PTOX	periodic trap oxidizer 周期捕集式氧化器
PIP	position indicator pulse （曲轴）位置指示器脉冲	PTS	parktronic system 电子驻车制动装置
		PU	pickup 轻型客货两用车，皮卡
PK	peak 峰值	PV	proportioning valve 比例阀
PKB	parking brake 驻车制动器	PW	power window 电动车窗
PLS	① pulsating air system 脉冲空气系统	PWM	pulse width modulated 脉宽调制的
	② pulse 脉冲，脉动	PW	① power position（自动变速器）动力位置
PM	① particulate matter 微粒		
	② permanent magnet generator 永磁发电机		② power 电源
PNP	park/neutral position 驻车挡/空挡位置	Q	
PN，P/N	① park/neutral 驻车挡/空挡	QA	quality assurance 质量保证，质保
	② part/number，part number 零件号	QDM	quad driver module 四驱动器模块
POA	pilot operated absolute valve 绝对先导阀	R	
POS	① positive 正（极）的	R	① radial tire 子午线轮胎
	② position 位置		② relay 继电器
POT	potentiometer variable resistor 电位计式可变电阻器		③ replacement 更换
			④ reverse 倒挡
PPM	① pats per million 百万分率		⑤ right 右（的）
	② pulses per minute 脉冲次数每分	R&B	recirculating ball 循环球
PPS	progressive power steering 电子控制液压动力转向系统	R&D	research and development 研究与开发，研发
		R&I	remove and install 拆卸和安装，拆装
PR	ply rating （轮胎）层级	R/B	relay block 继电器盒
PRESS	pressure 压力	R/R	rear engine/rear wheel drive 发动机后置后驱
PRNDL	park-reverse-neutral-drive-low （自动变速器）P.R.N.D.L 挡位，驻车挡-倒挡-空挡-行车挡-低挡	R-12	refrigerant-12 R-12 制冷剂
		RAM	random access memory 随机存储器

续表

英语缩略语	含　　义	英语缩略语	含　　义
RAP	① retained accessory power　附件保持电源 ② remote anti-theft personality　个性化遥控防盗装置	RU	① running　运转，运行 ② rust　锈，铁锈色
		RV	recreational vehicle　休闲[娱乐]车
RAV	remote activation verification　遥控激活验证	RVC	rear vision camera　后视摄像机
		RWD	rear wheel drive　后轮驱动
RAV4	recreational active vehicle 4WD　四轮驱动灵巧型休闲车	S	
		S	① stroke　行程 ② speed　挡
RB	roll bar　防滚杆（活顶篷车翻车保护）		
RCDLR	remote control door lock receiver　遥控门锁接收器	S4WD	selectable four wheel drive　选择型四轮驱动
RCM	restraint control module　约束（安全气囊）控制模块	SA	spark advance　点火提前角
		SABV	secondary air bypass valve　二次空气旁通阀
RDCM	right door control module　右门控制模块		
REC	recyle　再循环	SACV	secondary air check valve　二次空气单向阀
REGTS	recirculated exhaust gas temperature sensor　废气再循环温度传感器	SAE	Society of Automotive Engineers　（美国）汽车工程师学会
REM	rear electronic module　后电子控制模块	SAS	① slow adjust screw　怠速混合气浓度调节螺钉 ② steering angle sensor　转向角度传感器
REV	① reverse　倒挡 ② revolution　转		
RF	① right front　右前 ② radio frequency　无线电频率	SBC	sensotronic brake control　电子传感制动控制
		SC	supercharger　机械式增压器
RFA	remote function actuator（门锁）遥控功能执行器	SCB	supercharger bypass　机械式增压器旁通
RH	right hand　右手[方，侧]	SCM	seat control module　座椅控制模块
RHD	right-hand drive　右侧驾驶	SCR	① selective catalyst reduction　选择性催化剂还原 ② silicon controlled rectifier　可控硅整流器（晶闸管）
RKE	remote keyless entry　无线遥控门锁		
RLY	relay　继电器		
RM	relay module　继电器模块		
ROM	read only memory　只读存储器	SCV	① spark control valve　点火控制阀 ② swirl control valve　湍[涡]流控制阀
RON	research octane number　研究法辛烷值		
RPE	rotary piston engine　转子发动机		
RPM	① revolutions per minute　转/分（r/min） ② engine speed　发动机转速	SDM	sensing and diagnostic module　传感和诊断模块
		SDN	sedan　乘用车，轿车
RPO	regular production option　正规生产选装件	SEFI	sequential electronic fuel injection　电子顺序燃油喷射
RPS	rail pressure sensor　轨压传感器		
RR	right rear　右后		
RSE	rear seat entertainment system　后座娱乐系统	SEO	special equipment option　特殊装备选装件
		SET-DECEL	设定-减速
RSM	rain sensor module　雨滴传感器模块	SE，SEN	sensor　传感器
RSS	road sensing suspension　路感式悬架	SF	① splice pack　接线组[盒] ②（汽油机机油）SF级（按API分类，适用于1980—1988年美国设计规范车用汽油机）
RTD	real time damping　实时阻尼		
RTV	room temperature vulcanizing sealer　室温硫化密封剂		

续表

英语缩略语	含义	英语缩略语	含义
SFC	specific fuel consumption 比油耗率,燃油消耗率	SPT	seat belt pre-tensioner 安全带预收紧器
		Spt	sport 运动(模式)
SFI	① sequential fuel injection 顺序燃油喷射 ② sequential multiport fuel injection 顺序多点燃油喷射	SPV	special purpose vehicle 专用汽车
		SR	① sliding roof 滑动天窗 ② silver 银灰色(的)
SG	(汽油机机油)SG级(按API分类,适用于1989—1992年美国设计规范车用汽油机)	SRC	service fide control 运转平顺性控制
		SRI	service reminder indicator 维护提示器,保养指示灯
SGCM	starter/generator control module 起动机/发电机控制模块	SRS	supplemental restraint system 辅助约束系统(指安全带和安全气囊)
SGL	super grand luxurious 超豪华	SRT	system readiness test 系统准备状态测试
SGS	safe-guard system 安全防护系统		
SH	(汽油机机油)SH级(按API分类,适用于1993—1996年美国设计规范车用汽油机)	SS	shift solenoid 换挡电磁阀
		SST	special service tools 专用维修工具
SI	① spark ignition 火花点火 ② System International 国际单位制	ST	① scan tool 故障诊断仪 ② short trim (燃油修正)短期修正 ③ stability track 稳定性和牵引力控制装置
SIAB	side impact airbag 侧碰撞安全气囊		
SIDI	spark ignition direct injection 火花点火直喷	STC	stability and traction control 稳定性和牵引力控制(装置)
SIR	supplemental inflatable restraint 辅助充气约束装置	STLR	semitrailer 半挂车
SIS	① side impact sensor 侧碰撞传感器 ② spark ignition system 点火系统	STP	stop 制动
		STRG	① steering 转向 ② steering gear 转向器[机]
SJ	(汽油机机油)SJ级(按API分类,适用于1997~2002年美国设计规范车用汽油机)	SUV	sport utility vehicle 运动型多用途车,多用途跑车
SJ/B	smart junction block 智能型接线盒	SW	① 【德语】黑色 ② switch 开关
SKD	semi knockdown 半散件组装		
SLA	short long arm (悬架)长短(横摆)臂	SWB	short wheelbase 短轴距
SLP	① stop lamp 制动灯 ② shift lever position 变速杆位置	SWPS	steering wheel position sensor 转向盘位置传感器
SMFI	sequential multipoint fuel injection 顺序多点燃油喷射	T	
SOHC	single over head shaft 单顶置凸轮轴	T	① turbo-charge 涡轮增压 ② temperature 温度
SOL	solenoid 电磁阀,带活动衔铁的电磁线圈	T/A	transaxle 变速驱动桥
SOV	solenoid valve 电磁阀	T/F	tail front 尾前方
SPD	speed 转速,车速	T/M	transmission 变速器
SPEC	specification 规格,技术条件[参数]	T/R	tail rear 尾后方
SPI	① single point injection 单点燃油喷射 ② smoke puff limiter 烟雾限止器	TAB	thermal air bypass 热作用空气旁路
		TAC	① tachometer 转速表 ② throttle actuator control 节气门执行器控制
SPS	① service programming system(GM)维修编程系统 ② speed signal 转速信号	TACH	tachometer 转速表

续表

英语缩略语	含 义	英语缩略语	含 义
TAP	① throttle adaptive pressure 节气门适配压力 ② throttle angle position 节气门开度位置 ③ transmission adaptive pressure 变速器适配压力	TIM	① tire inflation module 轮胎充气模块 ② tire inflation monitoring 轮胎充气监测
		TIS	Tech-line Information System（GM）技术热线信息系统
		TL	tubeless tire 无内胎轮胎
		TMC	Toyota Motor Corporation 丰田汽车公司
TB	throttle body 节气门体	TN	tan 棕褐色（的），茶色（的）
TC	turbo charger 涡轮增压器	TOC	transmission oil cooler 变速器油冷却器
TCC	torque converter clutch 液力变矩离合器	TOHC	twin overhead camshaft 双顶置凸轮轴
TCCP	torque converter clutch pressure 变矩器锁止离合器压力	TORQ	torque 转矩，力矩
		TP	throttle position 节气门位置
TCCS	Toyota computer-controlled system 丰田计算机控制系统	TPA	terminal positive assurance 端子正极确认
TCI	transistorized coil ignition 晶体管点火线圈	TPM	① tire pressure monitor 轮胎气压监测器 ② tire pressure monitoring 轮胎气压监测
TCM	transmission control module 变速器控制模块	TPMS	tire pressure monitoring system 轮胎气压监测系统
TCS	traction control system 循迹控制系统或牵引力控制系统	TPNP	transmission park neutral position 变速器驻车挡空挡位置
TCV	timing control valve 正时控制阀	TPS	① throttle position sensor 节气门位置传感器 ② throttle position switch 节气门位置开关
TC，T/C	① traction control 牵引力控制 ② transmission control 变速器控制 ③ turbocharger （废气）涡轮增压器		
		TR	transmission range 变速器挡位
TD	① theft deterrent 防盗 ② turbo diesel 涡轮增压柴油机	TRANS	① transaxle 变速驱动桥 ② transmission 变速器
TDC	top dead center 上止点	TRC	traction control system 牵引力控制装置
TDI	turbocharged direct injection 涡轮增压直接喷射	TRK	truck 货车，卡车
TEMP	temperature 温度	TRS	transmission range selection 变速器挡位选择
TEMS	Toyota electronic modulated suspension 丰田电子调制悬架	TSI	turbo-charging fuel stratified injection 涡轮增压燃油层状喷射
TERM	terminal 端子，接线柱	TSS	turbine shaft sensor 涡轮转速传感器
TFI	① thick film ignition 厚膜点火 ② turbo-charging fuel stratified injection 涡轮增压燃油层状喷射	TT	tell tail warning lamp 尾部告知警告灯
		TURBO	turbo-charge 涡轮增压
		TV	① throttle valve 节气门 ② television 电视
TFP	transmission fluid pressure 变速器油压力	TVS	thermal vacuum switch 温控真空开关
TFT	transmission fluid temperature 变速器油温	TVV	thermal vacuum valve 温控真空阀
THA	（丰田ECU端子用词）进气温度传感器信号电压	TWC	three way catalytic converter 三元催化转化器
THM	Turbo-Hydra-matic 涡轮液力自动变速器	TWC+OC	three way + oxidation catalytic converter 三元氧化催化转化器
THS	Toyota Hybrid System 丰田混合动力系统		
THW	（丰田ECU端子用词）冷却液温度传感器信号电压	TWI	tread wear indicator 轮胎花纹磨损指示器
		TXV	thermal expansion valve 热膨胀阀

续表

英语缩略语	含 义	英语缩略语	含 义
\multicolumn{2}{c}{U}	VC	① viscous clutch [coupling] 黏液离合器
UHP	universal hands phone 通用型手机		② voltage, constant 恒定电压（常指 ECM 提供的 5V 电压）
U/H	under-hood 发动机室盖		
U/HEC	under-hood electrical center 发动机室电气中心	VCC	viscous converter clutch 变矩器黏液（锁止）离合器
U/S, U.S	undersize 减[缩]小尺寸	VCI	vehicle communication interface 车辆通信接口
UART	universal asynchronous receiver/transmitter（数据线连接器）通用异步收发器	VCIM	vehicle communication interface mode 车辆通信接口模式
UDC	upper dead center 上止点	VCM	① variable cylinder management 可变气缸管理
UD, U/D	under-drive 爬行挡，低速传动（传动比大于 1 的传动）		② vehicle communication module 车辆通信模块
UEGO	universal exhaust gas oxygen sensor 宽带氧传感器		③ vehicle control module 车辆控制模块
UI	unit injector 泵-喷油器	VCR	variable compression ratio 可变压缩比
UIS	unit injector system 泵喷嘴系统	VCRM	variable control relay module 可调控继电器模块
UJ, U-joint	universal joint< 万向节	VCT	variable cam timing 可变凸轮轴正时
ULEV	ultra-low emission vehicle 超低排放车辆	VCT-i	variable cam timing-intelligent 智能型可变凸轮轴正时（VVT-i，智能型可变气门正时）
UP	unit pump（柴油机）单体泵		
UPS	unit pump system 单体泵装置	VCV	vacuum control valve 真空控制阀
URPA	ultrasonic rear parking assist 超声波后驻车辅助装置	VDOT	variable displacement orifice tube 变排量节流孔管
USB	universal serial bus 通用型串行总线	VDV	vacuum delay valve 真空延迟阀
US, U.S, USA	United States 美国	VECI	vehicle emission control information 车辆排放控制信息
UTD	universal theft deterrent 通用型防盗	VES	① variable effect steering 可变助力转向
UV	ultraviolet 紫外线		② vehicle entertainment system 车辆娱乐系统
\multicolumn{2}{c}{V}	VF	vacuum fluorescent 真空荧光
V	① valve 气门，气阀	V-flex	viscous flex coupling 黏液柔性离合器
	② voltage 电压	VIN	vehicle identification number 车辆识别代码
V dif	voltage difference 电压差	VIPS	variable induction port system 可变进气口系统
V ref	voltage reference 参考电压		
V.L FUEL	very low fuel 极低燃油（量，液面）	VIS	variable geometry intake system 可变几何形状进气系统
V.Low Press	very low pressures 极低压，（轮胎）胎压极低	VLV	valve 气门
V6	V 型 6 缸发动机	VMV	vacuum modulator valve 真空调制阀
V8	V 型 8 缸发动机	VOL	volume 音量
VAB	variable air bleed 可变空气量孔	VR	voltage regulator 电压调节器
VAC	① vacuum 真空	VRS	vehicle remote start 车辆遥控起动
	② vehicle access code 车辆访问代码		
VAF	volume air flow 体积型空气流量		
VAT	vane air temperature 叶片（式空气流量计中）空气温度		
VATS	vehicle anti-theft system 车辆防盗系统		

续表

英语缩略语	含义	英语缩略语	含义
VSA	vehicle stability assist 车辆稳定性控制装置	W/P	water pump 水泵
VSC	vehicle stability control 车辆稳定性控制（装置）	W/S	windshield 挡风玻璃
		WDS	Worldwide Diagnostic System 全球诊断系统
VSES	vehicle stability enhancement system 加强型车辆稳定性控制装置	WG, WGN	wagon 旅行车
		WHL	wheel 车轮
VSS	vehicle speed sensor 车速传感器	WOT	wide open throttle 节气门全开
VSV	① vacuum solenoid valve 真空电磁阀	WOTS	wide open throttle switch 节气门全开开关（在节气门全开时接通）
	② vacuum switching valve 真空开关[转换]阀	WPR	wiper 刮水器
VTA	voltage, throttle angle （丰田）节气门位置传感器信号电压	WS	【德语】白色
		WSS	wheel speed sensor 轮速传感器
VTEC	variable timing and lift electronic control （本田）可变配气正时和气门升程电子控制装置	WT	water tank 水箱
		WU-OC	warm up oxidation catalytic converter 暖机氧化催化转化器
VTV	vacuum transmitting valve 真空传输阀	WUP	wake up 唤醒
VVA	variable valve actuation 可变气门驱动	WU-TWC	warm up three way catalytic converter 暖机三元催化转化器
VVT	variable valve timing 可变气门正时		
VVT-i	variable valve timing-intelligent 智能型可变气门正时	X	
		XM	一种用于美国、加拿大的卫星无线电服务
VVTL-i	variable valve timing & lift-intelligent （丰田）智能型可变配气正时和气门升程	X-valve	expansion valve 膨胀阀
		Y	
VW	Volkswagen【德语】大众（汽车公司及汽车品牌）	YE, YEL	yellow 黄色（的）
		Z	
W		ZEV	zero emission vehicle 零排放车辆
W/B, w/b	wheel base 轴距		

References
参考文献

[1] 黄立新．汽车专业英语［M］．北京：高等教育出版社，2004．
[2] 陈晟闽．汽车专业实用英语［M］．北京：机械工业出版社，2011．
[3] 粟利萍．汽车实用英语［M］．第2版．北京：电子工业出版社，2008．
[4] 吴金顺，常同珍．汽车专业英语［M］．第2版．北京：北京理工大学出版社，2011．
[5] 王锦俞等．实用汽车维修英语［M］．第2版．北京：机械工业出版社，2011．
[6] 黄立新．汽车专业英语［M］．西安：西安电子科技大学出版社，2006．
[7] 边浩毅．汽车专业英语［M］．杭州：浙江大学出版社，2012．
[8] 张金柱．汽车商务英语［M］．北京：机械工业出版社，2006．
[9] 宋红英．汽车实用英语［M］．北京：高等教育出版社，2009．
[10] 王怡民．汽车商贸英语［M］．北京：人民交通出版社，2004．
[11] 李玉柱，罗新闻．汽车专业英语［M］．北京：科学出版社，2007．
[12] 黄汽驰．汽车专业英语［M］．北京：机械工业出版社，2005．
[13] 米芙铮．外贸英语函电［M］．北京：机械工业出版社，2009．
[14] 于明进．汽车服务工程专业英语［M］．北京：人民交通出版社，2008．
[15] 杨丽华，董俊英．贸易实务英语［M］．北京：首都经济贸易大学出版社，2002．
[16] 张立玉．汽车4S体系英语［M］．武汉：武汉大学出版社，2013．
[17] 张国方．汽车销售与服务［M］．北京：人民交通出版社，2006．
[18] 贾遂钧．如何做好汽车维修业务接待［M］．北京：机械工业出版社，2008．
[19] 张国方．汽车营销学［M］．北京：人民交通出版社，2008．
[20] 郎全栋．汽车文化［M］．北京：人民交通出版社，2002．
[21] 马林才．汽车实用英语［M］．北京：人民交通出版社，2004．
[22] 张发明．汽车品牌与文化［M］．北京：机械工业出版社，2008．
[23] 陆华忠．进口汽车维修英语［M］．沈阳：辽宁科学技术出版社，2001．
[24] 韩建保．汽车实用英语［M］．北京：高等教育出版社，2005．
[25] 夏雪松．进口汽车维修实用英语［M］．北京：人民交通出版社，2004．
[26] 张立玉．实用商务英语谈判［M］．北京：北京理工大学出版社，2003．
[27] 宋进桂．汽车专业英语读译教程［M］．北京：机械工业出版社，2007．
[28] 刘波，杨智勇．汽车维修工［M］．北京：化学工业出版社，2012．

新能源与智能汽车技术 丛书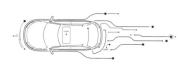

Interaction Design
in Intelligent Cockpit

智能座舱
人机交互设计

赵丹华　编著

化学工业出版社

·北京·

内容简介

　　科技发展给汽车座舱设计带来挑战，设计师需要应对新的设计对象、设计范式。本书在从传统到智能的座舱设计转向背景下，尝试提出智能座舱人机交互设计的方法论：基于空间、角色和动作的智能座舱交互设计和基于动作叙事的智能座舱交互设计。详细阐释了方法论的概念、使用的设计工具与流程，并附有案例。内容详实、严谨、深入浅出，图文并茂的呈现使读者能更顺利地理解和掌握智能座舱交互设计的新方法。

　　本书可作为高等院校工业设计、交互设计、数字媒体设计、车辆工程、软件工程专业学生的教材，也可作为用户体验研究员、汽车产品经理、汽车HMI设计师、汽车零部件设计师、车载信息系统设计师、导航/车载软件和App开发人员的参考书。

图书在版编目（CIP）数据

智能座舱人机交互设计 / 赵丹华编著． -- 北京：化学工业出版社，2024．11． --（新能源与智能汽车技术丛书）． -- ISBN 978-7-122-27496-0

Ⅰ．U463.83

中国国家版本馆CIP数据核字第2024GV2978号

责任编辑：张海丽　　　　　　　　　　　　文字编辑：袁　宁
责任校对：宋　玮　　　　　　　　　　　　装帧设计：王晓宇

出版发行：化学工业出版社（北京市东城区青年湖南街13号　邮政编码100011）
印　　装：北京宝隆世纪印刷有限公司
787mm×1092mm　1/16　印张9¾　字数225千字　2024年11月北京第1版第1次印刷

购书咨询：010-64518888　　　　　　　　　售后服务：010-64518899
网　　址：http：//www.cip.com.cn
凡购买本书，如有缺损质量问题，本社销售中心负责调换。

定　　价：79.00元　　　　　　　　　　　　　　　　　　　　版权所有　违者必究

前言

筹备这本书的伊始是全国正在热烈地向汽车电动化和智能化发起挑战，到这本书交给编辑的时候，国内正在上演着新能源车的混战，从价格战到出海战，新能源车已经成为一种成熟的业态，我们国家的新能源车产业链形成了闭环，中国自主品牌在各大车展上都绽放异彩。

从燃油车到新能源车，从机械化到智能化，我们正在经历一个范式改变的时代，即从动力时代到算力时代的改变。有意思的是，这两个时代之中，最典型的代表都是车，从早期的福特T型车流水线，到特斯拉的自动驾驶，车这个产品是当下时代科技和艺术的映射。智能技术为我们的座舱带来了无限多的可能，随着自动驾驶技术的不断迭代，人们从驾驶任务中逐渐得到解放，人们发现座舱逐渐成为生活的"第三空间"。可以冥想，可以野营，可以开会，可以小憩，在未来的智能座舱中，人们可以干什么，人们会有什么样的期待，设计师们可以进行什么样的畅想，都会和以前的那个时代有着巨大的差异。

《智能座舱人机交互设计》不仅关注造型和交互的问题，更关注出行体验和出行场景的问题，致力于基于场景的出行体验设计，探索人工智能技术下的人机交互新框架和方法，为智能时代的人车互动设计提供概念基础。

在本书的创作过程中，有幸得到了赵江洪教授的悉心指导，赵教授不仅以其丰富的专业知识和经验为本书提供了宝贵的建议，而且在书稿的修改和完善上给予了极大的帮助。同时，我也要感谢学生薛仲杰、刘雨菲、马羽佳、卓良、汪斯为、王炳权和李志扬对本书的编写工作的参与和贡献。此外，书中所呈现的部分研究成果，是湖南大学设计艺术学院智慧出行方向团队对智能座舱的深入探讨和实践的结晶。在此，我特别感谢所有智慧出行方向的团队成员。他们在座舱设计、技术开发、理论研究和创新探索方面的努力，极大地丰富了本书的内容。

　　本书探讨的是新能源车和未来智慧出行设计中的一个小部分，但仍然希望以这个小点映射出智能时代下设计活动、设计思考以及设计范式的转变。仅以此书来记录一个时代的开启。

赵丹华
2024 年 5 月 29 日
于岳麓山下

目录

第1章 智能座舱人机交互设计概论 ·· 001

    1.1 智能座舱交互设计——设计范式 ·· 002
        1.1.1 设计范式——设计迭代 ·· 003
        1.1.2 设计范式——实践反思 ·· 005
    1.2 智能座舱交互设计——设计对象 ·· 006
        1.2.1 设计对象——智能汽车 ·· 006
        1.2.2 设计对象——智能汽车技术架构 ·································· 011
        1.2.3 设计对象——智能座舱 ·· 013
        1.2.4 设计对象——智能座舱技术架构 ·································· 014
    1.3 智能座舱交互设计——设计场景 ·· 015
        1.3.1 交互设计场景——要素、场域和触点 ······························ 016
        1.3.2 交互设计场景——场景、叙事、价值 ······························ 018
        1.3.3 智能座舱人机交互设计方法论 ···································· 019

第2章 传统到智能的座舱设计转向 ·· 020

    2.1 汽车座舱技术演进 ·· 021
        2.1.1 传统机械化座舱 ·· 022
        2.1.2 电子化座舱 ·· 023
        2.1.3 智能辅助驾驶座舱 ·· 026
        2.1.4 智能驾驶座舱 ·· 027

2.2 汽车座舱的用户体验 …………………………………………………028
2.2.1 基础驾驶体验 …………………………………………………029
2.2.2 电子信息座舱的用户体验 …………………………………………030
2.2.3 智能座舱的用户体验 …………………………………………031
2.3 智能座舱的应用场景 …………………………………………………034
2.3.1 智能座舱人机共驾场景 …………………………………………034
2.3.2 智能座舱休闲娱乐场景 …………………………………………035
2.3.3 智能座舱办公／商务场景 ………………………………………036
2.3.4 车－家互联场景 …………………………………………………037

第 3 章 基于空间、角色和动作的智能座舱交互设计 …………………039

3.1 智能座舱人机交互设计概念 …………………………………………041
3.1.1 智能座舱的交互设计的操作定义 ………………………………041
3.1.2 智能座舱的交互设计问题 ………………………………………041
3.2 智能座舱人机交互要素 ………………………………………………042
3.2.1 智能座舱交互——空间 …………………………………………042
3.2.2 智能座舱交互——角色 …………………………………………043
3.2.3 智能座舱交互——动作 …………………………………………045
3.3 人机交互 SRA 设计流程 ……………………………………………050
3.4 空间交互接触点 ………………………………………………………051
3.4.1 交互触点的概念 …………………………………………………051
3.4.2 智能座舱的交互触点设计 ………………………………………052
3.5 人机交互 SRA 设计案例分析 ………………………………………055

第 4 章 基于动作叙事的智能座舱交互设计 ……………………………063

4.1 智能座舱人机交互——叙事设计理论框架 …………………………064
4.1.1 叙事的概念 ………………………………………………………064
4.1.2 叙事的内容 ………………………………………………………065
4.1.3 叙事方式 …………………………………………………………066
4.1.4 叙事的目标和意义 ………………………………………………068
4.2 智能座舱人机交互——叙事设计流程 ………………………………069
4.2.1 叙事设计的问题求解路径 ………………………………………069
4.2.2 叙事设计流程 ……………………………………………………071

        4.2.3　叙事设计工具——卡片 ……………………………………… 073
　　4.3　智能座舱人机交互叙事设计模型与设计策略 …………………………… 075
        4.3.1　智能座舱人机交互叙事设计模型 …………………………… 075
        4.3.2　智能座舱人机交互叙事设计策略 …………………………… 076
　　4.4　人机交互叙事设计案例分析 …………………………………………… 077
        4.4.1　场景和场景要素提取 ………………………………………… 077
        4.4.2　智能场景趋势调研 …………………………………………… 078
        4.4.3　设计概念生成与设计迭代 …………………………………… 079
        4.4.4　设计方案产出 ………………………………………………… 080

第 5 章　智能座舱人机交互设计工具 …………………………………………… 083

　　5.1　产品设计和设计工具 …………………………………………………… 084
        5.1.1　智能座舱造型设计的基本原则 ……………………………… 084
        5.1.2　产品设计工具 ………………………………………………… 085
　　5.2　座舱交互设计方法与工具 ……………………………………………… 090
        5.2.1　交互设计方法 ………………………………………………… 091
        5.2.2　交互设计工具 ………………………………………………… 095

第 6 章　智能座舱人机交互设计案例 …………………………………………… 102

　　6.1　亲子游戏座舱设计——Popo Racer ……………………………………… 103
        6.1.1　设计问题提出 ………………………………………………… 103
        6.1.2　基于人机交互框架应用的设计方案概述与创新点 ………… 103
        6.1.3　设计过程 ……………………………………………………… 107
　　6.2　车载智能机器人拟人化设计——电力规划局 ………………………… 112
        6.2.1　设计问题提出 ………………………………………………… 112
        6.2.2　基于人机交互框架应用的设计方案概述与创新点 ………… 112
        6.2.3　设计过程 ……………………………………………………… 116
　　6.3　绿色驾驶行为鼓励系统——"豹豹"车载智能语音助手 ……………… 118
        6.3.1　设计问题提出 ………………………………………………… 119
        6.3.2　基于人机交互框架应用的设计方案概述与创新点 ………… 119
        6.3.3　设计过程 ……………………………………………………… 122
　　6.4　个性化车载即时推荐系统——"盒你同行" …………………………… 126
        6.4.1　设计问题提出 ………………………………………………… 126

6.4.2　基于人机交互框架应用的设计方案概述与创新点 ……………… 127
6.4.3　设计过程 ………………………………………………………… 130

第 7 章　智能座舱未来发展趋势 …………………………………………… 133

7.1　智能座舱的车机发展趋势 …………………………………………… 134
7.1.1　智能化水平提升 …………………………………………………… 134
7.1.2　功能集成与定制化服务增加 ……………………………………… 136
7.1.3　数据安全与隐私保护加强 ………………………………………… 137

7.2　智能座舱体验发展趋势 ……………………………………………… 138
7.2.1　个性化与舒适性体验提出了新的人因要求 ……………………… 138
7.2.2　围绕便捷性的多模态交互出现 …………………………………… 140
7.2.3　多生态融合 ………………………………………………………… 141

7.3　L4+ 智慧出行展望 …………………………………………………… 142
7.3.1　汽车座舱从"移动空间"到"智能生活空间" ………………… 142
7.3.2　场景服务从"单点"向"交通网络"转变 ……………………… 143
7.3.3　出行场景从"单一"到"多种交通工具"涌现 ………………… 144

参考文献 ……………………………………………………………………… 146

第 1 章

智能座舱人机交互设计概论

1.1 智能座舱交互设计——设计范式
1.2 智能座舱交互设计——设计对象
1.3 智能座舱交互设计——设计场景

智能座舱人机交互设计有两个要讨论的主题，即"智能座舱"和"交互设计"，前者是设计对象范畴的问题，后者是设计过程范畴的问题。每个从事智能座舱人机交互设计的设计师，都必须清楚地了解这两个主题，并建构起自己的设计实践认识和理论框架，才能真正具备解决设计问题的能力。这意味着设计师要清晰地意识到，我们在做什么，我们要做什么。本章试图为全书提供一个可被讨论的设计问题，明确设计的意义，和便于掌握设计方法的概念框架。不过我们首先要认识到，智能化并不会给我们带来更多的"确定性"，世界也许会更加不可预测，而设计是"有意图的行动"，是"在不可预测的世界中引入有意图的变化"。因此，智能座舱人机交互设计的研究和学习，也应该是实践认识论的。勒温说："了解这个世界最好的方式就是去改变它。"

围绕智能座舱人机交互设计，本章先从设计过程（theories of how）的范畴讨论设计问题，即设计范式（design paradigm）的问题；然后，从设计对象（theories of what）的范畴讨论智能座舱问题，即设计对象的设计问题；最后，通过引入"场景"的概念和理论模型，讨论人机交互设计问题，并提出一种基于设计范式、设计对象和设计场景的"智能座舱人机交互设计方法论"。

1.1 智能座舱交互设计——设计范式

设计范式的问题是关于设计过程范畴的问题，即设计活动的行为方式、过程或方法的问题。比如，如何设计出符合用户需求的智能座舱？如何通过迭代设计策略获得迭代优势？因此，设计范式是指，试图找到实现特定价值或目标的途径和方法。对设计范式的研究就是，我们有意识地把"设计过程"与"设计对象"分开研究和讨论，以便从设计本体的视角理解设计，学习设计，寻找设计的价值。

设计是什么？这个问题的答案取决于"设计范式"与"设计对象"怎么联结，偏于产品的是产品设计，偏于交互的是交互设计，偏于智能座舱人机交互的是智能座舱人机交互设计。在这里，设计范式是"无本质"地存在，而设计对象并不具有本质意义上的规范性，设计对象是作为交流和表达"设计意图"的"物化"形式。假如我们承认智能座舱是人机交互设计的一种物化形式，就会建构相应的设计体系和设计流程，并获得设计话语权。从设计范式的角度，智能座舱人机交互设计的基本范式就是，寻找满足用户需求和实现用户价值的途径和方法。

设计范式（theories of how）的学习和研究一直是设计师非常关注的，比如《设计方法与策略：代尔夫特设计指南》中，推理设计、情境地图、文化探析、用户观察、用户访谈、问卷调查、焦点小组、用户旅程、思维导图、战略论、趋势分析和功能分析等，都是设计过程范畴的研究内容。同样的例子还有智能座舱的"体验设计"，本质上也是设计过程范畴的研究内容。体验设计并不直接获得"设计体验"，而是通过设计对象、人机互动和场景触点获得设计体验。

芬德利（Findeli）认为，人类的设计大体分为美（aesthetics）、逻辑（logic）和伦理（ethics）三个历史阶段：①美是设计发展的起源，是人类开始模仿自己对观察到的自然物"有意味的形式"的表征。比如，先民们在墓穴上撒红色矿物质的现象，就是一种象征性的、富有意味的形式，体现了先民们对生命和死亡的某种理解，"美"是设计的"第一性原理"。②设计发展的逻辑阶段，是人的理性认识能力发展阶段，是设计科学和技术科学发展的阶段，逻辑意味着因果关系和理性。③设计发展的伦理阶段，是表达人对所处环境和社会未来的困惑和解救的阶段。当人工智能几乎要终结人的智能傲慢时，又想回到人的价值和意义原点。下面将简要讨论两个通用的设计范式：设计迭代与实践反思。

1.1.1 设计范式——设计迭代

智能座舱是一个典型的"产品生命周期很长"的产品，可以不断迭代升级，具有智能科技和高端消费品的属性。因而，设计迭代是智能座舱的"自然属性"。不过，与生物体经历出生、成长、衰败到死亡的完整生命周期完全不同的是，智能座舱的生命周期可以通过设计迭代，获得新生命和产生新价值。迭代的概念是互联网思维的"信条"，也是智能座舱人机交互设计的重要思想。在概念上，设计迭代过程有点像我们日常生活中熟悉的做老面馒头的过程：上次发面时留下的面团作为这次发面的"老面"加入这次的面团，即智能座舱的设计迭代不完全是一种新旧设计的"替代"过程，而是一种自我迭代的过程。例如，人工智能大模型训练也被视为一种迭代过程，其中每个迭代步骤都会根据前一次迭代的结果来更新模型的权重和参数，以逐渐提高模型的性能和泛化能力。同样，智能座舱的 OTA（over-the-air technology，空中下载技术）通过网络从云服务器远程下载更新程序包，对智能座舱系统（硬件和软件）进行更新或升级，就像是给座舱安装一个可以不断更新的智能电脑系统。因此，在智能技术快速迭代的时代，是否具有优秀的迭代升级能力，在很大程度上决定了智能座舱的"产品生命周期"。

> **案例**
>
> 雷军称，小米作为全球前三的智能手机公司，最强的优势就是智能科技，小米在消费电子、操作系统、芯片、AI 等方面的能力都非常地强悍。一辆车的生命周期很长，只有下决心自研智能座舱和智能驾驶，才能做好迭代升级。

从方法论范畴，设计迭代是通过迭代的途径，实现"迭代优势"的目标，也称为"代际优势"。迭代优势甚至可以说是"降维打击"的竞争优势，这种打击往往是残酷的，给普遍存在的产品带来生存和发展的压力。中国已经进入设计和科技的"迭代加速"时代，中国算力总规模达到了每秒 1.97 万亿亿次浮点运算（2023 中国算力大会官方公布）。改革开放以来，我国的歼 20、5G、北斗卫星导航系统、神舟飞船、航母战斗群、量子计算、基因技术、电动汽车、电池、智能座舱等，初步显露出迭代优势，尤其是中国电动汽车形成的全产业链、全球市场、全谱系产品、多品牌生态和充分市场竞争的迭代优势，正是迭代跃升的重要标志性历史事件。

设计迭代的类型各有不同，如版本迭代、市场响应迭代、功能迭代、应急迭代等；设计迭代需要良好的设计团队，包括开发团队、测试团队、运维团队、市场团队、客服团队等；设计迭代需要具备优秀的数据分析能力，包括数据采集、数据清洗、数据建模、数据分析、数据输出等。但是,设计迭代最要紧的是,需要一个有远见和有"有意图行动力"的设计领袖。

从设计学习的范畴,优秀的设计师不仅善于重新理解前人在设计中对设计的理解,也善于重新理解自己曾经对设计的理解,进而形成自己的理解迭代,也可称为认知递归。"设计使人成为人"实质上是指,人的递归式学习使人在心智和行动能力上具备了设计能力,一种在自然中引入人的意图的能力。可以说,人工智能大模型学习的方式,就是亿万次迭代后出现的智能"涌现"。而智能涌现与人的设计能力,本质上都是递归性的。

设计问题求解(problem solving)研究认为,设计迭代是设计问题和问题解协同进化的问题。设计问题的"初始状态"和"目标状态"都是模糊和不确定的,需要通过一系列心理操作,将初始状态过渡到"中间状态",再将中间状态转换为目标状态,每个中间状态的"问题 - 问题解"共同定义一次迭代。图 1-1 中,每一次迭代都需要调用上一次迭代的解。所以,设计问题求解是一个在问题空间和解空间中协同进化的迭代过程。因此,设计迭代可以看作一个"递归"步骤,即调用上次设计(解 S_n)的一些特征属性来完成新设计(解 S_{n+1})。而当设计(方案)达到或满足一定条件时,停止迭代并输出设计,这是一个通用的设计迭代范式。

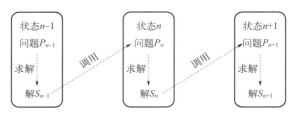

图 1-1　设计问题求解的协同进化模式

设计意图(design intention)研究认为,设计迭代本质上,是设计意图与认知解释的沟通问题,是指社会环境对设计"物种"的个体进行选择,适应环境的个体得以生存并繁殖后代,这是一个价值生成和价值判断的架构。其中,设计师的设计意图与用户的认知解释的沟通模式是自然选择的机制,如图 1-2 所示。图中"意图"与"形态"、"识别"与"解释"之间的实线,表示以造型特征为主的视觉特征的信息和知识传递;虚线表示以词语为主的概念语义的信息和知识传递。设计中,设计师通过视觉特征和概念语义来实现意图与形态之间的转换和迭代。因此,我们必须清楚,在设计迭代过程中,究竟什么是有意图的行动?什么是意图与有意图的行动之间的关系?值得注意的是,有观点认为,在实践理性领域,占中心地位的是有意图的行动而不是意图。

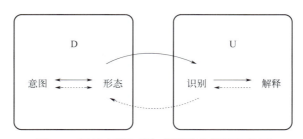

图 1-2　设计意图和认知解释的沟通进化机制

1.1.2 设计范式——实践反思

唐纳德·舍恩（Donald A.Schon）提出的"实践反思"（reflective practice，又称为实践反映），为设计研究提供了"实践中的认识"（knowing-in-practice）这样一条研究路径，即实践认识论，也为设计研究提供了一种设计范式作为研究对象。

舍恩认为，设计问题在解决过程中，问题定义是"命名事物"（name the things）和"框定情境"（frame the context）的反复过程，即设计思维活动所呈现出来的一种独特思维结构。智能座舱人机交互的设计活动中，大量存在这种"命名-框定"的设计范式。比如，"L4+级智能座舱"的命名"L4+"及其所框定的智能座舱交互场景，可能涉及自动驾驶、多模态交互、娱乐办公、舒适健康和个性化设置等场景化设计问题和自动驾驶分级基准，这都属于复杂的设计问题求解。

多斯特（Dorst）则将实践反思的行动结构描述为"命名（naming）—框定（framing）—行动（moving）—评估（evaluating）"四个步骤。舍恩通过口语分析实验发现，在反映性对话中，实践行动者对问题的"框定"与"重新框定"（re-framing），将会衍生出新的"行动中反映"。在舍恩的《反映的实践者》中，"框定"和"重新框定"是指对问题或情境的理解和认知的过程，也称为"架构"和"重新架构"。"框定"通常是指对一个问题或情境进行解读和定义。比如，当我们看到一个陌生人，我们可能会根据他的外貌、行为和举止等特征，对他进行一定的判断和预测，这个过程就是一种框定；而"重新框定"则是指对已经框定的问题或情境进行重新定义和理解。比如，当我们对一个陌生人有过一段接触和了解后，我们可能会发现之前的判断和预测是不够准确的，我们需要重新定义和认识这个人。因此，从设计过程的范畴，实践反思的"框定"和"重新框定"是一种迭代。

戈登·帕斯克（Gordon Pask）提出的"对话理论"（conversation theory）认为，对话结构需要至少两个参与者：第一个参与者向第二个参与者表述对某主题的理解；第二个参与者接受表述并产生自己的理解，并将这种对第一个参与者理解的理解表述给第一个参与者；第一个参与者接受到这个对理解的理解，并与自己原来表述的理解进行比较。从实践反思的观点，设计过程可以看作设计师与原型不断对话的原型迭代过程，就是反复做方案的过程（图1-3）。这种对话是场景化的，每次对话都有积极与消极的可能。这里，当设计师身处设计过程，通过原型建构自己的理解和表达时，设计师是对话的第一个参与者，设计师"一镜到底"的设计逻辑是对话的出发点；当设计师抽身于设计过程，以自我为视角俯瞰自己建构的原型（物化为作品）时，原型是对话的第二个参与者，因为所有的设计（原型）都有自己独特的语言表达，设计的表现力是对话的出发点。图1-3中，问题与原型之间形成"场景化反映对话"关系，原型与原型之间形成原型迭代关系，同时产生情境知识。

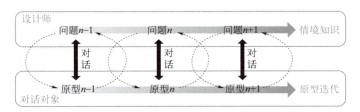

图1-3 设计实践反思的原型迭代框架

1.2 智能座舱交互设计——设计对象

在设计研究的范畴，设计对象并非一个静态的、现存的、具有固定意义的实体。它只存在于设计过程的交流和语言中，只有当设计对象被"物化"为具体产品后，它才会以实体的形式存在。例如，面对一个"L4+级智能座舱"的研发项目，在设计方案冻结之前，其设计对象和智能场景都是动态的、概念的、没有固定意义的，设计问题解决过程中的"命名—框定—重新框定"，意味着设计对象一直处于原型迭代的状态。另外，在汽车设计领域，也采用"对标设计"的方法，来解决设计对象的不确定性问题。例如，对标保时捷设计"性能车"，同时，对标特斯拉设计"智能电动车"，两条研发路径合二而一。所谓"对标设计"就是通过比较和研究同类产品和服务的标杆，为超越标杆并获得迭代优势提供设计基准和代际基准，即"框定"设计对象。比如，波音737MAX对标空客A320，小米SU7对标保时捷TAYCAN，商飞C919对标空客A320。因此，对标设计的本质是命名和框定设计对象，以明确设计目标。

> **案例**
>
> 　　2023年德国国际汽车及智慧出行博览会（慕尼黑国际车展）9月5日至10日在慕尼黑举行。本届车展主题为"体验互联出行"，来自38个国家和地区的750余家整车和零部件企业携最新车型与技术亮相。中国车企在电动化转型方面表现出色，受到广泛关注。
>
> 　　在这次展会，比亚迪、名爵、零跑、小鹏、阿维塔等众多中国汽车品牌，以技术创新和独特设计吸引了众多观众和媒体关注。比亚迪股份有限公司展示了6款电动车型，除此之外，还带来了电池车身一体化、智能扭矩分配系统、刀片电池等最新技术。车展期间，新一代智能电动汽车阿维塔12实现首发，其搭载了鸿蒙4.0系统等平台，为用户带来更多智能化服务和更自然的人车交互体验。宁德时代新能源科技股份有限公司携旗下车用电池"神行超充电池"参展。该款电池采用磷酸铁锂材料，可帮助电动汽车实现"充电10分钟，续航400公里"。诺博汽车系统有限公司在展会上全球首发了智巢3.0智能座舱及系列汽车电子创新产品，展示了最新迭代的智慧出行解决方案。
>
> 　　慕尼黑国际车展市场传媒总监迪姆·瓦格纳表示，全球出行行业正经历一场伟大变革，中国汽车市场在全球市场中举足轻重。
>
> 　　　　　　　　　　　　　　　　　《人民日报》2023年9月12日第017版（节选）

1.2.1 设计对象——智能汽车

人工智能大体分为五类：机器学习、深度学习、自然语言处理、计算机视觉以及自动规划和决策。也可分为：领域人工智能、通用人工智能和混合增强型人工智能。其中，领域人工智能ANI（artificial narrow intelligence），是为在特定领域内执行特定任务研发的人工智能，例如，图像识别、自然语音指令、智能驾驶汽车。另外，通用人工智能 AGI（artificial general intelligence），旨在应对多种甚至泛化问题，拥有推理、计划、解决问题、抽象思考、快速学习和从经验中学习的能力。

智能汽车的人工智能通常属于领域人工智能（ANI），也被称为狭义人工智能。这种 AI 是特定于应用程序或任务的，针对某一领域进行优化。在智能汽车领域，人工智能系统被专门训练和执行与驾驶、导航、障碍物识别、行人检测等相关的任务。这些系统通常基于机器学习和深度学习算法，通过大量的数据进行训练，以在特定领域内达到或超越人类的表现。

目前，大多数商业化的智能汽车和自动驾驶技术都是基于这种狭义人工智能。它们通过摄像头、雷达、激光雷达（LiDAR）等传感器收集数据，并使用 AI 算法进行实时决策和控制。这些系统能够识别交通信号、障碍物、行人和其他车辆，以实现安全有效的自动驾驶。

（1）智能汽车国家战略

从 2012 年到 2014 年，我国的智能网联汽车处于初步的"萌发"阶段。2015 年，我国汽车工业开始转型，国家主管部门积极推动智能网联汽车的发展规划和专项行动计划。随后，中国颁布了制造强国战略《中国制造 2025》，其中明确提出了要掌握汽车低碳化、信息化、智能化的核心技术，智能技术由此被纳入国家战略。特别是在"节能与新能源汽车"这一重要领域中，智能技术占据了显著地位。

2016 年，在工业和信息化部的委托下，由中国汽车工程学会牵头，500 位专家经过一年的努力，完成了大型联合研究项目——"节能与新能源汽车技术路线图"。技术路线图以 2020 年、2025 年、2030 年为关键时间节点，详细规划了汽车需求、产品应用及产业基础。2017 年，《汽车产业中长期发展规划》由工业和信息化部等三部委联合发布，进一步提升了智能网联汽车在国家战略中的地位，显示出我国政府对于"弯道超车"机会的特别重视。而在 2019 年颁布的《交通强国建设纲要》中，更是专门提到了加强智能网联汽车（包括智能汽车、自动驾驶、车路协同）的研发，旨在形成自主可控的完整产业链。2020 年，国家发展改革委、工业和信息化部、科技部等 11 个部委联合发布了《智能汽车创新发展战略》，明确指出智能汽车的发展不仅有助于汽车产业的转型升级，更是建设制造强国、科技强国、智慧社会，增强国家综合实力的重要途径。智能汽车已被视为"建成现代化强国的重要支撑"。在《关于积极推进"互联网+"行动的指导意见》《关于印发新一代人工智能发展规划的通知》《增强制造业核心竞争力三年行动计划（2018—2020 年）》等政策文件中，也都强调了要大力发展智能网联汽车。2021 年颁布的《中华人民共和国国民经济和社会发展第十四个五年规划和 2035 年远景目标纲要》中提到，要发展壮大战略性新兴产业，构筑产业体系新支柱，聚焦新一代信息技术、生物技术、新能源、新材料、高端装备、新能源汽车、绿色环保以及航空航天、海洋装备等战略性新兴产业，加快关键核心技术创新应用，增强要素保障能力，培育壮大产业发展新动能。2024 年 3 月 5 日，李强总理在第十四届全国人民代表大会第二次会议上代表国务院作《政府工作报告》，提出 2024 年要巩固扩大智能网联新能源汽车等产业领先优势，且提振智能网联新能源汽车、电子产品等大宗消费。

案例：上海国际车展显示——汽车行业正加快智能化电动化转型

全球1000多家整车和零部件公司参展、超过150款新车全球首发、展出800余款新能源车型、跨国品牌携全系电动化车型深耕中国市场、中国品牌智能电动汽车加快走出去步伐……4月27日落幕的上海国际车展显示，全球汽车行业正加快智能化电动化转型。

得益于一系列新能源汽车支持政策，更得益于中国品牌车企紧抓转型机遇推出适应消费需求的新技术、新产品，我国新能源汽车产销连续8年位居全球第一。2022年我国新能源汽车销售688.7万辆，同比增长93.4%，销量占比25.6%，提前3年完成2025年规划目标。2023年一季度，我国新能源汽车迎来开门红，产销分别完成165万辆和158.6万辆，同比分别增长27.7%和26.2%，市场占有率提升至26.1%。

当前，我国新能源汽车已进入全面市场化拓展期，行业企业正聚焦成本、效率与用户体验，加快创新步伐，提升产业链供应链韧性，推动产业发展再上新台阶。

"下一步，要更大力度、更高水平推动新能源汽车产业发展。"辛国斌表示，要加强顶层设计，建立新能源汽车产业发展部际协调机制，统筹推进产业发展全局性工作；强化技术创新，支持产学研用深度合作，开展车用芯片、固态电池、操作系统、高精度传感器等技术攻关；完善政策体系，制定加快充换电建设、公共领域新能源汽车推广应用等支持政策；深化国际合作，建设海外政策、法规、标准等信息共享服务平台，支持中国品牌开拓海外市场。

《人民日报》2023年5月17日第018版（节选）

智能网联汽车（intelligent and connected vehicle，ICV）是指，装备先进的车载传感器、控制器等器件，并融合现代通信与网络技术，实现车与X（车、路、人、云端等）的智能信息交流和共享，具备复杂环境感知、智能决策、协同控制等功能，可实现安全、高效、舒适、节能行驶，并最终实现替代人来操作的新一代汽车。从技术发展路径来说，智能汽车分为3个发展方向：网联式汽车（connected vehicle，CV）、自主式汽车（autonomous vehicle，AV）以及智能网联汽车。"网联式汽车"可通过网络系统感知周边环境，实施决策控制和非自主式自动驾驶；"自主式汽车"则可以独立于其他车辆，依靠车载传感器与车载控制系统，实现环境感知和决策控制，执行自动驾驶。目前，网联式驾驶辅助和自主式驾驶辅助相结合，是我国智能网联汽车发展的主流模式。智能化（即汽车自动驾驶技术）和网联化（即车联网）相结合是未来自动驾驶汽车产业发展的重要方向。

（2）自动驾驶分级与智能网联汽车分级

自动驾驶分级不仅是智能座舱交互设计的概念，更是用户理解自动驾驶和相应驾驶行为的概念。比如，设计师和用户都能够基本理解，汽车自动驾驶共有L0到L5六个级别，其中L3是自动驾驶的分界线，L3以下为"辅助驾驶"，L3以上为"自动驾驶"。值得注意的是，自动驾驶或智能驾驶不仅是一个自动驾驶分级的问题，更是一个高度"场景化"的技术概念和设计概念，是智能座舱交互设计的关键技术。

目前，智界 S7 集成了华为 HarmonyOS 4 智能座舱和 HUAWEI ADS 2.0 智能驾驶系统，实现了 L3 级自动驾驶。

2014 年，国际自动机工程师学会（SAE International）发布了 SAE J3016《道路机动车辆自动驾驶系统相关术语分类和定义》(*Taxonomy and Definitions for Terms Related to Driving Automation Systems for On-Road Motor Vehicles*)。此后，SAE International 陆续对该标准进行了多次更新，以适应自动驾驶汽车的发展。该标准将驾驶自动化分为六个级别，分别为 0 级——人工驾驶、1 级——辅助驾驶、2 级——部分自动驾驶、3 级——条件自动驾驶、4 级——高度自动驾驶、5 级——全自动驾驶，不同等级自动化水平所实现的功能逐级递增（表 1-1）。

表 1-1 SAE 分级标准（2018 版）

等级	自动化程度	具体定义	动态驾驶任务		动态驾驶任务接管	设计适用域
			驾驶操作	感知和判断		
0	人工驾驶	由人类驾驶员负责驾驶车辆	驾驶员	驾驶员	驾驶员	无
1	辅助驾驶	车机系统对方向盘和加减速中的一项操作提供驾驶支持，人类驾驶员负责其余的驾驶操作	驾驶员和车机系统	驾驶员	驾驶员	限定场景
2	部分自动驾驶	车机系统对方向盘和加减速中的多项操作提供驾驶支持，人类驾驶员负责其余驾驶操作	车机系统	驾驶员	驾驶员	限定场景
3	条件自动驾驶	车机系统完成绝大部分驾驶操作，人类驾驶员需要在适当的时候提供应答	车机系统	车机系统	接管期变为驾驶员	限定场景
4	高度自动驾驶	由车机系统完成所有驾驶操作，人类驾驶员无需对所有的系统请求做出应答，但限定道路和环境条件	车机系统	车机系统	车机系统	限定场景
5	全自动驾驶	由车机系统完成所有驾驶操作，人类驾驶员无需保持注意力	车机系统	车机系统	车机系统	限定场景

这里，SAE 分级标准是一个在"车机系统"和"人类驾驶员"之间分配驾驶任务的"分配表"，驾驶任务分配不同，人类驾驶员介入驾驶任务的程度不同，自动驾驶的级别也不同。而驾驶任务分配和人类介入程度都是完全取决于场景的，比如，城市道路与高速公路就是完全不同的驾驶场景，所以 SAE 分级标准表最后一项都无一例外地填写着"限定场景"。因此，智能座舱交互设计不是一个单一的"自动驾驶分级"问题，而是基于"限定场景"研发智能座舱交互系统，以满足用户真实的需求（表 1-2）。

表 1-2 面向自动驾驶分级的场景端

自动驾驶分级	场景端
L1 辅助驾驶	高速公路巡航、城市拥堵路段的跟车等
L2 部分自动驾驶	高速公路自动驾驶、自动泊车等

续表

自动驾驶分级	场景端
L3 条件自动驾驶	高速公路自动驾驶、城市自动驾驶等
L4 高度自动驾驶	封闭园区、港口、仓对仓运输等
L5 全自动驾驶	未来城市出行、长途货运等

2018 年 SAE 分级标准中：L0 级，车辆完全缺乏任何驾驶自动化技术。驾驶员一直在工作，并完全负责操控车辆。这包括转向、加速、制动、停车以及任何其他必要的驾驶或停车操作。一些 L0 级车辆可能提供有限或短暂的辅助驾驶功能，例如警告和警报，甚至是紧急安全干预。L1 级，车辆具有一个单一的自动驾驶辅助系统，如转向或加速（巡航控制）。L2 级，车辆通过持续帮助驾驶员加速、制动和转向来实现部分自动化。这一级别的车辆通常配备先进的驾驶辅助系统（ADAS），可以在特定情况下控制上述功能。L1 级和 L2 级技术都要求驾驶员在驾驶车辆时保持注意力集中并完全投入。L3 级，车辆自动处理所有驾驶任务。L3 级车辆具有"环境探测"能力，可以自行做出明智的决定，例如加速超过缓慢行驶的车辆。但它们仍然需要人工控制。驾驶员必须保持警惕，并准备在系统无法执行任务时接管控制。L4 级，车辆可以实现在自动驾驶模式下运行。而 L3 级和 L4 级的关键区别在于，如果出现问题或系统故障，L4 级车辆可以自动进行干预。L5 级，自动驾驶车辆完全控制所有驾驶和导航任务，做任何有经验的人类驾驶员能做的事情。L5 级车辆甚至不需要有方向盘或加速/制动踏板。乘客只需设定目的地，就可以工作、睡觉、看电影、玩游戏。

汽车智能网联的分级上，工业和信息化部组织中国汽车工程学会、清华大学等单位共同编写的《节能与新能源汽车技术路线图》中设置了《智能网联汽车技术路线图》一章，创造性地提出了自动驾驶与网联化双维度智能网联汽车分级（图 1-4）。

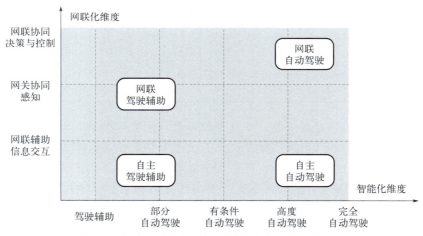

图 1-4 自动驾驶与网联化双维度智能网联汽车分级

在智能化维度上（图 1-4 横轴），国内编制的自动驾驶汽车分级标准是，基于驾驶自动化系统能够执行动态驾驶任务的程度，并根据在执行动态驾驶任务中的角色分配以及有无设计运行条件限制，将驾驶自动化分成五个等级。在网联化的维度上（图 1-4 纵轴），按照网联通信内容及实现的功能不同，可以分为三个等级。

（3）智能驾驶场景

这里，用一个实例来简要说明智能驾驶的场景概念。某品牌智能驾驶系统的高速领航辅助功能，可以在高精度地图覆盖的高速公路、城市快速路和城市高架桥的场景下，为驾驶员提供车道级导航及最优行车路线，完成驾驶员设定的导航任务，并在安全的情况下，实现智能进出匝道、智能辅助超车、智能最优变道、智能限速匹配、智能避让大车等，该智能驾驶系统属于辅助驾驶功能，需要驾驶员手握方向盘，观察路况。在这里，"高精度地图覆盖""高速公路、城市快速路和城市高架桥""进出匝道、辅助超车、最优变道、限速匹配、避让大车"以及"手握方向盘"和"观察路况"，都属于为该智能驾驶系统限定的"场景"，这意味着"高速领航辅助"的智能驾驶，本质上是一个基于场景的智能辅助驾驶系统。值得注意的是，该系统非常接近L3级别的自动驾驶，且不久就会升级为L3级别自动驾驶。这种情况下，企业将其命名为"L2+"级自动驾驶。

在智能座舱人机交互设计范畴中，绝大多数情况下，智能座舱的智能化都是基于场景定义的，而不仅仅是依据自动驾驶L0～L5的级别进行分级。这个现象表明，在智能驾驶技术快速迭代发展的同时，智能驾驶的场景越来越重要，越来越具有研发价值，如何通过场景化智能驾驶技术，满足用户需求，引导用户期望，沟通用户，是智能座舱人机交互设计的关键。

1.2.2 设计对象——智能汽车技术架构

智能网联汽车融合了自主式汽车与网联式汽车的技术优势，涉及汽车、信息通信、交通等诸多领域，其技术架构较为复杂。我国工业和信息化部、国家标准化管理委员会于2018年和2023年发布《国家车联网产业标准体系建设指南（智能网联汽车）（2018年）》《国家车联网产业标准体系建设指南（智能网联汽车）（2023版）》，明确了智能网联汽车"三横两纵"的核心技术架构（图1-5）。

（1）智能感知与信息通信层

智能感知与信息通信层的技术，主要是指环境信息和车内信息的采集与处理的相关技术，涉及道路边界检测、车辆检测、行人检测等。所采用的传感器包括但不限于车载毫米波雷达、车载激光雷达、车载摄像头。通常需要运用多传感器融合技术，通过车载信息交互终端，感知融合和分析处理，为后续的决策与控制环节提供依据。

（2）决策控制与执行层

智能网联决策控制与执行层技术，主要是依感知信息进行决策判断，确定适当工作模型，制定相应控制策略，替代人类驾驶员做出驾驶决策，按照决策结果对车辆进行控制的相应技术。L0～L2级自动驾驶的先进辅助驾驶技术和L3～L5级驾驶自动化功能都属于智能网联决策控制与执行层的技术范畴。例如车道保持、车道偏离预警、车距保持、障碍物警告等。

（3）资源管理与应用层

芯片、软件、数据、架构、平台等技术都属于资源管理与应用层的技术。这些技术是智能网联汽车核心共性资源的功能、性能及应用。平台架构主要包括智能网联汽车云控平台、电子电气架构、车内有线通信技术等。车用软件包括软件管理及软件层级的应用等。车用芯片主要涵盖了安全芯片、计算芯片等。

图 1-5 智能网联汽车技术架构

智能网联汽车在纵向上的核心技术架构为功能安全、预期功能安全和网络安全、数据安全。

（1）功能安全、预期功能安全

功能安全是指在电子电气系统故障（包括软件、硬件、系统故障）等功能异常的情况下，车辆能够安全运行、不会引发安全风险的一系列支撑措施。主要包括产品层面的功能安全分析、设计开发要求、测试评价方法，以及企业层面的功能安全管理要求和审核评估方法。预期功能安全则要求我们采取措施用于规避车辆因设计不足、性能局限及人为误用导致危害发生的不合理风险，要求采取产品层面的预期功能安全分析、设计开发要求、测试评价方法，以及企业层面的预期功能安全管理要求和审核评估方法。

（2）网络安全、数据安全

车联网环境愈发复杂，因而以车端为核心，运用纵深防御理念保护其免受网络攻击或缓解网络安全风险十分重要。其中，可以关注的安全保障类措施有规范企业及产品相关的体系管理和审核评估方法；安全技术有车用数字证书、密码应用等，元器件级、关键系统部件级、整车级安全技术以及入侵检测等综合安全防护技术等。

随着智能化和网联化普及，汽车成为生产、收集、分析处理和传输数据的移动端口，也是获取和存储用户个人信息和行为习惯的重要载体。我国对数据提出明确的安全保护要求，且对重要数据和个人信息提出重点安全保护要求。数据通用要求、数据安全要求、数据安全管理体系规范、数据安全共享模型和架构等标准，是智能网联汽车发展中必不可少的规范。

1.2.3 设计对象——智能座舱

汽车智能化的发展催生了"智能座舱"这一全新概念,这一变革不仅重塑了人与车的关系,还创新了用车方式,为汽车人机交互的创新发展开辟了广阔的前景。随着自动驾驶技术的崛起,人与道路体系之间的直接信息交流逐渐减少,而人与车、人与人、车与车之间的信息流交互却日益频繁。值得注意的是,智能汽车的自动驾驶等级越高,智能座舱的用户需求就越发多元化,对个性化、情感和体验的追求也在不断演变。

智能座舱现已成为个人的数字化空间,并承担着人机交互设计的重要角色。汽车座舱的数字化、智能化和互联化特点越来越显著,其功能定位正在从以驾驶任务为中心,转变为以满足用户需求为中心。这种转变意味着人与车的关系也正在从以驾驶为主转变为一个更复杂的"事件-场景-动作"人机交互系统。因此,汽车座舱已不再是传统意义上的单纯驾驶空间,而是正在逐步演变成一个集交通驾驶、工作学习、休闲娱乐于一体的智能生活"第三空间"。这一变革预示着未来的汽车座舱将更加智能化、多功能化,将成为我们日常生活中不可或缺的一部分。

"智能座舱"是指,传感器、执行器和显示器集成,能主动感知人、车、环境状态,并通过人工智能和人机交互进行提示、决策和活动的人员乘坐空间。中国计算机学会智能汽车分会对"智能座舱"的定义是:一个集成了多种IT技术和人工智能技术的车内数字化综合平台,旨在为驾驶员打造智能化的行车体验,并提升行车安全性。围绕这一概念,国内外已经开展了大量研究工作,例如,在车辆的AB柱和后视镜上安装摄像头,以提供情绪识别、年龄检测、遗留物检测和安全带检测等功能。从市场现有汽车产品的角度,亿欧智库也为"智能座舱"设定了一套认定标准,即只有当车型同时配备了中控台彩色大屏、支持OTA升级以及智能语音识别系统时,才能被认定为配置了智能座舱。

当前的智能座舱主要集中在座舱内饰与座舱电子两大领域的创新与整合上,它构建了一个以用户为中心的人机交互(HMI)体系。通过收集各类数据并上传至云端进行深度处理与计算,智能座舱能够为用户提供高度场景化的服务,从而在安全性、娱乐性和实用性等多个方面,极大地丰富了用户的座舱体验。

> **案例:智能座舱产品**
>
> 伟世通的智能座舱包括四个核心:多屏显示和数字仪表、座舱域控制器、自动驾驶安全域控制器和信息娱乐系统。伟世通将多个显示器集成在一块面板上,该设计带来了无缝且高质量的视觉体验。
>
> 哈曼国际将ADAS、OTA、音响技术和车载信息娱乐系统进行融合,推出综合性的智能驾驶平台。
>
> 佛吉亚推出的概念座舱采用智能触控表面技术,座舱将电容触摸开关内置于材料的表面,使汽车内饰具有极简的科技感。座舱主显示器屏幕采用AMOLED,视觉效果极好。该座舱还采用了超薄隐形屏幕和车内互联共享系统(图1-6)。

图 1-6　佛吉亚推出的概念座舱

北汽将智能语音助手、环境感知和健康监测技术结合使用，推出 Hi·Me 智能健康座舱。语音助手不仅能控制影音和空调，还能通过它调用环境感知系统，将环境参数提供给用户。

华为专为智能座舱打造了 HarmonyOS 智能座舱系统，该系统打造了一个将多种智能终端互联互通的互联世界。比如，搭载 HarmonyOS 的手机与车机中控屏能够实现"一碰传"功能，将手机上的地点发送到车机端，直接开启导航。

恒驰 5 量产车采用高通第三代骁龙数字座舱平台，可以实现多感官人机交互，如语音交互和人脸识别。三联屏支持多应用同步显示，后续可通过 OTA 升级实现手势识别功能。人性化 AI 智能助理小驰，应用百度 AI 语音，当驾驶员疲劳时会立即发出警示。

1.2.4　设计对象——智能座舱技术架构

智能座舱在传统汽车座舱的基础上不断进化而来，具有更智能、更舒适、更能够洞察和满足用户需求的特征，全面改善了用户的使用体验。

硬件方面，传统座舱系统的硬件分散化明显，座椅、音响、仪表等车身电子共同构成了传统座舱的硬件系统。软件方面，传统座舱的软硬件高度耦合，可拓展性差，无法满足消费者的个性化需求。而目前整车的电子电气架构（E/E）从传统分布式走向域集中式，主流车企大多处于域集中架构阶段。采用域控制器可以实现优化功能协同、控制成本，同时能够支持数据共用、整车功能协同，也使智能座舱的软硬件层的解耦成为可能。

可以预见到，智能座舱的未来将充分利用语音交互、机器视觉、触觉监控等多模态交互技术来实现车内环境的全面感知。这些技术将与高级别的自动驾驶系统深度融合，协同工作，将座舱打造成一个集家庭温馨、娱乐休闲、工作学习和社交互动于一体的多功能空间。

> **案例：智能座舱域控制器方案将成为主流方案**
>
> 在智能座舱方面，能够集成众多 ECU、传感器、控制器的座舱域控制器应运而生，以座舱域控制器为中心的智能座舱系统将成主流趋势，这一系统将在统一的软硬件平台上实现座舱电子系统功能，成为融入交互智能、场景智能、个性化服务的座舱电子系统，逐渐满足用户对汽车座舱"第三空间"的定义，市场发展空间广阔。同时全球汽车软硬件厂商已经与众多车企合作，开始布局智能座舱域控制器市场。国外厂商中，伟世通、大陆、博世等在全球座舱域控制器市场占据主导地位，已在奔驰、吉利、通用等国际知名车企的众多车型上实现量产应用；国内厂商方面，德赛西威、东软集团、航盛电子、华为等企业也陆续推出了各自的座舱域控制器一体化解决方案，已搭载至理想、红旗、东风等车型。
>
> 引自《向"第三生活空间"迈进，智能化大潮座舱先行》天风证券研究报告
> 2022 年 6 月 14 日

正如前文所述，汽车电子电气架构（E/E）正经历从传统分布式到域集中式的演变，并有望在未来升级为中央集中式架构。这一变革导致智能座舱的软硬件架构发生显著变化，实现了软硬件的分离开发。在新的架构下，汽车底层硬件不再依赖单一功能的芯片进行简单逻辑计算，而是需要更强大的计算能力。同时，软件也不再局限于特定硬件，而是变得可移植、可迭代和可扩展。这种转变意味着传统的以电子控制单元（ECU）为核心的研发组织将逐渐让位于新型的研发模式，该模式包括通用硬件平台、基础软件平台以及各种应用软件。随着软硬件解耦成为行业趋势，汽车正迈入"软件定义汽车"的新时代。在集中式电子电气架构和空中下载技术（OTA）的支持下，软硬件在零部件层面得以充分解耦，硬件逐渐标准化，而软件则逐渐独立成为核心零部件产品。

在这个架构升级的背景下，硬件层的芯片和软件层的操作系统将共同支撑座舱域控制器的功能。作为未来汽车运算和决策的中心，域控制器的功能实现依赖于主控芯片、软件操作系统、中间件以及应用算法等多层次软硬件的紧密结合。系统芯片（SoC）已成为当前域控制器的主流方案，它集成了 CPU、GPU、NPU、存储器、BC、DSP 以及网联组件如 Wi-Fi 和 BT 等模块，以满足汽车智能化趋势下跨域融合的需求。从长期来看，座舱主控芯片有望进一步融合到中央计算芯片中，从而提升运算效率并降低成本。

在软件方面，它正成为构建智能座舱生态圈的关键力量。通过进一步联动各座舱硬件，座舱软件能够实现诸多个性化功能，如多屏互动、仪表服务以及智驾信息的多屏显示等，从而构建座舱的智能新生态。这一变革也重塑了汽车软件产业链，吸引了互联网和信息通信技术（ICT）企业的加入。同时，具备软件研发能力的整车企业也通过掌控车型软件开发架构来获取产业链的核心利益。

1.3 智能座舱交互设计——设计场景

海尔集团创始人认为，没有完美的产品，只有永远向完美迭代的场景，没有人会买

一个单一的产品，用户要的一定是一个场景。也可以说，没有一个完美的"手机支架"，不过，2024年3月上市的小米SU7创造了一个"手机支架场景"，一个最容易被忽视的，但有情感价值和用户需求的场景触点。

1.3.1 交互设计场景——要素、场域和触点

智能座舱设计既有人机交互"时间、空间、场所"范畴的"场景"意义，也有人机交互"事件、情节、体验"范畴的"叙事"意义。以智能座舱为代表的智能产品，只有建构一个完整的设计场景结构，才能让用户真正捕获产品体验和价值。一个可以描述、可以定义和可以建构的"设计场景"理论框架，是设计研究的基础性课题。

如图1-7所示，我们定义了交互设计场景的概念框架，包括三个场景要素及其对应的三个场域和三类场景触点。通过设计场景来表征设计问题和解决设计问题，也是认知科学和设计研究的核心概念，是使用设计工具来建构设计对象的活动。概念框架中的"场景接触点"，简称为"触点"或者"场景触点"，是指广义人机交互界面上的"位置点"。

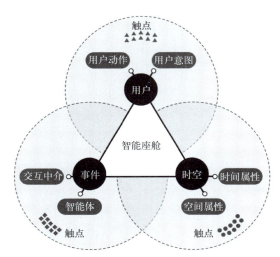

图1-7 基于要素、场域和触点的交互设计场景

（1）用户

"用户"属于场景"人物"范畴的场景要素，主要指"用户动作"和"用户意图"的用户行为学属性（图1-7）。用户的"人物"概念首先表现为"角色"意义，例如开车出行的父亲和开车上班的员工，可能属于同一个人的两种人物角色和故事情节；用户动作和用户意图，其实就是人的需求的行为学"标签"。值得注意的是，用户动作是可观测的"显性"行为，而用户意图是不可直接观测的"隐性"行为。例如，手指"交互触点"串联的"动线"，其路径、速度和力度的行为特征是可以直接观测的，但是这组动作的舒适性和体验感就不然。

用户要素对应的场域被称为"用户场"。用户场一方面是用来描述"人性"（human nature）和"情感"（emotion）的；另一方面是用来描述用户意义和用户价值的。

用户场中，可以触动用户情感和触发用户意义的人性元素和情感元素被称为"用户

触点"。大体可以分为两类：①人性触点，人性的优点和缺点、炫耀和低调、冒险和避险等，属于心理动机范畴，例如理想（Leading Ideal）智能座舱的"家庭主驾"设计；②情感触点，喜怒哀乐等，属于情绪范畴，例如高合（HiPhi）"座椅进入"设计。

智能座舱的用户是指驾驶和乘坐智能汽车的人，虽然用户和人都是指人类，但含义和用法是不同的。用户不仅有心理学、人类学和社会学定义，还可以是使用者，也可以是目标用户，亦可以是终端用户，甚至是一个用户账号。"用户研究"的常用工具包括Personal 故事板等。

（2）事件

"事件"属于叙事"情节"范畴的场景要素（图1-7）。叙事情节是指交互事件的起始、发展、转折和结束。主要是指用户通过"交互中介"和"智能体"，产生交互事件和交互体验的过程。其中，"交互中介"是指人机交互的媒介，包括手势、语音和一些其他模态的交互形式，例如蔚来（NIO）智能座舱的交互机器人"NOMI"；"智能体"是指车载系统具备的算力和人工智能模型。值得注意的是，交互中介是人的行为机制和任务机制的基础，是交互事件的载体；智能体是人的决策机制和思考机制的基础，是交互形式的载体。

事件要素对应的场域被称为"事件场"。事件场中，可以触动用户情感和触发用户行为的交互中介元素和信息元素称为"交互触点"。交互触点的"交互属性"和"交互特征"是建构叙事情节的关键设计问题。例如，智能座舱隐藏式门把手的"迎宾模式"，存在车主、把手、音乐、灯光、座椅五个基本"交互触点"。其中，车主接近座舱的方向和距离、门把手的响应时间和人机尺寸、音乐的调性和节奏、灯光的调性和动态，以及座椅后移空间等人机交互属性和交互特征，都是建构叙事情节和串联交互触点的设计关键。

（3）时空

"时空"属于"形式感"范畴的场景要素（图1-7），主要指"时间属性"和"空间属性"。第一，用户通过交互事件获得的时间感、空间感和形式感，既是物理的客观的，也是心理的情感的；第二，用户经历叙事情节的"真实"过程，即用户自我意识和体验的过程。时间属性与叙事情节的注意力、节奏、转折、生动性和情感等概念关联在一起，例如光阴似箭和度日如年；空间属性与"人在"空间的概念，与物理空间、心理空间、社交空间等概念关联在一起，例如漫无边际和拘束不安。

时空要素对应的场域被称为"形式场"。即时间感和空间感是人们获得形式感的认知基础，也是一切艺术形式的心理基础，例如对比、节奏、调性等，所谓高山流水、白驹过隙、日光荏苒。时间和空间往往不仅是指场所本身的存在，也是指场景的感知"形式"和感知"层次"，例如小鹏（XPENG）智能座舱的"过夜模式"。

形式场中，可以触动用户情感和触发用户行为的意象元素称为"形式触点"。例如，"大漠孤烟直，长河落日圆"生发出来的雄浑壮丽的意境，其意象元素是大漠、孤烟、长河、落日，亦即时空尺度的形式感意象。智能座舱"中控屏"尺寸大小，往往是最"容易"产生高科技"意象"的形式触点，特斯拉最先采用了15.5英寸❶的大中控屏，哪吒 GT 中控屏尺寸为17.6英寸。因此，形式触点是一种"意象"触发的形式感，而意象是客观存在的物象及其时空形式。

---

❶ 1英寸=2.54cm。

总之，本节定义了交互设计场景的三个场景要素——用户、事件、时空，三个场域——用户场、事件场和形式场，三类场景触点——用户触点、交互触点和形式触点，提出了一个比较完整的设计场景的概念框架，为场景叙事设计方法的研究提供了理论基础。

1.3.2　交互设计场景——场景、叙事、价值

舒尔茨（Norberg Schultz）认为，每一个场景都是一个故事。这个故事既可以与日常生活"场所"关联在一起，也可以与日常生活"事件"关联在一起，构成所谓"场景叙事"。因此，设计场景的设计活动本质上具有"场景叙事"的特征。场景叙事意味着，人处于具体的场所时，这个场所就是所谓的"人在"场景，而不仅仅是物理意义的空间和时间。"人在"场景中所发生的行为、情感和状态都是"真实"的事件，这种真实性可以产生"刻骨铭心"的记忆，引起独特的场景感和体验感，并且都属于被时间和空间"标记"出来的个体经验。因此，场景是一种特殊的"精神场所"，是以"人在"为中心的存在形式。

格尔尼诺（Greeno）认为：设计的本质是解决问题，而问题解决的过程意味着一系列有目的和有指向性的认知操作。从格尔尼诺的设计定义出发：①场景叙事设计的本质是解决问题；②解决问题的目的性，主要指场景的"互动性"特征，即设计的目的在于如何建构人的互动行为；③解决问题的指向性，主要指叙事的"情节性"，即设计始终"指向"通过互动性的叙事情节，来触发用户的产品体验和用户价值。因此，"场景互动"和"叙事情节"是场景叙事设计解决问题的主要认知特征。

多斯特（Dorst）在 *Design Studies* 上发表的论文中提出，设计的本质是建构一种产生价值的架构（framing）。同样，场景叙事设计的本质是，一种通过"场景互动"与"叙事情节"产生"价值"的场景叙事架构。其基本设计逻辑可以形式化表达为：

$$\{互动 + 情节\} = 价值$$

以智能座舱为例，其"隐藏式门把手"设计，既颠覆了"形式服从功能"的造型原则，也违反了可供性（affordances）的语义原则。但是，当车主靠近座舱时，隐藏的门把手会徐徐打开，同时播放音乐和点亮踏步灯，构成了一个完整、互动、新奇和感性的"场景叙事情节"（迎宾模式）。可见，场景叙事设计与功能主义、可供性原则等设计方法之间，存在着完全不同的问题求解路径。值得注意的是，这种设计方法和解题路径的不同，并不意味着哪一种设计方法是更正确或者更先进的，这本就不是所谓科学性和先进性的问题。

得益于自动驾驶技术、5G通信技术和云计算的融合发展，座舱内部的区域划分、布局设计和用户交互方式都在发生变化，催生出新的、多元化的驾驶与非驾驶场景。换句话说，"座舱"将不再局限于单一的"驾驶"场景，而是在对车辆智能、道路智能和乘客智能方面进行持续完善与扩展。它正逐步发展为能够实现不同场景间的流畅切换，连接"家居、娱乐、工作、社交"等多个生活场景的"第三生活空间"（图1-8）。

图 1-8 座舱内"第三生活空间"场景

1.3.3 智能座舱人机交互设计方法论

本节提出一种基于设计范式、设计对象和设计场景的"智能座舱人机交互设计方法论"（图 1-9）。其中，设计范式是一个"设计过程"范畴的问题；设计对象是作为交流和表达"设计意图"的"物化"形式的问题；而设计场景（theories of scenario）是设计问题解决中，问题命名（name）和问题框定（framing）的价值架构问题。

图 1-9 智能座舱人机交互设计方法论

从方法论范畴，智能座舱人机交互设计方法论是指，通过设计范式、设计对象和设计场景的途径，创造并交付满足用户需求和实现用户价值的设计方案。

在这个框架中，设计范式与设计场景的关联，体现在设计意图的确定、设计流程的规划以及设计方法的选用等设计过程方面；而设计对象与设计场景的关联则涉及用户特征、产品特性和市场需求等设计对象领域的问题。设计场景在这一方法论中充当了关键角色，它可以被视作设计范式和设计对象的"认知操作"桥梁。从本质上讲，设计场景是设计思维的承载者，其具体表现形式为一种设计的价值架构。最终，这些设计方案会转化为实体产品，即我们所说的设计对象，并以此为起点进入新一轮的设计迭代。

总之，设计是"有意图的行动"，是"在不可预测的世界中引入有意图的变化"。设计的价值在于涌现，在于有意图的设计迭代，在于持续生成的设计中间物和中间结果，由此人们获得了对于未知领域的认知迭代。设计师将这些知识封装在一个又一个的设计原型中，使得设计的结果一步一步获得其最终的物化形式。至此，有意图的行动形成了完整的闭环，设计价值在这些涌现中渐渐物化成型。

第 2 章

传统到智能的座舱设计转向

2.1 汽车座舱技术演进
2.2 汽车座舱的用户体验
2.3 智能座舱的应用场景

本章讨论有两个主题："座舱技术"和"用户体验"。前者是设计对象范畴的问题，即座舱技术演变和智能化问题；后者是设计过程范畴的问题，即从造型向体验的设计转向的问题，或者说从内饰造型设计向时空、场景、叙事的设计转向问题。这里必须指出的是，设计转向不是说现在的设计比过去的设计先进，而是体现设计自身的迭代进化。设计的持续迭代和进化，其实本质上是人类设计能力的进化和设计方法的进步。

本章围绕传统到智能的座舱设计转向，先从设计对象的范畴，按照传统机械化座舱、电子化座舱、智能辅助驾驶座舱、智能驾驶座舱四个阶段，讨论汽车座舱技术的演进；然后，从设计范式的范畴，按照基础驾驶体验、电子信息座舱的用户体验、智能座舱的用户体验的三个阶段，讨论从内饰造型向智能座舱人机交互的设计转向；最后，讨论智能座舱的应用场景，归纳出一般场景范式。

2.1 汽车座舱技术演进

20世纪末至21世纪初，计算机技术和网络技术在交通工具领域的广泛应用，以及车载信息技术的飞速发展，使得汽车的内部空间、人机界面、操作和交互过程都经历了革命性的变革。在用户需求和技术进步的双重推动下，汽车已逐渐从单一的产品演变为功能丰富的大型移动服务系统。

汽车座舱的造型与设计是复杂的。这种复杂一方面体现在其涉及机械结构、人机操控、电子电控等多种技术领域，又涉及产品设计、空间设计、交互设计和感知质量等多个设计领域；另一方面体现在汽车造型作为设计师的设计意图和用户的认知解释的认知对象，在设计师设计过程和用户解读过程中的存在方式是不同的。在汽车造型设计中，设计师通过视觉特征和概念语义来实现意图与形态之间的转换和迭代。在造型认知解释中，用户通过视觉特征和概念语义来实现识别与解释之间的转换和信息加工。可以说，汽车座舱的造型设计表现为一种特征和概念双重编码的认知活动。

从传统座舱到智能座舱，早期车的功能性决定了其布局，座舱的设计也和人对车的操纵息息相关，随着汽车信息化和自动化程度的逐渐提高，汽车设计师开始通过一系列方法统筹汽车内饰的造型与设计，但设计还是围绕技术应用以及降低汽车驾驶的技术复杂性展开。而智能座舱呈现出一种全新的趋势。随着自动驾驶和网联技术的发展，汽车不再仅仅是一个交通工具，而是一个可移动的、搭载多种服务系统的"第三空间"，因此，座舱的设计也需要适应这种变化，从传统的以功能性为主的设计转变为更加注重用户体验、舒适性和互动性的设计。

综上所述，座舱技术的革新促进了座舱造型与设计的演进，同时，从用户体验的角度审视座舱造型与设计的演进同样重要。技术进步为座舱设计开辟了新的可能性，而用户的体验需求则指引着技术的应用和优化方向。车从原先的单一产品发展成为当下具有多样化功能的大型移动服务系统，传统座舱演进为智能座舱的过程离不开用户体验和技术发展的双重作用。随着技术的不断进步和用户需求的日益多样化，智能座舱将扮演越来越重要的角色。

汽车作为机械工业发展的产物，自1885年德国人卡尔·本茨成功研制出世界上第一辆汽车以来,至今也不过百余年历史。技术不断发展,现在的汽车已从单一交通工具,成为了一个集信息获取、社会交流、媒体消费和个人娱乐于一体的综合空间,一个具有多样化功能的大型移动服务系统。汽车座舱从传统到智能,不再仅仅是多个零部件的简单集合,而是软件与算法能力不断提升下的服务载体。从座舱技术出发,可将座舱设计的演进分为传统机械化座舱、电子化座舱、智能辅助驾驶座舱、智能驾驶座舱。

2.1.1 传统机械化座舱

传统机械化座舱技术,主要依赖于机械式的控制器和操作界面,来实现驾驶员与驾驶系统之间的信息交流和指令传递。汽车座舱内提供车辆的基本运行信息,如发动机转速、车速、油量、水温等,这些信息通常通过机械式仪表盘来展示。这种交互方式相对简单直接,但功能和灵活性有限。具体来说有以下功能部件:

机械手柄和脚踏板:驾驶员通过机械手柄、脚踏板等物理控制器来操纵座舱内的各种功能。这些控制器通常通过机械连接或电线连接与座舱系统相连,驾驶员的操作会直接传递到系统并产生相应的反馈。

机械式开关和按钮:座舱内可能布满了各种开关和按钮,用于控制不同的功能,如空调、音响、灯光等。驾驶员需要熟悉每个开关和按钮的位置和功能,以便在需要时能够迅速准确地操作。

仪表盘和指示器:传统机械化座舱通常配备有模拟仪表盘和各种指示器,用于显示车辆的速度、发动机转速、油量、水温等关键信息。驾驶员需要时刻关注这些仪表盘和指示器,以便及时了解车辆的运行状态。

早期座舱除了座椅、仪表台等通用设计,还有头盔、防风护目镜、防护衣服、抓握手套等个性设计。座舱中的相关产品设计见图2-1(本书作者摄于都灵汽车博物馆)。

图2-1 早期机械化座舱技术

机械化座舱的设计重点在于保障驾驶的安全性和车辆的基本控制。技术集成度较低,各个功能模块相对独立。1908年,亨利·福特的T型车标志着汽车时代的正式到来。在这一背景下,车内用户界面主要聚焦于为驾驶员提供与主要驾驶参数相关的信息,如速度、油门和转速计数器等,以确保驾驶过程的安全与便捷。

> **案例：雪铁龙 DS 内饰设计**
>
> 1955 年雪铁龙 DS 内部仪表布置见图 2-2，这时出现了辅助驾驶信息设计的所谓警示灯模式，这意味着早期经验性、渐变式的驾驶信息判断，转变为"开关"式判断，极大降低了驾驶员的认知复杂度。同时，单幅方向盘直观地显示了汽车转弯角度，变速控制杆位于方向盘后，采用前进和制动的脚踏板设计。1955 年雪铁龙 DS 的车内设计标志着汽车内饰的技术雏形已经形成。

图 2-2　1955 年雪铁龙 DS 内部仪表布置

2.1.2　电子化座舱

电子化座舱，后又被称为信息化、数字化座舱，是在传统机械化座舱的基础上，通过引入电子技术发展起来的。车辆功能由电子控制单元管理，提高了车辆系统的响应速度和精确度。例如，传统机械化座舱的机械式仪表和物理按键逐渐被电子显示屏和触摸控制所取代，提升了信息显示的灵活性和用户操作的便捷性。所谓电子化座舱，其实可以称为机械化+电子化座舱。比如"手刹"变为"电子手刹"，但电子手刹存在踩油门自动解除、踩刹车（制动踏板）停车自动启动的操作习惯转变，因此，电子化座舱在提高驾驶的便利性和信息的丰富性的同时，也产生了许多交互问题。

随着技术的发展，汽车信息化和自动化程度的日益提升，座舱内的计量表逐渐从分散式显示整合为驾驶信息和辅助驾驶信息两大基本显示类型，这一变革也促使仪表台布局发生了相应调整。信息化技术的应用使得汽车座舱能够处理和显示大量数据，如导航信息、车辆状态；图形技术的进步使得座舱内显示屏的分辨率和图像处理能力得到提升；集成技术促进了座舱内多个电子控制单元（ECU）的整合，降低了线束的复杂性，提升了座舱系统的效率和可靠性，降低了汽车驾驶的技术复杂性。电子安全相关技术，如电子稳定程序（ESP）、防抱死制动系统（ABS）、牵引力控制（TCS）等的完善，显著提高了行车安全性。具体来说，电子化座舱阶段的标志性技术包括以下几种。

触摸屏显示器：现代电子化座舱广泛采用触摸屏技术，可以通过触摸屏幕实现导航、音频、电话、车辆设置等各种功能。

抬头显示器（HUD）：HUD 将车速、导航方向等即时信息，直接投影在驾驶员视线前方风挡上，驾驶员无需低头即可获取关键信息，提升了行车安全性。AR-HUD 是一种将增强现实（AR）技术应用于抬头显示（HUD）的汽车智能座舱系统，可将虚拟的图像和信息叠加到现实路面上。

语音交互：通过语音识别系统，驾驶员可以用语音指令来控制汽车的各种功能，如导航目的地输入、音乐播放、电话拨打等。

触觉技术：多功能方向盘上集成了多种功能按键，驾驶员可以通过触觉感知来操作这些按键，实现对音频、电话、巡航控制等功能的快速访问。

电子技术引入汽车座舱后，汽车设计师开始借助信息化技术、图形技术和集成技术，对汽车内饰的造型与设计进行全面整合。因此，机械化+电子化座舱的出现，标志着人类完成了现代汽车内饰造型设计的风格雏形和基本形制，包括车身设计、内饰设计、空间设计、CMF 设计、NVH 设计等。经典 T 型布局基本形成，设计强调仪表、中控。主副驾之间的中央控制台造型与其上排列的各类按键呼应，产生良好的融合。汽车内饰的发展代表车型及其造型特点见表 2-1，汽车内饰设计风格见表 2-2。内饰设计成为汽车造型设计的一个独立部门，有专门的设计团队。

表 2-1　汽车内饰的发展代表车型及其造型特点

时间/年	代表车型	内饰造型特点	部件造型特点	发展期
1885	The Benz Patent 奔驰一号	"粗陋"的机械结构，结构简易	喜爱使用名贵木材作为辅助装饰材料（珠光漆和珐琅），并镶嵌贵重金属，放置真皮座椅，以此来彰显车主显赫的身份	启蒙时期——诞生与初期发展
1908	Henry Ford 的 T 型车			
1915	劳斯莱斯 Silver Ghost			
1923	奔驰 15/70/100			
1937	克莱斯勒 Airflow Eight			
1948	大众甲壳虫 雪铁龙 2CV	造型简洁方正和功能至上，简单实用而又安全可靠，方向盘纤细硕大，仪表分散排布，造型元素以平面直角和圆形仪表盘为主，充斥了夸张的装饰元素	方向盘多为金属亮铬材质。内饰 CMF 开始呼应外饰 CMF	功能时期
1954	奔驰 300SL 凯迪拉克 Eldorado	汽车内饰设计开始向复杂精致、功能规整划分，受传动轴影响，内饰主线从横向，向 T 型和整体车内空间一体化发展	开始使用木纹、真皮材质，在换挡件等局部结构件上加装饰性材质	一体化时代
1959	沃尔沃 PV544			
1965	福特 Mustang			
1975	BMW 3 系 E21			
1983	丰田皇冠 S120	经典 T 型布局基本形成，设计强调仪表、中控。中央过道之间的造型融合，中控上排列各类按键	电子化时代特征明显，车内开始出现塑料-皮质组合	现代电子化
1991	奥迪 100 C4			
1998	丰田普锐斯			

续表

时间/年	代表车型	内饰造型特点	部件造型特点	发展期
2006	奥迪 A8 雷克萨斯 LS	比例均匀、线条流畅，开始体现人本思想，线条柔和优雅；造型圆润饱满，仪表集中排布，关注人机关系、舒适性、可视性和驾驶体验	方向盘、操作区为适应人机关系和可视性，开始以偏暗色亚光塑料为主；车身内饰颜色在这一阶段可视为"消失的颜色"阶段，装饰性亮色金属漆多用于一些功能键上，比如 CD 播放、旋钮等。座椅仍以皮质为主	人本时期
2006	雅阁			
2007	大众宝来			
2007	标致 307			
2007	现代伊兰特			
2007	凯美瑞			
2012	特斯拉 Model S	随着科技的发展，电动汽车的兴起和自动驾驶的逐渐普及，汽车内饰造型开始摒除原有的 T 型布局，重新进入新的汽车内部分区排布尝试，整体设计风格向一体化科感发展，以简化驾驶区、丰富体验区为主，在造型上更加大胆、丰富、多元化，以彰显未来科技感	1. 开始大胆采用高科技特种材质，比如大面积的特种玻璃、陶瓷的使用，达到从视觉上减轻车身内部的沉闷感。2. 大胆采用真实材料，搭配参数化手法，在内饰上，开始采用木材、水泥等真实材料，或模拟仿真真实材料的触感，并以参数化手法表现辅助科技，以增加情感互动。3. 在表面处理和颜色上，都采用了渐变的手法，丰富了使用者在内部空间中的体验	科技时期
2014	BMW Vision i8			
2019	Byton 本田 Urban EV 概念车 奔驰 F015 沃尔沃 Concept 26 概念车			

表 2-2 汽车内饰设计风格

设计风格	未来主义	现代主义	高科技风格	当代科技风格
社会意识	人类征服自然，崇尚工业机器生产			以人为本，追求和谐，崇尚自然
美学来源	均反映"机器时代"的美学，抽象主义			生态哲学，技术理性，数字美学
感知意象	未来感	现代感	狭义科技感	广义科技感
表现形式	多声与多节奏的抽象形体，运动趋向，内心不和谐的需求	理性主义与功能主义，标准化与批量化生产方式	复兴机器美学，暴露零件结构，表现并鼓吹高新技术	展现人类最高智慧，物质实体链接非物质世界的多元化表达，融合高情感与高技术
造型特征	机器语言，犀利，速度感，力量感	纯粹装饰极少，高度一致，几何化	复杂罗列、精细、夸张的造型特征	简洁、炫酷、智能、精准等开放式的语言特点

  汽车内饰造型与设计并非单一的产品设计，而是综合考虑人机工程学后在座舱内部所形成的整体设计。这通常涵盖了基于舒适度的座椅布置、基于操作准确率的控制按钮布局以及基于信息获取效率的仪表盘可读性设计等多个方面。通过反复的造型设计推

演，旨在打造出既安全便利又美观舒适的驾乘环境。汽车内饰也完成了从机械到驾驶环境的转变，基本上确立了汽车内饰形制的技术雏形。自此，汽车开始有了明确的"内外"之分，汽车内饰设计这一概念逐渐得到大众的更多关注，频繁出现在人们的视野中。伴随着机械工业的进步，汽车内饰设计开始向复杂精致、功能规整划分。同时，受传动轴布置影响，内饰主线从横向，向 T 型和整体车内空间一体化发展。

总之，通过机械化＋电子化座舱发展，人类几乎完成了对汽车的"物理边界"拓展，出现了以赛车、跑车和轿跑为代表的性能车，并将"驾驶感"或"操控性能"推到了极致，与此同时，在被动安全的极限上研发主动安全，汽车工业成为整个工业的引擎之一。而随着技术进一步发展催生的智能座舱，则不仅要继续追求汽车的物理边界，更要探寻汽车的"智能边界"，这是一次伟大的技术跃升，将根本改变人类的生活方式和出行方式，即所谓"第三空间"。

2.1.3 智能辅助驾驶座舱

智能座舱是近年发展出来的汽车座舱概念，是机械化座舱和电子化座舱的迭代跃升，正在以极快的速度进步、发展。智能座舱中的人工智能，是指被专门训练和执行与驾驶、导航、障碍物识别、行人检测等相关的任务。这些系统通常基于机器学习和深度学习算法，通过大量的数据进行训练，以在特定领域内达到或超越人类的表现。华为对自研智能座舱的描述是，鸿蒙 2.0 实现了人与车机的流畅交互，鸿蒙 3.0 实现了人与设备的自由互联，鸿蒙 4.0 实现了多人多屏多设备的智慧体验，下一次升级将通过"千悟引擎"，精准感知到座舱里的每一个人，在 10 秒内就可以复制个人的声纹，并进行个性化的服务。

为了研究方便，我们将智能座舱分为智能辅助驾驶座舱和智能驾驶座舱。智能座舱的智能概念既是一个越来越泛化的概念，比如通用人工智能；又是一个越来越场景化和专门化的概念，比如领域人工智能和智能座舱。采用智能辅助驾驶和智能驾驶来区分智能座舱的发展阶段，尽管不能完整体现座舱的智能化水平，但是智能驾驶是座舱智能化水平的基础，又是用户能够最直观感知的重要体现。

从 20 世纪 80 年代至 2015 年，随着传感器技术的飞速进步和芯片技术的广泛应用，智能化自动控制系统层出不穷，包括发动机控制、自动变速、动力转向、电子稳定程序、主动悬架、座椅位置调节、空调、刮水器、安全带、安全气囊、防碰撞、防盗、巡航行驶、全球卫星定位等功能。同时，车载音频/视频数字多媒体娱乐系统、无线网络以及智能交通等车辆辅助技术也相继涌现，使得汽车座舱逐渐展现出智能化和网联化的特点。在这一阶段，技术的涌现使汽车内饰造型开始摒除原有的 T 型布局，重新进入新的汽车内部分区排布尝试，整体设计风格向一体化科技感发展，以简化驾驶区、丰富体验区为主。

2015 年以来，随着电子电气系统的不断增加，它们之间的通信变得日益复杂，线束设计的难度也迅速提升，因此，汽车的电子电气架构不断升级以适应这些变化。博世在 2017 年提出了电子电气架构的演化图，将整车电子电气架构的发展划分为六个阶段：模块化阶段、功能集成阶段、中央域控制器阶段、跨域融合阶段、车载中央电脑和区域控制器阶段，以及车载云计算阶段。目前，汽车电子电气架构正在从分布式向域集中式转变。在车辆上，主要存在五个域：动力域、车身控制域、自动驾驶域、底盘控制域和座舱域。其中，驾驶辅助/自动驾驶域和座舱域直接关联到用户的体验感受，因此备受汽车制造企业的重视。这些技术的发展和变革，不仅提升了汽车的智能化水平，也为用户带来了更加便捷、舒适的驾乘体验。以下是智能辅助驾驶座舱的一些标志性技术。

自然语言处理：通过先进的自然语言处理技术，座舱系统能够准确识别并理解驾驶员的语音指令，实现更加自然和流畅的语音交互。

多模态交互：结合语音、手势、面部表情等多种交互方式，使驾驶员能够以更自然的方式与座舱系统进行沟通。

高清晰度显示：采用高分辨率的显示屏幕，提供清晰、细腻的图像显示，使驾驶员能够更容易地获取和理解信息。

AR/VR 技术：利用增强现实（AR）或虚拟现实（VR）技术，在驾驶员视野中叠加虚拟信息，提供更丰富、更直观的驾驶辅助和娱乐体验。

生物识别：通过指纹识别、面部识别等技术，实现个性化设置和安全验证，提高座舱的安全性和便捷性。

情感识别：利用传感器和算法分析驾驶员的情绪状态，根据驾驶员的情绪调整座舱环境或提供相应的驾驶辅助。

车联网技术：通过车载通信系统实现车与车、车与基础设施、车与行人的全面互联，提供实时交通信息、远程车辆控制和智能交通管理等功能。

云计算和大数据技术：利用云计算和大数据技术处理和分析车辆运行数据，为驾驶员提供更具个性化、更精准的驾驶建议和服务。

人工智能算法：通过机器学习、深度学习等算法，使座舱系统能够自主学习和优化，提供更智能的驾驶辅助和决策支持。

预测性维护：基于车辆使用数据和算法分析，预测车辆部件的寿命和故障风险，提前进行维护和更换，提高车辆的安全性和可靠性。

同时，另一个具有跨领域智能增强的技术就是智能座舱与手机生态的深度融合，其基本概念是通过技术手段将智能座舱与手机操作系统、应用程序和服务进行无缝连接，使车主能够在车内便捷地访问和使用手机上的功能和服务。这种融合旨在改善驾驶体验，让驾驶者在行车过程中能够安全、方便地享受各种便捷服务。

2.1.4 智能驾驶座舱

从智能辅助驾驶到智能驾驶，存在非常大的技术重叠区。智能座舱迈入高度智能化阶段，座舱技术取得显著进步，集成了先进的人工智能、大数据、云计算等技术，可以实现更加智能的驾驶辅助、个性化设置、智能互联等功能。

智能驾驶座舱里，空间的功能愈发丰富，除了作为用户驾驶操作的主要场所，还承载着浏览信息、收发短信、接打电话、导航、广播和音乐等众多次要任务。汽车座舱演变为一个集嵌入计算、通信和感知能力于一体的新型智能空间。这个阶段的汽车不仅能够独立执行驾驶任务，还为与其相关的移动生活模式提供了全方位服务，使智能座舱真正成为了集移动办公、生活起居、休息娱乐、社交通信于一体的移动生活"第三空间"。汽车已不仅是过往认知上的交通工具，更是可以应对多场景使用需求的智能网联移动终端。

在智能驾驶座舱内，人机交互技术呈现出多元化趋势，包括语音识别、手势识别、人脸识别、人工智能（AI）、增强现实（AR）、抬头显示（HUD）、高级驾驶辅助系统（ADAS）、车联网模块、SRV环视等多种技术。同时，座舱空间布局也呈现出多元化特点，涵盖了一体化中控显示、流媒体中央后视镜、音响、座椅、灯光等丰富内容。

案例：广汽埃安座舱

广汽埃安座舱内预设的四个场景主题模式，分别为小憩、暴雨、节能和性能，每个模式开启后，车机系统会协同启动相应的预设，来实现最契合主题的驾乘感受（图2-3）。

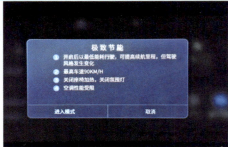

图2-3 广汽埃安的同时空下的系统协调

同时，智能座舱技术的发展，使得座舱功能与应用场景的多样性及用户体验之间的冲突开始凸显，智能座舱将以用户高层次情感需求作为产品差异化的内核。设计师则通过深入研究场景下的用户行为，发现用户实际需求、剖析使用过程、形成创新设计方案。在这样的模式下，智能座舱的设计形成以"场景-可控交互事件-用户行为"为基础的创意与设计模式。设计解决方案也呈现出从静态到动态的转变趋势。

2.2 汽车座舱的用户体验

汽车提供服务时，与用户体验最密不可分的就是汽车座舱。智能座舱既是智能的载体，又是用户直接感知智能和体验智能的场所。在智能座舱中，座舱芯片起到至关重要的作用。它们是汽车运算决策的中心，负责处理大量的数据和信息，以确保座舱内各项功能的协同和优化。为了实现流畅、高效的智能座舱体验，座舱芯片需要具备高性能的处理能力，包括强大的数据承载能力、快速的数据处理速度以及出色的图像渲染能力。

汽车座舱是人车交互的核心平台，它为驾驶者提供了与车辆进行交流和操作的主要界面，因此，消费者对汽车的直观感受很大程度上来自于座舱内的交互体验。在传统观念中，汽车主要被视为一种交通工具，座舱设计的重点在于实现驾驶员与外界的有效信息交流，以及完成基本的机械驾驶任务，这使得产品设计的核心集中在车辆作为运输工具的功能上。然而，现代汽车的发展已经超越了这一传统框架。随着数字化和信息化系统的广泛应用，原本的机械和电气控制系统已经逐步被智能技术所取代。车载信息系统、娱乐系统、语音控制以及多样的车载应用和软件，已经成为智能汽车的标配，这些技术的发展使得人机交互更加注重满足用户的个性化体验和需求。可以说，汽车座舱正在经历一场前所未有的变革。尽管技术变革使汽车座舱的设计关注点产生了变化：过去的座舱设计主要关注功能性和驾驶操作；智能座舱的设计更加重视乘客的体验和互动，目标是创造一个充满智慧、舒适且高度互联的移动空间。但在从传统座舱向智能座舱演进的过程中，坚持以用户为中心的设计理念是不变的，始终将用户需求和体验放在首位。座舱在设计过程中，始终要深入分析用户的行为逻辑，以确保各项功能都能够符合用户的操作习惯和预期。

座舱内用户体验的发展可以划分为三个主要阶段：①基础驾驶体验阶段，重点在于实现基本的驾驶操作和信息交流；②电子信息座舱的用户体验阶段，这一阶段开始引入车载信息系统和娱乐功能，提升了驾驶的信息化水平；③智能座舱的用户体验阶段，这一阶段的座舱不仅提供高度个性化和智能化的交互体验，还强调与用户的生活环境和需求紧密相连，打造一个全方位的智能生活空间。

2.2.1 基础驾驶体验

基础驾驶体验是对应于机械化座舱技术阶段的驾驶体验。在传统机械化座舱中，驾驶者的体验主要集中在感受车辆的驾驶性能上，如操控性等，座舱的功能和舒适性相对有限。

最早的汽车主要基于马车形制，为了避免乘客干扰驾驶员复杂的机械操作，形成了驾驶舱和乘员舱"分区"的布局雏形。驾驶舱位于车体（车身）前部，是驾驶员的工作区，驾驶员可以面向行进的方向（通过前窗）观看前方；而乘员舱位于车体（车身）后部，是乘员的"自由区"，乘客既可以面向行进方向，也可以背向行进方向，甚至垂直于行进方向，通过侧向窗观察车外环境。早期汽车总布置见图2-4。

图 2-4　早期汽车总布置

> **案例：第一代汽车的"内饰"与驾驶行为**

自 1885 年造出第一辆"汽车"后的很长一段时间，不论是日常行驶还是竞速比赛，汽车驾驶都是"两个人的事"。第一代"汽车"见图 2-5（本书作者拍摄于都灵汽车博物馆）。汽车诞生初期，驾驶时需要随时观察油箱压力（油表）、水冷系统的温度（水温计）和引擎状态等各种计量表，以确保汽车的正常运行。初代的汽车仪表是分散组装的，开关和油表位于仪表台上，而水温计则安装于散热器旁。这是由于当时技术条件的限制，为了更精确地采集数据，各种车内仪表都选择装在靠近部件的位置。各种不同类型的仪表安装位置既分散又远离驾驶员的现象，使得仪表的数值读取对于一个驾驶员来说是很困难的。因此，车手（驾驶员）一定需要一名副驾驶，以共同完成汽车的仪表观察和相关操控，副驾驶还负责维修机器故障。

图 2-5 第一代"汽车"

1956 年，福特公司成立了人机工程部，标志着汽车设计开始从对车的关注转到了对人的关注。人机工程学是倡导"使机器适应人"的科学，强调工具的辅助意义，避免工具的强制性，借助数据化的人机标准，调和人和机器的矛盾，使机器更易于被人使用。

通过使用人机工程学原则，座椅舒适度、控制按钮布局合理性和仪表盘可读性等有所提升。但基础驾驶体验阶段的用户体验依旧更多地集中在直接、基础的操作和功能上。

2.2.2 电子信息座舱的用户体验

信息化驾驶体验对应于机械化 + 电子化座舱技术阶段的驾驶体验。座舱开始提供更多的驾驶信息，如导航、车辆状态等，驾驶者可以更方便地获取所需信息，提升驾驶的便捷性和安全性。随着驾驶操作难度的显著减轻，驾驶员的体验从单纯的操作体验上升为更为丰富的驾驶体验。人在驾驶过程中产生了执行驾驶任务外的其他需求，车内开始置入除驾驶外的其他功能，而新的辅助功能使驾驶员单纯的驾驶行为变成了驾驶 - 娱乐行为。早在 1924 年，雪佛兰汽车就率先搭载了收音机设备，这被认为是驾驶者除驾驶车辆外所进行的首个次要交互任务，彰显了汽车内部设计与科技的演进。

随着时间的推移，特别是在 20 世纪 80 年代，车内电子集成、智能辅助驾驶以及车载娱乐信息系统等技术的飞速发展，空调系统、音乐（CD/MP3）、通话、车载导航等功能逐渐融入汽车，使得驾驶愈发成为一种享受和情感体验（图 2-6）。在这一过程中，早期汽车的机械部件逐渐被功能更为完善的电气部件所替代。值得注意的是，由于电气化是渐进式地替代原有机械部件，因此这些新引入的电气化产品起初都是相互独立的。然而，随着越来越多的电气化产品集成于汽车这一载体，汽车内部设计逐渐朝着为驾驶者提供更为丰富、便捷和愉悦的驾驶体验的方向发展。

图 2-6　早期汽车搭载收音机的广告

2.2.3　智能座舱的用户体验

智能化驾驶体验对应于智能辅助驾驶和智能驾驶座舱技术阶段的座舱用户体验。智能座舱可以给驾驶者提供更加智能化的服务：智能化的辅助驾驶体验，如自动避障、车道保持辅助、自动泊车、智能召唤等，甚至能够在特定的路况和环境条件下，执行所有的动态驾驶任务；多样化的交互方式，如语音控制、手势交互，增强了交互体验；同时，还可以根据驾驶者的习惯和喜好进行个性化设置，如自适应巡航的跟车距离或车速。这使得驾驶员的驾驶任务进一步减少，降低了驾驶过程中的疲劳感，且驾驶员可以在车辆自主行驶时处理其他非驾驶相关的活动，如工作、阅读或休闲娱乐。可以说这一阶段的用户体验不再是单纯的驾驶体验，而是以智能化驾驶体验为主的综合体验。

事实上，在这个智能化时代，汽车座舱作为一个"集成进化"空间，各种服务系统和功能部件以"插件"的形式集成到汽车内部，来满足更加多样化的用户需求。特别是自 5G 技术出现以来，汽车的全面智能化和高度集成化趋势使得汽车开始转变为集娱乐、办公、生活、社交于一体的人机交互智能产品。因此，座舱的设计与用户的体验也进入了一个全新的阶段。

智能座舱中用户体验的变化与自动驾驶技术的发展息息相关。自动驾驶从 L0 级别发展到 L5 级别，人机之间的交互比例逐渐发生变化，意味着驾驶员和乘员的注意力得以从驾驶任务中逐渐解放。曾任福特汽车美国设计总监的 Moray Callum 提出，当驾驶员不需要驾驶时，内室就变成了驾驶员和乘客的平等"空间"。未来到了 L5 阶段，车内人员将驾驶任务完全交给智能驾驶系统，汽车座舱的定义将发生根本性的变革。它不再仅仅是一个驾乘空间，而是转变为纯粹的乘用空间；其空间布局从围绕驾驶任务转变为围绕用户需求，从已定义空间转变为可定义空间。

人与车的关系也从以驾驶任务为主的交互系统，转变为以可控交互事件、场景和动作为基础的复杂人机交互系统。多通道人机交互（multimedia user interaction）设计，包括语音识别、手势输入、可穿戴设备、视线追踪等新的交互形式，成为汽车人机交互的主要研究方向和领域。

智能座舱形成了以信息为基础、以交互内容为核心、以座舱空间为载体的用户体验空间。自然语言识别技术使得乘客可以通过语音与座舱系统进行交互，实现更加便捷的操作；手势控制技术则进一步丰富了交互方式，让乘客能够通过简单的手势完成一系列复杂的操作；虚拟助手则能够主动为乘客提供信息和服务，改善乘客的乘车体验；个性化推荐技术则能够根据乘客的喜好和需求，为其提供量身定制的内容和服务；生理检测和脑机接口技术则能够实时监测乘客的身体状态和意图，为乘客提供更加贴心和个性化的服务。

随着交互技术的发展，驾驶车辆可以不完全依赖实体化的传统人机界面，从而减少认知负担和驾驶分心。汽车空间在交互信息组织结构、任务操作的特点与信息操作的方式等方面，同样具有其自身的特点。交互技术和智能技术改变了汽车用户的驾驶情境。

案例：奥迪 Urbansphere 概念车

奥迪 Urbansphere 概念车不同于传统的燃油车，电动能源的布局使得座舱内部空间宽敞。在内部设计上，它区别于传统的方向盘、脚踏板和仪表盘共同组成的中控部分，在自动驾驶过程中，方向盘、脚踏板和常规仪表盘都可隐藏，极大增强了车内空间的空间感和自由度，如图 2-7 所示。

图 2-7 奥迪 Urbansphere 内饰

座椅也能以多种方式轻松满足乘客多样的社交需求。相互交流时，乘客可旋转座椅，面对面交谈。而那些想要私密空间的乘客则可以通过头枕后方的隐私屏获取信息，头部上方区域的屏幕将其与身旁的其他乘客隔绝开来。当乘客之间想要共享车载信息娱乐系统时，一块大尺寸的透明 OLED 屏便会从车顶垂直降至两排座椅之间，如图 2-8 所示，通过一块横穿整车内部的"影院大屏"，后排两名乘客可一起参加视频会议或观赏电影。该大屏还可分屏使用。在无需使用大屏时，由于其透明的设计，乘客可直接清晰地看到前方。乘客还可以选择将屏幕向上收起，与玻璃车顶融为一体。该座舱既是一个移动尊享室，也是一个移动办公室，因此成为用户出行途中的"第三生活空间"。

图 2-8 奥迪 Urbansphere 后排座椅

尽管自动驾驶技术尚未完全实现 L5 级别的全自动驾驶，但汽车座舱已经逐渐演变为一种全新的空间领域，成为家庭和工作场所之外的"第三空间"。这个概念，即"移动的起居室"（mobile living room），正受到学术界和汽车制造商的广泛关注。这种新兴的汽车座舱设计观念赋予了车辆内部更多样化的功能与体验。自动驾驶的技术发展使得人们可以在行车过程中更多地专注于放松或工作及娱乐等活动。因此，汽车座舱——"移动的起居室"设计的核心在于如何优化车内空间布局、舒适性、娱乐性和工作性，以满足用户在车内不同场景下的需求。理想化的智能座舱设计应根据终端用户的出行场景，运用更多数据通道，主动地洞察与了解终端用户的实际需求，并通过软硬件协作解决实际问题，从而使终端用户获得更好的使用环境和驾驶体验。

案例：小鹏 P5

小鹏 P5 的智能第三空间结合了睡眠、娱乐、生活、户外、用户 DIY 五大场景。小鹏 P5 的智能座舱提出"动静皆宜，智趣无忧"，内部配置了亲肤材质的可调节座椅和香氛，折叠空间内放置了床垫、隐私帘、头枕、被子等，为睡眠场景提供了条件（图 2-9）。

图 2-9 小鹏 P5 车内"起居室"

在睡眠场景下，为保证安全，在进入睡眠模式前，系统也会进行电量提醒，如电量过低，则限制用户进入长时间睡眠模式，同时小鹏 P5 的守护型智能香氛系统可以监测车内一氧化碳和二氧化碳浓度，进行异常提醒或智能调节。

小鹏 P5 为生活场景在后排配置了冰箱、小桌板、车载加热器、太阳能车顶等设施。一家人上车后，前排驾乘者——爸爸开车，儿童和妈妈坐后排。妈妈在后排打开冰箱拿出早餐食品，放入车载加热器加热 10 分钟，再打开小桌板享用；而全车音响、后排的座椅和投影仪能支持在夜间的时候，乘客在后排进行沉浸式的观影。

2.3 智能座舱的应用场景

智能座舱的使用场景和技术可能性正在不断拓展。从目前智能座舱的实际应用中，以及各大车企所提出的智能座舱概念里，可以清晰地看到人机共驾、休闲娱乐、办公/商务以及车-家互联等四大主要应用场景。这些场景不仅丰富了用户的驾驶和乘坐体验，也预示着智能座舱未来的发展趋势和无限可能。

2.3.1 智能座舱人机共驾场景

（1）人机共驾技术场景

感知与决策融合：在人机共驾场景中，车辆通过先进的传感器（如雷达、摄像头、超声波传感器等）实时感知周围环境，包括障碍物、交通信号、道路标记等。这些信息与驾驶员的意图和操作相结合，通过高级算法进行处理，以实现人机之间的协同决策。

动态权限分配：系统根据驾驶环境和驾驶员的状态，动态调整自动驾驶系统和驾驶员之间的控制权限。例如，在复杂的交通情况下，系统可能会更多地介入驾驶过程，以确保安全；而在简单的路况下，驾驶员则可能拥有更多的控制权。

实时交互与反馈：人机共驾系统通过直观的人机界面（HMI）与驾驶员进行实时交互，提供驾驶建议、警示信息以及系统状态更新。这种交互确保驾驶员始终了解系统的运行状况，并能够根据需要调整自己的驾驶行为。

（2）人机共驾应用场景

自动驾驶辅助功能：在人机共驾模式下，驾驶员可以启用自动驾驶辅助功能，如自适应巡航控制、车道保持辅助等。这些功能可以减轻驾驶员的驾驶压力，特别是在高速公路或拥堵的城市道路上。

复杂路况应对：当遇到复杂或突发的路况（如前方事故、道路施工等）时，人机共驾系统可以与驾驶员共同应对。系统可以提供额外的感知信息和驾驶建议，帮助驾驶员做出更明智的决策。

驾驶员状态监测与接管：系统持续监测驾驶员的生理和心理状态（如疲劳、分心等）。当检测到驾驶员可能无法安全驾驶时，系统会发出警示并准备接管驾驶任务，以确保行车安全。

提供个性化驾驶体验：人机共驾系统可以根据驾驶员的偏好和习惯进行个性化设置。例如，系统可以学习驾驶员的加速、制动和转向习惯，并在自动驾驶时模拟这些习惯，以提供更加自然的驾驶体验。

综上所述，人机共驾场景在技术层面强调感知与决策融合、动态权限分配以及实时交互与反馈；在应用层面则注重自动驾驶辅助功能、复杂路况应对、驾驶员状态监测与接管以及提供个性化驾驶体验。

> **案例：特斯拉自动辅助驾驶系统（Autopilot）**

Autopilot（自动辅助驾驶系统）是特斯拉独有的一项技术，2014年10月 Autopilot Hardware 1.0（简称HW 1.0）发布以来就一直在全球电动车行业中拥有不小的关注度。现在该功能已经是特斯拉完全自动驾驶能力（full self-driving capability）中的重要功能之一。使用Autopilot时驾驶员在车辆行驶过程中无需自己操作就可以让车辆自己判断是否驶入/驶出高速或者超车，同时做出相应的驾驶动作，这些都是在驾驶者监控下实现的。目前特斯拉官网上公布的Autopilot具有如下几个功能：

① 自动辅助导航驾驶。系统会根据路况建议驾驶者变更车道以优化导航路线，适时调整以避免车辆被堵在速度较慢的车辆后方。在启用了相关功能的情况下，系统还可以根据驾驶者设定的目的地，自动控制车辆驶入高速公路分岔路或出口。

② 自动辅助转向。借助先进的摄像头和运算能力，系统可以在更为拥挤、复杂的路况中自动辅助转向，或始终让车辆保持在车道内行驶。

③ 智能召唤。使用智能召唤，即使停车场地的环境较为复杂且车位空间有限，系统也能够自行导航并及时避开障碍物，最终让车辆来到驾驶者的身边，如图2-10所示，用户于B点使用智能召唤功能，可将车从A点召唤至B点。

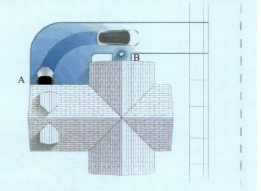

图2-10 特斯拉Autopilot智能召唤功能

2.3.2 智能座舱休闲娱乐场景

（1）休闲娱乐技术场景

多媒体系统集成：智能座舱通过高度集成的多媒体系统，提供电影、音乐、游戏等丰富的娱乐内容。这些内容可以通过车内的高清显示屏、高品质音响系统来呈现，为乘客带来沉浸式的娱乐体验。

人机交互技术：借助先进的语音识别和自然语言处理技术，乘客可以通过简单的语音指令来操控智能座舱的娱乐系统，如播放音乐、选择电影或游戏等。此外，智能座舱还可能支持手势控制，进一步丰富人机交互方式。

个性化推荐算法：智能座舱能够根据乘客的历史偏好和行为数据，通过算法智能推荐适合的娱乐内容，让每个乘客都能享受到个性化的休闲娱乐体验。

连接技术与云服务：通过车联网技术，智能座舱可以实时获取网络上的娱乐资源，并保持系统软件的实时更新。同时，乘客的个人账户信息可以同步到车载系统中，实现无缝的娱乐体验切换。

（2）休闲娱乐应用场景

长途旅行中的娱乐：在长途驾驶或乘坐过程中，乘客可以通过智能座舱观看电影、听音乐或玩游戏来打发时间，提升旅行的舒适度。

家庭出游的欢乐时光：在家庭出游时，智能座舱的娱乐系统可以提供适合全家人的娱乐内容，如播放动画片或家庭电影，营造温馨的车内氛围。

等待时间的消遣：在停车等待或充电期间，乘客可以利用智能座舱的娱乐功能来消磨时间，避免无聊和焦虑。

社交娱乐的互动平台：智能座舱还可以作为社交娱乐的平台，乘客可以在车内与朋友进行在线游戏对战、共享音乐播放列表等互动活动，增强社交体验。

综上所述，智能座舱的休闲娱乐场景通过先进的技术集成和丰富的应用场景设计，可为乘客提供多样化、个性化的娱乐体验。

案例："inside the future" 的虚拟触控辅助娱乐交互体验

宝马 2017 年的概念车中展示了名为"inside the future" 的虚拟触控辅助娱乐交互体验，该研究项目主要包含 HoloActive 触控技术（实现悬浮式虚拟中控屏）、BMW Sound Curtain（个性化音效装置）以及后排折叠大屏幕这三项技术。其中最有特点的就是 HoloActive 触控技术（图 2-11），可实现通过虚拟屏幕模拟真实触感操作达成信息娱乐交互功能。

图 2-11　HoloActive 触控技术

2.3.3　智能座舱办公 / 商务场景

（1）办公 / 商务技术场景

移动办公技术支持：智能座舱提供稳定的网络连接，确保在车内也能随时接入互联网，处理办公事务。通过车载高速网络，乘客可以在座舱内收发电子邮件、参与视频会议，或实时访问公司内部的办公系统和云存储服务。

智能语音助手集成：为了提升办公效率，智能座舱集成了智能语音助手，乘客可以通过语音指令来创建日程、记录笔记或查询重要信息，实现便捷的语音交互体验。

多任务处理能力：智能座舱的中控系统具备强大的多任务处理能力，支持同时运行多个办公软件，如文档编辑器、表格处理软件和演示文稿工具等，满足商务人士在车内处理多种工作任务的需求。

舒适的办公环境：为了确保在车内办公的舒适性，智能座舱还提供了人性化的座椅设计和环境控制系统，如自动调节的座椅角度、温度控制和氛围灯光等，以营造出一个舒适的办公环境。

（2）办公/商务应用场景

移动会议室：对于需要频繁出差或在外场工作的商务人士来说，智能座舱可以作为一个移动会议室。在车内可以随时加入或发起视频会议，与团队保持紧密沟通，确保工作的高效推进。

路途中的文档处理：在前往会议或商务活动的途中，乘客可以利用智能座舱内的办公系统，审阅或编辑重要文档，有效利用碎片时间，提高工作效率。

紧急事务处理：面对突发的紧急工作事务，即使在行车过程中，乘客也能通过智能座舱快速响应，如紧急审批文件、回复重要邮件等，确保工作的及时性和连续性。

商务休闲两不误：在完成工作任务的同时，智能座舱还能提供轻松的音乐或舒适的座椅按摩功能，帮助商务人士在紧张的工作之余，也能享受到片刻的放松和舒适。

综上所述，智能座舱在办公/商务场景中，通过先进的技术支持和舒适的环境设计，可为商务人士提供一个高效、便捷的移动办公空间。

> **案例：广汽绿境 SPACE**
>
> 2022年6月在广汽科技日（GAC TECH DAY）上首发亮相的广汽绿境 SPACE 如图2-12所示。其新车内饰采用了云山珠水织物面板设计理念，座舱内配备了概念化座椅、围坐式沙发和茶几。该款概念车站在未来出行的视角，展示了未来出行中的移动商务办公场景。
>
>
>
> 图2-12　广汽绿境 SPACE

2.3.4　车–家互联场景

（1）车–家互联技术场景

无缝连接技术：智能座舱通过先进的通信技术（如蓝牙、Wi-Fi、5G等）实现与家庭智能设备的无缝连接。这种连接允许车辆与家中的智能设备进行数据交换和控制操作。

物联网（IoT）集成：借助 IoT 技术，智能座舱能够与家中的各种智能设备（如智能灯具、智能门锁、智能家电等）进行连接和互动，形成一个智能化的生活环境。

远程控制功能：通过手机 App 或其他远程控制平台，用户可以在车内或远离车辆时远程控制家中的智能设备。例如，在回家的路上通过智能座舱提前打开家中的空调或热水器。

数据安全与隐私保护：在车-家互联场景中，智能座舱采用先进的数据加密和隐私保护技术，确保用户数据的安全性和隐私性。

（2）车–家互联应用场景

智慧出行与家居协同：当用户准备出行时，智能座舱可以与家中的智能设备协同工作，如自动调整家中温度、关闭不必要的电器等，以节省能源并确保家庭安全。

远程控制与管理：在外出期间，用户可以通过智能座舱远程控制家中的智能设备。例如，检查家中摄像头的实时画面、调节室内温度或灯光等。

到家模式预设：当用户接近家时，智能座舱可以与家中的智能设备通信，自动开启"到家模式"，如打开门锁、调整室内光线和温度等，以提供舒适的家居环境。

个性化生活体验：智能座舱可以根据用户的喜好和习惯，与家中的智能设备共同打造个性化的生活体验。例如，自动播放用户喜欢的音乐、调整室内氛围灯光等。

综上所述，智能座舱在车-家互联场景中，通过无缝连接技术、物联网集成和远程控制功能等技术手段，可为用户提供更加智能化、便捷和个性化的生活体验。同时，智能座舱还注重用户数据的安全性和隐私性保护，确保用户在享受智能化服务的同时，个人信息也得到充分保护。

案例：ConnectedDrive 服务功能

宝马与三星旗下智慧家庭装置整合服务商 SmartThings 进行合作，配备 ConnectedDrive 服务功能（图 2-13）的车型可通过连接设备打开和关闭家庭报警系统，以及在家庭紧急情况下接收警报。

图 2-13　宝马 ConnectedDrive

第 3 章

基于空间、角色和动作的智能座舱交互设计

3.1 智能座舱人机交互设计概念
3.2 智能座舱人机交互要素
3.3 人机交互 SRA 设计流程
3.4 空间交互接触点
3.5 人机交互 SRA 设计案例分析

本章讨论一个主题，可简称为"人机交互 SRA 设计"（space，role，action）。人机交互 SRA 设计方法，采用智能座舱人机交互设计方法论和智能座舱交互设计场景的概念框架（详见第 1 章），探讨智能座舱交互设计方法，属于设计范式范畴的问题，即设计过程和设计方法问题。这里，设计方法主要包含以下几个方面。

思维模式：SRA 设计方法提供一套系统的场景化的设计思维模式，通过空间、角色和动作三个场景要素，框定设计问题，挖掘用户需求，捕获空间交互触点，提出设计方案，评估方案的可行性。

步骤和流程：SRA 设计方法提供了明确的设计步骤，包括研究、分析、构思、原型制作、测试和迭代等。

技术和工具：SRA 设计方法提供了一种"汽车交互时空动作蓝图"的设计分析工具，也包括用户访谈、问卷调查、头脑风暴、故事板、原型工具等一般设计工具的应用，有助于设计师更有效地收集数据、生成创意和评估设计。这一部分会在第 5 章进行专题讨论。

创新策略：SRA 设计方法提出了"空间、角色和动作三要素汽车人机交互设计框架"，通过多维度地思考、发现或赋予要素新概念，设计者能够更深入地了解不同场景下的用户体验，从而洞察到更多的机会点来拓展设计空间，从多个维度启发和推动创新思考。

评估与迭代：SRA 设计方法强调对设计方案的持续评估和迭代。通过用户反馈、测试和分析，设计师可以不断优化设计方案，直至达到最佳效果。

总之，基于空间、角色和动作的设计方法，是以"空间交互触点"为核心的一套解决设计问题的"设计逻辑"，可以有效地将复杂的汽车交互过程进行拆分，帮助设计师更加科学清晰地梳理思路，从而提高设计效率。时空动作蓝图通过将空间、角色和动作进行可视化处理，不仅可以帮助设计师进行设计思考，也可以帮助团队内其他背景的成员理解设计方案，从而降低沟通成本，提升沟通效率。对于"空间交互触点"的设计研究意义，只要看到苹果智能手机发明的"触摸开启"和小米 SU7 发明的"手机支架"，就会明白最容易被忽视、最不起眼，但也许是最大流量和用户需求价值的，可能只是一个小小的空间交互触点（图 3-1）。

图 3-1　苹果智能手机和小米 SU7 设计的"空间交互触点"

在这里，我们将智能座舱人机交互设计作为一个系统性的方法提出，旨在通过整合设计流程和设计场景，为智能座舱的人机交互提供高效、直观且用户友好的设计方案。智能座舱人机交互设计方法能够确保设计者在设计过程中充分考虑用户的需求和期望，同时确保设计方案在实际使用中的可行性和有效性。这有助于提高智能座舱的人机交互质量，改善用户体验，推动智能座舱技术的不断发展。

3.1 智能座舱人机交互设计概念

3.1.1 智能座舱的交互设计的操作定义

智能座舱人机交互（human-computer interaction）是人车交互的载体。它不仅与车辆驾驶安全密切相关，也是用户体验、用户感知和信息交互的重要媒介。如图 3-2 所示，是智能座舱人机交互的概念模型。

智能座舱人机交互设计旨在优化人与汽车之间的交互沟通过程。有学者以设计为出发点，提出了未来智能汽车的人机交互九大发展趋势，分别为"从运载工具到交通系统""连接与分离""共享服务""无处不在的显示""接管与移交""实体媒介交互""个性化""多通道融合交互""智能情感交互"。

图 3-2　智能座舱人机交互的概念模型

智能座舱人机交互的目标是促进人机之间安全、直观和流畅地交互，改善整体驾乘的体验。智能座舱人机交互是一个复杂且动态的领域，需要跨学科协作和创新，智能座舱人机交互相关研究也成为人因学、人机交互、心理学、用户体验和服务设计研究的交叉领域。

从交互设计范畴来看，智能座舱可以被定义为"智能服务空间"，即智能座舱能够精准感知到座舱空间里的每一个人（角色）的每一个动作，并结合大数据与用户偏好，通过多屏显示、自然语音、座椅、氛围灯等媒介与用户交互，使用户获得无缝流畅、多模态融合、情感识别、安全可信的驾驶体验和交互体验。与此同时，智能座舱也可以被定义为"智能移动空间"，座舱能够主动感知车外环境，通过分析环境以及其他周边车辆，结合驾驶员判断，实现人与车、车与路的交互。智能服务空间和智能移动空间，是我们正确理解人机交互设计的"设计对象"和"设计范式"的操作定义。

3.1.2 智能座舱的交互设计问题

首先，智能化导致非驾驶场景增多。SAE L3 级以上智能驾驶汽车，驾驶员的注意力更多地转向与驾驶无关的活动，甚至在 L5 级可实现自动驾驶，这给交互设计的概念带来了根本变化。这个问题本质上是人的角色转换。传统汽车用户界面设计，核心目标是最大限度地减少对驾驶员的"分心"设计；但智能驾驶的用户界面，驾驶员更像是一位乘客，因此，交互设计需要关注"非驾驶活动或任务"（NDRA）。与此同时，智能座舱实现了舱内外的信息共享，导致用户接收的信息量、信息复杂度和注意力负担随之迅速增加，这带来了智能座舱"无处不在的显示"现象，且多人多屏多设备互动，成为未来智能座舱的发展趋势。图 3-3 中，理想 L9 在驾驶区域配备了 13.35 英寸的高清 HUD 屏和方向盘交互屏，前排配备了两个 15.7 英寸的车辆中控屏和附加娱乐屏，后排配备了一个 15.7 英寸的后舱娱乐屏，实现前后排的跨屏互动和五屏联动。理想汽车的设计并非个例，在 2022 年国际消费电子展（CES）上，宝马发布了"影院模式"（theater mode）未来车内娱乐系统。在影院模式下，宝马通过 31 英寸超宽的悬浮屏幕和配备 5G 互联的环绕音响系统，在座舱内形成了一个极富沉浸感的私人影院。在前排用户可以调节屏幕的同时，后排用户还可以通过触控位于车辆的车门扶手处的数字界面，对悬浮屏幕的远近和角度进行个性化调节。事实上，多屏多人互动是一个社会性"角色"的问题，领导与属下、同学与同学、父母与孩子等，这种互动是非常复杂又非常生动的。

图 3-3　理想 L9 五块智能屏（图片来源：理想汽车官网）

其次，单一交互体验和座舱整体交互体验是存在矛盾的。智能座舱交互设计的目标应是提供一种完整的座舱用户体验，一个内聚、无缝和智慧的用户体验，而不是凌乱无序的屏幕和控件的堆砌。这本质上是智能座舱的空间、空间触点、空间动线的关系问题。智能座舱中的交互体验不仅仅是与单一屏幕的交互体验，而是将显示、控制、灯光、声音、触觉反馈等各种组件集成为一个连贯且易于感知的整体，从而为驾乘人员提供安全、舒适、愉悦的乘坐体验。大量文献研究表明，仅研究传统手动驾驶的场景，如驾驶员的认知工作量、注意力分散、情绪状态等，可能无法解决智能座舱中的整体用户体验问题。

3.2　智能座舱人机交互要素

3.2.1　智能座舱交互——空间

智能座舱一般分为三个设计空间：驾驶员空间、前排乘客空间和后排乘客空间（图 3-4）。智能座舱的空间是一个人造空间，其设计问题并不仅仅是空间认知与空间构建的哲学和观念问题，更是一个实际的产品设计问题。这涉及以下几个概念。①智能座舱内饰（car interior），是汽车车身的重要组成部分。智能座舱内饰主要包括以下子系统：仪表板系统、副仪表板系统、门内护板系统、顶棚系统、座椅系统、立柱护板系统、其余座舱内装件系统、座舱空气循环系统、行李箱内装件系统、发动机舱内装件系统、地毯、安全带、安全气囊、方向盘，以及车内照明、车内声学系统等。内饰空间研究包括空间特征、空间布局和空间形态等关键问题。②智能座舱空间设计（space design），即以空间为存在方式的设计。任何造型必然存在于一定空间中，造型是空间设计的途径。③空间形态是关于"空间张力""空间尺度""空间私密性"等空间关系的，是脱离了具象感知的造型表现的概念。

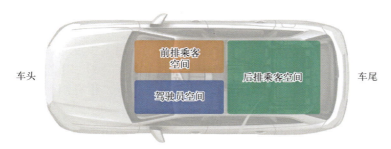

图 3-4　智能座舱的三个设计空间

座舱空间还可被分为物理空间（physical space）和数字空间（digital space）。物理空间是智能座舱的实体构造体现的。在物理空间中，驾驶员和乘客可以通过触摸、语音、按压、手势、情感等方式与座舱进行交互。数字空间是智能座舱中虚拟的、与计算机相关的信息空间，包括导航系统、娱乐系统、车载通信、智能驾驶系统等。数字空间中的信息以数据形式存储和呈现，并时刻与物理空间发生互动，但不受物理空间的限制。数字空间的交互主要依赖于软件和界面设计。另外，智能移动空间，特别是车联网、社会空间、信息空间之中的所谓移动空间，特指个体的特属空间与所处的社会环境、人文环境和信息环境之间的交互关系。

3.2.2　智能座舱交互——角色

智能座舱的用户会出现不同的角色身份，每种角色的关注点和交互限定也会有所不同。一般来说，可以将智能座舱交互的角色按操作任务分类为驾驶员和乘客。毕竟可能还需要漫长的时间，才会出现几乎不受限定的全智能的自动驾驶，驾驶员才会完全等同于乘客。

（1）驾驶员

驾驶员是智能座舱驾驶任务的执行者，驾驶员的需求和体验始终是交互设计的核心关注点。在智能辅助驾驶的等级下，驾驶员的主要任务是驾驶，最关注的仍是驾驶安全和驾驶感的问题。驾驶过程中，驾驶员需要同时处理多种实时动态信息，如路况、导航、娱乐、乘客的行为等，因此，驾驶员的认知负荷是交互设计的重要研究方向。如何通过改变界面设计、信息呈现方式等来降低驾驶员的认知负荷，从而提高驾驶安全性，以及如何减少驾驶员分心和增强其对于系统的信任，都备受关注。

随着自动驾驶等级的提升，驾驶员可以从事其他的非驾驶任务，但驾驶员仍应该随时保持"智能服务"和"移动空间"的持续注意力，以便于提高接管自动驾驶和处理交互事件的反应速度，因此，需充分关注驾驶员在复杂环境下的感知、认知和决策过程。

（2）乘客

乘客在前后排空间限定下可以被进一步区分为前排乘客和后排乘客。

前排乘客会极大地影响驾驶员的用户体验，因为前排乘客可以在更大空间中与驾驶员进行互动。这就意味着除了社交娱乐活动外，前排乘客也可能辅助驾驶员驾驶，但同时也是驾驶员分心的潜在来源。因此，驾驶员可以将有些交互任务，通过中控触摸屏，"分配"给前排乘客，尤其是将需要精确操控和具有复杂要求的交互任务配置给前排乘客，提供交互任务的互操作，为驾驶员和前排乘客同时提供积极的用户体验。同时，支持驾驶员与前排乘客的协作，帮助驾驶员减少认知负荷和分心，让前排乘客成为更好的驾驶助手。所以，建构驾驶员和前排乘客的人机共驾场景，将有助于为驾驶员和乘客空间开发交互技术，并使前排乘客成为联合驾驶员（co-driver）。

后排乘客主要处在娱乐休闲场景中，交互设计需要考虑如何提供更加自然的交互方式和更加便捷、舒适、愉悦的乘车体验。为了增强后排乘客的用户体验，有研究者提出了交互式车门的概念，使乘客能够参与并探索周围的环境。同时交互式车门可以显示行进路线上的兴趣点，除后排显示屏外，支持AR的侧窗还可以显示更多详细信息。另外，基于周围环境的交互方式也能改善后排乘客的体验，例如，一个以乘客为对象的信息娱乐系统，能够提供对电影库的访问并推荐景点、酒店或餐馆，推荐位于以当前汽车GPS定位点为圆心的特定半径内的兴趣点。

同时，因为乘客具备家庭和社会属性，所以还应考虑行为受到限制的特殊人群，比如儿童和老人。儿童由于认知水平以及能力水平不足，在汽车交互设计中常常会受到很多设计限制，年幼的孩子不具备表达自己喜好的技能，而且他们也无法长时间地执行任务，很容易分心。人类从婴儿期到成年期会经历不同发育阶段，表现出不同水平的认知、运动和社交能力。由于儿童不具备与成年人相同的精细运动技能，因此他们无法有效地使用为成人设计的触摸屏设备和应用程序。根据《人机交互手册》（*The Human–Computer Interaction Handbook*），处于前运算阶段（2～7岁）的儿童应该能够点击相对较大的特定目标。最好避免复杂的键盘输入，因为他们在这个年龄段无法很好地阅读。针对儿童特性开发的一款新颖的车载游戏（Mileys），集成了位置信息、增强现实和虚拟角色，让儿童乘客乘坐汽车时感到更有趣，并加强家庭成员之间的联系，鼓励安全和生态驾驶，将儿童与他们的环境而不是他们的娱乐设备联系起来。除了儿童外，老人通常也会受到行为不便和行动缓慢的限制，所以在设计时也需要进行特殊考虑。

值得注意的是，智能座舱内的角色并非独立的，而是紧密联系并相互影响的。图3-5中，驾驶员和乘客形成的智能座舱"操控关系"，包括双方同意的控制（consensual control）、令牌环控制（token-ring control）、分级控制（hierachical control）、专制控制（autocratic control）、无政府控制（anarchic control）。目前，智能座舱的前后排关系中，当前文献中较少提到的，一个主要的挑战将是让驾驶员和前排乘客可以实时了解后排乘客当前的状态和正在进行的交互行为，但同时也要保证后排乘客的隐私性。因此，在进行设计时不仅需要考虑每一种角色独有的特征和需求，也需要将所有的角色进行整体性考虑，深入分析各角色之间发生的协同互动所带来的影响。

图 3-5 驾驶员和乘客的五种协同形式

3.2.3 智能座舱交互——动作

场景要素中，用户的动作概念主要涉及用户动作和用户意图两个方面。系统通过监测生理和行为信号（眼神、打哈欠、情绪），发现驾驶员疲劳程度过高时，通过语音提醒驾驶员并调整座椅舒适度。这一系列智能检测和避险动作，有显性和隐性的差别，一般以用户是否"意识到"的动作为区分标准。显性动作输入是指，用户在"有意"和"知情"状态下主动进行的交互动作，比如，通过触摸屏幕动作设置导航路径，包括触控、手势、语音等。隐性动作输入是指，用户在"无意"和"不知情"的状态下发生的交互动作，主要涉及凝视、用户行为和生理信号等方面，例如，人脸识别疲劳驾驶检测系统利用摄像头图像传感器的图像处理和分析技术，实时监控和测量驾驶员脸部特征变化，如眼睛闭合频率、凝视方向、打哈欠频率等。当这些特征达到一定标准时，系统就会判定驾驶员处于疲劳状态，并及时发出报警提示的交互动作。

（1）触摸和控制

触摸和控制是最基本的动作交互类型，触摸与控制类别代表了基于手的触觉的输入技术，如按钮、滑块、旋钮、柄状控制、拇指轮、踏板、多功能控制器和触摸屏。尽管触摸和控制在很多新型交互技术中可能显得传统，但对于需要快速反应和明确操作反馈的情况，触摸和控制依然具有一定优势。

多点触控设备支持大约十种核心触摸手势，使它们能够响应大多数触摸命令，例如点击、双击、拖动、轻拂、捏合、张开、按下、按下并点击、按下并拖动和旋转、使用单手或双手的手指。

（2）手势

手势作为一种直观且自然的交互方式，已引起越来越多的关注。通过捕捉驾驶员和乘客的手势动作，手势识别技术可以实现对车辆功能的控制和设置，从而降低驾驶员在驾驶过程中的注意力分散。采用摄像头、深度传感器、红外传感器等设备，手势识别系统能够准确地识别各种预定义的手势，如滑动、捏合、旋转等。这使得用户可以在不触摸物理控件的情况下，操控车载信息娱乐系统、调整座椅、控制空调等。然而，要实现高效且易用的手势识别交互，需要综合考虑手势的设计、识别准确性、用户习惯等多个因素，以满足不同驾驶场景下的交互需求（图 3-6）。

（3）语音输入

语音输入作为一种方便且高效的人机交互手段，正逐渐成为行业关注的焦点。通过识别和理解驾驶员和乘客的语音指令，语音输入技术可以实现对车辆功能的控制和设置，从而减少驾驶员在驾驶过程中对物理控件的依赖，提高行驶安全性。采用先进的自然语言处理（NLP）和语音识别技术，语音输入系统能够准确地识别各种语音命令，如导航、播放音乐、拨打电话等。此外，智能语音助手的引入进一步提升了语音输入的实用性，使得用户可以更自然地与车载系统进行对话式交互。然而，要实现高效且易用的语音输入交互，研究者需要综合考虑识别准确性、语境理解、多语言支持等多个因素，以满足不同驾驶场景和用户的需求。

图 3-6　手势识别交互

语音输入占用的注意力通道较小，是一种有用的输入方法，大语言模型一旦渗透智能座舱，将极大地提高系统的复杂交互能力。

（4）凝视

凝视一般被用于显性输入，系统也可以在用户没有任何主动意图的情况下，追踪用户的眼神。目前"注视交互"的能力足够强大，已经集成到智能座舱中。驾驶员的眼睛状态已经可被诸如困倦警告之类的应用程序追踪到。类似的，通过隐式存储和突出显示最后一次查看的屏幕位置，可以加快注意力从屏幕上切换回来的速度。在执行一项需要持续监督的视觉、安全关键任务的同时，执行注视交互是具有挑战性的（图 3-7）。

图 3-7　通过 obii Pro Glasses 3 眼动仪进行眼动捕捉

（5）行为和生理信号

行为是指驾驶员的面部表情、眼球运动、身体位置和姿势，而生理信号是指心率、血压、脑电、肌电等。触摸、手势、语音和凝视这四种动作均属于用户主动的显性输入，而行为和生理信号主要用于定义用户的隐性输入，即系统通过摄像头、毫米波雷达等传感器，在用户无意识的情况下，收集用户的行为和生理信息，并对信息输入给予个性化的反馈。例如，在检测到驾驶员分心或疲劳时，智能车辆助理（IVA）可以选择提供视觉或振动触觉警报，系统还可以对驾驶员发出语音对话，提醒保持警觉。此外，如果系统通过车内姿态识别，检测到驾驶员处于非最佳身体姿势，可以通过智能座椅将驾驶员推向正确的身体姿势，以使其获得最佳的驾驶注意力。同样，如果通过表情识别发现用户情绪激动或悲伤，车机系统可以推荐舒缓的音乐，控制车内温度，营造放松的环境。表 3-1 中，总结了智能座舱的各种动作类别。值得注意的是，这些动作类别并非相互排斥。实际上，智能座舱交互系统往往会综合处理多种输入方式，以实现更自然流畅的人机交互。通过整合语音识别、手势控制和视线跟踪等技术，汽车交互系统提高了用户与汽车之间沟通的自然性，为用户带来更加便捷、直观和安全的体验。

表 3-1 汽车交互中的动作要素

动作	定义
触摸和控制（touch&control）	按键、旋钮、触摸屏等
手势（gesture）	用户通过手势（如挥手、滑动手指等）控制车辆的某些功能
凝视（gaze）	用户眼睛的输入，如眼神等
语音输入（speech）	用户可以通过语音命令与汽车进行交互
行为（behavior）	用户的面部表情、身体姿态等
生理信号（physiological）	心率、血压、心电、肌电等

综上所述，智能座舱中的人机交互设计框架可以归纳为三个核心要素：空间、角色和动作。空间包括数字空间和物理空间，它们共同构成了座舱内的交互环境；角色主要指驾驶员和乘客，他们在座舱内与各种系统进行交互；动作则涵盖了用户在座舱内与不同设备进行交互的各种行为和释放出的生理信号。图 3-8 为基于空间、角色和动作三要素的人机交互设计。图中，座舱内的角色通过动作将信息输入给座舱空间。空间中的传感器会将用户的动作转化为电信号并传递到相应的系统中。系统接收到信号后，通过数字空间将反馈信息传递给用户，从而实现智能座舱中的人机交互。然而，在交互过程中，物理空间会通过人机工程学等相关规则来约束动作发生的边界，以确保操作的舒适性和安全性。同时，角色之间还会进行协作和互动，不同角色的特征和需求也有所差异。

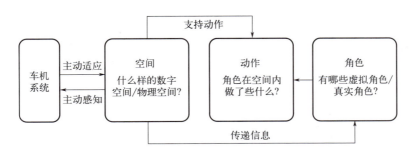

图 3-8 基于空间、角色和动作三要素的人机交互设计框架

人机交互设计关注特定条件下人与行为的互动关系，依据交互过程中的不同要素特征，快速搜寻和发掘人机交互相关信息。曾经以驾驶员为中心的仪表设计是座舱中主导的设计范例，仪表盘和中控屏的空间位置都在驾驶员前方。然而，随着车辆变得更加复杂和功能丰富，对额外显示器和控件的需求导致了座舱布局的重新配置，随之带来了新

的设计范例，例如将信息娱乐和气候控制装置放置在驾驶员和前排乘客都可以访问的中控屏上，将关键驾驶信息投射到挡风玻璃上的平视显示器，以及为后排的乘客提供娱乐屏幕。而智能驾驶技术的发展加速了汽车交互设计范式的演变，因为对传统的以驾驶员为中心的控制需求已经减少，并且出现了新的交互形式，例如语音识别和手势控制。我们能够感受到当下智能座舱设计的空间布局不断变化，设计焦点从单个组件转移到汽车交互设计的整体体验。

案例：极狐考拉——亲子场景

考拉是极狐品牌第一款场景驱动的车型。基于用户驱动、场景驱动和观念驱动，考拉首创"亲子出行场景"的系统性解决方案，将以奶嘴座舱、后排堡垒、情绪空间和家庭游乐场等专属场景化产品优势，满足"宝爸宝妈"对家庭出行生活和驾驶平衡的需求。见图3-9、图3-10、图3-11。

图3-9 极狐考拉的物理空间配置

图3-10 极狐考拉的物理空间与数字空间

随着进入多孩时代，家庭以及亲子出行需求得到了无限放大。针对带娃出行的各种"崩溃"瞬间，极狐考拉以形成温暖的亲子移动空间为出发点，提供了一个系统性的前后排亲子人机交互场景解决方案。极狐考拉也充分考虑到了"宝妈"们的实际需求：当侧滑门开启时，后排儿童座椅将自动向车门方向旋转，方便妈妈抱着孩子入座；而当车门关闭后，座椅也将回归原来的位置。上车后，在座舱物理空间中，儿童位于后排安全座椅，车内座舱空间考虑到前排驾驶位年轻妈妈群体的需求，在中控部分布置了多种可放置儿童物品的可变形置物区，同时布置了可变形中空桌板，便于进行冲泡奶粉等操作，同时加大的前后排空间和可向后移动更多的座椅，让座舱号称百变的"育儿袋"。

在数字空间中，位于前排的数字屏幕中的车内助手则能一键投屏查看后排儿童状态，避免妈妈开车时因回头观察儿童情况可能造成的事故和危险。并且，摄像头可以智能识别儿童入睡状态，快速自动调整空调、音响（多媒体声道转换至主驾头枕音响，后排更安静）、氛围灯，适应儿童当下状态。同时车机系统还会对日程，比如早教课、体检、打疫苗等环节进行智能化安排，形成个人专属的备忘录。

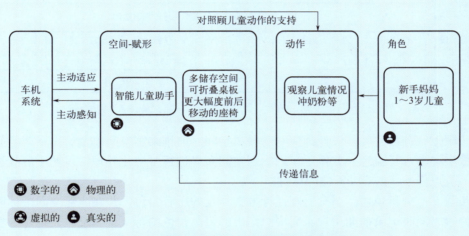

图3-11 极狐考拉亲子人机交互设计框架分析

极狐考拉的亲子人机交互设计首先通过对用户角色，即年轻妈妈和1～3岁儿童的需求愿景和相应动作进行分析，进行了座舱内前后排物理空间的配置。儿童出行过程中需要带许多物品并且妈妈需要及时照顾儿童，产生向后排移动的用户动作，而座舱内数字空间则通过智能车机系统帮助妈妈查看后排儿童的状态，自动根据儿童的状态对车内整体氛围进行调整，同时通过智能化规划帮助亲子共同获得一段良好的行程中的体验。

因此，智能座舱交互设计中，硬件和软件的整合，以及空间的利用，多角色、多触点的分析，都是改善用户体验的重要因素。然而，由于缺乏对复杂空间、角色和动作进行分析的方法和指导，使得在设计汽车交互方案时效率较低，并且存在无法充分利用设计维度并因此错过重要创新点的风险。因此我们需要重新审视传统框架中的缺陷，并针对汽车交互的新特点，如非驾驶场景的增加、多屏多人交互的新趋势等，形成新的设计框架，重新构建人车交互设计的理论体系。

3.3 人机交互 SRA 设计流程

根据交互设计场景的概念框架，通过分析空间、角色和动作三要素，我们提出了汽车人机交互 SRA 设计流程（图 3-12），并通过设计实验初步验证了其有效性和可行性。图 3-12 的上半部分为传统汽车交互设计方法，表示人机交互 SRA 设计流程是传统流程的"概念发散"的拓展；下半部分则是基于空间、角色和动作三个要素的汽车交互设计方法与流程。以下简要描述人机交互 SRA 设计流程。

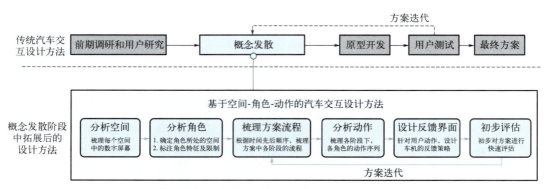

图 3-12　基于空间、角色、动作的汽车人机交互 SRA 设计流程

步骤①：分析空间。设计师应对驾驶员空间、前排乘客空间以及后排乘客空间内所有的数字屏幕进行梳理，并按照车内物理空间布局进行可视化处理，以便于后续进一步分析。节点任务：提交交互空间文件。

步骤②：分析角色。明确交互设计方案涉及的所有角色，并在座舱空间中标明各角色的位置，同时记录前期用户研究中总结出的每个角色的特征、需求以及特殊人群可能面临的行为限制等信息，这将有助于设计师更好地从用户的角度进行方案设计，激发共情力和洞察力，进行概念方案发散。节点任务：提交角色定义文件和初步概念方案。

步骤③：梳理方案流程。设计师根据输入的交互场景和设计目标，按照时间先后顺序，梳理方案中各阶段的流程并进行详细记录。节点任务：整理提交概念方案文件。

步骤④：分析动作。设计师需要根据概念方案，梳理角色的关键动作和空间交互触点序列。将所有动作序列连接起来，便构成了整体的用户体验。值得注意的是，概念方案涉及多角色交互时，应标注在该阶段发生的动作，这些动作所处的情境较为复杂，受到空间和角色限制较多，对整体座舱体验影响较大，在后续评估中应重点关注。节点任务：提交角色动作分析报告。

步骤⑤：空间交互触点分析（设计反馈界面）。空间交互触点分析属于人机界面分析的范畴。根据角色的动作来制定车机的多模态反馈策略，同时，对角色动作与空间交互触点的对应关系进行明确的梳理，便于后续评估判断概念方案的合理性。节点任务：提交空间交互触点分析报告。

步骤⑥：初步评估。在团队内，评估概念方案，针对每个方案的输入动作和空间交互触点，进行深入的分析与讨论，并结合人机交互规则或用户体验评估规则，对方案进行初步评估。同期，进行用户测试。完成评估后，可以将评估意见收集分类，再进行新一轮设计迭代。节点任务：提交评审意见报告。

3.4 空间交互接触点

空间交互接触点，又称空间交互触点。苹果智能手机发明的"触摸开启"和小米SU7发明的"手机支架"，都是经典的交互触点设计。智能座舱的汽车交互设计已不再是简单的单一屏幕的交互设计，而是涉及多个组成部分和多种交互方式的复杂交互系统，且系统中的每一个交互环节都会影响用户体验，同时，也为创新设计提供了许多机会点。空间交互触点是智能座舱交互场景的体验构成点、体验观察点、体验分析点和体验评估点。

"服务设计"面临同样的问题，并通过引入"接触点"的概念，将复杂抽象的服务过程，提炼为了不同的服务接触点，帮助设计师共情用户并发掘设计机会点。在服务过程中，用户与服务提供者之间存在多个接触点，这些接触点是用户获得服务体验的重要部分，也是用户感知服务质量的关键因素之一。

智能座舱同样可被定义为"智能服务空间"，因此，可以引入服务设计的概念和思想，解决智能座舱服务空间的设计问题。本节引入了"接触点"的概念，并将此概念在汽车交互的背景下重新定义，为交互设计提供理论模型支撑。

3.4.1 交互触点的概念

（1）服务设计的接触点定义

在服务设计中，接触点（touchpoint）是指用户在与服务提供者进行互动过程中的交互场景点。Shostack（1984）通过引用一个四年期研究项目，使用卡片法，研究了服务创新的接触点的重要性和潜力。接触点不仅构成了服务设计创新的更广泛、更完整的模型和手段，也是服务提供者和客户之间的接触点，用户会利用许多不同的接触点作为使用场景。例如，获取银行服务的接触点包括其实体建筑、网站、自助机、银行卡、客户助理、呼叫中心、电话协助等。每当用户与接触点相关联或互动时，就产生服务体验，并形成用户与服务和服务提供者之间的关系。接触点是服务设计的核心方面之一，因此，服务设计可以定义为"跨时间、跨接触点"的体验设计。

"接触点"字面意思就是事物之间相互接触的点，是利益相关者与服务系统进行交互的载体。接触点可以是有形的，也可以是无形的，大体可分为物理接触点、数字接触点、情感接触点、隐形接触点和融合接触点等。为了更有效地优化各个接触点，服务设计师需要采用多种方法和工具，如用户画像、服务蓝图、用户旅程地图等。通过这些工具，设计师可以深入了解用户在不同接触点上的需求和体验，从而识别潜在的问题和改进机会。

(2) 人机交互与用户体验的接触点

本书提出的智能座舱交互设计场景的概念框架中,"场景接触点",简称为"触点"或者"场景触点",是指广义人机界面上的"位置点",分为用户触点、交互触点和形式触点三类。

通常,用户体验(user experience,简称 UX/UE)是指,用户使用产品或服务时,通过用户界面和场景触点所感受到的整体体验,涉及可用性、满意度、可信度和积极情感反应。而人机交互是人与计算机交互界面的概念,强调作业效能(human performance)。这里,人机界面和用户界面不是一个完全相同的概念,当然,二者之间有着密切的关系,在我们的讨论中也不做特别的区分。因此,智能座舱人机交互的交互触点或者场景触点,可以被看作人机界面触点和用户界面触点两者的交集。人机交互设计的目标是创建一种用户友好的交互界面,以便用户能够轻松地与计算机系统进行交互。用户体验的目标是确保用户在与产品或服务进行交互时,能够获得良好的体验。因此,设计人员需要考虑产品或服务的各个接触点,以确保它们既是用户友好的,又能够满足用户需求和期望,从而改善产品或服务的整体用户体验。在设计接触点时,需要考虑用户的心理和行为习惯,以及用户在使用过程中的感受和反馈,从而使产品或服务能够更好地满足用户需求并提高用户满意度。

用户触点的使用及来源主要通过用户场景来实现。随着近几年用户体验设计的蓬勃发展,复杂堆砌的功能已经不再帮助产品提升体验感,更多的则是从用户场景出发,通过对接触点的深入分析而设计出实用的产品体系,才能带来更好的用户体验。

总之,服务设计、人机交互和用户体验中,接触点(touchpoint)的核心概念是大致相通的。在三个领域中,接触点都指的是用户与产品、服务或品牌在互动过程中的各种交互场景的触点。这些场景包括各种在线和离线渠道、实体和虚拟环境,以及人际互动等。接触点在整个用户体验或服务体验过程中起着关键作用,直接影响到用户对产品或服务质量的感知和评价。

这三个领域在处理接触点时的侧重点可能略有不同。在服务设计领域,往往更关注服务提供者与用户之间的互动,以及服务在整个生命周期内的各个阶段。在用户体验和人机交互领域,重点通常放在产品或系统本身的各个方面,如界面设计、功能实现和性能优化等。

3.4.2 智能座舱的交互触点设计

基于空间、角色和动作三个要素,我们可以建立一个树形结构定义智能座舱的交互行为。通过我们提出的智能座舱交互触点的概念,对座舱的设计进行进一步的分析。

(1) 构建交互行为的树形结构

智能座舱按照驾驶员空间、前排乘客空间、后排乘客空间三个区间进行区分,因此,智能座舱的人机交互行为可以用"空间 - 角色 - 动作"的范式来定义(图 3-13)。

(2) 空间交互接触点:动作触点和反馈触点

如图 3-14 所示,从空间 - 角色 - 动作的树形结构中,可以提取出空间交互接触点的概念。空间交互接触点包括动作触点和反馈触点,图中上部为交互输入,即动作触点;

图中下部为交互输出,即反馈触点(表 3-2)。

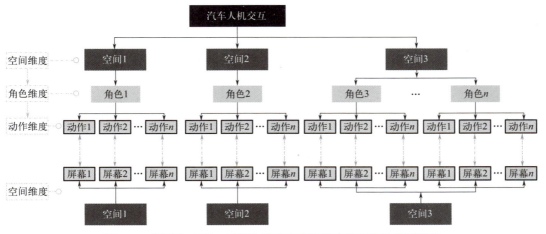

图 3-13 "空间 - 角色 - 动作"范式定义下的交互行为的树形结构

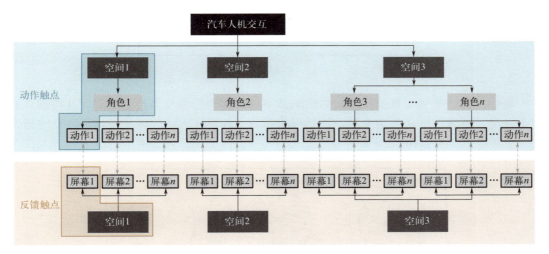

图 3-14 动作触点与反馈触点

表 3-2 空间交互接触点总结表

要素	具体分类				
空间	驾驶员空间	前排乘客空间	后排乘客空间		
角色	驾驶员	前排乘客	后排乘客		
动作	触摸和控制	手势	凝视	语音输入	行为和生理信号
屏幕	数字仪表盘	HUD	中控屏	副驾娱乐屏	后排娱乐屏	扶手屏

动作触点中包含空间、角色和动作的三重信息。在座舱空间中,角色会通过动作将信息输入给系统,在此输入过程中,空间会定义角色活动的边界,而角色的特征和状态

会决定动作的种类。

反馈触点是指在用户与智能汽车进行互动时，系统提供给用户有关其动作或操作状态的信息。屏幕上输出的信息是对角色输入动作的反馈，因此，动作和屏幕具有相对应的关系。反馈触点在交互设计中非常重要，因为它们可以帮助用户了解他们的行为是否已成功、是否需要更改其输入或操作方式，以及系统是否正在处理他们的请求。

在图 3-14 中，反馈触点包含空间和屏幕的两重信息。具体来说，汽车内部的空间布局会影响屏幕的位置和尺寸，屏幕作为汽车交互的重要载体，设计师在进行反馈信息设计时，应充分考虑空间影响下的屏幕布局带来的交互舒适度的问题。值得注意的是，智能座舱中的反馈并不仅仅是屏幕上的视觉信息。

综上所述，如图 3-15 所示，空间交互接触点包括动作触点和反馈触点。动作触点由空间 - 角色 - 动作构成，反馈触点由空间 - 屏幕构成。

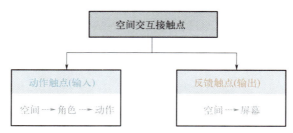

图 3-15　空间交互接触点

最后，智能座舱交互设计还面临多屏幕布局、多角色参与以及多空间交互接触点的复杂情况。而基于空间、角色和动作的智能座舱交互设计方法较传统设计方法具有以下几个显著优点（图 3-16）。

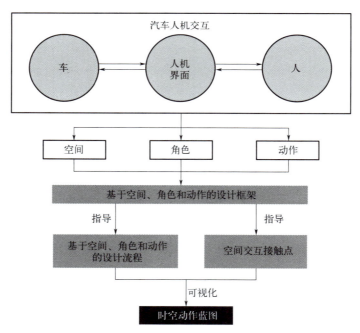

图 3-16　基于空间、角色和动作的智能座舱交互设计框架

① 支持创新：通过多维度思考、发现或赋予要素新概念，设计者能够更深入地了解不同场景下的用户体验，从而洞察到更多的机会点来拓展设计空间。这样的方法能够从多个维度启发和推动创新思考。

② 激发想法：这种思考方式在概念发散阶段可以激发交互设计师产生大量想法并将其实现。同时，它还可以帮助交互设计师在设计过程中梳理思路，将智能座舱内的复杂活动进行要素拆解，从而促进团队内的沟通和交流，提高设计过程的效率。

③ 多角度思考：从多个角度进行思考，使整个方案更合理、更具前瞻性。这样的方法可以加快方案迭代速度，避免因单一视角导致的盲点和问题。

④ 系统性统筹：采用空间、角色和动作的设计系统有助于设计师在整个设计过程中保持系统性思考，从宏观和微观层面统筹考虑，实现各个要素之间的协调和一致性。采用考虑空间、角色和动作的设计框架对于汽车交互设计具有重要意义，这种方法可以帮助设计师更好地应对复杂的座舱环境，发挥创新能力，提高设计效率和质量。

3.5　人机交互 SRA 设计案例分析

从设计研究的学习观看，所谓人的递归式学习是人在心智和行动能力上具备的设计能力，这件事只能发生在实践的范畴，即实践认识只能发生在实践者的实践行动中。这意味着，任何设计理论和方法都是为了让设计师可以更清晰地意识到，我们在做什么，我们要做什么，但是究竟怎么做并没有唯一正确的路径，只能通过设计实践来建构个体和团队的"设计方法论"。

设计项目背景：依托于湖南大学设计艺术学院与德赛西威汽车电子公司的合作，以"Smart Solution"为主题，突出展现企业的核心科技优势，设计出符合企业调性的智能座舱技术的展示空间。项目分为前期调研、方案推导和方案设计三个部分。根据前期调研，设计目标交互场景确定为亲子娱乐场景、办公场景和旅拍场景。

（1）空间布局卡片

空间布局卡片，用于可视化分析座舱空间，包括驾驶员空间、前排乘客空间和后排乘客空间。首先梳理数字屏幕的布局，并按照座舱物理空间布局绘制俯视图。座舱空间布局卡片可以一目了然地看到车内所有屏幕的位置关系，有利于提高后续设计效率，如图 3-17 所示，座舱空间中有前排屏、方向盘屏、流水屏和后排屏。

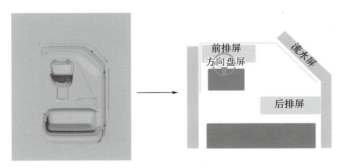

图 3-17　座舱空间

（2）角色用户画像

角色用户画像帮助设计团队了解用户真正的需求，对智能座舱体验的期待，通过生动、细致的需求描述，协助设计团队共情，以创造更加人性化的设计。

图 3-18 展示了两个角色的用户画像：前排的驾驶员家长与后排乘坐的儿童。驾驶员家长以 35 岁左右的在职男性为典型，他们常在周末与家人前往城市近郊露营。这类家长的痛点在于，孩子在后排无聊时容易哭闹，对驾驶造成干扰。他们期望能在行车过程中，通过简单易懂的小游戏与孩子互动，以提升驾驶的安全性。后排儿童以 5～7 岁的儿童为典型，这些在互联网环境下成长的孩子，对游戏和娱乐有较强的兴趣。他们的痛点在于乘车过程中的无聊，并渴望与父母的互动。然而，驾驶中的家长往往难以分心照顾孩子们的情绪，因此孩子们期望在车上也能体验到有趣的游戏。

图 3-18　座舱内角色的用户画像

（3）时空动作蓝图

时空动作蓝图的结构如图 3-19 所示，包括交互流程、角色动作和空间交互接触点三部分。借助时空动作蓝图可视化的方式，设计师可以将复杂的汽车交互方案进行清晰的梳理和可视化表达，设计团队可以针对相关创意与设计洞见开展讨论，评估备选方案，提出概念设计方案。时空动作蓝图的使用流程如下。

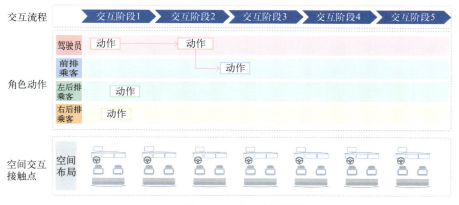

图 3-19　时空动作蓝图

① 填写内容前阅读时空动作蓝图右侧使用指南的内容。如图 3-20 所示，Tips 部分介绍了如何填写角色的动作，以及如何绘制空间交互接触点。图 3-21 为时空动作蓝图中的快捷使用工具包组件。

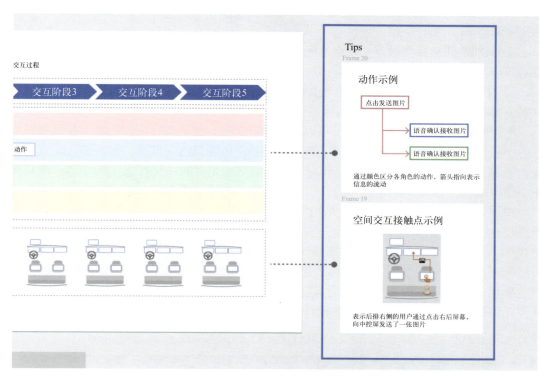

图 3-20　时空动作蓝图使用指南

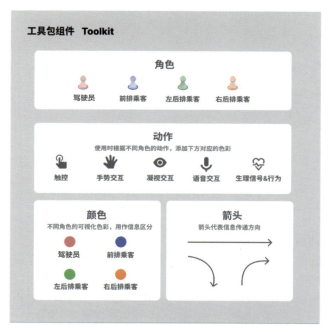

图 3-21　时空动作蓝图中的快捷使用工具包组件

②定义阶段：根据输入的设计目标和设计概念，划分和定义用户完成任务或实现目标的过程的各个阶段。

③定义动作：梳理并描述每个角色的动作序列，每个动作都使用不同颜色的方框区分。同时，将相关联的动作通过箭头进行标注，关联动作不限于单个角色，包括多角色的交互动作。

④识别空间交互接触点：根据空间、角色和动作的描述，识别空间交互接触点，在空间布局卡片中加以标注。

⑤检查与评估：根据人机交互的原则，以及角色用户画像中的痛点和需求，对整理方案进行快速评估，并根据评估结果进行迭代设计。

根据图3-22所示方案，驾驶员可以通过手势交互，在游戏音乐的伴奏下发出随机颜色的小球。这些小球会依次经过前排屏、流水屏，最终到达后排屏。在后排，儿童可以旋转屏幕上的轮盘，用与小球颜色相对应的轮盘区域来接收由父母发出的小球。成功接住小球即可获得分数。

在项目中，空间布局对角色动作产生了具体限制。对于驾驶员而言，由于前排屏距离较远，触摸操作不方便，因此，所有需点击确认的按钮均被布局在易于触及的方向盘屏上，以便驾驶员操作。而前排屏则主要用于展示阅读性信息。对于后排乘客，虽然侧面的流水屏在空间上可触摸，但因其角度导致阅读性差和触摸难度大，故流水屏主要用于展示与车内氛围相关的动态信息，例如小球移动的动画，而不会显示需要乘客详细阅读的文字信息。这样的设计旨在优化用户体验，降低操作难度。

时空动作蓝图是汽车交互的可视化工具，可以帮助我们梳理多个角色与多个屏幕之间的复杂交互过程

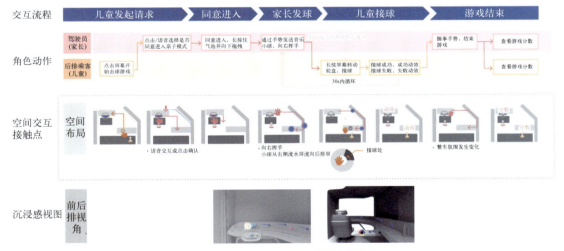

图 3-22　亲子场景下的时空动作蓝图

（4）低保真界面设计

在时空动作蓝图的基础上，我们进行了低保真界面的设计，并以交互文档的形式进行输出。在界面布局阶段，我们保持了与车内屏幕布局的一致性，以便于我们更好地理解和规划不同屏幕间的信息联动。在设计过程中，我们始终关注用户需求与痛点，并以此为核心进行低保真界面的推演，同时参照时空动作蓝图，特别关注空间交互接触点，

以确保设计的可用性和用户体验。

以驾驶员发球界面为例（图 3-23），当驾驶员向右挥手时，前排屏和方向盘屏会给出手势识别成功的视觉反馈，并随机显示一种颜色的小球。随后，小球会沿着流水屏向后排屏移动，后排屏上则显示出等待接球的轮盘。

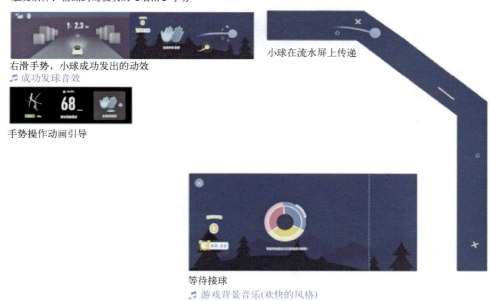

图 3-23　驾驶员发球界面

在后排乘客转动转盘接球界面（图 3-24），小球从流水屏滑动至后排屏，此时儿童可以通过转动后排屏上的轮盘来尝试接球。如果轮盘上与小球颜色相同的区域成功接到小球，则视为接球成功，屏幕上会显示出接球成功的动效。若接球区域颜色与小球不符，小球则会被弹开。

当后排儿童连续成功接球时，会触发连击奖励（图 3-25）。此时，后排屏上会显示奖励动效并播放奖励音效。游戏分数会实时显示在屏幕左侧，同时游戏倒计时会在分数下方显示，这样的布局旨在保持前排屏、流水屏和后排屏之间的视觉连贯性。

游戏结束时（图 3-26），若驾驶员做出握拳手势或游戏倒计时归零，游戏将终止。此时，前排屏和后排屏会显示本次游戏的得分，而方向盘屏和后排屏上则会提供"退出游戏"或"再玩一次"的操作选项。

（5）座舱效果图

最终整体座舱效果，如图 3-27 和图 3-28 所示。智能座舱整体呈半开放环绕式，以简洁的白色基调为主。座舱配备前排主驾驶位单人智能座椅、后排双人座椅。在迎宾模式下，前排座椅可以后退向外旋转迎接用户乘车，该座椅还支持在辅助驾驶条件下用户自定义选择向右旋转面向座舱内侧或后排。座舱采用了流水屏环绕设计，通过环绕语义方便了座舱前后排用户交流，座舱内的多场景信息通过流水屏在座舱内得到更好的传递。同时座舱内配备的桌板屏幕是可以前后移动的，用户可以基于自己在不同场景下的需求操作它。该座舱可以很好地实现亲子娱乐场景互动。设计方案及效果可扫描二维码观看。

扫码观看视频

后排乘客转动转盘接球

触发条件：小球从流水屏飞入后排屏

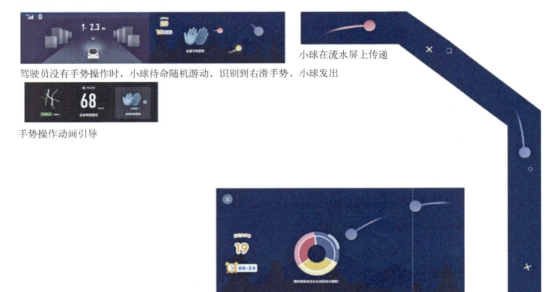

驾驶员没有手势操作时，小球待命随机游动，识别到右滑手势，小球发出

小球在流水屏上传递

手势操作动画引导

小球从流水屏上弹到后排屏上

接球成功时

接球成功后，小球与转盘融合，转盘对应区域出现小动效
🎵 成功发球音效

接球失败时

接球失败时，小球被弹飞

图 3-24 后排乘客转动轮盘接球界面

分数显示&连击奖励

触发条件：后排乘客连续成功接收3次小球

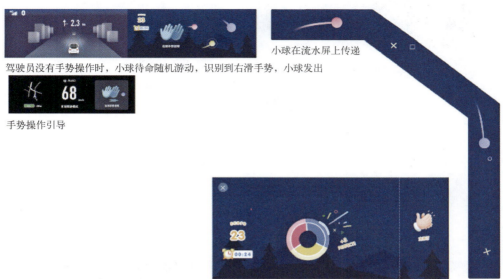

图 3-25 分数显示 & 连击奖励界面

游戏结束&显示得分

触发条件：游戏结束

图 3-26 游戏结束 & 显示得分界面

图 3-27　座舱屏幕效果图

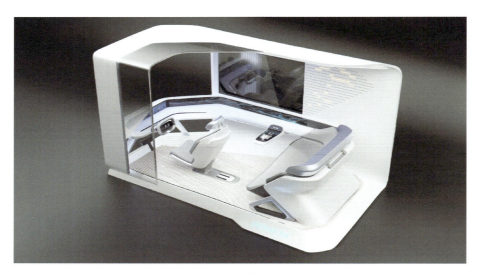

图 3-28　座舱效果图

第 4 章

基于动作叙事的智能座舱交互设计

4.1　智能座舱人机交互——叙事设计理论框架
4.2　智能座舱人机交互——叙事设计流程
4.3　智能座舱人机交互叙事设计模型与设计策略
4.4　人机交互叙事设计案例分析

本章讨论的主题是叙事设计，即"智能座舱人机交互叙事设计"。用叙事理论对人机交互进行系统性"解读"和"建构"，有助于从场景的"事件情节""人物角色"和"时空结构"三个关键认知点，建构智能座舱交互设计场景的认知，提高设计过程的概念生成和概念沟通的有效性，为创新设计提供创新策略。基于动作叙事的智能座舱交互设计方法主要包含以下几个方面。

思维模式：智能座舱人机交互叙事设计的思维模式，就是用叙事的"设计逻辑"，把交互设计场景的用户、事件和时空三个要素统合为"同一体"，以实现设计意图与认知解释的共情和共鸣。

步骤和流程：包括叙事设计的问题求解路径和叙事设计流程两个部分。其中，问题求解路径包括：①以时间为线索全流程穷尽式问题框定；②事件全要素梳理的设计机会点框定；③叙事要素沉淀和重组的新概念生成；④减少创作压力的叙事模式；⑤创新概念故事叙述。叙事设计流程包括：①多角色利益相关者分组；②素材卡片与阐述；③用户行为机会卡排列重组；④座舱造型卡标注说明与概念完善；⑤创新概念故事叙述。

技术和工具：用户行为机会卡和座舱造型卡。

创新策略：叙事设计研究本质上是围绕设计概念创新和设计概念交流的。本方法提出了智能座舱人机交互叙事设计模型与设计策略，并通过模型图进行可视化表达。

评估与迭代：在设计问题求解路径和叙事设计流程中，叙事设计方法强调对设计方案的持续评估和迭代，包括全链路压测、用户反馈、测试和分析，设计师可以不断优化设计方案，直至达到最佳效果。

4.1 智能座舱人机交互——叙事设计理论框架

4.1.1 叙事的概念

广义上，叙事是用"讲故事"的方法组织和呈现信息的方式。在文学领域里，叙事是按时空逻辑来呈现某一事件或人物的方式。从词性上判断，叙事可以用作动词，也可以用作名词：动词是指叙事动作的本身，即讲故事的方式；名词是指叙事动作的对象，即故事的内容。随着叙事学体系的发展，这种源于文学的概念逐渐扩展到心理学、文化、艺术和设计等领域。20世纪90年代兴起的叙事设计，是通过设计作为表达性的媒介以及联系内在和外在世界来呈现故事，通过组织和编排一系列事件情节，使用户产生心理上的共鸣和情感体验。

讲故事是一种行为，它涉及叙事的内容和表达形式两个方面。在叙事研究中，通常"故事"的概念是用来指代叙事的内容，而"情节"的概念是用来指代叙事的形式。因此，叙事与设计在内容和形式的问题上是高度一致的，叙事学和设计学不可避免地会产生相互交叉与融合。好的设计就是讲故事，用生动有力的表现形式，将叙事元素融入设计中，设计实用的好用的产品，传递信息并引起情感共鸣，获得良好的用户体验。

4.1.2 叙事的内容

叙事的内容是早期叙事学研究的重点之一，叙事内容即"讲什么故事"，是故事所要传递的内容信息。每一个场景都是一个故事，每个故事都有事件情节、人物角色和时空结构。

"人、物、环境"共同构成了事件，是事件的基本组成要素（如图4-1），而这些要素在时间和空间维度下的变化过程，则构成了故事的情节发展。在智能座舱交互设计中，用户在特定的场景下与智能座舱发生互动，产生不同的行为动作与交互反馈，从而构成完整的"事件"。用户、场景、座舱三者紧密相连，且相互影响，任一个因素的变化都会改变"事件"的产生与呈现。

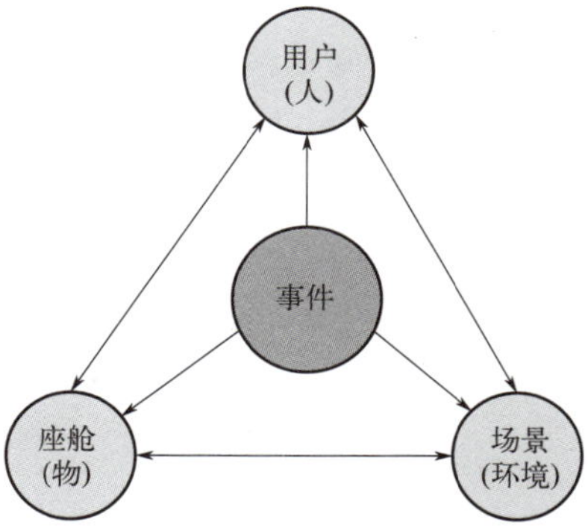

（1）事件的"用户"要素

图4-1 智能座舱"事件"的三要素

用户是事件的主体，也是故事情节的主要参与者，用户的行为、思想和情感推动故事情节的发展。叙事中的"用户"是具体的，包含性别、年龄、职业、性格特点等属性，只有基于完整的属性表达，才可以更加真实地呈现出用户的行为特征，也有助于设计师了解用户的基本需求，增加事件的可信度。

（2）事件的"场景"要素

场景是用户及座舱所处的空间或场所，是用户体验或使用智能座舱的环境。场景包含时间框架、空间环境、现实场景、虚拟场景等，在不同的故事背景与叙事目的下，场景可以有不同的定义，多种场景间也可以存在交叉兼并。叙事设计强调的是在具体场景中整合资源，以深入理解用户和特定场景的用户潜在需求。

（3）事件的"座舱"要素

叙事中"座舱"的概念并不局限于"座舱实体"，"座舱"是"用户"的交互对象，它可以是座舱实体或功能部件，也可以是车机系统、服务系统等。在叙事设计中，"座舱"通常是整个叙事活动的设计对象与最终目的之一，通过对"用户"和"场景"的分析，来确定"座舱"的具体功能和呈现形式，给用户创造出全新的功能体验。

情节是故事的重要组成部分，是整个故事的骨架。故事是一个发展的、动态的过程，情节是一个故事的主要线索，它描述了事件发展的顺序和逻辑，阐述了整个故事的起因、经过、结果。情节是故事内各个元素——"用户""场景""座舱"在时间和空间维度下变化的过程（图4-2），是不同时间段下人物行为和环境变化的总和。在叙事设计中，以用户需求和行为动机为基础，围绕使用场景设置故事情节，因此，一定程度上情节可以被视作智能座舱的用户使用流程。

图4-2 "情节"的意义结构

"事件情节"描述了事件发展的顺序和逻辑,阐述了整个叙事内容的起因、经过、结果。事件情节的研究涉及以下关键术语。

(1)动作接触点

接触点通常是指两个不同对象之间接触的位置或区域。"动作接触点"指"用户"与"座舱"实体或车机服务的接触位置。

(2)空间动线

动线(circulation)的概念最初是指人在建筑空间中的行走路线。动线是空间与时间两个维度的结合,通过动线设计可以引导用户的行为与心理。"空间动线"指以时间逻辑连接的"动作接触点"(图4-3)。

图4-3 智能座舱中的"空间动线"

(3)空间关系

空间关系通常指两个或多个对象在空间中相互的位置和方向关系。"空间关系"指"座舱"不同的实体功能部件之间的相对位置,如座位之间的并列排放或前后排放。

4.1.3 叙事方式

叙事方式即"如何讲故事"。在确定叙事内容、完成故事构建后,需要思考如何讲述故事。叙事者、叙事立场、叙事创造、叙事视角的差异都会影响讲述故事的具体方式——包含口语叙事、文本叙事、视觉叙事等。

① 叙事者。叙事者即讲故事的人。智能座舱人机交互中,叙事者的可能身份有设计师、用户、工程师、营销师、管理者等。考虑到不同人员的知识与技能差异,根据具体任务选择不同身份的人来做叙事者是非常重要的。设计师作为整个设计活动的参与者与推进者,在各个设计阶段对叙事设计任务有着较深的理解,因此,从创意到构思再到验证阶段,都可以作为叙事者参与其中;用户拥有实际使用经验以及直接深刻的洞察与感受,可以将其转化为故事想象,并快速构建出智能座舱交互事件情节,因此,智能座舱用户最适合在需求洞察与方案构思阶段作为叙事者来参与设计环节;而拥有不同专业知识背景的其他项目参与者,如工程师、营销师、管理者等,作为设计项目的利益相关者,有自己的利益诉求和产品理解,可以作为叙事者对叙事设计内容提出自己的限制与要求。

② 叙事立场。通过深入分析用户在交互式叙事中所扮演的角色,我们能够推导出故事的基础特性。叙事立场可根据其属性进一步划分为探索型和本体型两大类。在探索型立场上,用户的主要任务是发掘或学习故事的内容及其构成要素,有时甚至需要重建或重新编排事件顺序。而在本体型立场上,用户则拥有改变故事状态的决策权,并能够留下可追踪的历史记录。这样的分类有助于我们更全面地理解用户在交互式叙事中的不同

参与程度和影响力。

③ 叙事创造。叙事创造可以分为创造性叙事和非创造性叙事。在创造性叙事中，叙事者通过叙事来逐步明确故事内容与情节发展，叙事者可以对事件内容进行重建或重新编排，有能力做出改变故事状态的决策。因此，创造性叙事也通常运用于叙事设计的方案构思阶段。在非创造性叙事中，叙事者在叙事活动前就会被给予叙事材料，并会被要求在规定的叙事模式或其他系统限制下进行叙事，事件的交互结果也在叙事活动前就已经被确定。非创造性叙事是一种对事件的演绎过程，参与者在叙事活动过程中对故事内容进行反思，因此，非创造性叙事更适用于叙事设计的展示与验证，从而发现方案问题并提出改进策略。

④ 叙事视角。叙事视角可分为外部视角和内部视角。在外部视角下，叙事者处于故事之外，在一个与故事内人物角色不同的层面上进行活动。叙事者站在外部的视角设计故事内人物角色的行为活动，叙事者与用户对故事的感知视角相同，保证了客观性，同时有利于用户理解设计方案内容。在内部视角下，叙事者会代入并扮演故事中的人物角色，这种方式可以使叙事者更加直观深刻地感受到故事内人物角色的感受与体验，有助于发现叙事设计的问题或提出创新思路。

不同的叙事媒介会产生不同的叙事方式，语言、文字、图像、音乐等都可以成为交互事件的载体，根据叙事任务与叙事内容的特点与差异，可以选择不同的媒介或将其组合来进行叙事。不同的叙事方式可以帮助用户更好地理解每种叙事类型的特性，也可以强化故事特征与讲述目的，使内容更具说服力。常见的叙事方式包含口语叙事、文本叙事、视觉叙事、多媒体叙事等。

口语叙事：口语叙事是指通过口头表达形式来传达设计师的想法、愿景和设计思路。这通常发生在会议、演示或其他面对面的沟通中，设计师会使用口语语言结合手势、表情和其他非语言性的方式来呈现设计方案。口语叙事也被运用于用户访谈、概念产出等设计阶段，实时叙述故事情节可以帮助建立听众（访谈者）的信任和理解，讲述者可以根据听众的反应，调整故事的节奏并回答他们的问题。此外，讲述者还可以与听众共同创作故事，提供情境和结构，鼓励听众插入自己的经历和故事。

文本叙事：文本叙事是指通过文字来讲述一个故事或交互事件的方式。其优势在于能够以单一陈述的形式对内容进行编辑，并可以广泛应用于前期调研、概念产出、文档报告撰写等设计阶段。

与具象的视觉符号相比，文字能够带给人们更广泛的思考空间。然而，文本叙事与用户的沟通是间接的，无法获得用户的及时反馈，单一的叙事形式也可能导致信息传递过程中对文本原义的误解。因此，在使用文本叙事时也可以结合口语、视觉等叙事形式，产生多方位的展示效果，起到更好的启示、传递作用。

视觉叙事：视觉叙事是指通过视觉元素（如图像、颜色等）来讲故事。视觉叙事通常依靠视觉元素之间的组合和运用，创造出生动、清晰或抽象的表达效果。故事板是一种常用的视觉叙事工具，是指用图片或简短文字来描绘一段故事情节，以便更好地展示、传达和沟通叙事内容。故事板对用户行为进行了详细的描述（图4-4），设计师可以通过制作故事板来模拟用户场景和行为，以促进对用户需求的理解。同时，故事板也是一种对设计方案的可视化表达，故事板可以建立设计团队与受众等其他利益相关者之间的有效沟通的方式。

图 4-4 视觉叙事—故事板

多媒体叙事：多媒体叙事可以采用视频、声音和文本等多种元素，创造出更加生动、具有情感共鸣的叙事效果（图 4-5）。在智能座舱设计方案展示中，使用多媒体叙事可以完整地呈现故事发展的场景、流程与座舱状态变化过程。

图 4-5 使用视频叙事呈现智能座舱设计方案

4.1.4 叙事的目标和意义

（1）叙事创造了一种信息组织模式

叙事创造了一种不同于其他交流形式的独特信息传达模式，提高了复杂设计内容的可理解性。人类理解现实的方式只有两种：其一，通过逻辑推演与经验累积；其二，通过讲故事来组织感官、身体和认知获得的事件记忆的线索。叙事是认知组织主要过程之一，通过将时间、事件视为情节的一部分来赋予它们意义。

因此，叙事可以被视为一种认知工具。通过故事，人们能够更高效地记忆与理解信息，原因在于故事能够将信息融入生动有趣的具体情景中，进而提升信息的可接受性和可理解性。叙事需遵循一定的结构,例如,开头、主体和结尾的组织形式,为信息的传达提供了明确的架构。叙事的结构有助于信息接收者理解不同信息在整体故事脉络中的相互联系。此外,叙事还能借助隐喻和象征来构建意义,通过符号或隐喻来传达更为宏大的概念或思想,从而以凝练且有力的方式表达复杂的意蕴。因此,在设计领域,叙事成为一种有力的工具,它能够协助设计师更为精准地传递信息,引导观众聚焦设计中的关键要素,体验事件的动态情节过程,进而深入解读设计内容,领悟设计的宗旨与深层含义。

(2) 叙事能够与用户建立情感连接

叙事在设计领域不仅能传递信息和意义,更能与用户建立更紧密的情感连接。通过"讲故事",设计师更容易与观众产生情感共鸣,进而提升设计的亲和力与社会影响力。故事围绕人物与情节展开,真实的场景、人物内心体验及成长过程描述,都能触动观众情感。叙事与体验紧密相连,只要有"事",就有体验。叙事设计深入挖掘用户的使用与情感体验,将生活经验融入设计,创造出易于被大众理解的新产品形式,实现设计师与用户之间的情感沟通。

产品的情感体验并不是产品本身所具备的物理属性,而是通过与产品交互的"事件",从而赋予用户情感体验。时间维度是"事件"和"记忆"的共同通道,在产品设计过程中融入"事件"的表达,通过"事件"与"记忆"的相互作用,可以引发用户与产品的情感共鸣,从而增强用户与产品之间的情感连接。

(3) 叙事可以维持团队创新力

持续创新是一项重要而艰巨的任务,创新过程是多方面的,包括对产品和服务的新创意,以及根据技术能力及生产条件做出的技术创新。因此,创新需要具有不同观点和知识背景的团队协调努力,以促进重新组合想法和产生新颖性创意。然而团队也可能失衡,叙事恰恰是一种促进团队互动的有效形式。

一方面,讲故事的方式可以拓展思考的深度和广度,从而激发出创新思维和改变传统方法的勇气,并转化为开拓新领域、解决新难题的实际行动。同时,叙事为团队提供了一种生成记忆,将从过去特定实例中积累的想法转化为当前和未来的努力,并保留了创新的多样性。另一方面,叙事促进了团队成员的共同理解,从而提高了合作效率、推动了创新故事的传播。特别是在早期团队中,由于团队成员责任和利益不尽相同,在缺乏对设计对象的共识的情况下,叙事是团队里思想翻译的强大机制。

4.2 智能座舱人机交互——叙事设计流程

4.2.1 叙事设计的问题求解路径

智能座舱人机交互设计的问题求解路径,大体可分为问题洞察和问题沟通两条路径。其中,问题洞察又被细分成:以时间为线索的全流程穷尽式问题框定和事件全要素梳理的设计机会点框定;问题沟通则被细分为叙事要素沉淀和重组的新概念生成,促进概念生成的叙事模式以及设计方案讲解与达成共识。

（1）以时间为线索的全流程穷尽式问题框定

所谓以时间为线索是指交互事件发展的时间顺序；所谓穷尽式问题框定是指按照时间顺序梳理交互事件的全过程。例如，按照使用顺序梳理识别、进入、启动、驾驶、接管、车内活动、车外活动、泊车 8 个场景，分析用户体验，挖掘设计机会。互联网界普遍采用的所谓"全链路"分析，通常指的是从起点到终点的整个流程或路径的分析。所谓"全链路压测"，更是会模拟海量的用户请求和数据对整个业务链进行压力测试，以确保系统的稳定性和性能。

（2）事件全要素梳理的设计机会点框定

从设计问题启发到创新概念生成的过程中，需要对问题进行凝练和转化，使问题变成可以被直接运用的设计机会点。智能座舱的设计问题或创新机会点通常以"交互事件"的形式被记录，例如"用户使用手势快速拍照""亲子进行语音互动游戏"等，因此，以交互事件为基础，可以围绕"用户、场景、座舱"要素，尤其是事件的情节要素（情节是一个交互事件的主要线索，它描述了事件发展的顺序和逻辑，阐述了整个故事的起因、经过、结果），充分利用文字、图片、视频等媒介准确和形象地记录交互事件。通过这样的方式，问题和创新机会点可以转化为直接被使用的设计素材。

（3）叙事要素沉淀和重组的新概念生成

设计团队的创新概念启发与生成过程，不一定是连续的，也不一定是顺利的，甚至团队的成员组成也会发生变化。一方面，这个过程中的不同环节时间间隔过长会导致"丢失"已经生成的概念和设计机会点；另一方面，智能座舱设计概念内容复杂，个体通常难以形成完整的事件理解和描述。因此，要构建包括要素沉淀、要素重组和概念故事的设计素材组织模式（图 4-6）。可以采用叙事卡片法，对事件要素及相关创意机会点进行整理与沉淀，通过卡片挑选、摆放、排序以及写和画，搭建出不同创意的智能座舱场景故事。

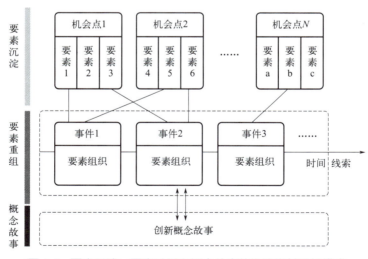

图 4-6　要素沉淀、要素重组和概念故事的设计素材组织模式

（4）促进概念生成的叙事模式

在创新概念生成阶段，参与者知识背景各异，复杂的设计工具和任务对于参与者有

很重的认知负担,难以迅速输出完整设计方案,并可能因此使参与者感到挫败,影响设计参与度。采用故事结构来组织和呈现思想,可简化复杂概念,使其变得有意义且易于理解。叙事还能帮助参与者清晰把握故事走向和重点,防止创作过程陷入混乱。

(5)设计方案讲解与达成共识

人类天生倾向于理解以故事形式呈现的信息。在智能座舱概念设计的阐述中,叙事作为一种独特的信息传递方式,显著提升了复杂设计内容的易懂程度。故事所具备的固定框架和起承转合的结构特点,有助于听众理解设计元素在整体背景下的联系,进而可更深入地理解设计内容和领悟其目的与意义。同时,通过叙事,设计元素被巧妙地融入故事情节,这不仅增强了设计的吸引力,还在叙事者与听众之间建立了情感纽带,有助于设计师把握创新概念的核心体验。

4.2.2 叙事设计流程

智能座舱人机交互设计的概念生成,是一个交互事件要素的组织过程,大体分为五个步骤。图4-7体现了以概念生成为核心的智能座舱人机交互叙事设计流程。

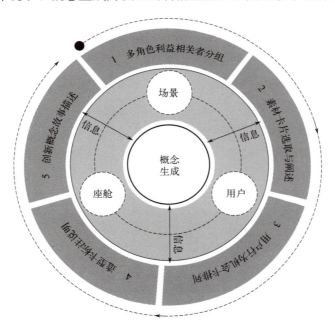

图 4-7 智能座舱人机交互叙事设计流程

(1)多角色利益相关者分组

在智能座舱创新概念的生成阶段,对团队人员构成有明确的要求。该阶段需要吸纳所有利益相关者,包括设计师、工程师等。这些人员不仅具备智能座舱设计所需的专业知识和社会经验,能够弥补团队在设计知识方面的不足,确保知识的均衡分布,这是团队有效沟通与协作的基石。而且,他们能根据明确的团队任务,从实际场景出发,为创新概念的生成提供基本方向指引(图4-8)。

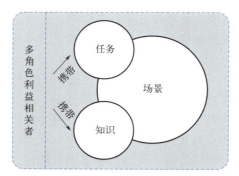

图 4-8　多角色利益相关者携带场景知识和任务

在智能座舱创新概念生成阶段，设计师在团队中主要扮演促进者的角色。他们不仅参与场景故事的构建，还负责推动团队协作，促进成员间的交流与互动，以催生新的观念和创意。在这一阶段，会将不同成员分成多个设计小组，小组成员通过选择素材卡片、共同讨论等方式生成创新概念。集中讨论的形式有助于汇聚多元背景的成员，促进深入交流和互动，从而达成共同理解，实现设计方案的整合与改进。为确保每个设计小组都具备全面的智能座舱设计知识，组员应涵盖不同知识领域，包括设计、技术、管理和用户经验。同时，考虑到小组讨论和决策的效率，每组人数控制在 3～5 人较为适宜。这样的配置能够确保项目的顺利进行，同时促进创新思维的产生和发展。

（2）素材卡片选取与阐述

参与者根据对智能座舱产品的理解或使用期望，从素材库中选择相关的用户行为机会卡，为后续的概念故事生成提供创意输入。在选择前，小组可预先设定一个主题场景类别，并据此筛选卡片，以确保所选卡片内容能构成连贯的完整故事。选择后，每位参与者需阐述所选卡片内容及选择理由，同时可基于个人理解对卡片内容进行重新描述或拓展。此举旨在深化参与者对卡片内容的思考，并从他人的叙述中汲取灵感。此外，通过相互观察和倾听，团队成员能就某一设计概念达成共识，从而加强团队间的沟通与协作。

（3）用户行为机会卡排列

参与者通过小组讨论，筛选卡片并整理创意概念。在构建故事时，他们利用卡片作为故事事件的输入，依据时间顺序排列组合卡片，明确故事发展路径，构思初步方案。每组应围绕固定场景和同一故事展开交流讨论，鼓励输出个人想法，以提高设计效率并确保故事完整。排序方式便于参与者以时间为线索整理素材，直观表达和记录所构思的故事。同时，卡片作为共享设计材料，使参与者在后续方案讲述与互动评价时，能基于对卡片内容的初步了解，更轻松地理解其他组别的方案。

（4）造型卡标注说明

为明确创新概念的应用场景及用户在座舱中的具体状态，我们需在相应的用户行为机会卡下放置座舱造型卡，并在卡片上明确标注动作接触点，以此完善创新概念的构成要素并实现可视化方案呈现。在此基础上，参与者应充分利用各自不同的知识背景，从专业角度出发对创新概念的细节进行构思或改进，以提升方案的专业性和实用性。例如，技术人员可以从技术层面对创新概念的技术可行性进行评估，或引入新技术来支持概念的升级；而智能座舱的用户则可根据自身使用经验和期望，对创新概念的功能定义进行完善。

（5）创新概念故事描述

每组推选一名代表，结合用户行为机会卡和座舱造型卡，详细阐述创意概念。其他小组参与者在观察和倾听过程中，对他组方案形成初步认识。在叙述时，应采用外部视角，即以第三人称描述故事内容。这种方式能确保受述者与叙事者对故事的感知视角一致，从而降低受述者的理解难度，更有效地传达创新概念的核心内容。由于参与者身份和知识背景的差异，他们可能对特定问题产生不同的理解，这种差异可能会影响后续设计活动的顺利进行，导致重复讨论和设计方案的争议。为了解决这一问题，可以采用公开描述的方式，让参与者利用自身知识和经验对问题进行定义和阐述。这样，这些知识就会成为团队共享的信息，帮助大家形成一致的理解。同时，口语叙事的方式还能在叙事者与听众之间建立情感联系，有利于团队进行更深入的设计讨论和诠释。

4.2.3 叙事设计工具——卡片

叙事设计的"卡片法"是一种在界面设计中常见的方法，它通过将文本内容与图片（或图形）进行整合，让信息传达更加直观。卡片法中所使用的卡片可以在叙事设计的不同阶段起到不同的作用。在智能座舱设计中使用的卡片有用户行为机会卡、座舱造型卡等。

（1）用户行为机会卡

图 4-9 为用户行为机会卡的模板，这是本研究在智能座舱问题发现阶段所采用的叙事卡片。鉴于协同设计的需要，我们选择了实体卡片作为简单易用、具有可操作性的讨论辅助工具。每张卡片的尺寸为 16cm×10cm，内容涵盖"场景类别""标题""文字描述""示意图片"和"行为流程描述"五个部分，通过文字、图像和色彩三种信息方式呈现。其中，"场景类别"标明卡片所属主题，并通过特定色彩便于使用者进行快速识别；"标题"概括了卡片中描述的用户行为；"文字描述"部分详细解释了用户行为的机会点；而"示意图片"则直观地展示了标题和文字描述的内容，帮助使用者更深入地理解和感受相应情境；"行为流程描述"将用户的行为以时间线的方式分解为一个个流程并阐述，使得每一阶段的行为特征和内容更加清晰明了。

图 4-9 用户行为机会卡及其使用案例

用户行为机会卡是对智能座舱中"用户"要素的凝练表达，它直接展现了"行为"层面，并从侧面反映了需求（如图 4-10）。需明确的是，使用用户行为机会卡并不创造场景，而是基于前期调研所确定的场景，来洞察用户行为的机会点。此类卡片为创新概念生成提供了来自"用户"视角的灵感，是一种可循环使用的设计启发工具。

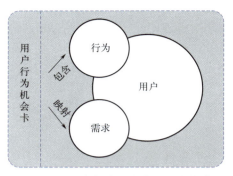

图 4-10　用户行为机会卡的要素构成

（2）座舱造型卡

用户行为机会卡主要描绘了座舱内用户的状态，而要展现座舱实体与车机状况，则需借助座舱造型卡。如图 4-11 所示，卡片的尺寸也设定为 16cm×10cm，由文字、图像和色彩三种信息元素组成。卡片内容包括"风格"和"座舱图片"两部分。其中，"风格"一项用于描述所展示的座舱造型的审美特征，而"座舱图片"则是由设计团队提供的座舱设计示意图，涵盖了多种典型的空间布局。这些图片有助于使用者在构思故事时，更清晰地理解用户与座舱以及座舱内部各实体部件之间的空间关系。此外，使用者还可以在卡片上标注出用户与座舱的交互点，从而辅助进行概念推导和叙事表达。

图 4-11　座舱造型卡及动作接触点标注

座舱造型卡是设计师对座舱实体与车机在空间布局和造型风格上的创新探索，同时也反映了设计师对新兴技术在座舱实体应用上的表现形式的思考（图 4-12）。这类卡片不仅为后期创新概念生成过程中的参与者提供了"座舱造型"维度的灵感启发，还为他们考虑创新概念如何具体呈现在座舱实体上提供了有力支撑。

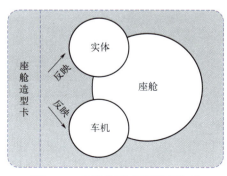

图 4-12　座舱造型卡的要素构成

4.3 智能座舱人机交互叙事设计模型与设计策略

4.3.1 智能座舱人机交互叙事设计模型

智能座舱创新概念生成的复杂性和多样性，赋予了"叙事"更深远的含义。智能座舱交互设计的叙事设计范式，不仅指通过构建故事来创造新的设计概念，更涵盖了设计要素之间的关联与形式转换，以及具有不同知识背景的利益相关者之间的协同合作。此外，它还涉及多种工具在概念生成过程中的设计要素表达和协同使用方式。本小节综合本章对智能座舱创新概念启发和概念生成流程的研究，构建智能座舱人机交互叙事设计模型（图 4-13）。

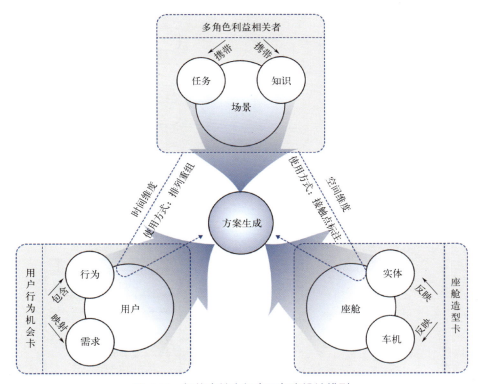

图 4-13　智能座舱人机交互叙事设计模型

从要素的构成上，创新概念生成需要包含场景、用户、座舱三类要素。用户层面上，用户行为机会卡的创建直接反映了用户的机会行为，同时也是用户需求映射体现；座舱层面上，座舱造型卡反映了座舱的实体与车机状态，是设计师对智能座舱造型风格、功能、空间布局状态的一种探索与解读结果；场景层面上，拥有不同专业背景的多角色利益相关者携带了设计项目的任务与智能座舱知识等，以此为基础多角色利益相关者产生对于场景的解读与定义。

4.3.2 智能座舱人机交互叙事设计策略

对智能座舱创新概念生成阶段与概念方案迭代阶段的设计策略进行总结,最终形成了智能座舱人机交互叙事设计策略(图4-14)。

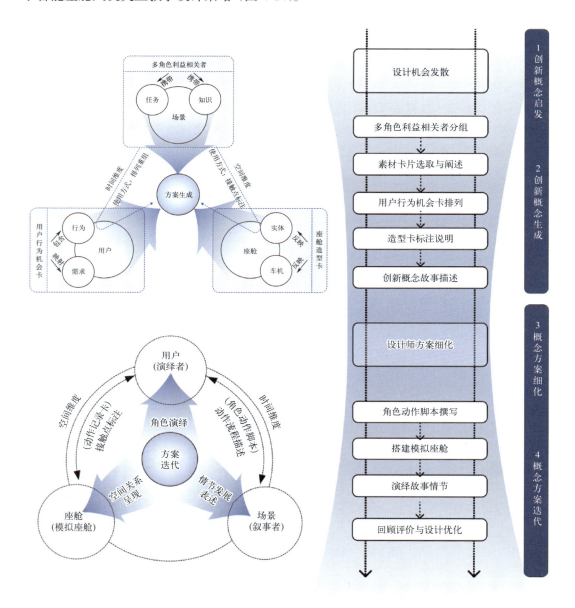

图 4-14 智能座舱人机交互叙事设计策略

智能座舱产品的设计与开发是一个复杂且多阶段的过程,涵盖概念设计、原型制作和设计验证等环节。本章着重探讨智能座舱在创新概念设计阶段的要素、工具和流程。该阶段可细分为概念启发与生成、方案细化与迭代两个子阶段。虽然这些子阶段在项目流程上呈现连续性，但在实际操作中可以独立进行。依据不同子阶段的特性，可灵活调配设计参与者和组织模式。在概念启发与生成阶段，需广泛吸纳具有不同知识背景的利益相关者参与，以确保多元知识输入和多视角审视创新概念，从而提升创意的多样性并促进团队对设计目标达成共识。方案细化与迭代阶段则以设计师为主导，通过洞察现存问题，提出设计优化的思路，实现设计的逐步收敛。

智能座舱创新概念启发与生成是一个自下而上的设计过程，它从具体场景出发，结合用户行为和座舱状态来构建方案的初步形态。在实际操作中，多角色利益相关者首先解读选定场景，选取相应的用户行为机会卡和座舱造型卡，作为创新设计的要素输入。接下来，以叙事时间线为基准，对用户行为机会卡进行重新排列，构建出事件的基本流程和初步的创新概念故事。随后，利用座舱造型卡来诠释座舱的各种状态，并通过标注动作接触点来反映用户在座舱中的空间行为位置。这一过程最终形成了对智能座舱创新设计概念的全面而深入的解读。

智能座舱概念方案细化与迭代是一个自上而下的设计过程，它侧重于从用户视角深入剖析方案要素存在的问题，并利用要素间的相互作用来进行优化。在具体流程中，设计师首先会代入用户角色并构建角色动作脚本。接着，按照故事发展的时间线进行演绎，叙事者以旁白方式描述场景与情节变化，推动整个演绎过程。同时，利用动作记录卡详细记录用户的动作、接触点及体验感受。最终，形成对用户、场景和座舱三要素在时间和空间维度上的全面洞察，以此为基础对方案进行细化与迭代。

4.4 人机交互叙事设计案例分析

该项目来源于德赛西威与湖南大学的合作项目，项目以 2023 年上海车展德赛西威全尺寸智能座舱展台为设计目标，具有一定的前瞻性与充分的落地性。项目可分为场景和场景要素提取、智能场景趋势调研、设计概念生成与设计迭代、设计方案产出四个阶段。

4.4.1 场景和场景要素提取

在场景和场景要素提取阶段以实地访谈的形式进行调研，框定智能座舱展台的目标价值场景。对 10 位企业专家就场景、设计、技术三方面展开结构化访谈，记录访谈内容原文，在整理出的访谈文本中对于关键语句进行筛选，然后将复杂的从句拆解成多个简单句并提取描述性词语。最终结果：场景层级上以智慧和智能感为关键词，包含 Z 世代、办公、第三空间等主题场景选择方向，并需要保证场景体验的完整流程；座舱风格上以科技感为关键词，要求通透感、简洁感、层次感；座舱车机提供智能行车助手、多屏化、屏幕化、人车管理等多种应用技术。对 2016 年以来主机厂、头部供应商和造车新势力三类品牌展出座舱进行调研，调研内容涵盖 17 个参展品牌和 48 个参展座舱，分别对其主题场景、座舱风格和应用技术进行统计分析。结合企业调研结果，最终制定了以下场景及座舱设计要素。

4.4.2 智能场景趋势调研

（1）座舱主题场景

如图 4-15 所示，2016—2020 年 CES 展的座舱场景类别、主题数量明显增多，呈现出多样化趋势，如车内休闲、车内办公、情绪感知、多场景融合等。项目定义的目标场景有：亲子——以家庭亲子为目标人群，解决儿童游戏、儿童教育与亲子互动等家庭出行问题；轻游戏——以游戏为交互形式，面向不同的使用需求与场景，如缓解疲劳、多人互动、儿童寓教等，进行车内轻度游戏体验；旅途——以路途出行为典型使用场景，对全流程路途出行体验（如旅程规划、旅程体验、旅程记录与分享等）进行改进；人车共驾——面向实际驾驶员驾驶问题，如情绪调节、驾驶习惯引导等，用新兴技术辅助人车共驾体验改进。

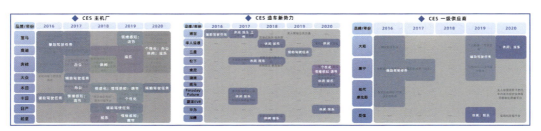

图 4-15　2016—2020 年 CES 展座舱主题场景变化趋势

（2）座舱布局类型

如图 4-16 所示，座舱布局类型主要分为：展示台，主要展示显示部件，不设完整 IP 操作台；半舱，完整的 IP 操作台及其相连部件（前排或双排座椅），非封闭座舱空间；全舱，完整的内饰部件、空间和氛围营造，全流程场景体验；概念车，整车展示。项目组最终确定，选用全舱或半舱的形式进行智能座舱备选方案设计。

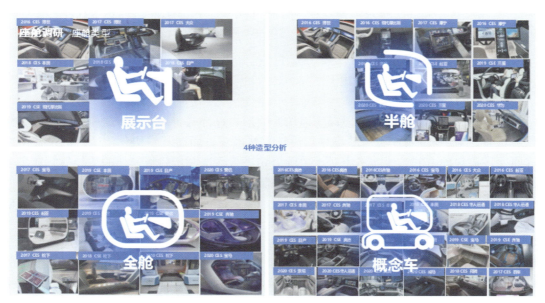

图 4-16　2016—2020 年 CES 展座舱布局

（3）智能感造型风格

如图 4-17 是座舱造型变化趋势，可以看出智能座舱的造型整体呈现从复杂向简约转变的趋势，从电子化座舱精致机械的风格向简约工业和有机生命变化。直接智能感的造型语义，最终确定以干净、流畅、宁静、舱内空间连续性为目标智能座舱的造型特征。

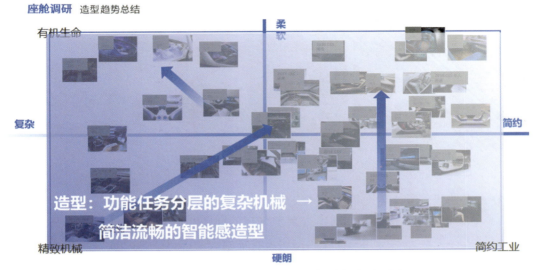

图 4-17　2016—2020 年 CES 展智能座舱造型风格变化

（4）交互技术趋势

交互技术趋势包括：交互界面介质无形化，不局限于传统的屏幕交互或是机械按键，使用车窗、灯光、复合式触控材质等，作为人车交互界面介质；人工智能人格化，"人格化"人工智能作为人车交互媒介，带来更好的情感体验，比如虚拟助手、车载机器人、全息管家等；多通道物理交互反馈，比如触觉反馈、虚拟按键带振动反馈、超声波触觉反馈、3D 触摸显示技术等；主动交互，自主感知、自主判断、自主响应、语音识别并主动反馈等。

4.4.3　设计概念生成与设计迭代

如图 4-18 所示，在这个阶段，组织有 6 个设计小组，每个小组都提出了独特的智能座舱创新设计方案。以其中一个名为"FLU-MOON"的典型方案为例，其设计特点如下：该方案以四人出游为场景主题，当座舱启动时，用户可点击开启"3D"数字仪表屏，该屏幕会根据用户头部的位置进行画面调整，实现个性化显示。用户登录个人账户后，座椅和外后视镜会自动根据驾驶员的体型进行预调整，提供最佳的驾驶视角。在沉浸模式下，座舱通过四维通感技术，即"声、色、香、触"，为乘客打造全方位的感官体验。环景模式的开启，则通过座舱内的大屏与多屏协同显示，营造出 360° 的全景视野。此外，座舱还能智能监测用户心情，并据此调整舱内氛围，改善乘坐体验。到达目的地后,座舱会自动记录整个出游过程,为用户提供珍贵的回忆。

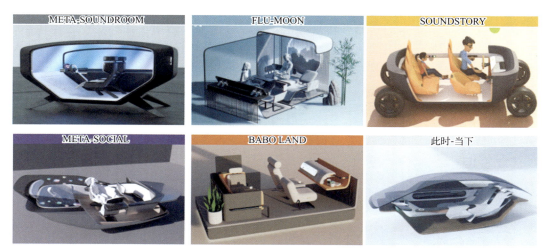

图 4-18 智能座舱设计方案(6 组)

在方案迭代阶段,运用叙事演绎法对设计方案中的空间关系、用户动作及动作接触点进行了深入剖析,并精准识别出方案中存在的问题。以 FLU-MOON 设计方案为例,我们发现了以下几个关键问题:首先,在手势拍照环节,当侧窗拍照完成后,照片传输到个人屏幕时,交互动作的设计尚待明确;其次,使用个人屏幕查看和编辑照片时,前排乘客位置的个人屏幕设置不合理,由于距离过远导致操作不便;最后,在相册上传环节,当手机已经连接至车载系统时,需要明确手机和车载相册之间的数据交互方式。基于这些问题,项目组对设计方案进行了有针对性的优化与迭代。最终,经过改进的 6 个设计方案均获得了德赛西威企业高层的高度认可,这初步验证了我们的设计方法和迭代流程的有效性。

4.4.4 设计方案产出

(1)场景定义与设计

智能座舱实现了多场景体验的无缝切换,具体分为办公模式、旅拍模式和亲子模式,用户可根据需求自主选择。通过多模式切换,旨在展示智能座舱在不同使用场景和任务中的功能多样性。设计的核心在于,多乘客与多屏之间的交互。在旅拍模式和亲子模式下,分别构思了共创分享旅行照片和亲子互动游戏的多人体验活动;而在办公模式下,设计了单人车内办公和在线会议的功能。

(2)用户定义及设计

基于多用户互动的场景需求,我们对舱内目标用户进行了相应的多角色设定。在旅拍模式下,用户被设定为结伴出行的好友,其中驾驶员用户不仅负责驾驶和旅途规划,还需与乘客用户协作进行旅行拍摄。乘客用户可以主动分享照片或发起相册共创。当共创模式启动时,座舱将切换至自动驾驶状态,驾驶员座椅自动后旋,以便与后排乘客共同进行创作活动。在亲子模式中,家长担任驾驶员并作为游戏主导者,通过"车内飞泡"游戏与孩子互动,孩子在后排屏上接收并响应来自不同方向的"飞泡"。而在办公模式里,用户则位于驾驶座,当线上会议开始时,座椅会侧旋以面向座舱侧方的显示屏,用户可在后排进行操作(图4-19)。

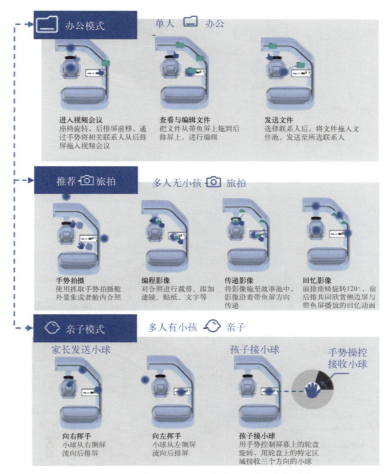

图4-19 三种场景下的用户定义及其动作流线

（3）座舱造型设计

针对前期定义的简洁流畅的智能感造型风格,制作风格意象情绪板(图4-20),主要以简洁干净的形态作为参考,强调整体呈现出的几何感与宁静流畅的视觉感受,其材质和色彩表达也具有一定的参考价值。半透明化的通透材质、天蓝色的色彩语义以及几何形态的简洁构型,很适合应用在座舱造型设计工作中。

（4）座舱车机 HMI 设计

如图4-21所示,为旅拍模式下,线上会议的车机 HMI 呈现。图中,用户在投递照片的屏幕上,拖动选中的方案向右移动,屏幕右侧与座舱中间流水屏智能表面相连接,投递后的个人票数以光点的形式传递到流水屏上,并最终归档到相应的位置,这种可视化的投票形式增强了用户的交互实感,同时体现了舱内交互状态下独特的交互连续性。

Smart Solution关键词

干净　流畅　宁静
舱内空间感　连续性　智能化表达

图 4-20　德赛西威智能座舱的风格意象情绪板

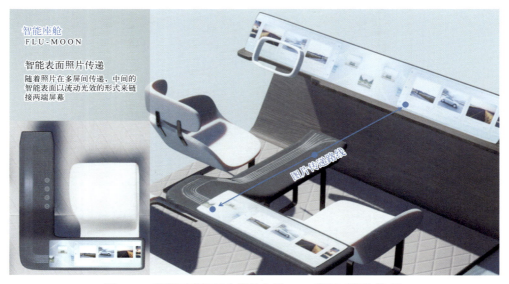

图 4-21　德赛西威智能座舱的车机 HMI 设计（旅拍模式）

第 5 章

智能座舱人机交互设计工具

5.1　产品设计和设计工具
5.2　座舱交互设计方法与工具

设计学习不是行为学习，而是能力学习。在智能座舱人机交互设计方法论下，设计仍然是一个实践认识的过程，仍然是在不可预测的世界中引入有意图的变化。这意味着，要真正理解智能座舱人机交互设计的设计范式、设计对象和设计场景，只能通过"做设计"。"做设计"则离不开设计工具，本章将简要介绍智能座舱人机交互设计工具。

人与座舱之间的互动是复杂和多元的。我们已经通过智能座舱的人机交互设计框架，深入探讨了"用户、事件、时空"这三个场景要素之间的相互作用。智能座舱的设计不仅仅局限于造型设计的范畴，它还涉及人与座舱交互的各个方面。智能座舱设计需要遵循"美、理性、伦理"的三大设计理念和设计标准。在座舱设计的不同阶段，需要使用不同方法及工具，具体分析智能座舱产品设计和交互设计在座舱内分别的作用，以及二者相辅相成改善整体的用户体验的特点。

5.1 产品设计和设计工具

5.1.1 智能座舱造型设计的基本原则

汽车造型设计，即传统汽车设计中的形状赋予或造型过程，是汽车设计开发的关键环节，同时也是设计理论研究和辅助设计技术的重要应用领域。尽管它属于产品造型设计的范畴，但汽车作为"交通工具"的独特性，如技术复杂性、多学科设计优化、用户需求的多元性及文化背景的丰富性，使得其内部空间设计与普通消费品形态设计存在显著差异。特别是汽车造型或款式具有独立意义，且座舱设计中融入了越来越多的交互体验等非物质元素。因此，座舱造型设计是一个综合性的创新过程，既反映了车辆的美学和功能需求，也体现了设计师的创意和技术水平。为支持设计师在汽车造型设计中的创新和探索，该领域已广泛采用多种基础设计工具。智能座舱的造型设计基于以下四个原则。

（1）人机工程学原则

智能座舱的设计必须首先围绕驾驶员和乘客的需求展开，同时兼顾操作习惯。在设计过程中，深入应用人机工程学原理至关重要，以确保操作控件的布局既合理又便捷，有效降低用户在长时间使用中可能出现的疲劳感。例如，中控屏、物理按钮和触摸屏等关键设备的位置设计，都应遵循人机工程学原则，使得驾驶员能够在驾驶过程中轻松、直观地进行操作。

（2）空间环境设计原则

智能座舱的造型设计同样需要兼顾舱内的舒适性与安全性。这涉及座椅设计、灯光布局、空气质量和噪声控制等多个方面。座椅不仅要提供良好的支撑性，还要确保长时间乘坐的舒适度，以减轻驾驶疲劳。灯光设计应追求柔和而不刺眼的效果，确保充足的照明且不影响驾驶员的视线。此外，对空气质量和噪声的控制也是提升座舱舒适度的关键因素。

（3）智能技术原则

智能座舱的设计应充分利用包括人工智能、大数据、互联网在内的现代科技，以实现信息的智能化处理和交互。这涉及语音识别技术的应用，允许用户通过简单的语音指令来控制设备，以及智能推荐系统的整合，根据用户的个人喜好和习惯提供定制化服务和建议。

（4）整体造型设计原则

智能座舱在整体造型上倾向于采用简洁而流线型的设计语言，旨在降低风阻并提升能源效率。座舱内部的空间布局需精心规划，以营造一个宽敞且舒适的乘坐环境。同时，智能座舱的设计还注重细节的打磨，如选用高品质材料和精致装饰，以增强座舱的整体质感和高端感。

总体而言，智能座舱的产品设计原则是一个多维度的综合考量，它基于人机工程学、空间环境设计、智能技术以及整体造型设计等方面，旨在为用户打造一个集舒适、安全与智能化于一体的驾乘体验。下面对智能座舱产品设计中常用的产品设计工具进行逐一介绍。

5.1.2 产品设计工具

（1）草图

草图在设计初期是一种重要工具，用于表达和阐述设计的初步理念或形态概念。它不仅能捕捉设计的初步意图，还能呈现形体的大致比例和基本准确度。同时，草图蕴含进一步探讨的空间，充满无限可能性。

在汽车造型设计中，草图反映了设计师对理想车型的想象。但设计的核心在于满足用户需求，因此草图需展现设计师的创意，更要反映用户的实际需求。这表明，草图不仅是设计思维的表现工具，还是关键的交流媒介。它帮助设计师与团队、利益相关者及用户沟通，确保设计与市场趋势和用户需求相符。

作为交流工具，草图简洁地阐释设计意象和概念，不必过分追求细节。在设计各阶段，草图形式多样，从宏观概略到拥有接近效果图的精细度，如快速草图、主体草图等。不论何种类型，其核心都是将设计师的构思以易懂的方式呈现，以推动设计的进展。在设计意象阶段，草图能迅速捕捉关键形体特征。从不同视角审视草图，设计师可构建初步形体架构（图5-1）。进一步利用草图拓展这些架构，可形成富含意象元素和创新方向的设计草图（图5-2）。

在设计深化阶段，草图的可修改性和沟通便利性使得设计师能迅速优化调整方案。此外，草图也作为深化设计的工具，助力设计师增添细节，并探讨体量与型面的关系（图5-3）。

（2）造型意象板

"造型意象板"是设计师通过组合图像、文字和样品等元素，以便直观展现设计造型意象的视觉工具。其核心功能在于将抽象的设计概念具象化、具体化为可视形式，从而有效地传达设计理念。此工具在造型设计和交互设计领域均具有重要应用价值。造型意象板的制作灵活多变，无固定模式，主要通过图像化手段捕捉智能座舱场景的感知信息，将设计师对色彩、质感、风格等方面的考量与设想进行具象化展现（图5-4）。

图 5-1　初步形体架构草图

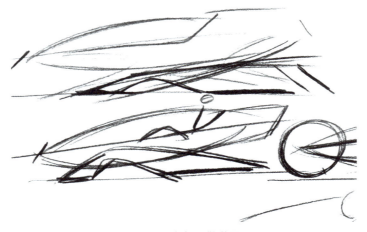

图 5-2　意象发散草图

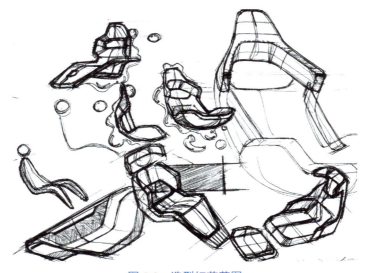

图 5-3　造型细节草图

风格定义-意向看板
IMAGEBOARD

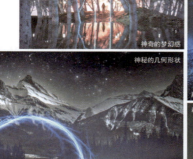

图 5-4　座舱设计造型意象板

造型意象板作为一种设计工具，其核心特征主要体现在图像的强大视觉表现力及其所承载的情感表达上。此工具的效用在于通过图像形式来捕捉并传递设计信息，从而有效弥补设计任务书等文本描述的不足，使那些难以言传的设计元素与理念得以具象化呈现。从本质上看，造型意象板可以被视作一种"取景"过程，它借助精心挑选与布局的图像，以视觉化的手段展示设计意图和信息。这种方法不仅有助于激发视觉灵感、形成特定风格与设计概念，还能通过视觉解读与故事情境的构建，增强对设计内涵的深层次理解。值得一提的是，造型意象板在设计流程中的应用并不限于前期（如概念设计等）环节。它在整个设计过程中都发挥着激发创意灵感与传达设计理念的重要作用，并且是设计团队协作沟通中不可或缺的工具。

在汽车造型与交互设计领域，意象板构建涉及概念意象板和视觉意象板两大核心部分。以设计科技感电动车人机界面为例，概念意象板在设计初期至关重要。比如，围绕"科技感"主题，搜集并展现相关设计概念意象。为此，造型与交互设计师需协作，精选体现科技元素的产品与交互技术图片，筛选与分类后，挑选出与主题紧密相关的场景、角色及氛围图像。意象板不仅要满足交互设计需求，还需将手势控制及显示技术概念可视化。此过程可帮助设计师深入理解并表达设计主题，确立统一设计基调，并明确软硬件界面的设计差异。

视觉意象板主要聚焦于通过"视觉语言"来表达设计概念。它运用特征线条、型面及图形元素等视觉符号，来细致刻画设计意图。在筛选和整理视觉意象板素材时，造型与交互设计师会基于各自对科技、灵动、优雅等形容词的独到理解，采用不同的取景策略。造型设计师可能借助家电、家具或概念车的特征线条与型面，来呈现产品的灵动与优雅特质；而交互设计师则可能通过游戏、网页或车载系统的界面，展示图形语言的灵动与优雅。这一过程实际上是设计师将素材与设计意象相结合的创造性工作。

综合概念意象板与视觉意象板，两者共同构建了一个展现统一风格、概念和视觉场景的工具，极大促进了设计师间的沟通交流。这不仅保障了软硬件界面风格与设计元素的一致性，更为汽车人机界面交互设计的软硬件融合注入了强大动力。

(3) 油泥模型工具

模型制作是汽车设计流程中的关键环节，紧随汽车总体与车身布局设计以及尺寸确定之后。油泥模型，作为一种重要的设计工具，为设计师提供了真实且直观的设计思想展示方式。通过它，设计师能精确验证造型方案是否满足尺寸、人机工程学及法规要求。模型的引入，为设计师提供了实物参照，这不仅强化了设计的直观感知，还优化了设计评价与反馈机制，从而有助于缩短产品开发周期。在模型评估中，评价者通过感知实体模型的线条、比例、色彩、材质和空间关系，获得对设计概念的三维理解。同时，通过草图与模型的对比，设计师能更清晰地传达造型关系与功能创意，确保设计的空间与功能逻辑合理。

汽车外形设计包含诸多复杂形态特征，这些细节在二维媒介上难以完整清晰表达。即便能在平面上呈现，也存在视觉差异，可能影响设计师对作品的理解和评价。油泥模型则能将平面设计图的元素转化为实际物体，在三维空间中展示造型方案，为设计师和决策者提供更直观的空间感受和真实的立体视觉效果，从而消除平面设计图中可能的视觉误差。

油泥模型（图 5-5）是使用油泥材料通过仿真手段呈现汽车造型的有效工具。通用汽车公司是最早应用此技术的先驱。20 世纪 30 年代，通用汽车公司的厄尔（Earl）首次将雕塑家使用的油泥引入汽车设计，用于塑造三维模型。经技术改进，油泥模型逐渐成为汽车设计中的标准工具，取代了早期使用的木板和石膏材料。油泥模型因其灵活性和可修改性，已成为全球知名汽车公司的首选模型，并广泛应用于其他工业造型领域。在中国，该技术自 20 世纪 70 年代起得到应用，已成为汽车设计与开发中不可或缺的工具。

图 5-5　油泥模型

油泥因其易塑形和易修改的特性，作为造型材料和设计工具在汽车设计中广受欢迎。加热后的油泥可轻松附着于骨架泡沫上，冷却至室温后表面逐渐硬化，这时便可用特制工具（如刮刀等）进行精细雕琢（图 5-6）。此外，油泥模型不易风干和龟裂，表面光滑，经适当后期处理后，能充分展现设计的造型方案，这是其另一显著优势。

图 5-6　油泥模型的加工

在汽车造型设计的初期阶段，油泥模型具有举足轻重的地位，对后续的数字化建模、工程设计乃至生产制造均产生显著影响。高质量的油泥模型不仅对其他团队具有极大的助益，而且能有效缩短设计周期，降低开发成本，并显著提升汽车的最终设计品质。油泥模型在汽车设计开发中的核心作用体现在：辅助设计师将二维设计构想转化为三维实体，便于企业决策层对设计方案进行评估与选择；在工程师与设计师之间搭建沟通的桥梁；为市场调研提供关键支持；在风洞实验中扮演重要角色；有助于验证数字模型的精确性。

油泥模型可根据不同的标准进行分类。按照功能和用途，可分为外饰模型、内饰模型、展示模型、验证模型和风洞模型等。以尺寸大小为依据，外饰模型常见的比例有 1∶1、1∶3、1∶4 等（图 5-7），而内饰模型则有 1∶1 和 1∶2 两种比例。

图 5-7　外饰模型 1∶4 模型和 1∶1 模型

从汽车开发流程的视角出发，油泥模型可按时序划分为前期概念创意模型、后期产品主导模型和最终设计呈现模型。若从工作规模与精细度来考量，模型则进一步细分为整车模型（图 5-8）与局部更改模型（图 5-9）。整车模型多用于全新车型的开发，而局部更改模型则主要应用于已上市量产车型的改型设计，以满足消费者对新鲜感的渴求并缓解审美疲劳。全新车型研发涉及大量资金、人力、物力和时间的投入，而局部更改模型在维持车身主体结构不变的基础上，仅对如发动机舱盖、保险杠或灯具等部件进行局部调整，旨在以最低成本为消费者带来显著的视觉更新。

图 5-8　整车模型（来源：作者拍摄于慕尼黑宝马博物馆）

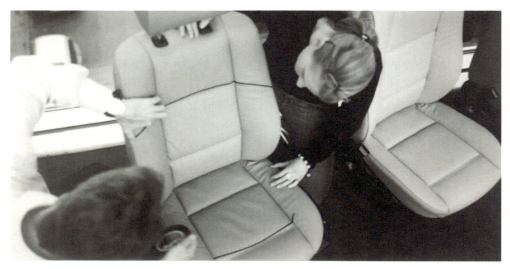

图 5-9　局部更改模型（来源：作者拍摄于慕尼黑宝马博物馆）

5.2　座舱交互设计方法与工具

汽车交互设计是交互设计的一个重要分支，它专注于用户与舱内空间或车机系统的人机交互，且这些交互主要在"封闭""有限"的座舱内进行。在此环境下，用户的操作行为通常与使用场景紧密相关，并具有明确的目标导向性，如获取信息或完成任务。设计师在设计交互界面时，需全面考虑用户的直接与间接操作，以及单步与多步任务，以确保交互界面的直观性和易用性。由于座舱内交互的特殊性，设计需围绕特定设计场景，如人机共驾、休闲娱乐、办公 / 商务以及车 - 家互联等四大主要应用场景，并需涵盖屏幕交互和车内各种实体与非实体元素的互动。智能座舱的交互设计则主要涉及人机界面、交互方式、任务分配与协同，以及错误处理和容错机制等关键方面。

（1）人机界面

智能座舱的人机界面设计必须充分考虑人类的认知和操作行为特点，以便用户能轻松与座舱系统进行高效交互。设计过程中，应全面权衡人的感知、认知和决策能力，同时兼顾机器的计算、推理和控制功能，旨在实现人机之间的顺畅协同。界面设计需以直观性和易用性为目标，旨在降低操作复杂度，从而优化用户体验。

（2）交互方式

智能座舱融合了语音识别、手势控制、触摸屏操作等多种交互方式，旨在满足不同用户的个性化需求和操作习惯。这些交互方式各具优势：语音识别使用户能通过口头指令便捷地操控座舱系统，手势控制实现了通过简单手势即可执行操作的目标，而触摸屏操作则为用户提供了一种直观且可视化的交互界面。

（3）任务分配与协同

智能座舱中的部分任务涉及人机协同，这要求建立清晰的任务分配与协同机制。一般而言，人类在高层次决策和任务监督方面发挥主导作用，而机器则专注于数据处理和执行具体细节。此种分工旨在最大化人机双方的优势，从而提高工作效率并确保操作的安全性。值得注意的是，SAE自动驾驶分级中，并不是完全按照人因工程的任务分配原则，即最大化人机双方的"优势"的分配原则，而是主要聚焦在"驾驶操作"和"感知判断"上，人类驾驶员的"介入"程度。这意味着智能座舱的人机任务分配与协同，尤其是场景化的设计思维，仍然是一个十分重要的设计问题。

（4）错误处理和容错机制

由于智能座舱中潜在的人机交互错误或机械故障，建立有效的错误处理和容错机制至关重要。这些机制旨在迅速发现并纠正错误，从而确保座舱系统的稳定运行。以语音识别系统为例，一旦发生误识别，座舱系统应提供即时的纠错功能，或支持用户重新输入指令。此外，对于可能出现的故障或异常情况，座舱系统还需配备预警系统和应急处理措施，以应对各种不确定性。

汽车座舱的交互设计遵循阶段性原则，因此，下面将按照设计流程顺序，系统介绍相关方法。由于人机交互设计与人的紧密联系，用户研究在设计过程中占据举足轻重的地位。在深入洞察用户需求与行为，并从中提炼设计思路后，故事板和界面设计成为智能座舱创意设计阶段的核心工具。创意设计转化为产品原型，并对设计概念和原型进行评估时，设计师可利用多种评估手段来确定最终交互设计的价值所在。

5.2.1 交互设计方法

（1）用户画像方法

用户画像是分析目标用户的有效工具，它有助于设计师精准定位设计对象。通过用户画像，可以描绘并概括用户在智能座舱内的潜在行为、价值观念和具体需求（图5-10）。由于智能座舱用户群体的多样性，设计工作需展现出个性化和适应性。因此，在设计流程中，为智能座舱创建用户画像显得尤为重要。

图 5-10　智能座舱用户画像生成

目标愿景关键词

惊喜感　未知的
有趣的　新奇的

目前存在的问题

1. 驾驶过程中，体验单一，重复行为使人感觉乏味
2. 接触事物成本高，需要提前花时间做很多攻略与规划

期待的需求

1. 日复一日地重复路线的过程中，能发生不一样的惊喜体验
2. 在恰当的场合，唤醒自己那些"三分钟热度"的想法，并给予自己付诸实践开始行动的可能

　　用户画像的构建应遵循以下步骤：首先，通过问卷调查、用户访谈及用户观察等多种研究方法，广泛搜集用户相关信息；接着，基于所收集的信息，深入理解用户，包括其特征、行为模式、价值观、需求及个性等；然后，从这些丰富的信息中，精心筛选出与项目紧密相关且最具代表性的目标用户特性；最后，依据这些特性构建 1～3 个精准的用户画像。

　　在用户画像的构建过程中，首先需要为设定的用户角色命名，并建立用户画像的基本构架，明确内容要点和信息层次，以确保对用户特性的精确描述。完成构架后，需进一步增加人物插图及文字说明，以揭示角色的背景信息，并可引用前期调研中收集的用户"原话"，以增强其真实感。若现有信息不足以全面反映用户特性，可考虑补充更详尽的个人资料，如年龄、教育、职业及家庭状况等，并尽量涵盖每位用户的价值观念和需求。

　　为强化用户画像在智能座舱设计中的运用效果，有以下实用建议：选用最能代表用户特性的原话，以加深对其印象；在构建用户画像时，应从整体到局部进行，先形成总体认知，再逐步细化，以免过度陷入调研的琐碎细节；此外，研究指出，选用与角色相匹配的图片和采用具有视觉吸引力的版面布局，能有效提升用户画像的受关注度和使用频次；最后，保持用户画像的连续使用，例如将其融入故事板制作中，有助于提升设计方案的连贯性和整体性。

（2）用户访谈方法

　　通过面对面访谈，设计师能够深入洞察用户对智能座舱的认知、期望与动机，以及他们在使用过程中所遇到的问题（图 5-11）。此方法同样适用于从专家处收集宝贵信息。尽管面对面访谈通常涉及线下交流，但鉴于时间、成本和实际条件的限制，线上虚拟访谈也不失为一种可行的选择。然而，线上访谈可能会对访谈效果产生一定影响，因此设计师需进行更多预设工作，以确保这些影响在可控范围内。

图 5-11　在真实车辆内进行的用户访谈

用户访谈作为一种灵活且有力的研究方法，能够在设计的各个阶段为设计师提供来自用户的深刻见解。项目启动之初，用户访谈可协助设计师了解用户对当前智能座舱的评价、使用情境及期望。进入概念设计阶段后，访谈则可用于检验设计方案，通过用户的反馈来评估其可行性与有效性。

在开始访谈前，为提高信息收集效率，设计师需有针对性地招募特定用户群体。问卷调查和筛选是高效策略。用户访谈的主要步骤如下：首先，明确访谈目标并据此制定访谈提纲，通过预访谈测试其有效性，并进行必要的优化；其次，招募 3～10 名受访者进行正式访谈，每次访谈约 1～1.5 小时，全程录音或录像以备后续回顾，利用语音转录工具可简化整理流程；最后，采用适当方法对访谈结果进行分析总结，可主观梳理信息，或将内容导入数据分析软件进行深入分析。

在智能座舱设计领域，用户访谈主要关注用户对智能座舱的使用经验和习惯。为确保访谈效果并获取有效信息，建议在真实车辆或模拟驾驶环境中进行访谈。这样做不仅便于用户现场演示使用细节，还能深化用户对座舱空间的直观感受。若实车条件受限，可运用座舱相关视频或图片作为访谈辅助材料。若访谈内容与座舱空间密切相关，可在室内利用不同材料模拟座舱环境，以帮助用户更好地体验和表达。鉴于智能座舱融合了物理空间与虚拟交互，访谈时需特别注重提升用户对空间的认知和感知。

（3）交互原型测试方法

在设计流程的各个环节，设计师均有机会构建交互原型，并通过测试收集反馈。然而，将原型与概念发展阶段的初步原型结合使用，往往效果更佳。此阶段，基本的交互理念已确立，而一个简易的原型（例如纸模、模拟屏幕、虚拟按键等）对于细节的确认和理念的验证至关重要。这类快速搭建的原型，不仅能在一定程度上模拟交互流程，还能检测设计师预设的交互行为是否可行（图 5-12）。通过此类测试，设计师不仅能直接收集用户对交互方式的反馈，对理念进行迭代优化，还能更有效地与目标用户或其他利益相关者沟通和展示未来产品的交互模式。

在产品设计或屏幕交互设计中，简单的交互原型即可满足模拟需求。然而，智能座舱的交互设计关乎空间行为，与空间尺度紧密相连。因此，理想的方法是在合适的座舱内直接构建交互原型，通过调整车内结构来模拟人机交互。若无法在车内或实车尺寸的台架上构建原型，可在特定空间内大致标出座舱尺寸，使用线条或胶带进行简单标记。若能在实车或台架上进行测试，并布置可交互元素，如屏幕、按钮等，将能更真实地模拟车内交互情境。

图 5-12　使用搭建的原型进行汽车内交互方案的原型测试

实车测试能展现真实的车内细节与驾驶氛围，同时准确呈现外部环境，但车内现有风格可能影响用户反馈。相比之下，台架测试更具自由度，但难以模拟车外环境。若设计方案与外部环境紧密相关，台架测试效果可能欠佳。

面对复杂、难以实现的低保真或高保真交互界面，可采用"绿野仙踪"技术进行用户交互测试。该方法通过后台人员对用户操作给予适当反馈，营造"交互正在运行"的错觉，从而使用户反应更接近真实场景，成为一种高效低成本的模拟测试方式（图 5-13）。

图 5-13　使用"绿野仙踪"方法模拟车内语音交互

5.2.2 交互设计工具

（1）线框图

与常规交互设计流程相仿，汽车交互设计通常始于手绘线框图（图5-14）。手绘或软件绘制的线框图均能以较低成本帮助设计师明确各页面信息展示、结构布局及整体用户界面使用流程。

图 5-14　手绘线框图

线框图作为交互设计的基础框架，反映了用户行为模式与设计核心需求，促进设计师团队与利益相关者的高效沟通，共同开发出以用户为中心的原型和产品。在创意阶段，设计师可利用线框图快速确定特定页面的信息层级及不同交互阶段的基本表现形式。线框图应力求简洁明了，避免过多色彩和视觉元素，以确保信息的直观呈现与理解。简单的方框和线条即可代表图片和文本，必要时可辅以文字说明。

在明确关键页面和信息层级后，线框图应进一步展现这些页面、流程及阶段间的内在联系。尤其需强调的是，页面间的连线至关重要，它们揭示了页面跳转的逻辑，并展示了如何顺畅地引导用户进入新的交互环节。绘制连线时，设计师需为这些连线指定具体的交互方式，如页面上的特定组件，或车内的实体按键、触控感应装置等（图5-15）。

由于汽车交互设计的空间特点，线框图中还可融入车内的核心结构信息，例如中控屏、方向盘及仪表板的相对布局（图5-16）。此类基于空间布局的汽车内部线框图，能清晰标识交互点，同时便于设计师将交互元素布局于屏幕外，从而充分利用汽车空间的扩展性。

线框图旨在清晰地展现潜在交互解决方案的框架，以供团队深入讨论、持续改进，并基于交互流程及视觉设计提供反馈。在制作交互线框图时，设计师应遵循以下原则：聚焦于功能、可访问性、整体布局与导航设计，从而提升用户体验的便捷性；尽早构建清晰的信息架构，实现对信息的合理分类与组织；将屏幕界面划分为几个主要的内容区块；借助链接、图像占位符等细节元素，对内容区块进行精细调整；添加注释，以辅助团队成员更快地解读线框图的意图；维持线框图的简洁性，避免过度关注琐碎细节，确保工作效率。

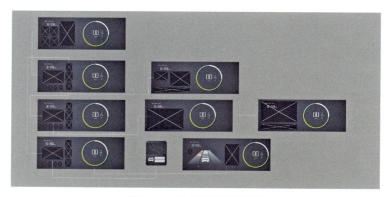

图 5-15　汽车界面线框图

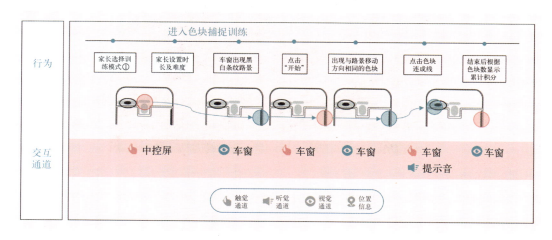

图 5-16　汽车内部线框图

（2）故事板

作为一种视觉叙事工具，故事板能够有效地帮助人们理解设计在实际应用情境中的表现。与传统的文字叙事相比，故事板通过视觉化的方式讲述故事，更为直观且生动，这正是其独特魅力。故事板在形式上与漫画相似（图 5-17），它聚焦于用户与设计概念之间的交互，从而有助于设计师更深入地了解目标用户群、产品使用情境及最佳使用时机。完整的故事板包含明确的用户角色、按时间轴顺序进展的故事、明确的文字注释，并使用统一的视觉风格。

作为一种全周期研究方法，故事板展现出强大的适应性和成长性。设计师能借助故事板深入体验用户与产品的交互，从而持续优化和完善设计，并汲取宝贵灵感。在智能座舱这类复杂立体结构中，故事板对于凸显和集中呈现关键人机交互区域尤为有益，可帮助观察者明确把握空间构造和操作方式的变化。

故事板应用流程如下：首先，明确故事中的核心元素、创新思路、模拟使用场景以及至关重要的用户角色。其次，选定故事及欲传达的信息，如展示现存问题、新设计带来的解决方案，或全新体验。重要的是要简化故事，确保信息传达简明扼要。确定内容后，绘制故事大纲草图，按时间轴顺序展现，细化每格内容，并辅以文字注释，使故事层次分明、循序渐进。

上车设定目的地　　　　手动驾驶 风速光效随车辆速度变化 根　　切换到自动驾驶模式
　　　　　　　　　　　据设定还会有对应气味

光效声效提醒后 风模式由直吹风转为　可以根据手势来改变风量和场景模式　自动泊车场景下风和光效呼吸式渐隐
环绕模拟自然风

图 5-17　故事板

在智能座舱设计创新中，故事板常被用于描绘车内空间，增强用户对车与人的相对位置及车内空间尺寸的感知。设计者需精心选择视角，如挡风玻璃视角展示前排动作，或从车外展示车内社交互动。鉴于车内细节繁多，设计者需学会在故事板中设置视觉焦点。

（3）原型绘制工具——Figma

原型制作的首要步骤是对线框图中的核心页面进行详细设计。常用的设计工具有 Adobe XD、Sketch、Figma 和墨刀等。Figma 因其简洁的交互组件创建流程、出色的可视化效果以及强大的在线协作能力，而受到众多设计团队的偏爱。

在 Figma 提供的画布上，设计师能够添加多样的参考内容，导入线框图，建立对应页面，并精确设定文字、图片样式及组件形态（图 5-18～图 5-20）。所创建的样式可在系统中存储，并能迅速应用于其他页面，根据需求进行调整。在单一画布上完成所有页面的设计，有利于保持设计的统一性。

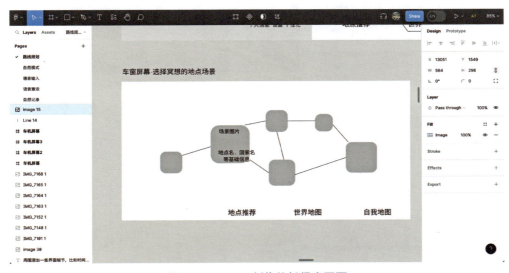

图 5-18　Figma 制作的低保真页面

图 5-19 Figma 制作的高保真页面

图 5-20 将交互页面置入汽车空间内进行展示

（4）交互原型工具

在完成了详尽且细致的交互页面设计后，便可进一步构建交互原型。原型作为产品的直接展现，通过不断的迭代优化，可逐步逼近最终的产品形态。虽非最终产品，但原型已具备对外展示的功能。功能性交互原型能有效验证多个维度，如：交互流程的流畅性与易操作性；交互组件的易懂性，以及是否存在误导风险；整体交互体验是否符合预期，能否引发用户的期望情感反应。

为制作一个动态的、能展示视觉与动效的交互原型，选用在线交互原型工具是明智之选。ProtoPie，作为当下流行的高保真交互原型设计软件，不仅支持软硬件交互，还能从多种主流原型设计软件中导入内容（图 5-21）。

Figma
一款全平台可使用的矢量图形编辑器和原型设计工具

Sketch
macOS 专用的矢量图形编辑器，具有原型设计和协作的功能

Adobe XD
一站式 UX/UI 设计平台，可以进行移动应用和网页设计与原型制作

墨刀
AI 专业原型工具，支持多场景原型设计

即时设计
可云端编辑的专业级 UI 设计工具

Pixso
具备一站式原型设计、交付能力，是新一代在线原型设计协作工具

图 5-21 市场上常见的主流原型设计软件

ProtoPie 针对车机 HMI（人机界面）进行了专门优化，以满足车内交互中多屏幕、多组件操作的需求。它支持跨屏幕交互，并允许设计师在平板或屏幕硬件上预览设计。这样，可以在模拟车内空间、高仿真座舱台架或真实车辆中，通过简单组合移动屏幕，进行沉浸式交互模拟测试（图 5-22）。

图 5-22　使用模拟方向盘与界面进行交互

ProtoPie 还支持使用物理按钮操作屏幕，为设计师提供了更大的灵活性，能够充分利用车内的物理按键和感应组件，创造出更多样化、更真实的交互方式（图 5-23）。同时，其集成的语音交互功能可以识别用户语音指令，实现语音识别交互，更加符合汽车交互设计的特殊需求（图 5-24）。

图 5-23　用 ProtoPie 和座舱台架实现车内交互模拟

图 5-24　用 ProtoPie 实现语音交互

　　智能座舱设计是一项多维度挑战，它要求设计师在美学与交互之间达成精妙平衡。一个出色的智能座舱设计需融合以下要素：

　　首先，安全性和合理性是其设计基础。设计师需保证所有交互功能均不干扰驾驶，同时确保紧急情况下的迅速响应与操作便利。

　　其次，外观吸引力对用户满意度至关重要。智能座舱造型应符合现代审美，并运用创新材料和色彩搭配，创造独特视觉体验。

　　再者，人机工程学原则对保障驾乘者舒适度极为关键。设计师需精细考虑座椅布局、控制面板位置及显示屏视角等，以降低用户体力和认知负荷。

　　此外，直观、流畅且智能的交互体验是设计核心。这要求设计师深刻洞察用户需求，通过精妙设计的界面与交互逻辑，实现用户与座舱系统的轻松沟通。

　　最后，设计应具备前瞻性，能适应未来技术发展和用户需求变化，如整合人工智能、大数据分析和物联网等新兴技术，以提升座舱智能化水平。

第6章

智能座舱人机交互设计案例

6.1 亲子游戏座舱设计——Popo Racer
6.2 车载智能机器人拟人化设计——电力规划局
6.3 绿色驾驶行为鼓励系统——"豹豹"车载智能语音助手
6.4 个性化车载即时推荐系统——"盒你同行"

6.1 亲子游戏座舱设计——Popo Racer

扫码观看视频

在新时代家庭出行的背景下，本案例针对后排儿童因无法获知前排路况和车辆动态而感到无聊，甚至出现晕车症状的问题，进行了深入的设计研究。基于儿童作为用户角色的互动需求，设计师对空间、角色和动作进行了细致的分析，并提出了一种创新的设计策略，旨在通过游戏化的互动动作设计，增强前排父母与后排儿童之间的联系。

具体而言，设计师利用智能车机系统进行车外环境的感知，并预测父母的驾驶行为习惯。以此为基础，系统能够生成相应的游戏音效和车内游戏图示，提前告知儿童即将发生的环境变化。儿童可以根据这些音效和图示，参与到一个互动打击游戏中。这样的设计不仅为车内创造了愉快的互动氛围，而且为亲子旅途增添了美好的共同记忆。

6.1.1 设计问题提出

在家庭出行的场景中，父母出于安全考虑往往会选择将儿童安置在汽车的后排座位。然而，随着新能源车的广泛使用，与传统燃油车相比，新能源车的高扭矩特性使得车辆加速和减速更加迅速，同时电机的噪声较低，这改善了驾驶体验，但也可能导致车内乘客对外界环境的感知与实际不符，增加了晕车的风险，尤其是在后排的儿童更容易感到不适。此外，由于车辆的物理空间限制以及父母需要专注于驾驶的任务，后排的儿童在感到不适时往往无法得到及时的安抚，而父母也会因为无法及时了解儿童的状态而感到焦虑。

为了解决这一问题，Popo Racer 的设计团队提出了一种创新的解决方案，特别关注儿童在新能源车座舱后排的感知信息环境以及他们的情绪和行为状态。该设计提供了一种联结前后排的亲子游戏交互方案，旨在帮助儿童在特定的车内环境中享受更加愉快的旅程。同时，设计团队基于智能座舱的人机交互框架，对交互系统的安全性进行了细致的考量，确保儿童在后排的乘坐体验安全、舒适且愉快。

6.1.2 基于人机交互框架应用的设计方案概述与创新点

（1）空间

Popo Racer 的设计旨在为家庭亲子出行提供互动娱乐，其核心应用场景是在座舱空间内，父母与儿童通过简单的游戏互动来缓解后排儿童的无聊情绪或晕车等不适症状。该系统通过综合分析驾驶行为与游戏互动的平衡性，设计出一套系统性的前后排空间亲子交互游戏方案。

具体而言，家长在确保驾驶安全的前提下，可以主动启动 Popo Racer，与儿童一同参与车内的互动游戏。这样的设计不仅能够安抚儿童的不安情绪，还能为他们带来更加愉悦和舒适的车内旅程体验（详见图 6-1）。

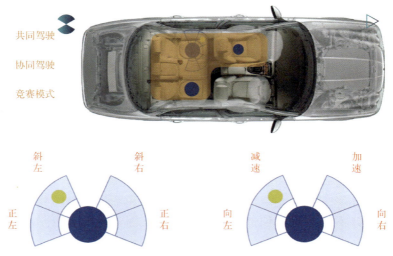

图 6-1　Popo Racer 使用场景

在 Popo Racer 的设计理念中,针对前排家长与后排儿童在空间上的分离以及他们之间的互动需求,座舱的物理空间设计旨在促进信息向后座的流动。为此,设计团队在有限的车内空间内搭建了一种"介质",用以传递由驾驶行为转换而来的多种信息。这一设计提升了现有门板和中控部分的利用效率,结合智能表面技术,将这些物理部件转变为数字空间中的互动游戏符号显示介质,有效地将信息传递给后排的儿童。

同时,考虑到家长对儿童状态的感知需求及驾驶安全性,数字空间设计允许前排家长通过屏幕实时观察到自己驾驶行为的记录和转换,了解传递给后排的信息内容,同时掌握儿童的游戏状态,实现家长与儿童之间的双向信息交流。这种设计不仅增强了家长对儿童的感知,也为双方提供了一种新奇的互动游戏体验(参见图 6-2)。

图 6-2　Popo Racer 造型设计

(2)角色

方案深入考虑了儿童用户的生理特征、情感需求和兴趣偏好(参见图 6-3)。设计师提出了一种创新的转换机制,将车机系统提前感知到的路面信息和家长的驾驶行为转换为数字游戏信号，并通过数字空间传送至后排。利用音效和图示等直观的符号信息，不仅增强了儿童对路况信息的感知，也转移了他们的注意力，有效缓解了可能的不适症状。此外，通过儿童与父母共同参与的游戏动作，父母能够更好地安抚儿童的不安情绪。

图 6-3　Popo Racer 用户画像

（3）动作

在该场景下，涉及的动作要素分为家长的驾驶行为预测、转换和儿童的游戏动作。

通过调研得知"提前告知儿童汽车的行驶方向有助于减轻晕动病的症状"。鉴于儿童对色彩、动画和图形的高度敏感性和偏好，设计团队打造了一套符号系统，由具有象征性意义的图标、颜色和动画构成，旨在对应并传达各种驾驶行为和信息，如车速、加速度和行驶方向等。前排家长的驾驶行为、决策和操作被转化为数字信号，并通过智能座舱的数字空间传递给后排的儿童。儿童可以通过这些直观的符号系统感知当前的以及即将发生的车辆行进状态。此外，趣味化的图标和互动游戏设计能够吸引儿童的注意力，引导他们参与到与驾驶状态相关的游戏交互中，缓解儿童的晕车等不适症状，减轻无聊情绪（图 6-4 ～图 6-6）。

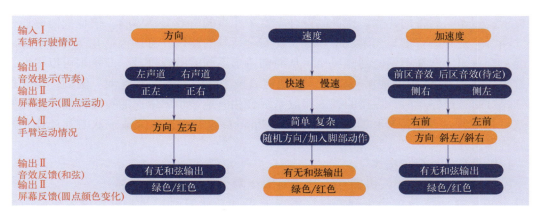

图 6-4　Popo Racer 驾驶信息 - 游戏信息对应

图 6-5　Popo Racer 驾驶信息 - 游戏信息 - 动作对应

图 6-6　Popo Racer 故事板

考虑到儿童的生理特性和可触及范围，首先对物理空间内的游戏显示和声音播放进行了设计。利用智能表面技术和可折叠屏幕的特性，使得儿童能够在后排的任意可触达位置轻松触发游戏。在数字空间层面，系统将家长的"驾驶动作"转化为游戏符号和声音提示，传递给后排的儿童。这样的设计丰富了儿童的游戏交互体验，使他们能够通过视觉和听觉两种感官参与到游戏中。家长在安全行驶的路段，可以根据儿童的游戏完成情况，有意识地选择不同的驾驶风格，从而创造出不同的游戏符号。儿童则可以根据这些符号，使用 Popo 棒完成游戏动作，实现前后排之间的亲子游戏互动。例如，当家长在红绿灯前减速停车时，后排的智能座舱系统会相应地显示出减速的符号并播放减速的音效。儿童通过观察符号和听到音效，使用 Popo 棒进行敲击，完成一次游戏动作，并因此获得积分。

（4）整体方案框架描述

Popo Racer 的亲子人机交互设计主要围绕两个核心用户角色展开：家长与儿童。设计分析了这两个角色的生理特征、需求愿景和动作习惯，并充分考虑了座舱内前后排的物理空间特性。通过数字空间的游戏化设计，Popo Racer 解决了前后排之间的物理"距离感"问题，同时也克服了家长在驾驶过程中无法及时安抚儿童情绪的局限。

智能车机系统能够提前感知并预知家长的"驾驶动作"，并将这些动作转换成游戏化的数字信息，再传递给后排的儿童。这样的设计使得儿童能够通过参与游戏实时感知车辆的行驶状态，有效缓解晕车等不适体验。同时，在物理空间上，显示布置的优化让家长能够实时了解儿童的游戏进展和情绪状态（参见图 6-7）。

此外，家长端的设计也考虑了驾驶行为的感知，这不仅提升了驾驶的安全性，还有助于增强旅途中的整体体验。

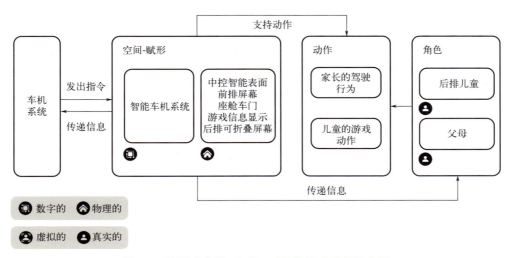

图 6-7　基于"空间 - 角色 - 动作"设计框架的应用

6.1.3　设计过程

Popo Racer 在整体设计过程中以"空间 - 角色 - 动作"作为核心设计框架。这一框架通过明确用户所处的空间，深入理解和满足用户的需求，以及梳理用户的动作，围绕不同用户角色及其相应的动作逻辑进行设计。在智能座舱内，Popo Racer 成功打造出两个核心空间：一是"数字空间"，即通过游戏化设计构建的互动界面；二是"物理空间"，即座舱内与游戏互动直接相关的显示区域。整体设计过程中融合了传统的汽车交互设计方法和基于"空间 - 角色 - 动作"的设计理念。

（1）前期调研与用户研究

在设计过程中，设计团队首先致力于深入挖掘座舱内亲子间前后排沟通的实际挑战，以及儿童在车中遭遇晕车时的不适感原因和可能的缓解措施。

为了深入理解这些问题，设计团队开展了一系列用户研究和市场调查，采用了访谈、观察、问卷调查等多种研究方法。通过与亲子家庭的深入访谈，团队成员了解了他们的沟通习惯，并结合问卷调查的数据分析，最终确定了采用游戏化手段来加强前后排之间的沟通。此外，还通过文献研究，深入探讨了晕车的成因以及可能的缓解策略。

（2）设计问题抽取

在理解座舱内亲子沟通所面临的现实问题之后，设计师们进一步深化了对设计问题的探讨。这一过程涉及对设计目标的明确梳理，对可能的解决方法进行初步的创意发散，并通过严格的评估筛选出那些可行性较高的方案。

在 Popo Racer 项目中，设计团队最终将设计问题明确定义为：如何将儿童在行驶过程中可能出现的晕车状态，通过游戏化的内容转换，从而不仅可以改善儿童的晕车不适感，同时也能增强座舱内前后排亲子之间的沟通互动。

（3）空间 – 角色 – 动作流程分析

在设计的这一关键阶段，设计师引入了"空间 - 角色 - 动作"的设计框架，以系统化地构建解决方案。通过用户空间分析、角色分析、方案流程梳理以及动作分析，设计师们对反馈界面进行了初步评估，从而为前述设计问题创造出有针对性的解决策略。

① 用户空间分析。设计团队首先依据用户研究的成果，构建了用户角色原型，并以此作为分析座舱空间的基础。在这一分析中，特别关注了两个关键的空间位置：家长所在的前排以及儿童所在的后排。前排空间设计需满足驾驶需求，因此包含了仪表、中控屏等关键接触点；后排空间则通过智能表面、立体声音响等接触点，来满足儿童的游戏互动需求。同时，前后排之间的数字接触点设计，确保了驾驶信息与游戏信息的顺畅传递。以下是初步空间布局的示意图（图6-8）。

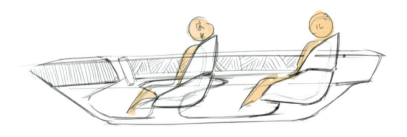

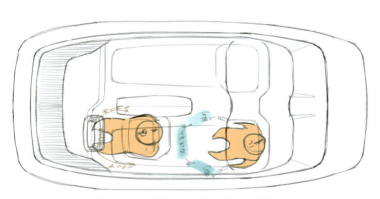

图 6-8　座舱初步空间布局示意图

② 角色分析。在对座舱内的空间和接触点进行了明确的界定之后，设计师紧接着对空间内的角色进行了深入分析。根据角色的特性和场景的具体需求，设计师在空间内标出了潜在的互动区域、动线等关键要素。在 Popo Racer 的情境中，家长的主要行为是控制车辆进行驾驶，这是驾驶信息产生的主要源头。家长的次要行为包括设定游戏模式和关注游戏的反馈，这些行为的位置和接触点相对固定。对于儿童而言，安全性是首要考虑，因此他们的空间位置被固定在座位上。为了参与游戏，儿童需要通过视觉和听觉的观察，并结合手部和脚部的动作来完成游戏操作。这一分析过程揭示了在整个体验过程中，角色可能使用到的接触点以及相关动作。

③ 方案流程梳理。在对座舱内的空间和角色有了初步的构思之后，设计师按照时间线的顺序，对家长与儿童在空间中的互动、接触点以及相应的系统操作进行详细的梳理和安排。整体流程被划分为几个主要阶段：游戏启动前的准备、驾驶信息的输入、游戏模式的选择、游戏中的动作演示、游戏动作的输入、游戏结果的输出以及游戏结束后的结算。详细流程的内容在图 6-9 中展示。

④ 动作分析。在确立了座舱内的空间布局和接触点之后，设计师分析了家长和儿童在各个流程节点下的具体动作，以构建时间动作序列。这些动作序列对于物理空间的布局和数字空间内信息传递的设计至关重要。在 Popo Racer 项目中，动作分析的范畴不仅限于定义交互方式，还需要确定驾驶信息与游戏动作内容之间的映射关系。设计师需要输出不同驾驶行为所引发的游戏元素的具体移动方向、速度以及反馈模式。此外，在同一阶段内，还需考虑前后排家长与儿童这些不同角色的动作之间的相互关系及其关联性（参见图 6-10）。

⑤ 设计反馈界面。在全面定义了空间、角色和动作的框架之后，设计师着手进入具体反馈界面的设计阶段。这一阶段的设计工作涵盖图形用户界面（GUI）、语音用户界面（VUI）以及通过硬件交互提供的触觉用户界面（TUI）。部分界面如图 6-11 所示。

⑥ 初步评估。在完成了设计方案的基础框架之后，设计师采取了一系列快速原型开发和评估方法，以便及时发现并解决方案中存在的问题。这包括使用纸面原型、故事板演绎以及专家评审等技术。通过这些方法，设计师有针对性地对设计方案进行了迭代，调整了空间布局、场景流程和角色动作等。

（4）原型开发与用户测试

在方案得到初步优化后，设计师依据方案内容制作了实体模型和可交互的原型。通过这些原型，开展了用户测试，以识别在实际应用中可能遇到的问题，并基于用户测试的反馈对方案进行了进一步的迭代和改进。

（5）最终设计输出

经过多轮的设计迭代和精心优化，设计师最终完成了 Popo Racer 的全套设计（详见图 6-12）。该设计方案全面覆盖了座舱空间的造型设计、交互设计以及用户界面设计等多个方面。

Popo Racer 是一款深植于智能座舱设计理念的创新作品，它细致入微地考虑了座舱内不同用户角色及其行为动作的多样性。该设计特别针对座舱内儿童在行车过程中可能遇到的晕动病问题，同时巧妙地考量了座舱前后排的空间布局，以及父母无法时刻陪伴在孩子身边的现实情况。

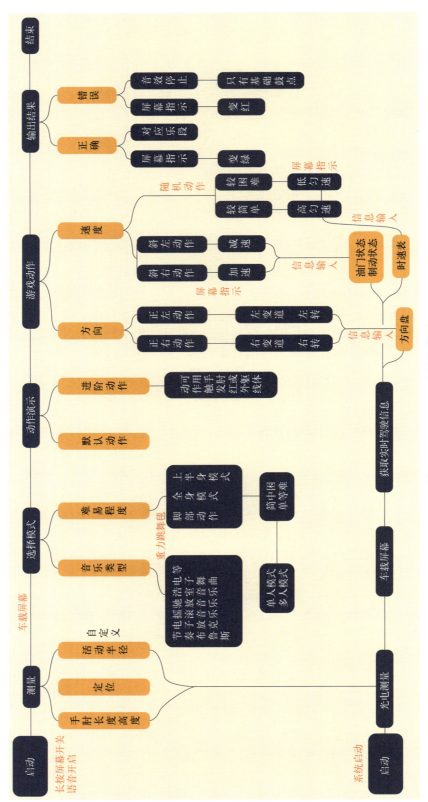

图 6-9 Popo Racer 体验流程图

110　智能座舱人机交互设计

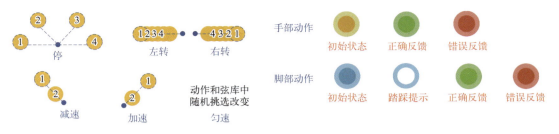

图 6-10 Popo Racer 动作序列和反馈信号

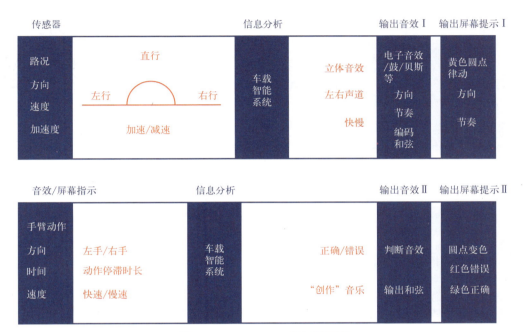

图 6-11 Popo Racer 交互界面图

图 6-12 Popo Racer 座舱设计

为了有效应对这些挑战，Popo Racer 的座舱系统能够精准区分座舱内的用户角色，如"父母"与"儿童"，并准确判定他们的位置。车机系统可实时监测父母和儿童的状态，当孩子出现不适时，系统便会自动启动 Popo Racer 游戏。这款游戏创新性地将驾驶

第 6 章 智能座舱人机交互设计案例　111

位上家长的驾驶动作转化为游戏信号，这些信号随后被传递至后排儿童所在的空间。后排的儿童通过互动式的游戏界面，能够预先感知驾驶行为并与之同步，从而创造出一种全新的互动体验。这种设计不仅有效缓解了儿童的晕动病，还显著增强了家庭成员之间的互动乐趣，为亲子出行增添了更多的情感纽带和愉快回忆。

6.2 车载智能机器人拟人化设计——电力规划局

本案例专注于电动汽车的电力使用场景，旨在改善因续航里程信息误差、能耗反馈延迟等信息显示问题，以及缺乏情感化提示所导致的不佳驾驶出行体验。设计团队基于用户角色——驾驶员对于电力数据获取的需求，以及对信息透明度和真实性的追求，进行了细致的空间、角色、动作分析。利用智能座舱交互设计框架，设计了与之匹配的车载机器人话术和表情反馈机制。

扫码观看视频

通过定义不同的电力使用场景和主要耗电因素，该方案将电力信息通过视觉和听觉等感官通道，以智能情感化提示的方式传递给驾驶员和乘客。这些信息通过数字空间中的固定接触点展现，从而增强用户对车机系统的信任感、使用意愿以及驾驶过程的趣味性。

6.2.1 设计问题提出

相较于传统燃油汽车，电动汽车的用户在体验过程中，主要的负面感受往往源自与电能相关的各种场景。目前，现有的车机系统在电力数据信息展示方面存在一些不足，如行驶里程信息的误差以及耗电行为反馈的延迟等问题。这些问题导致用户因为无法获得确定的电力消耗信息、对车机系统缺乏信任等原因，而经常处于一种持续的负面情绪状态。

针对这些挑战，本案例的设计团队特别关注用户角色——驾驶员在信息获取方面的需求。设计任务不仅包括改善座舱内的自然交互体验，还涵盖了情感反馈的维度。设计的核心聚焦于车载机器人的情感化表现，旨在通过机器人的互动和反馈，增强用户的情感体验。为此，团队提出了"电力助手"这一创新概念。

6.2.2 基于人机交互框架应用的设计方案概述与创新点

（1）空间

考虑到用户角色——驾驶员在驾驶过程中的主要任务，信息传达和交互发生的接触点在空间布局上应保持相对固定，以减少对驾驶注意力的分散。同时，座舱内的前排乘客也有获取信息和进行交互的需求。设计团队结合驾驶员和前排乘客在物理空间中的视触可达性范围，决定在数字空间上将显示介质布置于中控台区域。这样的布局不仅便于驾驶员的操作，也方便前排乘客与电力助手进行交互（参见图 6-13）。

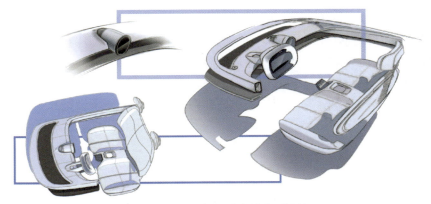

图 6-13　电力规划局座舱造型设计

（2）角色

通过深入的市场调研，发现新能源汽车的主要用户群体具有一些鲜明的特征：他们对新鲜事物持开放态度，乐于尝试尖端科技产品，并对出行体验有较高的期望（参见图 6-14）。针对这类用户角色，改善其出行体验的关键在于解决电力相关信息数据的真实性、透明性问题，并优化显示交互效果。此外，还需在座舱内增强用户在智能技术的自然交互、场景适应性以及情感反馈等方面的体验。

基于这些洞察，提出的设计方案专注于满足真实用户角色——驾驶员在电力信息感知、情感反馈以及多场景适应和切换等方面的需求。为此，设计团队创造了虚拟角色——车载机器人小 e。小 e 的角色定位是全车的电力管家，同时拥有人格化的形象设计。它能够感知并响应不同的驾驶场景和驾驶行为，提供以电力规划为基础的丰富、有趣的语音和表情反馈。小 e 的设计旨在增强交互的趣味性和故事性，从而提升用户对车机系统强大功能性的感知，并激发他们使用的意愿。

图 6-14　电力规划局用户画像

（3）动作

在电力规划的设计方案中，小 e 的核心功能是感知不同驾驶者的驾驶行为。这涉及对驾驶行为和动作的深入分析，以便构建多样化的驾驶场景。小 e 通过这些场景，为驾驶员提供个性化的建议，并通过情感化的反馈方式，传达车辆的电力状态以及对未来旅程的可行性评估。

小e的反馈设计，结合对驾驶动作的细致分析，旨在确保驾驶员能够获得关于车辆电力状况的清晰理解，并得到必要的信息支持，以规划接下来的行驶路线。

① 环境感知与情感化设计提示。在方案设计过程中，设计师注意到外界环境温度对汽车电力消耗有显著影响，为此对外界环境温度进行了细致分级，并通过车机系统对外界温度进行感知。基于这些感知数据，虚拟角色小e通过趣味的视觉设计——根据外界温度变化调整其衣物搭配，穿上与外界温度相匹配的服装——来进行互动。小e通过这一穿衣服的动作，不仅向用户直观地提示了外界温度变化，同时也暗示了车辆电力状态的相应调整，改善了真实用户的使用体验（图6-15）。

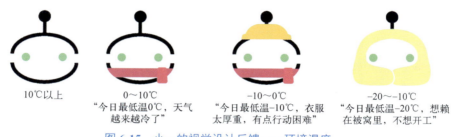

图6-15 小e的视觉设计反馈——环境温度

② 用户驾驶及车辆控制行为反馈。在智能座舱的设计中，驾驶员的真实驾驶行为对车辆的电力使用有着直接影响，同时一些无意识的高耗能驾驶行为可能会加速电力的消耗。为了优化这一过程，车机系统将驾驶员的驾驶行为和车辆控制行为纳入了综合计算分析。

虚拟角色小e的设计旨在通过视觉辅助元素和表情反馈，直观地向驾驶员展示电力消耗的情况。在不同的场景下，小e会呈现不同的形象和变化，例如"蒲公英"散开和"潜水冒泡"等视觉效果，以及"眩晕"等表情，从而在数字空间内增强车机系统的透明性并提升用户的信任度。

以"潜水冒泡"为例，当车辆负载较轻时，小e会在水面上自由游动，通过台词"我现在身轻如燕，长征都不在话下"来形象地表达电力充足，续航能力强。相反，当车辆负载加重，小e则会像铅球一样沉入水底，并表现出挣扎的动作，以此向驾驶员传达电力消耗可能受到影响的信息，并暗示需要调整驾驶模式以适应当前的负载情况（图6-16）。

③ 里程与耗能预估。在智能座舱的设计中，驾驶员对于实时电力数据有着高度关注，因此设计的虚拟角色小e着重于以动作和表情反馈的形式来匹配电力数据的实时变化。小e通过续航里程的实时预估以及一系列如"微笑""流汗"等富有表现力的动态表情，直观地向驾驶员传达续航里程信息的变化，从而更直接地呼应了用户的心理预期和情绪变化，将视觉的直接传达化为了有温度的沟通，如图6-17所示。

情感化设计/载重

通过小e的吃水量表示载重增加或减少,增加乘客与增加物品的语音表达不同

情感化设计/驾驶风格

急刹车/急加速时触发此状态,小e模拟人在乘车过程中的运动状态

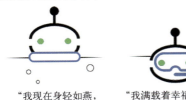

"我现在身轻如燕,长征都不在话下"

"我满载着幸福,与你们一路相伴"
"挑货小能手,就是我"

急刹车　　急加速

"我要晕车了,开慢一点好吗?"
(连续驾驶中触发此状态超过5次)

图 6-16　小 e 的视觉设计反馈(1)

VUI设计/能耗等级

常态显示时,根据百公里能耗分为三个等级:一级——悠闲喝咖啡/二级——初始状态/三级——加油干活(显示最大耗能原因)

VUI设计/里程变化

车内操作后,里程实时预估,续航里程提升——微笑/续航里程降低——冒汗

一级能耗　　二级能耗　　三级能耗

里程显示　　续航提升　　续航降低

图 6-17　小 e 的视觉设计反馈(2)

(4)整体方案框架描述

电力规划局的设计方案深入考虑了驾驶员在信息感知、科技体验、自然交互和情感反馈等多个维度的心理特征、需求愿景和行为实现,并据此进行了细致的分析。基于这些分析,团队设计了虚拟角色机器人小 e,旨在通过对驾驶员驾驶行为的分析,设计出小 e 在不同场景下的动作反馈。这样的设计策略旨在增强驾驶员在电力使用场景中对电力状况的感知,同时提升他们对车机系统的信任度、加强情感联结和趣味互动,从而全面改善用户的出行体验和提高用户使用意愿(参见图 6-18)。

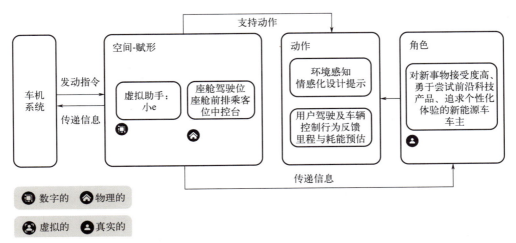

图 6-18　基于"空间 - 角色 - 动作"设计框架的应用

座舱内的数字空间利用智能车机系统实时监测车外环境、车辆状态以及驾驶员的"驾驶动作",并将其转换为相应的语音话术、辅助性视觉标志和表情反馈。这种设计理念不仅能够有效缓解用户的忧虑情绪,还能填补情绪交流的空白,进一步改善用户的使用体验。此外,座舱内的物理空间布局也有利于信息在不同乘客间的流通,促进前排乘客对驾驶员的辅助,共同营造一个和谐愉悦的座舱氛围和出行体验。

6.2.3 设计过程

电力规划局方案致力于改善电动汽车的出行体验,为此,设计团队细致梳理了不同用户角色的需求和用车场景。在此基础上,定义了两类关键角色:一是真实角色——驾驶车辆的驾驶员;二是虚拟角色——车载机器人小e。通过深入分析这两类角色在座舱中的交互动作与流程,旨在解决电动汽车使用过程中与电能相关的各种问题。

(1)前期调研与用户研究

在项目的初期阶段,设计师采用了桌面调研法来精确勾勒新能源车车主群体的用户画像。调研结果显示,这一用户群体对新鲜事物和智能科技具有较高的接受度。此外,团队还发现,在电动汽车的使用体验中,用户的主要负面体验往往与电能相关,如充电不便、充电时间过长、表显里程与实际里程存在差异等问题。基于这些发现,团队将目标用户群体定位为那些注重出行体验并乐于尝试前沿科技的电动车车主。对于这些用户而言,电能相关问题是他们驾驶体验中亟待解决的核心问题。

(2)设计问题抽取

在面对电动车充电时间较长和续航里程不稳定等技术难题时,传统的设计方法可能难以提供根本性的解决方案。因此,设计师们转变思路,将关注点投向了情感化设计领域。通过深入研究用户画像和对市场上的竞争对手产品进行分析,设计团队孕育出了一个创新的概念——"电力助手",使其在处理与电能相关的各种使用场景时,能够与用户进行情感化的互动和表达。

(3)空间 – 角色 – 动作流程分析

这一阶段,设计师开始引入"空间 - 角色 - 动作"框架,创造针对上述设计问题的解决方案。

① 空间分析。座舱内部的空间布局对于车载机器人的有效展示和互动至关重要。为了确保机器人位于驾乘人员的视线交汇处,设计师精心选择了中控台区域作为其展示窗口。在该区域,特别设置了一块圆形显示屏,专门用于呈现车载机器人小e的形象,这样既便于小e进行情感表达,也方便用户清晰观察和与之互动。

② 角色分析。考虑到用户在驾驶和操控车辆过程中产生的数据是了解驾驶行为和电能消耗的关键,设计师为虚拟角色小e赋予了鲜明的人格特征。在此基础上,根据不同的电力使用场景,设计师定制了相应的对话脚本和表情反馈。通过小e,驾驶员可以及时获取能源消耗状态和异常用电警告,从而增强了用户对车辆能耗的直观感知。

③ 方案流程梳理。设计师对电动汽车耗电的关键因素进行了细致的分类,确定了环境温度、载重、驾驶风格和车内空调四个主要场景。针对这些场景,设计师采用流程图的形式,对用户的驾驶行为、车载机器人小e的响应行为以及系统的判断逻辑进行了详

尽的分析和排列。这一流程的梳理旨在优化用户体验，确保小 e 能够在各个场景下提供恰当的反馈和建议。具体流程见图 6-19。

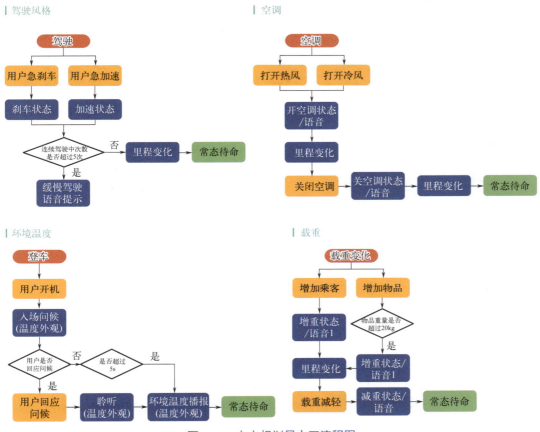

图 6-19　电力规划局交互流程图

④ 动作分析。在电力规划局的方案中，用户的中心活动是驾驶车辆，而车载机器人小 e 作为虚拟角色，其设计动作更为细致和复杂。设计师针对驾驶员的行为，对小 e 的动作反馈进行了细致的分类，主要分为表情和话术两大类。

针对不同的用电情景，设计师为小 e 塑造了一系列静态形象特征，如尴尬、高兴、悲伤等表情状态，并巧妙地融入了辅助视觉元素，如衣物、蒲公英等自然物象，以增强情感表达。在动态表现上，设计师依据场景特性和情感化设计原则，创作出了各具特色的动作反馈，旨在提升整个交互过程的趣味性和故事性。

在话术设计方面，小 e 的对白会根据驾驶风格和场景而有所变化。例如，在需要传达"承诺"感的场景中，小 e 会通过表达将更加努力或更加留心的言辞，来强化这一情感效果。

⑤ 设计反馈界面。完成上述设计定义后，设计师着手开发具体的反馈界面，这包括了小 e 在各用电场景下的关键状态和相应的动态表现。设计成果详见图 6-20。

VUI设计/环境温度

环境温度通过小e衣着的变化进行表达，每日首次进入车内触发此状态

10℃以上　　0~10℃　　-10~0℃　　-20~-10℃
　　　　"今日最低温　"今日最低　"今日最低
　　　　0℃，天气　　温-10℃，　温-20℃，
　　　　越来越冷了"　衣服太厚重，想赖在被窝里，
　　　　　　　　　　有点行动困难"　不想开工"

情感化设计/驾驶风格

急刹车/急加速时触发此状态，小e模拟人在乘车过程中的运动状态

　　　　　急刹车　　　急加速

"我要晕车了，开慢一点好吗？"
（连续驾驶中触发此状态超过5次）

情感化设计/载重

通过小e的吃水量表示载重增加或减少，增加乘客与增加物品的语音表达不同

"我现在身轻如燕，　"我满载着幸福，与你们
长征都不在话下"　　一路相伴"
　　　　　　　　　"挑货小能手，就是我"

情感化设计/车内空调

以蒲公英为意象，开启空调后，将蒲公英吹散，象征电量快速消耗

初始状态　　开热风　　开冷风
"关了空调，我又是　"起风了，风儿吹走了电力"
一条好汉"

图 6-20　小 e 设计输出

（4）原型开发与用户测试

在原型开发与用户测试阶段，设计师根据方案内容制作了动效视频和可交互原型，并通过组织用户测试与问卷调查，对方案的交互体验及用户对小 e 行为的评价进行了评估。

（5）最终设计输出

经过多轮的设计迭代和优化，设计师最终完成了电力规划局的全面设计输出，涵盖了座舱空间造型、交互设计以及车载机器人设计等方面。

电力规划局方案是一个旨在减轻电动车用户里程焦虑的智能座舱车载机器人概念设计。该设计通过车载机器人小 e 的情感化交流，尝试降低用户在电能相关场景中的负面体验。小 e 被设定为全车的电力管家，具备人格化特征，能够根据各种驾驶场景和行为，通过表情和话术直观地向驾驶员反馈耗电情况，从而更真实地贴近用户的心理预期，有效缓解用户的担忧情绪。

6.3　绿色驾驶行为鼓励系统——"豹豹"车载智能语音助手

在全球气候变暖日益加剧的当下，消费者对环保的意识不断增强，政策法规的推动以及智能技术的日新月异，共同促使节能减排从抽象的口号转变为时代的潮流，从未来的可持续趋势逐步转变为当前的切

扫码观看视频

实行动。本案例聚焦于油电混合汽车的节能减排，以车载智能语音助手"豹豹"这一卡通形象与用户建立互动，通过"豹豹"主动提供节能减排的建议，引导并激励用户采取相关的绿色驾驶行为（图 6-21）。通过趣味性的互动和内置的成就系统，进一步促进用户形成长期的绿色驾驶习惯，为可持续发展做出积极贡献。

图 6-21　绿色驾驶行为鼓励系统——"豹豹"车载智能语音助手

6.3.1　设计问题提出

全球变暖是人类当前面临的严峻挑战之一，其带来的冰川消融、海平面上升和极端气候事件频发等问题，对全球居民产生了广泛而深远的影响。在此背景下，社会各界都应积极参与到节能减排的行动中。节能减排的行动不仅限于工业和企业，它已经扩展到日常生活的每一个角落，尤其是在出行方式上。当前的出行场景中存在三个主要的设计痛点：首先，用户往往缺乏对节能减排重要性的认识，并未意识到自己的出行行为对环境的具体影响，导致缺乏采取绿色驾驶行为的动力；其次，用户对于如何通过改变出行习惯和采取具体措施来减少碳排放缺乏了解；最后，即便有环保意识，但在实际生活中，持续践行绿色驾驶行为仍面临诸多挑战。

为了激励用户长期坚持绿色驾驶行为，"豹豹"车载智能语音助手的设计重点在于传播环保的生活理念，同时强调用户在体验中的个性化和自由度，避免给用户带来被强制执行环保理念的束缚感。设计采用了类似小海豹的可爱形象和类似QQ宠物的互动逻辑，通过"豹豹"与用户的互动，使用户在情感上与"豹豹"建立联系，从而更愿意接受其绿色驾驶的建议。此外，主动交互的形式能够有效提升用户的参与度，从而有助于用户养成并维持绿色驾驶的习惯。

6.3.2　基于人机交互框架应用的设计方案概述与创新点

（1）空间

"豹豹抱抱"方案将使用场景设定在低碳减碳的大背景下，特别是在座舱空间内，通过用户与小海豹虚拟形象的简单互动，增强用户对减排行为的感知，明白日常用车行为对环境的影响，并学习如何通过绿色驾驶行为实现有效的节能减排。该方案在"碳排放、碳行为"的大背景下，在满足用户日常驾驶需求外添加绿色出行、绿色驾驶的概念。

方案中，"豹豹"的互动涉及物理空间和数字空间。通常情况下，"豹豹"会在车机屏幕中与用户相伴，及时响应用户需求，提供导航和绿色驾驶的建议。在座舱内，用户可以通过中控显示屏、车窗投影、氛围灯等与"豹豹"进行交互，这一过程以语音交互为主，手势交互为辅。同时，数字空间中的"豹豹"通过一系列的引导和反馈，辅助用户完成体验。

（2）角色

方案设计中涵盖了两类角色，分别是驾驶员用户和"豹豹"智能语音助手。在调研中发现，驾驶员用户对于减排缺乏感知、对节能行为了解不足、难以维持环保行为。为此，方案融入了游戏化设计，创造了以极地野生动物海豹为原型的虚拟角色"豹豹"。海豹作为极地动物，其生存受到全球变暖和冰川融化的严重威胁。通过这一角色设计，能够激发用户保护极地动物的英雄主义情结，通过"为极地动物保护其冰川家园"的概念鼓励绿色驾驶行为。节能减排的效果可以通过数据或视觉化的形式直接反馈给用户，增强用户对环保行为意义的理解。作为智能语音助手的"豹豹"，能够自然地提供节能减排的建议，辅助用户轻松实施减排措施，降低环保行为的个人成本。

此外，方案进一步细分了用户群体，区分了注重节能反馈的实用型用户和注重身份认同的环保型用户。针对这两类用户的不同绿色驾驶动机，"豹豹"的语音模式和角色性格也会做出相应的调整。对于实用型用户，提供实际的建议和准确的数据反馈，增强其成就感；而对于环保型用户，则加强情感联结，提供情感价值和积极的环保反馈，确保满足这两类用户的需求。

（3）动作

① "豹豹"在数字空间内的移动和行为。在智能座舱内，虚拟角色智能体化身为"豹豹"智能语音助手，为用户带来温馨的陪伴感。每当用户步入车内，车机屏幕激活时，"豹豹"便在虚拟的"冰川家园"中现身，向用户致以亲切的问候。在数字空间里，"豹豹"展现出丰富多彩的行为模式：它不仅在用户进入时表示欢迎，还会在驾驶过程中表现出愉悦的情绪，甚至在用户休息时陪伴一旁小憩。这些细腻的行为设计丰富了"豹豹"的形象，使用户产生情感共鸣，从而更愿意关注"豹豹"的福祉，关心动物的自然栖息地，并采取车辆减碳措施，以实际行动助力野生动物的环境保护。如图 6-22 展示了"豹豹"在数字空间中的行为示例。

② 用户在车内执行绿色驾驶行为获得奖励。当用户上车时，车机屏幕渐次亮起，展现出冰川场景，与此同时，"豹豹"被唤醒，它在虚拟的冰川世界中向用户问好。在这一设计构想中，用户被塑造成环保的英雄，肩负着保护远在极地的"豹豹"免受气候变化威胁的使命。这一使命的完成，依赖于用户在驾驶过程中践行绿色驾驶行为。每当用户采纳"豹豹"的绿色驾驶建议，比如选择开窗通风而非开启空调，或者采取平稳驾驶以节省电能，方向盘右侧的原型屏幕上便会有冰块落下。用户可以通过手势操作，将这些冰块"投掷"到大屏幕上，随后"豹豹"会接住冰块，并将其转化为新的冰山，增添至虚拟冰川之中（图 6-23）。用户的自发环保行为同样能够触发这一奖励机制。通过这种

直观的反馈，用户能够感受到自己行为对"豹豹"栖息地的积极影响，从而激发用户的同情心和责任感。看到"豹豹"在冰川家园中快乐生活，用户会感到满足，这种英雄主义心理驱使用户更加积极地投身于绿色驾驶行动。

图 6-22　"豹豹"在数字空间中的行为展示

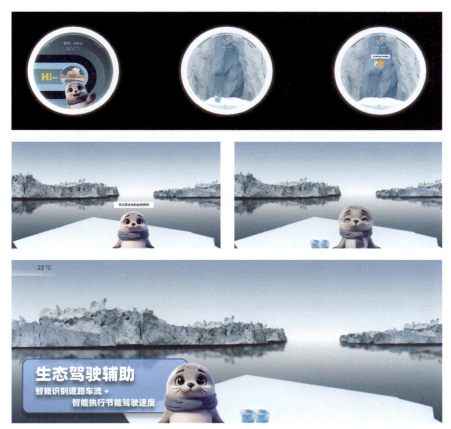

图 6-23　系统给予用户的绿色驾驶奖励可以积累为冰块，形成冰川

③ 整体方案框架描述（图 6-24）。该方案利用"豹豹"智能语音助手，构建了一个旨在鼓励绿色驾驶行为的系统。它针对用户的心理和行为特征，设计了一套游戏化的交互体验。用户通过与"豹豹"互动，接受绿色驾驶的建议，在车舱内开展绿色驾驶实践，使得节能减排的努力和效果得以具体化，增强了用户的成就感。通过这样的机制，培养用户形成长期绿色驾驶的习惯，进而为环境保护做出持续的贡献。

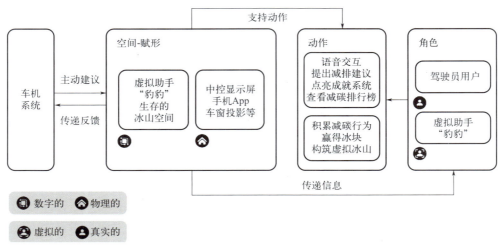

图 6-24　基于"空间 - 角色 - 动作"设计框架的应用

在用户上车后，车机屏幕缓缓亮起，伴随着冰山生成的特效，"豹豹"在屏幕中向用户打招呼。"豹豹"会实时推荐适宜的空调温度和车内减排设置，同时鼓励用户采纳绿色驾驶行为，或自动切换至生态驾驶模式。用户持续接受绿色驾驶建议或主动采取减排措施，都能在系统中积累冰块作为奖励。用户可以用手势将这些冰块"投掷"给"豹豹"，后者接住后会向用户表达感谢，并将积累的冰块转化为新的冰山，重建其虚拟的冰川家园。这一系统为用户提供了长期而可持续的正向激励，促进了节能减排行为的持续发展。

6.3.3　设计过程

（1）前期调研与用户研究

依据先前的调研数据，设计师们已经明确了绿色驾驶行为鼓励系统——"豹豹"车载智能语音助手的目标用户群体（图 6-25）。这一群体主要分为两类：一类是实用型用户，他们注重通过环保行为节约能源和开支，对消费持谨慎态度，并期望看到环保行为带来的实际效益；另一类是年轻的环保型用户，他们充满活力，具有强烈的社会责任感，认为环保是每个人的责任，并希望在环保行动中获得积极的反馈。然而，在现有的交互系统中，碳排放数据的展示尚不够直观，缺乏便于分享和交流的实体媒介，对于减碳大环境的表现也不够全面，同时，在车舱内对绿色生态驾驶的引导也存在不足。设计师们希望这一交互系统能够以友好的方式向用户提供建议，直观地展示用户行为的意义，并在长期使用中陪伴用户持续进行减排行动。

图 6-25 用户画像分析

（2）设计问题提炼

基于对"碳排放、碳行为"概念的理解，设计师们进一步梳理了设计问题，包括明确设计目标、初步探索具体解决方法，并从中筛选出具有一定可行性的方案。

在绿色驾驶行为鼓励系统——"豹豹"车载智能语音助手的设计中，最终确定的设计问题集中在：提升用户对环保行为的感知、增强用户对车内绿色驾驶行为的认识，并激励用户持续保持绿色驾驶行为。

（3）空间–角色–动作流程分析

在这一阶段，设计师引入了"空间-角色-动作"框架，以创造解决上述问题的方案。

① 用户空间分析（图 6-26）。设计师首先依据用户调研的结果，构建了初步的用户画像和角色原型，并以此为基础对座舱空间进行分析。在这个场景中，物理空间和数字空间是两个关键的交互领域。物理空间中，用户通过中控屏、圆形信息屏等进行交互，接触点涵盖了座椅、空调、音响、氛围灯、中控屏等。数字空间中，"豹豹"通过语音引导和反馈协助用户完成行车过程中的减碳行为。特别是，当系统为用户的绿色驾驶行为提供奖励——冰块时，用户可以通过手势将虚拟冰块投入到屏幕中，这一动作连接了物理与数字空间，增强了互动体验。

图 6-26 可交互屏幕的初版交互原型设置

② 角色分析。在确定了空间和接触点之后，设计师对空间内的角色进行了深入分析，根据角色特征与场景需求，明确了互动发生的位置和动线。在"豹豹"方案中，鼓励用户进行绿色驾驶行为是交互设计的核心。通过游戏化的设计手法，引入了虚拟角色"豹豹"，利用其家园故事和与用户的互动来增强用户的英雄主义心理，提升用户的环保意识。同时，"豹豹"会根据实时天气、行车状态、驾驶目的等因素，为用户提供动态的用车建议，以实现减排目标。

③ 方案流程梳理。在对座舱空间和角色有了初步构想之后，设计师通过时间线的形式对用户、接触点以及操作流程进行了细致梳理。整体流程被划分为行车前、行车途中、行车后三个阶段，涵盖了唤醒"豹豹"、出行指引、绿色驾驶建议、冰块投掷互动等环节。

④ 动作分析。在流程梳理完成后，设计师进一步分析了用户在各个节点中的动作，形成了时间序列。这些交互动作将影响座舱的空间布局以及数字空间的信息显示权重。在"豹豹"智能语音助手方案中，设计师定义了"豹豹"在不同交互阶段的显示位置，以及在出行指引、绿色驾驶建议等环节的交互布局，还有不同屏幕中显示的信息内容，包括在天气变化时给予用户的减排建议等。

⑤ 设计反馈界面。完成上述工作定义之后，设计师开始了方案的设计工作，包括交互界面和交互逻辑的设计。部分界面如图 6-27 所示。在这一阶段，设计师探索了多种颜色和风格，特别是对"豹豹"形象进行了精心选择和多轮迭代，以期达到最佳的传达效果。

图 6-27 "豹豹"形象风格探索及迭代

（4）最终设计输出

经过一系列设计迭代和精心优化，设计师最终完成了"豹豹"智能语音助手及其所属的绿色驾驶行为鼓励系统的全面设计工作。该系统涵盖了交互流程设计和用户界面设计等关键环节。在用户界面的呈现上，采用了统一的灰蓝色调，营造出和谐的视觉体验。界面中的"豹豹"端坐于冰山之上，持续为用户提供亲切的陪伴感。用户通过采取绿色驾驶行为，不仅能对"豹豹"做出积极的回馈，还能帮助其扩展冰山领地，形成了一个良好的互动循环。图 6-28 和图 6-29 展示了"豹豹"智能语音助手案例的页面设计。

图 6-28 "豹豹"冰川环形屏界面展示

图 6-29 "豹豹"圆形信息屏界面展示

第 6 章 智能座舱人机交互设计案例

"豹豹"车载智能语音助手是一个专为智能座舱系统设计，旨在鼓励绿色驾驶行为的系统。该系统针对两类用户群体：一是注重节能反馈的实用型用户，二是注重身份认同的环保型用户。"豹豹"以极地动物海豹的形象呈现，在驾驶过程中向用户提供绿色驾驶建议，同时通过其背景故事和生活环境，展现绿色驾驶对基地环境的积极影响，将环保这一宏大概念与用户情感相连，从而帮助用户建立或维持绿色驾驶习惯。

6.4 个性化车载即时推荐系统——"盒你同行"

本案例针对信息碎片化时代下年轻人"三分钟热度"的现象，旨在打破他们下班后生活重复单调的模式。系统基于年轻用户群体生活乏味、缺乏时间规划的问题，进行了座舱内的空间、角色、动作分析。座舱能够实时捕捉用户的"三分钟热度"灵感，并将其存入灵感库。在用户下班途中，系统根据大数据推荐及与用户兴趣相关的周边活动规划，并通过盲盒方式从灵感库中随机抽取，构建个性化车载即时推荐系统，提供多样化的规划方案，减少用户规划时间成本，丰富他们下班后的生活体验。

扫码观看视频

6.4.1 设计问题提出

在信息碎片化时代，尽管人们有机会接触到更多有趣的事物，但上班族忙碌的工作往往使他们忘记了那些瞬间涌现的新想法和灵感。下班后，他们渴望体验新鲜事物，但往往在完成网上搜索和四处询问的"攻略"后，对事物的热情也随之消退，反而给疲惫的一天增加了额外的负担。

"盒你同行"的设计关注年轻职场人士在驾驶过程中的单一和乏味问题，提供基于实时地理信息的"三分钟热度"攻略服务。该服务帮助用户在下班通勤时做出体验新鲜事物的决策，激励上班族迈出体验生活的第一步，打破日常生活的单调性（图 6-30）。

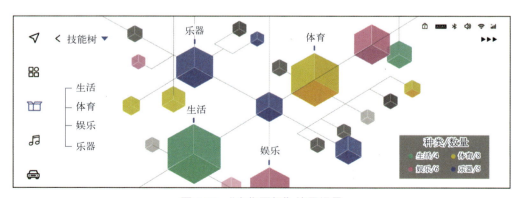

图 6-30 "盒你同行"使用场景

6.4.2 基于人机交互框架应用的设计方案概述与创新点

（1）空间

"盒你同行"的使用场景主要定位于城市通勤小型车辆，座舱设计专注于每日下班后的通勤时段。座舱空间设计以驾驶员为中心，支持与"盒你同行"系统的互动。整个座舱的信息传递主要集中于前排，因此将副驾驶座位后移。这种空间布局不仅为乘客提供了更为舒适的乘坐空间，也让驾驶者处在车内的中心位置，更容易接触到车载智能交互系统。此外，驾驶员右侧空间设计了独特的盲盒抽取按钮，方便驾驶员快速进行抽取操作。在数字空间上，驾驶员可以在视觉可触达范围内通过前排屏幕看到输入的灵感库和盲盒抽取的推荐结果（图 6-31、图 6-32）。

图 6-31 "盒你同行"灵感盲盒抽取空间示意

图 6-32 "盒你同行"造型设计

（2）角色

通过对年轻上班族的调研访谈，发现他们面临的最大挑战在于，他们拥有尝试新鲜生活的愿望，渴望生活变得更加丰富多彩，但信息碎片化时代下的众多灵感常常被新想法的实践难度所阻。"盒你同行"旨在为那些充满"三分钟热度"想法，却因工作繁忙和缺乏实现方法而陷入单调生活的人群提供解决方案（图6-33）。

图6-33 "盒你同行"用户画像

针对这一挑战，"盒你同行"团队对职场年轻人这一用户群体的生活习惯和行为进行了深入调研。针对用户不便在车内动作，支持用户在车内无感输入灵感。用户可以直接通过语音输入，不需要执行更多的输入动作，方便用户记录每天都会冒出的新鲜想法。同时基于对职场年轻人这类用户的兴趣调研，这类型的用户往往被困在了两点一线的重复生活之中，仿佛一眼能够看见生活的尽头，因而他们的生活缺乏新事物，缺乏惊喜感。座舱采用盲盒扭蛋方式，联动平时的拆盲盒动作，吸引用户更加愿意尝试新事物。"盒你同行"希望解决用户常常被新想法的实践难度所阻的困扰，通过实时地理信息的攻略，让他们能够随时实践自己的新想法，从而让生活变得更加丰富多彩。

（3）动作

在"盒你同行"系统中，用户将执行三种核心动作：收集日常生活中的短暂兴趣灵感、从灵感库中抽取灵感盲盒以及记录灵感体验。

① "三分钟热度"灵感的收集。用户在座舱内可以直接通过语音输入记录灵感，利用语音识别技术轻松捕捉那些瞬时的想法。此外，用户也可以通过手机或其他移动设备快速记录灵感，这些记录将同步至车机系统中。用户可以随时通过前排中控屏查看个人灵感库，了解灵感的创建时间和数量（图6-34）。

图6-34 "盒你同行"灵感输入

② 灵感盲盒抽取。在下班通勤途中，当系统检测到路况良好并切换至 L3 级别辅助驾驶模式时，用户可以启动"盒你同行"进行灵感盲盒的抽取。抽取过程中，用户需先推动方向盘，随后中控屏将平移至用户前方，旋钮升起以供操作。用户旋转旋钮以完成抽取，抽取结果将显示在屏幕上（图 6-35～图 6-37）。用户可以选择立即前往，此时系统会提供相应的导航信息。

图 6-35 用户抽取灵感盲盒

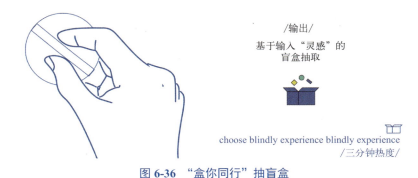

图 6-36 "盒你同行"抽盲盒

基于"灵感"的智能推荐提供可行的规划

图 6-37 "盒你同行"灵感抽取结果

③ 灵感体验的记录。抽取盲盒查看推荐是用户迈出探索新鲜事物脚步的第一步。用户根据推荐体验新鲜事物后，可以在回到座舱时通过旋钮开启灵感体验的记录功能。完成记录将获得与灵感盲盒对应的卡牌奖励（图 6-38），而"盒你同行"系统则会自动记录每次体验，形成用户个人的灵感树。

图 6-38 "盒你同行"灵感卡牌奖励

（4）整体方案框架描述

"盒你同行"专注于服务那些对新鲜事物抱有"三分钟热度"的用户群体。系统通过分析用户的行为和习惯，对车内空间进行优化设计，利用无感输入和盲盒抽取的交互方式，将用户的通勤时间转变为充满惊喜的全新体验。

用户可以在上车前通过手机记录灵感，进入座舱后，车载系统将同步手机端的记录，并通过语音输入继续快速捕捉用户的即时灵感。这些灵感将被自动分类并存储在个人灵感库中，方便用户随时查阅和抽取。当用户积累了一定数量的灵感后，可以通过盲盒抽取获取当日的"三分钟热度"灵感，并从系统中获取与灵感相关的实时地理推荐信息，进而选择前往相关目的地。这一系统不仅满足了用户对新鲜事物的探索欲望，还提供了实时地理信息推荐的便利，使用户能够体验从灵感产生到实现的完整过程（图6-39）。

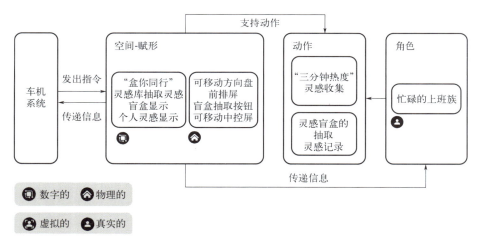

图 6-39 基于空间-角色-动作设计框架的应用

6.4.3 设计过程

（1）前期调研和用户研究

为了深入理解"三分钟热度"这一现象及其在现实生活中的体现和影响，设计师开展了一系列用户研究和市场调查。通过访谈、观察、问卷调查等多种方法，收集了人们对"三分钟热度"的感受、处理方式以及这一现象如何影响他们的日常生活和行为模式。

(2) 设计问题抽取

在深刻洞察现实问题的基础上，设计师将其抽象化，形成具体的设计问题。这一步骤涉及明确设计目标、确定具体待解决问题以及识别可能的设计限制。在"三分钟热度"案例中，设计问题主要集中在如何将这种瞬时的热情转化为持续且引人入胜的用户体验。

(3) 空间–角色–动作流程分析

这一阶段，设计师开始引入"空间-角色-动作"框架，创造针对上述设计问题的解决方案。

① 用户空间分析。小车作为城市通勤工具，设计师力求在其有限的空间内提供宽敞舒适的乘坐体验，同时为驾驶者带来全新的驾驶感受。为此，副驾驶座位被后移，这不仅增加了乘客的腿部空间，也使驾驶者位于车辆的中心位置，便于与车载智能交互系统进行互动。

② 角色分析。在确定了空间和接触点之后，设计师对座舱内的角色进行了详细分析。根据角色特征和场景需求，确定了互动发生的位置和动线。"盒你同行"专为那些拥有大量"三分钟热度"想法，但由于工作繁忙或缺乏实现途径而陷入单调生活的人群设计。用户需要自主操作屏幕，而位置与接触点相对固定。这一分析为整个体验过程提供了有关角色可能使用的接触点和执行的动作的洞察。

③ 方案流程梳理。设计师在此阶段已初步构思了座舱内的空间和角色，接下来以时间线形式梳理空间中的用户、接触点和对应的系统操作。整体流程分为输入、抽取和体验三大部分。

④ 动作分析。接下来，设计师需要对用户在空间内各流程节点下的动作进行深入分析，生成时间动作序列。这些动作将影响实际物理空间的布局和数字空间内信息的传递。为"盒你同行"设计简单便捷的操作方式，以确保用户能够轻松获得惊喜。

⑤ 设计反馈界面。完成空间-角色-动作的定义后，设计师着手设计具体的反馈界面，包括图形用户界面（GUI）、语音用户界面（VUI）以及硬件交互提供的触觉用户界面（TUI）。部分设计界面展示如图6-40所示。

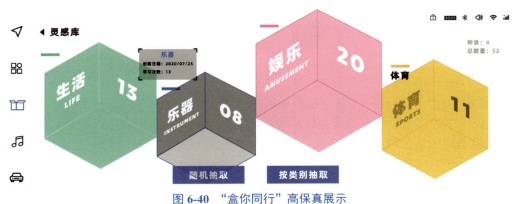

图 6-40 "盒你同行"高保真展示

⑥ 初步评估。完成设计方案大致内容的输出后，设计师运用纸面原型、故事演绎、专家评估等方法，迅速发现方案的潜在问题。针对这些问题，设计师进行了迭代，调整了空间布局、场景流程、角色动作等方面。

（4）原型开发和用户测试

在方案经过优化后，设计师着手基于方案内容创建模型和可交互原型，并通过原型进行用户测试。这一过程有助于发现真实环境下可能存在的问题，为随后的迭代提供了宝贵的反馈。

（5）最终设计输出

在设计的迭代和优化完成后，设计师呈现了完整的设计成果。这包括具体的产品设计、交互设计、用户界面设计等。在"三分钟热度"的案例中，设计师提供了一个全面的车载智能交互方案（图6-41）。

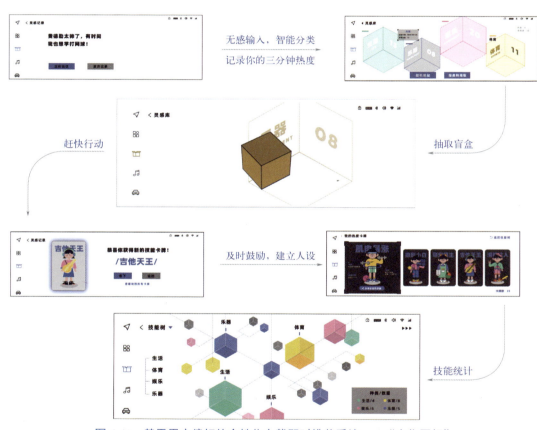

图6-41 基于用户偏好的个性化车载即时推荐系统——"盒你同行"

"盒你同行"方案是一个基于用户偏好的个性化车载即时推荐系统，旨在为职场年轻人提供一个智能座舱概念设计。该系统旨在消除用户查询出行攻略的疲劳，同时满足他们改善单调生活、降低出行成本的需求。座舱系统能够在车内和手机上记录用户灵感，创建灵感库，并通过盲盒抽取的方式提供实时地理推荐信息，从而在无形中降低用户的出行成本，为用户提供从灵感产生到实现的全过程体验。

第 7 章

智能座舱未来发展趋势

7.1 智能座舱的车机发展趋势
7.2 智能座舱体验发展趋势
7.3 L4+ 智慧出行展望

"未来世界汽车产业科技发展方向共识是绿色、互联、智能,其发展与变革需要以创新为驱动,也终将会延伸至人类整个出行方式的变革"。中国工程院院士陈清泉认为,要改变人类未来出行方式,仅限于研发与制造还远远不够,更要致力于通过智能网联技术实现智捷交通,进而打造未来智慧城市,最终才能真正实现人类未来出行方式变革的目标。

在智慧出行领域,电动汽车、智能汽车、智能交通和智慧城市等技术不断发展,为人们进入智能时代创造了条件。智能座舱是"技术+用户体验"的双驱动引擎,它可以为用户带来多种附加值和价值机会,满足人们出行时的学习、娱乐等多样化需求,提升出行的舒适度和乐趣。智能座舱的未来发展趋势有着诸多可能性。

7.1 智能座舱的车机发展趋势

7.1.1 智能化水平提升

在汽车科技迅速发展的当今时代,智能座舱已经成为驾驶体验中不可或缺的一部分。为了满足用户对先进科技的智能化需求以及提高驾驶安全性和便利性,汽车制造商正不断努力推动智能座舱的演进。目前车机智能化水平的提升主要体现在座舱软硬件升级和人机交互的多样化两方面。

(1)硬件和软件持续升级

智能座舱的硬件和软件都在不断进步。硬件上:物理按键逐渐减少;大尺寸中控液晶屏和全液晶仪表盘正在取代传统中控和仪表;座舱域控制器升级,可集中控制座舱内的多个电子设备;高级驾驶辅助系统(ADAS)集成更多传感器和摄像头,提供更多安全功能。软件上:车载操作系统不断升级,提供更好的稳定性和兼容性,设计也更加直观且易操作;通过汽车空中下载技术(OTA),厂商可以针对汽车内部的控制软件问题进行快速响应解决,也可以实现软件的功能更新;用户可以在车内对自己的系统进行升级,从而同步最新的资讯、功能,实现和手机一样的"永远在线"的体验;运用了人工智能(AI)算法的语音识别、自然语言处理和个性化推荐服务,给用户带来更自然的、符合个人习惯的交互体验。

> **案例:蔚来的 OTA 升级**
>
> 几乎每一个智能座舱品牌都做了 OTA 系统,以便支持企业对功能进行持续的升级和同步。如图 7-1,在蔚来的一次 OTA 升级中,它的自动泊车功能新增了对斜线车位的支持。在版本更新之中,OTA 能帮助车辆新增可用的 App,解锁自动泊车、解锁对更多场景的技术支持等,使得在品牌进行快速多轮的功能迭代之后,无论先购买还是后购买的车主都能享受同样的智能体验。

图 7-1 蔚来在 OTA 升级中新增了自动泊车时的新功能

未来智能座舱的软硬件架构还将持续升级，通过采用智能化、模块化、开放式的设计，促进多方合作和生态共建。这将为用户提供更丰富的功能扩展和服务集成，使座舱能满足用户更具个性化的需求，促进座舱技术的创新和发展。随着技术的不断进步和生态系统的成熟，我们可以期待智能座舱在软硬件架构方面的持续演进，为用户带来更优秀的智能驾驶体验。

案例：小鹏 Xnet2.0

小鹏发布的 Xnet2.0 运用了大模型技术并且融合了目前业内最高精度的纯视觉占据网络，感知范围扩大了 200%，新增了 11 种感知类型，如清扫车、儿童、减速带甚至小动物等。而在此之上，小鹏智驾的整体架构也迎来了革新——被称为"终极架构"的 XBrain。在 XBrain 架构下，除了负责感知的 Xnet2.0，小鹏还推出了 XPlanner——一套基于神经网络的规划和控制架构，可以融合分钟级别的时序，结合动态交通和静态环境感知信息，像人类一样合理规划车辆的运动轨迹，该智能座舱系统所属的"XOS 天玑"将接入 XGPT 灵犀大模型"AI 小 P"。此外，在同系统架构的未来产品开发层面是一台内部装载有一台六旋翼飞行器的 6×6 越野车（图 7-2），其主体采用了增程式动力架构，它或许将成为小鹏在混动架构上的初次尝试。它不仅本体可以载 4~5 人，内部的六旋翼飞行器还可以坐 2 人。飞机与汽车的解耦，让它们在技术上具备更高的智能化水平以及量产可能，当然，也更容易满足法规要求。

图 7-2 小鹏未来产品开发——越野车

（2）人机交互方式多样化

智能座舱的交互系统设计，经历了传统的触控交互时代，随着语音交互、人脸识别等技术不断突破并被应用到智能座舱中，座舱中的人机交互方式也变得更加多样化。这些技术使得驾驶员可以通过语音命令甚至面部表情来控制车机系统，提高了操作的便捷性和安全性。未来智能座舱将应用更多交互技术，进入多样化交互的阶段。

多样化交互是下一代人机交互方式的理想模型，简单说，就是综合利用手势、眼球跟踪、语音等多种方式来进行交互。应用多样化的交互方式有以下两点优势：一方面可以提高交互准确性，例如单独的语音交互，不可避免遇到噪声、回声、识别不清晰等状况，而通过获取图像、眼神、表情甚至血压心率等传感器信息与语音信息互补，可以融合多种不同的信息源，降低误交互率；另一方面，多个交互方式之间是互补的，可通过结合不同交互方式的优势，更便捷、更高效地为驾乘人员提供所需信息。

案例：蔚来智能香氛

蔚来智能香氛是气味交互设计的典型案例，可以实现多种香味的自由切换，用户可以通过在中控屏操作或与 NOMI 交互，使三种香味在系统内自由切换，且实现场景联动、智能调节和记忆功能（图 7-3）。而当监测到驾驶员的疲劳状态时，还可以自动释放提神醒脑的香氛，以确保驾驶安全。在未来，气味交互将不仅仅是智能香氛，它将变得更加个性化和人性化，也将实现场景化互动。比如，通过监测驾驶员状态，以实现疲劳驾驶气味提醒、快乐氛围加倍等功能；当打游戏时，可以通过佩戴 AR+ 气味来实现更好的游戏体验；在不同天气、不同季节提供不同的气味等。

图 7-3 蔚来智能香氛、AR+ 气味交互

7.1.2 功能集成与定制化服务增加

信息存储技术、车载计算平台、车联网硬件的发展使智能座舱正在成为一个高度集成的信息中心。座舱不仅可以提供传统的导航、音乐、电话等功能，还开始集成支付、娱乐、信息服务等多样化的功能。例如，一些智能座舱系统已经支持在线支付功能，驾驶员可以在车内直接完成餐厅预订、电影票购买等操作。

随着消费者个性化需求的增加，智能座舱也开始提供定制化的服务。驾驶员可以根据自己的喜好和习惯来设置车机系统的界面、功能布局等，使得车机系统更加符合个人使用习惯。相较于传统的车上服务由后台定义、只能做到千人一面，个性化主动服务是 AI 场景引擎的特长，它更注重对用户使用习惯的学习与挖掘，以满足千人千面的用车需求。用户体验也将随着 AI 技术的不断沉淀得到持续改善。伴随 AI 技术加持汽车智能化升级，"规则驱动—数据驱动—智能助理"的场景引擎技术演进路线成为主流，帮助车企打造智能体验感满满的 AI 行车助手。AI 场景引擎也会特别注意服务的时机，在不干扰用户的前提下，提供适时的贴心服务。不仅如此，AI 技术赋予行车助手自学习能力，使主动推荐的服务越来越精准。

案例：斑马智行

未来驾驶情境中屏幕上多个通知有时候同时弹出，会干扰安全驾驶，斑马智行深刻洞察诸多用户的这一痛点，找到了解决问题的关键——场景。未来以场景为中心，基于对用户的理解，用数据和算法驱动主动服务，为主驾用户提供高频、刚需、原子化、触手可及的服务是斑马智行为车企全新打造的行车助手的产品理念。其采用的 SOA 原子化软件架构从底层打破了各功能间的界限，让跨域融合成为可能。斑马智行自研的 AliOS 智能座舱操作系统（图 7-4）支持 SOA 软件架构，采用多核异构融合架构，在系统之上打造的行车助手可通过统一的系统级交互框架，运用 AI 场景引擎，串联起原子化的服务，满足用户的个性化需求。围绕用户的多种行车场景，如上车、拥堵路段、停车、长时间驾驶等，行车助手可基于 AI 场景引擎主动为用户推荐个性化音乐、场景化车控功能及快捷建议。当汽车感知到相关场景时，行车助手便会弹出卡片，用户一触即达，不再需要寻找 App，可快速获得智能服务带来的满足感。

图 7-4　座舱中的 AliOS 智能座舱操作系统

面向未来，智能座舱作为一个全新智慧空间，既可以丰富人们在移动场景下的体验，又可以满足人们在静止场景中的多样化需求。

7.1.3　数据安全与隐私保护加强

随着智能座舱功能的不断增加，数据安全和隐私保护也成为了关注的焦点。未来的智能座舱将更加注重用户数据的安全性和隐私保护，采用更加先进的加密技术和隐私保护措施来确保用户数据的安全。

人车互信的建立是智能座舱设计中不可或缺的一部分。通过透明和可验证的数据管理流程，用户可以确信他们的个人信息得到了妥善的保护。这种信任的建立是双向的：用户信任智能座舱能够安全地处理他们的数据，而智能座舱则通过提供可靠的服务和保护来赢得用户的信任。因而数据安全和隐私保护是智能座舱技术发展中的关键要素，不仅是因为它们对于保障用户基本权利的重要性，也因为它们能显著改善用户体验。建立良好的人车互信是人车协同更好发展的基础。

数据安全是智能座舱技术的基石。随着汽车行业不断向自动化、互联网化发展，大量的个人数据，如位置信息、行驶习惯甚至生物识别信息，都被收集和分析。这些数据的安全性直接关系到用户的信任和接受度。采用强大的加密技术、数据访问控制以及网络安全策略，可以确保这些信息不被未经授权的第三方获取。这种安全保障不仅避免了数据泄露带来的风险，还增强了消费者对智能座舱产品的信任。

隐私保护是改善用户体验的关键。智能座舱通过收集和分析用户数据来提供个性化服务，如路线规划、音乐推荐等。然而，如果没有适当的隐私保护措施，这种数据收集可能会让用户感到不安。因此，开发商需要设计一套既能有效利用数据，又能保护用户隐私的机制。例如，通过匿名化处理数据，或让用户能控制哪些数据可以被收集和使用。这种对隐私的尊重不仅符合法律法规，更能提升用户对产品的好感度和满意度。

数据安全和隐私保护在提供个性化体验方面起着至关重要的作用。用户更倾向于使用那些能够提供定制化服务同时又不侵犯个人隐私的智能座舱系统。例如，系统可以根据用户的行驶习惯和偏好提供路线建议，但在处理这些数据时，必须确保用户的身份和行程细节得到保护。

随着智能座舱技术的不断发展，对于数据安全和隐私保护的需求将更加突出。未来的智能座舱将不仅仅是驾驶的辅助，更将成为个人数据的集中处理中心。在这样的背景下，确保数据安全和隐私保护将是改善用户体验、增强市场竞争力的关键。数据安全和隐私保护不仅是智能座舱技术发展的必然趋势，更是改善用户体验、赢得市场的重要策略。

综上所述，智能座舱的"车机"发展趋势主要体现在智能化水平提升、功能集成与定制化服务增加以及数据安全与隐私保护加强等方面。这些趋势将共同推动智能座舱向更加智能、便捷、安全和舒适的方向发展。

7.2 智能座舱体验发展趋势

7.2.1 个性化与舒适性体验提出了新的人因要求

智能座舱将通过人工智能、大数据等技术，为乘客提供更加个性化的出行体验。用户可以根据个人喜好和习惯进行个性化设置，如调节座椅位置、后视镜角度、空调温度、照明颜色和强度，自定义仪表盘和信息娱乐系统的布局和显示信息。同时，在舒适性方面，智能座舱将通过识别、检测技术收集乘客信息，进行自动环境调节，优化座舱环境，以及提供舒适的座椅和空间布局，让乘客在座舱内更加舒适和愉悦。例如，动态香氛系统可根据用户偏好或驾驶模式释放不同香味，改善驾乘体验；自适应音响系统能够根据乘客位置和车内噪声水平自动调整音量和音质；座椅的技术升级提升了用户驾驶和乘坐车辆时的舒适度，通过内置加热系统，用户可以在冬天享受温暖的座椅；通过内置按摩装置，用户可以在车内得到腰背的自定义按摩服务。

而随着技术的不断发展，未来智能座舱的个性化和舒适性体验将更加多样化和精细化，这也给座舱人机界面和布局等方面提出了新的人因与工效要求。

座舱应用了更先进的显示和交互技术而具有更强大的功能。在新型交互技术应用方面，应当遵循人因工程的设计原则，使座舱的显控系统设计更加合理、更加人性化，并需要解决引入新技术后设计的工效测试与评估问题。从座舱智能人因设计方面，我们可以从以下角度出发：座舱自动化/智能化功能的宜人性设计、管理功能界面/交互的人因设计、工效测试评估等。

在目前的座舱中我们已经能够看到很多部件围绕新技术在人因设计方面做出了新的探索，例如，"零重力座椅"、向日葵屏、曲面显示、无人机人机协同等。随之座舱的标准也将逐渐纳入有关新型交互、智能系统方面的人因要求。

案例：深蓝向日葵屏

2023年6月25日，深蓝S7电动汽车正式上市。它配备的15.6英寸向日葵屏更是吸引了众多消费者的目光。这款大尺寸的中控屏幕不仅具备了高分辨率和出色的显示效果，更为用户带来了前所未有的便捷与乐趣。向日葵屏的名字源于它的独特设计。这款屏幕可以像向日葵一样向两侧转动，从而根据驾驶员或乘客的需求调整最佳观看角度（图7-5）。这种设计极大地增强了驾驶过程中的操作便利性，无论是查看导航信息、车辆状态，还是进行娱乐功能的操作，都能轻松实现。

深蓝向日葵屏无疑在软件体验和人性化设计上下足了功夫。这款屏幕不仅让驾驶变得更加便捷、安全，也为乘客带来了前所未有的娱乐享受。在未来，我们有理由相信，随着技术的不断进步和消费者需求的不断变化，汽车的软硬件将会围绕人因工程有更多的设计创新和突破。

图 7-5　深蓝 S7 配备的向日葵屏

> **案例：深蓝 S7 "零重力座椅"**

深蓝汽车是长安汽车的子品牌，专注于打造新能源汽车。深蓝汽车在能源增程和内饰舒适性配置上都有着独特技术。深蓝 S7 的座椅号称"零重力座椅"（如图 7-6），在人机工程学设计基础上，配合四向腿托，使乘客在乘坐时，身体压力均匀分布到身体的各个部分，提供人性化的车内乘坐舒适度。另外，座椅还支持手机、屏幕、物理按键多种调节方式，也能在切换观影模式时一键调节至舒适观影形态。座椅还兼具通风、按摩等功能，可以满足不同年龄段乘坐者的多样化乘坐需求。

图 7-6 深蓝 S7 的"零重力座椅"

7.2.2 围绕便捷性的多模态交互出现

随着传感器技术和人工智能技术的进一步发展，未来智能座舱必将融合多种感知手段，从以语音为主的交互模式转向以视觉感知为核心，以语音及其他多种感知方式为辅助的多模态交互模式，形成独立的立体式的感知层。乘客可以通过语音、手势等多种方式与座舱内设备进行交互，实现各种功能操作。多模态的交互方式将大大提高操作的便捷性，使乘客能够更加方便地使用智能座舱的各种功能。

此外，全息、AR、智能表面等介质无形化交互，在提供自由有趣的交互方式的同时也在无形中创造了具有更高操作性和自由度的座舱服务体系，拓展了未来交互方式的可能性。

在可预见的未来，智能座舱将基于用户体验，引入更多智能交互方式，以实现更加自然、智能、便捷的交互。

> **案例：宝马品牌在座舱内多模态交互探索**

2016 年，宝马在 CES 展会上展示的概念车可通过车载感应器识别 3D 手势，达成驾驶员操作触控和手势交互；2017 年，宝马在交互方式上持续探索，通过虚拟触控达成娱乐交互；到 2020 年，宝马展示了名为 BMW i3 Urban Suite 的特别版车型"城市套房"，设计师让 i3 座舱变成一个个人化的极度舒适的休憩空间，以满足乘客的个人化需求；在2022年的CES展上，宝马发布了"影院模式"（theater mode）未来车内娱乐系统，在影院模式（图7-7）下，宝马通过31英寸超宽的悬浮屏幕和配备5G互联的环绕音响系统，在座舱内形成了一个极富沉浸感的私人影院。

图7-7　宝马"影院模式"未来车内娱乐系统

7.2.3　多生态融合

智能座舱已经进入"万物互联、跨界融合"的新竞争周期，下一个技术变革时代已经开启。智能座舱将与手机生态、智能家居生态进行深度融合，实现更加无缝无感的互联场景体验。例如，乘客可以在手机和座舱之间实现导航、音乐和视频通话等应用的自动流转和接续使用，这将大大改善乘客的使用体验。同时，深度网联化和智能交通融合也是未来智慧城市和智能座舱技术发展的重要方向。随着互联网和智能交通技术的不断发展，智能座舱将与互联网和智能交通系统实现紧密结合，打造深度网联化的车辆系统。

在构建互联与多生态融合的智慧愿景下，各路厂商仍在探寻更多可能。就连不起眼的开关面板，都被"赋予"了远程控制、家居联动等一连串IoT层面的互联功能。智能座舱被华为、蔚来、小米等造车新势力，乃至老牌车企吉利等，打造成"人车家"生态图景中万物互联落地的"新钥匙"。汽车、手机是目前生活中两个高频的"智能终端"，而驾乘空间与家居空间、办公空间交织在一起，就形成一个立体网状的生态结构（图7-8）。

图7-8　以车为中心的移动互联

> **案例：小米打造人车家互联生态**
>
> 2024年3月28日上市的小米SU7通过人车家生态互联功能，实现了车辆、手机、智能家居设备之间的紧密连接。用户不仅可以通过手机实现远程解锁、车内智能控制等功能，还可以实现车家联动，用户可在家备车，一句话打开车内空调、座椅加热；还能在车内控家，随时调用家中摄像头，一键实现门铃对讲；全自动化特性能设置地理围栏，SU7进小区自动激活回家模式。车载智能系统的不断优化以及与智能家居设备的融合，将为用户带来更加智能便捷的生活体验。
>
> 随着智能科技的不断发展，人车家生态互联功能也将不断升级和完善。未来，人们或许可以在车内直接操作智能家居设备，实现更便捷、智能的生活方式。

综上所述，智能座舱的"体验"将朝着个性化、舒适性、多维交互、便捷性以及多生态融合等方向发展。这些发展趋势将共同推动智能座舱技术的不断进步和应用范围的扩大。

7.3 L4+ 智慧出行展望

7.3.1 汽车座舱从"移动空间"到"智能生活空间"

汽车的属性不再仅局限于交通工具，而是与人和周边环境形成了新的关系。一方面，随着智能驾驶技术向L4+的方向发展，人们的注意力可以从驾驶中解放出来，车内的使用场景也随之增加，这使得移动情景下的用户体验更加丰富多彩。在车内，人们可以像在建筑空间内一样，享受舒适便捷的环境，轻松地处理工作、学习或娱乐事务。另一方面，随着多元化的人机交互技术、车载光技术、沉浸式的AR/VR技术等的成熟和应用，智能座舱的功能形态也将变得更加丰富有趣。除了动态场景，汽车在静态场景中的功能将得到更大的拓展。

面向未来，座舱将完全成为一个智慧空间，内饰的形态也将逐渐摆脱方向盘+仪表盘+屏幕的传统组合，而呈现出新的空间布局，使得用户在乘车时的空间和时间价值将大大提升，丰富的拓展场景让智能座舱真正成为虚实融合的智能生活空间。

在娱乐场景下，用户不必亲临现场也可以感受演唱会、音乐会等的氛围，现场音乐也不再是唯一的选择，动作交互也可以在增强现实技术下更具沉浸感，多屏幕交互、VR、AR和全息等技术在座舱内的应用，充分证明了这一点。座舱可以成为用户的专属郊游空间、探险空间、自然驿站、旧货贩卖站等。

在带娃出行场景下，车内空间布局设置有专属的儿童区域，车身传感设备和车内交互设备可以有效结合，准确识别车外的自然和人文环境信息，并及时通过屏幕交互同步到车内儿童用户，拓宽儿童的知识获取通道。

在移动办公场景下，座舱布局基于休息和工作两种模式。座椅不再是定向排布，车窗作为投影屏幕被充分利用，iPad和手机等移动终端将轻易接入办公生态系统，一键隐私玻璃和 ID 识别充分保证用户的会议和数据私密性；智能座舱升级为在路上的移动办公空间，用户在他们奔向机场、餐厅、家庭的途中，高效地完成休息和工作（图 7-9）。

图 7-9　办公休息场景

在社交场景下，人与人的距离在出行过程中被无限拉近，用户可以通过外部摄像头记录车外环境并对记录的视频进行剪辑、分享，充分拓展行车过程中的场景，比如堵车也不再无聊，附近的车友可以通过车机互动，AR/VR 技术的加成可以让用户和朋友感觉彼此近在咫尺。

基于场景体验的设计策略是当前汽车设计领域的热门话题。这种设计策略强调个性化定制和情境感知，通过先进的传感器技术和人工智能算法，座舱可以感知到用户的行为、喜好和情绪，并根据这些信息进行个性化定制。根据特定地区或文化背景，座舱应按照当地用户的需求和偏好进行定制化设计，以确保座舱能够适应特定地区的文化特征和使用习惯。要求设计师深入理解特定地区的文化、用户习惯和技术发展，以创造出既符合当地特色又具有前瞻性的座舱设计。

7.3.2　场景服务从"单点"向"交通网络"转变

随着数字化以及智能化的技术深入渗透到智能座舱中，场景驱动下的服务将更加智能和高效，真正实现从"单点"到"系统"，再到"场景融合网络的体验服务"。华为《智能世界 2030》报告提出如下转变：

第一，随着网联化基础设施的逐步完善和智能驾驶渗透率的提升，智能网联从单车智能走向多车协同，将进一步推动智能驾驶广泛商用和智慧交通体系的建设。构建泛在的 V2X 连接能力，连接人、车、道路基础设施，通过在云端构建车云协同智能驾驶平台，打通端到端应用场景，通过全息环境感知、全局资源调度、动态业务地图、多车协同驾驶、车道级路径规划、信号协同控制、业务仿真测试等服务能力，将有效加速多车协同的智能驾驶商用落地。

第二，汽车智能化发展使得实时服务场景识别更为高效和精准。智能座舱通过与其他车辆的通信，实现车辆与车辆之间的信息交流和协同。通过车辆之间的互联互通，智能座舱可以获取周围车辆的行驶状态、车速、位置等信息，从而实现智能的交通流优化和安全驾驶。通过对车辆数据、位置信息以及周边环境的识别和分析，进而判断用户所处的场景，主动预测用户的需求，从而提供精准的服务。

第三，互联互通的全新操作系统能够打通更多服务场景，基于新交互方式的应用生态应运而生，互联世界所激发出的更多服务将承载到智能汽车上，让汽车成为新的智能载体。伴随着数字世界的到来和数字经济的不断发展，数字化全景生态日渐丰富，场景驱动下的智能车联功能和服务将更加智能、高效和便捷。

案例：未来座舱服务

根据以上三点带来的转变，我们通过案例站在用户或者消费者视角对未来座舱的服务进行大胆畅想：如果用户在预约远途出行服务的同时，希望在车上和朋友享用一顿牛排大餐，那么，出行服务商会依据消费者的出行目的和个性化偏好，提供一辆匹配其驾乘习惯的共享餐车，并在规划好的行驶路径周边，选择一家备受好评的西餐厅预订食材；这家餐厅会依据车辆预计抵达交货地点的时间进行备餐，无人机会准时将餐饮送到指定位置，车辆自动开启天窗，无人机进行餐饮配送，并在车内完成牛排的制作，车辆继续向目的地出发。

7.3.3　出行场景从"单一"到"多种交通工具"涌现

未来交通出行场景将更加多样化，除了传统的汽车、火车和飞机等交通工具外，新型交通工具如磁悬浮列车、超级高铁、飞行汽车等逐渐涌现，也将走进我们的生活。这些新型交通工具具有更高的速度、更大的运力和更短的旅行时间等特点，它们将城市的出行方式从二维拓展至三维，真正将垂直城市带入到大众视野，将为人们的出行提供更多选择和便利。例如，超级高铁利用磁悬浮技术和真空管道运输乘客，能够实现比飞机更快、更安全、更舒适的出行体验。飞行汽车则可以在城市上空飞行，避开地面交通拥堵，为紧急医疗救援、应急抢险等提供快速通道。在未来的出行场景中将呈现多种交通工具并存的局面。

案例：小鹏旅航者 X2

在"1024小鹏汽车科技日"上，小鹏汇天公布了一辆陆空两用的飞行汽车。而在这之前，小鹏旅航者X2（图7-10）还在迪拜完成了海外首飞。X2采用了封闭式座舱设计，其飞行系统在折叠状态下与普通汽车尺寸相当，在飞行状态下仅需通过折叠变形系统，即可打开机臂切换到飞行模式，用于垂直起降。另外，其并未安装车轮，而是一个固定式的"U"形起落架。在设计上，采用了鸥翼式车门+两座桶式座椅和三屏式设计，科技感十足，而其纯电式设计则非常符合绿色出行。在飞行状态下，可以通过方向盘和右侧挡杆配合以实现在空中前进、后退、转弯，以及上升、悬停、下降等。在使用中，用户通过App来计划和预订旅程（运营平台系统会根据用户的特征、时间、交通拥堵状况、成本、乘坐需求等要素来自动给出最佳交通解决方案），将空中模块、地面模块或其他交通工具连接至乘客座舱。

图 7-10　小鹏旅航者 X2

总之，未来交通出行场景的发展将更加智能化、环保可持续、多样化和人性化。这些新型交通工具的出现将使人们彻底告别拥堵现象，为人们提供更加便捷、高效、舒适的出行体验。未来多种交通工具的涌现将给用户的生活方式带来极大的便利。

参考文献

[1] 赵丹华.汽车造型的设计意图和认知解释[D].长沙：湖南大学，2013.
[2] 赵丹华，江雨豪，顾方舟，等.设计迭代：揭示设计意义的理论线索[J].装饰，2023（12）：19-24.
[3] 赵丹华，顾方舟.汽车内饰的造型设计与设计研究[J].包装工程，2019，40（16）：43-61.
[4] 顾方舟.设计问题求解的问题表征研究[D].长沙：湖南大学，2023.
[5] 马羽佳.基于空间、角色和动作的汽车人机交互设计研究[D].长沙：湖南大学，2023.
[6] 卓良.基于动作叙事的智能座舱创新设计策略研究[D].长沙：湖南大学，2023.
[7] 黄颖捷.汽车内饰的空间模式与空间设计[D].长沙：湖南大学，2019.
[8] 王正通，赵丹华，李添天.汽车内饰造型中的空间动线研究[J].包装工程，2020，41（16）：223-229.
[9] 谭征宇，戴宁一，张瑞佛，等.智能网联汽车人机交互研究现状及展望[J].计算机集成制造系统，2020，26（10）：2615-2632.
[10] 谭浩，谭征宇，景春晖.汽车人机交互界面设计[M].北京：电子工业出版社，2015.
[11] 谭浩，孙家豪，关岱松，等.智能汽车人机交互发展趋势研究[J].包装工程，2019，40（20）：32-42.
[12] 唐纳德·A·舍恩，夏林清.反映的实践者[M].夏林清，译.北京：教育科学出版社，2007.
[13] 周济，李培根.智能制造导论[M].北京：高等教育出版社，2021.
[14] （美）布什（Bush P.M.）.工效学基本原理、应用及技术[M].陈善广，译.北京：国防工业出版社，2016.
[15] 王选政，等.出行创新设计[M].北京：机械工业出版社，2024.
[16] 陈芳，雅克·特肯.以人为本的智能汽车交互设计：HMI[M].北京：机械工业出版社，2021.
[17] 泛亚内饰教材编写组.汽车内饰设计概论[M].北京：人民交通出版社，2012.
[18] 李克强，戴一凡，李升波，等.智能网联汽车（ICV）技术的发展现状及趋势[J].汽车安全与节能学报，2017，8（1）：1-14.
[19] 蔡萌亚，王文丽.汽车智能座舱交互设计研究综述[J].包装工程，2023，44（6）：430-440.
[20] 肖瑶，刘会衡，程晓红.车联网关键技术及其发展趋势与挑战[J].通信技术，2021，54（01）：1-8.
[21] 吴卫，李黎俊雄.湖湘红色文创产品设计中叙事设计的方法与实践[J].装饰，2021（9）：42-45.
[22] 李世国，费钎.和谐视野中的产品交互设计[J].包装工程，2009，30（01）：137-140.
[23] 辛向阳.交互设计：从物理逻辑到行为逻辑[J].装饰，2015（01）：58-62.
[24] 张晓聪.汽车智能座舱发展现状及未来趋势[J].汽车纵横，2019（8）：42-45.
[25] 解迎刚，王全.基于视觉的动态手势识别研究综述[J].计算机工程与应用，2021，57（22）：68-77.
[26] 蒋以兆.自动驾驶技术中的感测器件分析[J].集成电路应用，2017，34（01）：86-90.
[27] 《中国公路学报》编辑部.中国汽车工程学术研究综述·2023[J].中国公路学报，2023，36（11）：1-192.
[28] 缪立新，王发平.V2X车联网关键技术研究及应用综述[J].汽车工程学报，2020，10（01）：1-12.
[29] 覃京燕，朱向未，李丹碧林.信息可视化中交互设计方法探议[J].装饰，2007（3）：22-23.
[30] 李四达，丁肇辰.正版现货服务设计概论：创新实践十二课清华大学[M].北京：清华大学出版社，2018.
[31] 邓成连.触动服务接触点[J].装饰，2010（6）：13-17.
[32] 栾之珑，师丹青.多维度下展开的非线性叙事——新媒体时代的体验性叙事设计[J].装饰，2017（4）：30-33.
[33] JENSEN M V. A physical approach to tangible interaction design[C]//Proceedings of the 1st international conference on Tangible and embedded interaction. New York, NY, USA: Association for Computing Machinery, 2007: 241-244.
[34] CARROLL J M. Five reasons for scenario-based design[J]. Interacting with Computers, 2000, 13（1）: 43-60.
[35] LUNDGREN S, HULTBERG T. FEATURE Time, temporality, and interaction[J]. Interactions, 2009, 16（4）:

34-37.

[36] KRISCHKOWSKY A, TRÖSTERER S, BRUCKENBERGER U, et al. The Impact of Spatial Properties on Collaboration: An Exploratory Study in the Automotive Domain[C]//Proceedings of the 2016 ACM International Conference on Supporting Group Work. New York, NY, USA: Association for Computing Machinery, 2016: 245-255.

[37] JAAFARNIA M. Form & Space in Industrial Design[M]. 1st ed. Tehran: Sima ye Danesh, 2007.

[38] CARD S K, MACKINLAY J D, ROBERTSON G G. A morphological analysis of the design space of input devices[J]. ACM Transactions on Information Systems, 1991, 9(2): 99-122.

[39] PRABHAKAR G, BISWAS P. A Brief Survey on Interactive Automotive UI[J]. Transportation Engineering, 2021, 6: 100089.

[40] PRABHAKAR G, RAMAKRISHNAN A, MADAN M, et al. Interactive gaze and finger controlled HUD for cars[J]. Journal on Multimodal User Interfaces, 2020, 14(1): 101-121.

[41] DEY A. Understanding and Using Context[J]. Personal and Ubiquitous Computing, 2001, 5: 4-7.

[42] SCHILIT B, ADAMS N, WANT R. Context-Aware Computing Applications[C]//1994 First Workshop on Mobile Computing Systems and Applications. 1994: 85-90.

[43] WINOGRAD T. Architectures for Context[J]. Human–Computer Interaction, 2001, 16(2-4): 401-419.

[44] SHACKEL B, CHIDSEY K D, SHIPLEY P. The assessment of chair comfort[J]. Ergonomics, 1969, 12(2): 269-306.

[45] 代尔夫特理工大学, 工业设计工程学院. 设计方法与策略: 代尔夫特设计指南[M]. 武汉: 华中科技大学出版社, 2014.

[46] ALSHENQEETI H. Interviewing as a data collection method: A critical review[J]. English Linguistics Research, 2014, 3(1): 39-45.

[47] VISSER F S, STAPPERS P J, VAN DER LUGT R, et al. Contextmapping: Experiences from practice[J]. CoDesign, 2005, 1(2): 119-149.

[48] PRUITT J, ADLIN T. The persona lifecycle: Keeping people in mind throughout product design[M]. Elsevier, 2010.

[49] VAN DER LELIE C. The value of storyboards in the product design process[J]. Personal and Ubiquitous Computing, 2006, 10: 159-162.

[50] BOESS S, PASMAN G, MULDER I. Seeing things differently: Prototyping for interaction and participation[J]. Design and Semantics of Form and Movement, 2010, 85.

[51] SCHELLEKENS M. Human–machine interaction in self-driving vehicles: A perspective on product liability[J]. International Journal of Law and Information Technology, 2022, 30(2): 233-248.

[52] LIM Y K, SATO K. Describing multiple aspects of use situation: Applications of Design Information Framework (DIF) to scenario development[J]. Design Studies, 2006, 27(1): 57-76.

[53] CARROLL J M. Five reasons for scenario-based design[J]. Interacting with Computers, 2000, 13(1): 43-60.

[54] KRISCHKOWSKY A, TRÖSTERER S, BRUCKENBERGER U, et al. The Impact of Spatial Properties on Collaboration: An Exploratory Study in the Automotive Domain[C]//Proceedings of the 2016 ACM International Conference on Supporting Group Work. New York, NY, USA: Association for Computing Machinery, 2016: 245-255[2023-02-28].

[55] KERN D, SCHMIDT A. Design space for driver-based automotive user interfaces[C]//Proceedings of the 1st International Conference on Automotive User Interfaces and Interactive Vehicular Applications. New York, NY,

USA: Association for Computing Machinery, 2009: 3-10[2023-07-12].

[56] BERGER M, BERNHAUPT R, PFLEGING B. A tactile interaction concept for in-car passenger infotainment systems[C]//Proceedings of the 11th International Conference on Automotive User Interfaces and Interactive Vehicular Applications: Adjunct Proceedings. New York, NY, USA: Association for Computing Machinery, 2019: 109-114.

[57] HOFFMAN G, GAL-OZ A, DAVID S, et al. In-car game design for children: Child vs. parent perspective[C]//Proceedings of the 12th International Conference on Interaction Design and Children. New York, NY, USA: Association for Computing Machinery, 2013: 112-119[2023-11-20].

[58] BRANDT E, GRUNNET C. Evoking the future: Drama and props in user centered design[C]//Proceedings of Participatory Design Conference (PDC 2000). New York: ACM Press, 2000: 11-20.

[59] LEWIN T, MCGOVERN G. Speed Read Car Design: The History, Principles and Concepts Behind Modern Car Design[M]. Motorbooks, 2017.

[60] LUCERO A, ARRASVUORI J. PLEX Cards: A source of inspiration when designing for playfulness[C]//Proceedings of the 3rd International Conference on Fun and Games, 2010: 28-37.

[61] VAAJAKALLIO K, MATTELMÄKI T. Design games in codesign: As a tool, a mindset and a structure[J]. CoDesign, 2014, 10 (1): 63-77.

[62] HARITAIPAN L, SAIJO M, MOUGENOT C. Leveraging creativity of design students with a magic-based inspiration tool[C]//DS 93: Proceedings of the 20th International Conference on Engineering and Product Design Education (E&PDE 2018), Dyson School of Engineering, Imperial College, London, 2018: 265-270.

[63] DENG Y, ANTLE A, NEUSTAEDTER C. Tango cards: A card-based design tool for informing the design of tangible learning games[C]//Proceedings of the 2014 Conference on Designing Interactive Systems, 2014: 695-704.

[64] CLATWORTHY S. Service Innovation Through Touch-points: Development of an Innovation Toolkit for the First Stages of New Service Development[J]. International Journal of Design, 2011, 5: 15-28.

[65] VAN DER LUGT R. Developing a graphic tool for creative problem solving in design groups[J]. Design Studies, 2000, 21 (5): 505-522.

[66] CASH P, MAIER A. Understanding representation: Contrasting gesture and sketching in design through dual-process theory[J]. Design Studies, 2021, 73: 100992.

[67] GRIGG J. Materials and tools as catalysts of invention in graphic design ideation[J]. Design Studies, 2020, 70: 100960.

[68] LEE S, YAN J. The impact of 3D CAD interfaces on user ideation: A comparative analysis using SketchUp and Silhouette Modeler[J]. Design Studies, 2016, 44: 52-73.

[69] FINDELI A, BOUSBAKI R. The Eclipse of the Object in Design Project Theories[J].The Design Journal, 2005, 8: 3, 35-49.

[70] DORST K. Describing design: A comparison of paradigms[M]. Delft: Technische Universiteit Delft, 1997.

[71] PASK G. Conversation theory[J]. Applications in Education and Epistemology, 1976.

[72] GREENO J G. Natures of problem-solving abilities[M]. In: WKEstes (Ed.), Human information processing. Hillsdale, NJ: Lawrence Erlbaum Associates, Handbook of learning and cognitive processes, 1978, 5: 239-270.

[73] DORST K. The core of 'design thinking' and its application[J]. Design Studies, 2011, 32 (6): 521-532.

[74] RYAN M L. Beyond myth and metaphor: Narrative in digital media[J]. Poetics Today, 2002, 23 (4): 581-609.

[75] CLATWORTHY S. Service innovation through touch-points: Development of an innovation toolkit for the first stages of new service development[J]. International Journal of Design, 2011, 5 (2): 15-28.